PYRAMIDS
AND **POPPIES**

THE FIRST BRIGADE

Cheer! Oh, Cheer for the gallant men,
Boys of the First Brigade
Their deeds ring out o'er the silent glen,
Echoed in ev'ry glade;
Thousands of miles from Afric's shore,
And all to Afric's pride;
At Delville Wood, for evermore,
They fought, they bled, they died.

The lurid light of the bursting shell
Saw the 'Springbok' lines advance,
And on they went, thro' the lanes of Hell,
The fairest fields of France,
And man to man, steel to steel,
When all the Earth grew dim,
They fought, and died, with hero zeal,
And true Colonial Vim.

And we, who follow those who fell,
Shall bear their prestige through,
Historians one day may tell,
Of yet one more Fampoux;
Esprit-de-Corps in every mind,
Each manly trait displayed,
With each fond hope to God resigned,
Advance, the First Brigade.

By 'SEROWE'

PETER K A DIGBY

PYRAMIDS
AND POPPIES

The 1st SA Infantry Brigade in Libya, France and Flanders 1915-1919

HELION & COMPANY

Helion & Company Limited
26 Willow Road
Solihull
West Midlands
B91 1UE
England
Tel. 0121 705 3393
Fax 0121 711 4075
Email: info@helion.co.uk
Website: www.helion.co.uk
Twitter: @helionbooks
Visit our blog at http://blog.helion.co.uk/

Originally published by Ashanti Publishing (Pty) Ltd 1993
This reprint published by Helion & Company 2016
Designed and typeset by Battlefield Design, Gloucester (www.battlefield-design.co.uk)
Cover designed by Paul Hewitt, Battlefield Design (www.battlefield-design.co.uk)
Printed by Hobbs The Printers Ltd, Totton, Hampshire

Cover illustration by K J Lightfoot

ISBN 978-1-910294-62-8

British Library Cataloguing-in-Publication Data.
A catalogue record for this book is available from the British Library.

For details of other military history titles published by Helion & Company Limited, contact the above address, or visit our website: http://www.helion.co.uk.

We always welcome receiving book proposals from prospective authors.

This book is dedicated to
my late mother
Olwen Digby
who was the inspiration to me
during its writing
and to my late father
Captain Roland D Digby
a veteran of both World Wars

THE NEW SPRINGBOK

THE SPRINGBOK: 'I caused a bit of a sensation when I went Home in football togs,
and I hope the new outfit will give the Kaiser a schrik'.
(War and Election cartoons by Santry, CNA, 1915)

Contents

Foreword

ATTENTION: Peter Digby from Janice Farquharson, 24/3/93.
Pyramids and Poppies.

Dear Peter,

Last year you paid me the rather daunting compliment of asking me to write a foreword for your book Pyramids and Poppies. I agreed, subject to my reading the book first – and approving it. Well I have and I do; you, as a fellow First World War enthusiast, will know that such approval is not lightly given.

Here then, some brief comments by way of Foreword which is not – as your publishers might imagine – a routine exercise in approbation, but an attempt at a personal assessment of your important and perceptive study of a fascinating segment of South Africa's past. I have no doubt whatsoever that you will find a wide and appreciative audience.

I know that writing this book has been a long and arduous haul. We both know that it has been worth while.

Yours, Janice

Foreword by way of formality

This is the story of the 1st South African Infantry Brigade from its formation in 1915 to the final demobilisation in 1919 when the first of the Wars to End War was, officially, over. The 1st SAI had an exceptionally varied war. It was mustered in Potchefstroom, had a preliminary blooding in the deserts of North Africa; finally reached its original destination, the Western Front where it was involved in the Somme battles of 1916 and subsequent, fiercely bloody, actions in France and Flanders. For some individuals there were further strange interludes in Russia, then in the throes of revolution, which continued into 1919.

The remarkable range and the variety of experience, for the Brigade as a whole, and for individual members, will come as a surprise to many. Certain First World War battles have an enduring significance for the participants. For Australians and New Zealanders – the ANZACS – Gallipoli was very much 'their' battle. In France Vimy Ridge is for ever associated with the Canadian assault the bitter Easter in 1917. For South Africans, raw volunteers thrown into the bloodbath of the threatened Somme line in July 1916, it was and still is (though for differing, and regrettable political motives) Delville Wood.

For those with any interest, let alone an obsession, with the First World War, it is maddening that for the general public, Delville Wood was the sole battle the South African troops fought in France, or anywhere else for that matter. As Digby remarks, 'it appears that this is the only action to have penetrated the national consciousness'.

One of the great virtues of this fascinating, often harrowing, study is that Captain Digby sets Delville Wood in the context of Springbok service on the Western Front as a whole. He even gives a reasoned analysis of the casualties the SAI took in the Wood, discounting the myth of 3 000 dead and sensibly deciding that 'the real figures will never be known'. One must hope the ineffable SABCTV whose commemorations of Delville Wood too often verge on insulting ignorance, will take note.

There were so many other encounters, notably the furious assaults at Warlencourt and the 'backs to the wall' action at Marrières Wood,which have long awaited their proper recognition.

Digby handles his complicated narrative and his immense corpus of material with ease and insight. The story is told both from the Official level and with the worm's eye view of the ordinary squaddy.

His use of some remarkable letters, many previously unpublished, gives the story greater immediacy and brings to life those clear-eyed young warriors who fought so well and endured so much.

The South African military tradition is a long and honourable one. Digby recounts with laudible restraint the reprehensible attempts of the first Nationalist Minister of Defence, Erasmus, to destroy the very character of the Army that had fought so well in two World Wars. It is ironic that, in the 1980s, Delville Wood itself should have been part of a cynical propaganda exercise when a new, and to my mind hideously intrusive, 'National War Memorial' was erected at enormous cost within the innermost purlieus of the Wood itself.

The reader is directed to the Appendices. Digby explains why the Western Front battle honours of the First World War were never granted to the South African units involved; this in contrast to the sensible and honourable practices of the other Dominions, Australia and Canada in particular. He argues cogently –

and to my mind irrefutably – for assigning such honours to those regiments that have the right to carry those names which echo like a drum roll down the years. It is not too late to rectify a blatant injustice, even seventy years on.

Of course, there will be those who will dismiss this book as an exercise in vicarious bloodletting. That is their loss. My special field of academic study is the First World War and I have found Digby's wide ranging and compassionate but unsentimental study wonderfully nostalgic.

This is a splendid chronicle of unforgettable events. It demands attention.

Janice Farquharson
(MA, D Litt et Phil)

Author's note

This book would never have been written if John Pitts, former deputy editor of *The Star* had not suggested that I was the person to write it. He took a month to persuade me. I would have to find the time.

Although the exploits of the 1st South African Infantry Brigade in France and Flanders are possibly the most fascinating, in the World War I experience only one book *We Band of Brothers* by George W Warwick (1962) has been published since John Buchan's *The South African Forces in France* of 1920. A few writers have alluded to their Western Front experiences with the SA Forces in the odd paragraph or chapter in an autobiography. In 1978, G G J Lawrence published his experiences in the 1st SAI 1915-18 in four instalments in the South African Defence Force journal, *Militaria*. Both Warwick and Lawrence's experiences are autobiographical and do not give the whole story 1915 to 1919. Ian Uys's three fine books on Delville Wood focus on six days of the war with references to the subsequent exploits of members of the Brigade in passing. To work through many of the primary sources Buchan used, as well as the great wealth of fresh material, which forms the bulk of this book, has been a fascinating experience. Untravelled paths always have the greatest appeal.

It has been necessary to cut down the length of this saga of the 1st SA Infantry Brigade according to my publisher's requirements. I thank them for their guidance. Because of the necessary limitations that must be placed on such a book, the story of the SA Native Labour Contingent, Cape Coloured Labour Corps and Cape Auxiliary Horse Transport Companies is not covered, although they served in France. This is because they never encountered the SA Brigade during four years of war. In addition, their story is being told in another volume of this series of books, *South Africans at War*, as is that of the Cape Corps in Palestine. The story of the SA Heavy Artillery in France has been excluded with regret. However, this can be justified. Their service was in support of British Army formations for their entire Western Front experience. Only by chance, on three days, were they detailed to support the SA Brigade! Their story and that of other South African ancillary units which served with the British Army must wait with that of the SA Field Artillery in Palestine, to be told at a later date.

I have included the references to the Russian interlude and the Appendix on the RFC/RAF pilots because the former was a continuation of the war for members of the Brigade who wished to prolong the great adventure, while many members of the Brigade left the mud of the trenches to take to the air. For the preparation of the very informative Appendix on South African airmen I am greatly indebted to Ernest F Slatter of Pretoria.

I was fortunate to encounter two unique sequences of letters. They cover the period 1915 to 1918: the letters of Cyril Choat and A W Cloete-Srnith. Other such collections of letters from the front, written by members of the South African Forces in the First World War may exist, but they are unknown.

As Honorary Curator of the Transvaal Scottish Regimental Museum I have been able to consult the material that chronicles the story of the 4th SAI (SA Scottish), which I have assembled for the Regiment over the past twenty-five years. Finally, I have had the privilege, in this context, of meeting and talking to many veterans of the 1st SA Infantry Brigade. Two uncles of mine served in the Brigade. One was killed at Delville Wood. The story had to be told and I had to write it.

With such a complicated tale to tell I could not recount everyone's experiences or background in detail. Instead, I have told the story through the eyes of certain individuals so the reader can experience what it was like to have been there. It is my intention that those few will represent the thousands of men who served with the South African forces in France. Neither has the historical context of those momentous events been forgotten on the vast, muddy canvas of the Western Front.

Throughout the time *Pyramids and Poppies* was taking shape and assuming a personality of its own, my mother, Olwen Digby, was a constant source of encouragement and inspiration, as well as assisting with the proofreading.

I wish to thank the many people who have assisted me in the supplying of material or loan of photographs. I refer particularly to the following kind people: Nigel Pryde (for further information about A W Cloete-Smith); Mrs B Addison (for the loan of her copy of *Horse, Foot and Guns*); M L Hill (for material about Padre Eustace Hill); Mrs Margaret McCallum (for the Choat letters); Mrs W Winter (for the copy of Brig-Gen Dawson's diary at Marrières Wood); G S Whitford; Mrs T Avent; F V A Lilford; T Roffe; Y E Slaney and his daughter; Mrs Ann Bevan, for typing her father's reminiscences; E F Slatter; Ian S Uys; Mrs S Wallace; B K Thomas; V Phipson; Mrs C Cruikshank; F B Lee; P Bowles; G Donaldson; Miss E Hunt; W Addison; Al J Venter; R Cook; Mrs P Methuen; E Bernadi; J Lawrence; L D Rodger; N Clothier; and special thanks to Paul Fauchè for his encouragement and assistance with source material. This list would not be complete without thanking Commander W 'Mac' Bisset for the loan of photographs and his support while I was collecting research material; also Paul Blokland for photographing many of the illustrations that were destined for inclusion.

Last but not least, my gratitude and thanks to Estelle McKenna, who put the manuscript on disc. She lives up to the computer pogramme she uses: 'Word Perfect'. Thank you for your good humour and kindness.

The assistance of the following institutions has been invaluable: Transvaal Scottish Regimental Museum; SA Defence Force Documentation Centre; South African National Museum of Military History; St John's College Archives; Cape Archives; King Edward VII School Museum.

Peter K A Digby

Johannesburg
January 1993

Preface to Second Edition

Pyramids and Poppies was a revelation in that since it went out of print in 1994, I have been pestered to have the book reprinted.

The decision to choose a reprint of *Pyramids and Poppies* as the preferred option was not taken lightly. Before the first edition went to print in 1993, my publishers changed their minds and insisted that I remove one third of the text! (See Author's note.) In spite of this, *Pyramids and Poppies* was still a many-paged book: 444 pages including 222 illustrations and maps. For a mere 20 or 30 pages, the upheaval to the existing text and re-drafting of a very detailed index could not be justified. Furthermore, in the 22 years since the first edition appeared, no errors or omissions were brought to my notice. The only person who would have wished to make additions was myself! These may well appear as another book entitled *Commentaries on 'Pyramids and Poppies'*.

A handful of 'critics' who identified 'omissions' did not read the Author's note, which explained what was beyond the scope of the book and why; *Pyramids and Poppies* is essentially a 'people's history'. The book informs the reader what it was like to have been there – enabling them to participate in the experiences of the 1st South African Infantry Brigade. It is not a book written for academics where political correctness or ideological issues of the twenty-first century take pride of place, enhanced by that exact science known as 'hindsight', where battlefield strategies are torn to pieces after the event by an omniscient author. The Battle of the Scarpe and Lys have been purposely omitted, as terminology as these crept into historical writing after the First World War was over; they were not familiar to British and Empire soldiers during the war.

It is very gratifying that since *Pyramids and Poppies* appeared in 1993, it has been read with obvious enjoyment. P E Abbott, the historian, writing of the book in December 1994 in Spink and Son's Numismatic Circular of London, stated: 'The narrative makes compulsive reading principally for the personal memoirs on which it is based. These have an immediacy which few formation or for that matter regimental histories can match'.

That *Pyramids and Poppies* is just as relevant and useful to the researcher today came from an unexpected quarter: last year Dr Stuart Allan, Principal Curator of the National Museums of Scotland, stated that in setting up the centenary exhibition in the National Military Museum in Edinburgh Castle – subtitled 'Common Cause: Commonwealth Scots and the Great War' – he used *Pyramids and Poppies* as a reference source: '… Very early in the process of formulating the exhibition I referred to it consistently. It was a pleasure to read…'

On the matter of centenary celebrations of the First World War, it is a great sadness and disappointment to me that South Africa has done nothing to commemorate the sacrifice of its sons in the Great War 1914–1919. Regardless of colour, those who made the supreme sacrifice laid down their lives for their country and deserve to be remembered and recognised. All were volunteers and not subject to the stereotypical view of the war, as expressed by war poets such as Robert Graves, Wilfred Owen and Siegfried Sassoon.

Australia, Canada, New Zealand and India have done much – and intend to do much more – in the years leading up to the climax of the centenary commemoration in 2018, with the erection of new memorials in France and Flanders to remember their dead and keep memories bright. To date, South Africa has ignored the centenary and various suggested initiatives; these have received no encouragement. Twenty years into democracy, such commemoration must embrace the deeds and achievements of all South Africans; there is still time to remedy the situation.

It is hoped that even in a modest way, the second edition of *Pyramids and Poppies* will celebrate and commemorate the achievements of South Africans in the First World War. History is impossible to re-invent. Not all sections of the South African population, who served in France and Flanders during the period 1914 to 1918, saw frontline action.

I am indebted to Will and June Simpson, who were my hosts on my first visit to the Western Front and encouraged me to ensure that a second edition of my book was submitted for publication. My thanks to Duncan Rogers of Helion for his friendly support and Mike Taylor for extra photographs.

Peter K A Digby

Johannesburg
August 2015

(On the occasion of the centenary of the formation of the 1st South African Infantry Brigade in August 1915)

Chapter
1

These past ribbons nil

'This war is a Crusade - a privilege - these past ribbons nil'[1] - so spoke a South African colonel to his chaplain, of his previous campaign medal ribbons in the smoke and shell of battle, of the experience called the Great War. Hours later the colonel would lie dead. Some nine days later his battalion would emerge from Delville Wood four officers and thirty-eight men strong. Knowing this would not have changed the colonel's words. No war before or since has conjured up such emotion. Whether they were British or colonial born they felt the same - they wanted to be part of the experience.

They were afraid that the war would be over before they entered it. 'Something was going on that was too big to be missed - adventure on an heroic scale: secondly, the eagerness of a young man to test himself to try out, as it were his own guts. I do not think I was particularly patriotic.' So wrote South African author, Stuart Cloete, in his autobiography *A Victorian Son*.

Men made themselves available, to lose their lives if need be. It was also an answer to a call. Britain was in trouble.

Others involved from Britain itself were all, at that stage, volunteers. Yet somehow, at such a distance from the central theatre, in a divided South Africa, participation had been less evidently the obvious choice. For these men, as in 1939, it might have been so easily avoided.

It was a sombre welcome that awaited them on the Western Front. It seemed that a continent was bent on self-destruction. Others from the British Empire had made the same response as the South Africans. For the most part they were newcomers to the field of full-scale conflict - not veterans from other wars. They came to a testing ground that was of the severest, where heroism was the most unflinching. Their achievements exceeded all expectation.

The South African contribution, compared to Canada, Australia and New Zealand, was the smallest. The context of the post-rebellion, politically unsettled, four-year-old Union of South Africa made this an inevitable reality. However,

---

1   Warwick, George W, *We Band of Brothers* p166. Lt-Col F A Jones, DSO, OC 4th SAI was talking to Father Eustace Hill in Bernafay Wood on 11 July 1916 when the incident occurred.

South Africa's contribution, small as it was because of political and constitutional considerations, provided 67 306 white and 33 546 black and Coloured soldiers for service in German South West Africa with 47 521 white and 18 000 black and Coloured soldiers for service in German East and Central Africa.

A further 30 880 white and 5 823 black and Coloured soldiers volunteered for service in France.[1] The reputation they would gain there would be out of all proportion to their actual numbers.

By way of comparison, 418 000 Canadians went overseas, most to fight on the Western Front, 8 000 served in the Royal Canadian Navy while 24 000 served in the RAF and RFC. Canada raised and maintained a front-line army corps of four full divisions which suffered 200 000 casualties with 66 651 killed in action or died of wounds. Australia had an overseas army corps of five divisions, dispatching 331 781 soldiers for overseas service. New Zealand had forty-two per cent of its male population on active service, with 117 175 serving overseas as part of the New Zealand Expeditionary Force.[2]

In South Africa thousands were preparing to participate in this ultimate experience. The instant and terrifying destruction of one's companions of many months, was the naked horror that was not foreseen. Of course in war men die, but never before or since on a scale that was found on the Western Front, 1914 to 1918.

It was an experience that would be repeated again and again from August 1914 for nearly five years. A man who had been through it all once, knew that if he did come through, he would have to face it over and over again until the enemy got him or his own sergeant shot him for refusing to face it again.

Probably the most famous story of war that has come out of South Africa is *Commando*. King George V kept a copy as bedside reading at Windsor Castle, along with its sequel, *Trekking On*. Deneys Reitz, the author, who had written of his experiences in the Anglo-Boer War, then wrote in the companion volume about the Rebellion, German South West and East Africa and of that ultimate experience - the Western Front. Although a South African, an Afrikaner, Reitz went on in France to command 1st Bn Royal Scots Fusiliers, a British Regular Army unit, the 2nd Battalion which had been in action against his commando during the Natal Campaign of the Anglo-Boer War 1899-1902.[3]

1   *Union of South Africa and the Great War 1914-18 Official History p212* and *The Official Year Book Union of SA (1919-21:No5.)*

2   Cox R H W, *Military Badges of the British Empire 1914-18*

3   In World War I in East Africa he rose to the rank of lieutenant-colonel commanding the 4th SA Horse and in France he served as second-in-command of 7th Royal Irish Rifles, then the 1st Royal Scots Fusiliers with the rank of major and was promoted lieutenant-colonel commanding the unit from 5 October 1918 to January 1919.

Deneys Reitz described the experience that all those millions wished to be part of and, once tasted, wished to avoid. Names, dates and places would be different in each case, but that is unimportant.

On one occasion, in 1918, Reitz's unit was waiting to cross the sixty to eighty yards of no man's land in order to reach the allotted section of the Hindenburg Line. Tension became almost unbearable as zero hour approached. The men stood to. The British barrage engulfed the German front line. Ten minutes later, at 5.30 a.m., the barrage moved forward. The long awaited moment had arrived. The signal was given. Men clambered over the parapet and stumbled through the obstacle-strewn wasteland as the German barrage of exploding shells decimated their ranks. After a brief interlude of hand-to-hand fighting the objective was taken; Reitz and Bissett, his second-in-command, walked over the area their unit had crossed. As usual they were saddened by how many had fallen in the attack.

> At one place we came on a heap of flesh and clothing so mangled that, had it not been for two field-booted legs protruding from the awful mess, we could hardly have sworn that what lay here had been a human being. At first we could not determine whose remains they were, but seeing the

The ultimate experience – The Western Front – adventure on an heroic scale. A glorious charge of the Royal and Northumberland Fusiliers at St Eloi.
(Photo: Cloete-Smith Collection)

The naked horror of the instant and terrifying destruction of one's companions was not foreseen. (Photo Cloete-Smith Collection)

rim of a steel hat beneath, I did some grisly work with a stick and got the helmet clear. I found the name of one of our young officers inside it. Bissett, at that moment, must have felt someone walking over his grave, for he shivered and said: 'My God, I'm getting sick of this awful war'.[1]

Yet in the midst of that inferno of suffering there was the miracle of comradeship and brotherhood of the front line: the wonder of human companionship. Without that it would have been impossible to go on. It was to this climax of human experience, this final curtain of life that manhood flocked. They came in their thousands. The Union of South Africa was no exception.

Fall in and follow me, fall in and follow me,
Come along and never mind the weather all together
Stand on me, boys, I know the way to go,
I'll take you for a spree,
You do as I do and you'll do right.
Fall in and follow me.[2]

1   Reitz, D, Trekking On p256-259.
2   Soldiers Hymn Sheet, First SAI Brigade Association

Chapter 2

Potchefstroom

Potchefstroom. Unlikely gateway to the great adventure, all paths led to Potchefstroom. With the successful conclusion of the German South West Africa Campaign, all units of the ACF had been demobilised, ceasing to be liable for active service. However, as individuals, members of ACF units could volunteer for active service in Europe or in German East Africa. Many of the returned soldiers were determined to continue to serve in the war against Germany. At Potchefstroom they could make their resolutions a reality.

First to be formed was the 1st South African Infantry Brigade, consisting of four regiments, for service in France. Recruiting centres opened in every province. Initially, preference was given to veterans of the German South West Africa Campaign, as the Union Government feared the escalation of unemployment with the return of 100 415 white, Coloured and black servicemen and women in July 1915, after the German surrender. A total of only 337 of all races lost their lives during the campaign.

Botha and Smuts had added to the Union of South Africa a territory larger than Germany with about the same casualties as an average trench raid in France.

As early as April 1915, the Imperial Government had been approached about the supply of a South African force to continue the war on other fronts. Although considerable ill-feeling existed towards the British war effort within South Africa, especially in National Party circles, because of the recent Rebellion, by the second half of 1915 such feeling had subsided to the extent that the Union Government could risk the departure from South Africa of a considerable number of loyal and seasoned soldiers. In July 1915, the Union Government's offer was accepted by the Imperial authorities.

A 2nd and 3rd South African Infantry Brigade would be raised for service in German East Africa once the 1st South African Infantry Brigade had sailed for England. In the Great War, unlike the Second World War, men volunteered for service in a particular campaign, not for the duration of the war. A number did re-attest after serving in East Africa and arrived belatedly in France.

The flood of recruits was channelled to Potchefstroom in the western Transvaal.

It was here that an imperial garrison had been stationed after the Anglo-Boer War. The cantonments, until a year before, had been occupied by Imperial troops: part of the Imperial garrison of South Africa, that had remained in the country after the Anglo-Boer War. At the time of Britain's declaration of war against Germany in August 1914, the main military stations such as Potchefstroom, Roberts Heights, Wynberg and Tempe had British garrisons. By mid-October 1914 all British units had reached France with the 2nd Bn East Lancashire Regiment the last to leave. The latter arrived in France in the first week of November. Those of their young officers who were not killed would no doubt find themselves colonels before they were thirty.

On the outbreak of war, the Prime Minister of the Union of South Africa, Louis Botha, had offered to release all British units and hand over the defence of the Union to the recently established Union Defence Force.

Just as Simonstown was to see the departure of the Royal Navy some forty-five years later, so was South Africa witnessing the passing of an era: the last of the British Regular Army units on the point of departure from South Africa, never to return.

Departure of the last members of the Imperial Garrison, Roberts Heights, Pretoria in August 1914. Pte James Martin, Transvaal Scottish, in foreground.
(Photo: Transvaal Scottish Regimental Museum)

So, too, did Potchefstroom sadly bid farewell to its Imperial Garrison. The British troops had been the focal point of social life in Potchefstroom.

Potchefstroom cantonments, with its twenty-four miles of roads better kept than those in the town itself, was ideally suited to its new role as the training ground for the 1st South African Infantry Brigade. It had cost the British taxpayers one and a half million pounds. On the veld, in 1901, a city of galvanised iron had sprung up with rows of red-roofed houses, immense stables, hospitals, schools, recreation grounds, polo grounds, clubs, reading rooms, post and telegraph offices, and all the appurtenances of civilisation. The cantonments were built on what was formerly known as Vechtkopje, re-christened Derby Hill.[1] Like the Headquarters buildings of Northern Transvaal Command, Pretoria, which still stand, these wood and iron buildings were apparently dismantled at Poona and Karachi in India, shipped to Durban, transported north by ox-wagon and erected at Potchefstroom, Middelburg, Roberts Heights and Tempe, Bloemfontein. Other than those in Voortrekkerhoogte (Roberts Heights) Pretoria, the only other buildings to have survived are the general's house in Potchefstroom and Field-Marshal Smuts's house at Irene, which he had dismantled in Middelburg and re-erected on its new site outside Pretoria as his family home. Potch Camp is still used as a military base.

In 1915 the empty streets of the cantonments would fill with a new khaki population. It was South Africa's moment to honour her offer to send a brigade to France and Flanders.

At the receiving depot at Potchefstroom station, each party of volunteers was assembled for the march to camp. Many of those who marched along the dusty road had only recently returned from the German South West Africa Campaign.

W A 'Alf' Beattie, ex-4th SAI, recalled his reception.

> It was a bitterly cold dawn when the train pulled up at Potch and someone herded us into an open field and told us to stay there. When we were frozen to the marrow a lance-corporal arrived from our camp with coffee and a sack of bread. He opened a sack, broke the loaves into big chunks and chucked them at us. The bread fell on the dusty veld. My first reaction was a strong desire to pick up a lump and throw it back in the hope that I might mortally wound the Lance-Jack. Then it struck me that I was both hungry and thirsty so I shook the dust from my bread and swallowed the insult.

Of the parade ground at Potch Camp, Frederick Addison, a member of the 2nd SAI, had this to say:

---

1   Jenkins, Geoffrey, *A Century of History,* p100 quoted by Jenkins.

Recruits for the 1st SA Infantry Brigade, August 1915. Amongst the civilians are some wearing school cadet uniforms or uniforms from the recently concluded German South West Africa Campaign. (Photo: Transvaal Scottish Regimental Museum)

> Do you see that cloud of dust quickly drifting across the parade ground, and do you see under it boots and legs doing one hundred and forty paces to the minute, and you cannot help but hear the instructor, straight as a ramrod with pace stick under his arm, barking out orders like this 'left, right, left, right, that third man from the right in the second rank pick your feet up; you are walking like a baboon, left, right, left, right.' The clash of boots coming together rings out, the dust settles, and there comes to light a squad of human beings, grimed with sweat and dust, standing stock still, staring straight in front of them and not batting an eye-lid.[1]

Soon those who had joined the brigade settled down to camp routine: church parades each Sunday; much drill; ration fatigues; picket duty; instruction in the recognition of the various bugle calls and entertainment in the form of concerts and football matches.

The instructors were, in most cases, ex-British Regular Army NCOs. They had either been located or came forward of their own accord. In not a few instances they eventually joined the various regiments of the SA Brigade in some or other capacity in order to see frontline service. Pte Ernest Solomon wrote:

1   Addison, F, *Horse, Foot and Guns* p1.

Daily fresh parties arrived and daily the drilling squads assumed greater proportions, and soon the camp began to wear an animated appearance. In the meantime training went on apace; the evident keenness of everyone concerned made itself felt; intense enthusiasm prevailed. Came the day when the different regiments were formed; men were asked which they wished to join; the 1st (Cape), 2nd (Orange Free State and Natal), 3rd (Transvaal and Rhodesia), and the 4th (South African Scottish) were allotted quarters in separate parts of the camp enclosure; rifles, uniforms, caps, greatcoats, badges and the hundred and one articles of a soldier's kit were issued, officers put in an appearance, non-commissioned officers were appointed, platoons and companies put on a proper basis and, in that way, step by step, the 1st South African Infantry Brigade came into being.

General Smuts came down, inspected and addressed the Brigade in a few earnest and patriotic remarks, and before the end of August, there came the first rumour of a move that stirred up no little excitement.

It became known that 'A' and 'C' Companies of the 3rd Regiment were to leave. When the eventful morning arrived, General Lukin inspected the regiment and addressed the two companies concerned. It was then only that we received the first official intimation of our movements, for in the course of his remarks, he said 'You will be the first detachment of the 1st South African Infantry Brigade to land in England. I wish you all a pleasant voyage. Goodbye.'

'...the dust settles and there comes to light a squad of human beings' – Pte F Addison, 2nd SAI, Potchefstroom, August 1915. (Photo: Transvaal Scottish Regimental Museum)

The Hospital, Potchefstroom Military Camp, August 1915.
(Photo: Transvaal Scottish Regimental Museum)

> We marched straight from that parade to the station, and as we passed through those parts of the camp where the other regiments were stationed, and where our departure was not generally known, we were greeted with a fire of questions, to all of which we replied in as matter of fact a tone as possible. 'We're going to England'.[1]

The other regiments of the Brigade had still to receive their orders to leave Potchefstroom, along with the remainder of the 3rd Regiment. Until the order came, life continued.

Pte George W Warwick of the 4th Regiment (SA Scottish) recorded that: 'It was a source of wonder and joy the number of Dutch lads who joined the South African Scottish.[2] One such was questioned by a senior (British) officer during this inspection of new recruits:

Officer: What is your name?
Recruit: Botes, Sir.
Officer: What are you?
Recruit: Scottish, Sir.
Officer: Can you speak English?

---

1   Solomon, Ernest, *Potchefstroom to Delville Wood* p9-11 [edited]
2   Warwick ,George W, p16-19.

Recruit: No, Sir.

Officer: He must be a real Scotsman.

A most impressed officer marvelled at the fact that a SA Scottish unit was enrolling Gaelic speakers! That members of the Dutch population should have enrolled at all is amazing in that only thirteen years before Boer and Briton had been at war. Figures show that initially Dutch speakers represented fifteen per cent of enrolments and towards the end of the war this had risen to thirty per cent.

There were indications of the impending departure of the 4th SAI and other units of the Brigade. Inoculations were administered twice on one day, with two parades on Sunday 19 September: the usual church parade in the morning and another at 2.00 p.m., when the Mayor of Johannesburg and the Deputy Mayor of Pretoria addressed them. Tuesday, 21 September was a very hot day. There was a great parade at which Lt-Col F A Jones DSO, read out farewell messages from the Caledonian Societies in South Africa. The next day Col Jones announced on parade that the 4th SAI would be leaving Potchefstroom for overseas on the next Friday. The day before, Col William Dalrymple, honorary colonel of the SA Scottish had also bid his regiment God speed.

Arthur Betteridge, who had joined the SA Scottish, remembered those remote days of Potchefstroom Camp with nostalgia, in *Combat In and Over Delville Wood*, Vol I.

> I often smile when I think of those happy innocent days in camp where many good friendships were made; most of them were of short duration. So many of those eager lads were destined never to return to their homes. More than half of them lie at rest in the poppy-strewn fields of Flanders.

4th SAI on Parade, Potchefstroom, August 1915.
(Photo. Transvaal Scottish Regimental Museum)

The Brigade had departed, but the flow of recruits who streamed to Potchefstroom continued unabated. The supply of replacements for the inevitable casualties had to meet the demand so that the Brigade could be kept at full strength. One of those who arrived at Potchefstroom later in 1915 was No 7217 Pte A W Cloete-Smith, 2nd SA Infantry. Extracts from a series of letters he wrote to his mother paint a vivid picture of camp life at Potchefstroom:[1]

13-11-1915

We received our uniform this morning and were sworn in. I have joined the 2nd SAI because all the men in my carriage were doing so and they seem a really decent lot. We are in a room about fifty yards long, with twenty seven other men. The food is quite all right too. Just been putting the buttons on my uniform. Must close now.....

16-11-1915

It has rained every night since I have been here and has only just stopped now (9.15 pm) having started about four this afternoon. Don't worry about the pyjamas. There is not much chance of my getting leave as I hear we are all leaving today week to make room for the 10 000 they want for G[erman] E[ast] A[frica]. This, of course is not official. I have my full kit now with the exception of the shoulder badges and bayonet...I am wearing my own boots as the issue ones are the limit in more ways than one.
I must close now as it is time I got to sleep and most of the others are already in the land of dreams.

Best love to you and Dad and the others
Your affectionate son
A W Cloete-Smith

22-11-1915

We were told this morning that we had to get rid of all our civilian clothing, as a lot of the men have been taking off their uniforms and going down town as civilians. I shall sell mine to one of the Jews who come round every day.

---

1   The collection of letters is unique in that it covers the period 13 November 1915 to the end of the Great War. Cloete-Smith was an old boy of King Edward VII School, Johannesburg.

The Regimental Sergeant Major instructing men of the 4th SAI, Potchefstroom, August 1915. (Photo: Transvaal Scottish Regimental Museum)

A few terse remarks to the officers of the 4th SAI by Lt-Col FA Jones DSO, Officer Commanding 4th SAI, Potchefstroom, August 1915.
(Photo: Transvaal Scottish Regimental Museum)

These dealers were a fixture at Potchefstroom camp until the end of the War. It was a buyers market!

It was very difficult to keep clothes clean in camp as the private soldiers had to sit about on the floor even for meals.

29-11-1915

I am feeling like a piece of chewed string as I was inoculated again this morning. I am sweating like a pig, and feel absolutely rotten. I think it is partly due to the fact that just after I had been done we had to march down to the transport depot to hand in our rifles and I had to carry three rifles, notwithstanding the doctors orders that we were to do nothing for forty-eight hours...The Cape men have just fallen in and are leaving by a special [train] at eleven. This is in order to give them a chance of seeing their relatives before they leave for Europe. There is great excitement. There is cheering all over the camp just now as the Cape chaps are moving off...

30-11-1915

There are 165 of us going from the 2nd Regiment. There was a perfect 'picnic' here last night, as about ten of the chaps came in roaring drunk.

2-12-1915

Dearest Mother

Reveille was sounded this morning at 4.30 and at 6.30, we moved off for the station in full marching order i.e., greatcoats and two haversacks apiece. We have to get all we will want for about four weeks into the two haversacks, as we will not get our kit bags again until we are in camp in England. We left Potch at 8.20 and have just passed Bloemhof. They are giving us quite decent food on the train. We have had two meals, brekker and dinner. It is quite a change from camp food. There are three specials leaving Potch today, each carrying about 400 men ...Been turned out of our compartment to make room for two officers who are joining at Kimberley. We are due to arrive there at seven tonight. Have just passed Fourteen Streams and the Vaal. You must excuse the writing as it was done in the train... will write again as soon as we reach Cape Town.

The cover of this letter was stamped 'Beaufort West 3 December 1915'

Pte Cyril Choat of the 4th SAI recorded his Potchefstroom some four months later, highlighting other aspects that were to be repeated time and time again.

> Everyone was in high spirits and was singing and laughing along the way... When we had deposited our goods in the carriages we formed up and marched off in platoons and received tea and cakes from the ladies and also a small canvas bag containing some useful things such as soap, postcards and of course the usual tobacco and cigarettes. Papers, magazines, apples, chocolate and other things were distributed generally. Then came the farewells: all the ladies shook hands with us and our Instructor, a depot Sergt Major, almost cried. At Klerksdorp, a place about forty miles from Potchefstroom, I think, the ladies were (again) on the station in force. Although rather long, occupying two and a half days, the journey was quite nice.[1]

The kindness of the ladies along the route was fondly remembered by successive drafts. Without fail they were there.

And so this same story from arrival at Potch to departure, was to be repeated in varying detail through 1916, 1917 and 1918. Each draft would vie with each other in all they did, hoping that their draft would be the first to receive orders for departure for England! Adventure called. As the troop trains moved south, other trains with new recruits passed them on their way to Potchefstroom, to begin a new cycle.

J E P Levyns, who had signed up in July 1916 had no illusions as to the realities of the situation

> when, on the impulse of a moment, I went to the recruiting office... no doubt the spirit of adventure that is part of the make up of every healthy young man played its part in driving me to the decision to volunteer. But I was mainly moved by the same spirit of idealism that caused so many thousands of my doomed generation to offer their lives to their country. I believed with them that this war was like no previous one and that Great Britain had taken up arms to defend the noblest ideals of democracy against the grossest form of military tyranny and aggression that the world had

---

1   Mentioned in a letter from Cyril Choat to his parents 28 February 1916. The collection of letters is housed in the Transvaal Scottish Regimental Museum and covers the period 1916-18. Choat was a member of the 4th SAI.

seen since the defeat of Napoleon. I had no illusions about my chances of coming out of the war alive or unwounded. When Wood and I signed on, Cape Town and South Africa were still numb from the horror of the casualty lists published after the opening of the Somme offensive.

The regiment that I had volunteered to join, the South African Scottish (4th SAI) was, at first sight, a strange choice for a man of German descent, but natural for one who had been in the Cape Town Highlanders for two years.

Before leaving Cape Town, our draft was given a civic farewell. The chairman of the recruiting committee, a prosperous member of the business community, was supported on the platform of the city hall by a number of other important citizens, seated in rows beside and behind him. He thanked us for our patriotism and assured us that this was a war of high ideals that would end wars. We need have no fears for the loved ones we were leaving behind us. A grateful country would not only care for them but, when peace returned, would welcome us back like the heroes that we were. It would help us to pick up the threads of civilian life again.

These lofty sentiments were lost on a little man in the draft who was seated just behind me. The jacket of his faded navy-blue suit was adorned with a row of medal ribbons, amongst which I recognised those of the Boer War. As the speech ended, he announced, in a voice loud enough to be heard on the platform, that it was a lot of hypocritical balls and that bloody old bastard and his pals would let the war heroes rot in the gutter, the same as last time! He was still speaking when someone on the platform signalled to the city organist, who struck up 'Land of Hope and Glory' and followed it with the 'King'.[1]

1   Levyns, JEP, *The Disciplines of War* p28-31.

Chapter 3

The Brigade

The men who had joined the SA Brigade for service in France were of a particularly fine type. They represented a good cross-section of the full spectrum of life – miners, businessmen, civil servants, professional men, academics, students and farmers.

Major D R Hunt, OC of 'C' Company 4th SAI (SA Scottish) preserved the nominal roll of 'C' Company.[1] He made an analysis of the original 'C' Company on formation at Potchefstroom. Bearing in mind how the Brigade was constituted, these facts are borne out as typical of the Brigade as a whole, except perhaps for the number of Scots! The average age was between twenty and thirty. Slightly under half were South African born. Close on four-fifths of their number were unmarried. Except for twenty per cent, all gave details of previous military experience of some kind.

It should be noted that even where 'none' was recorded, every enrolment who had been at school between the period 1904 to 1915 in South Africa had certainly been a member of his school's cadet detachment, at a time when cadet training was far more advanced and of a practical nature, to fit the cadet for army life, than it is today.

Buchan, who assessed the quality of the various brigades in France, wrote of the SA Brigade:

> Few of the new brigades were better supplied with men of the right kind of experience, and no brigade showed a better standard of physical well-being. It should also be remembered that the level of education and breeding was singularly high. The Brigade resembled indeed the famous 51st Division of Highland Territorials, which was largely a middle-class division.

The Brigade Commander was the fifty-five year old Brig-Gen H T 'Tim' Lukin, CMG, DSO, a man with a long and distinguished record, who had fought in every South African campaign since 1879. At the time of his appointment, Lukin

---

1   In possession of the Transvaal Scottish Regimental Museum.

was Inspector-General of the Union Defence Force. From 1902 to 1910 he commanded the Cape Mounted Rifles. He always regarded his CMR period as the highlight of his military career.

A fellow officer, Col B C Judd, wrote of him with affection:

> He usually gave every problem ponderous consideration as he was a slow thinker. However, having solved the problem he would act quickly and successfully. (He was) quite fearless.[1]

The four officers-commanding chosen for the four regiments that were to mould the new units and take them to France, were men of similar experience. All were Permanent Force members of the Union Defence Force and District Staff Officers of various military districts in the Union of South Africa. Officers were mainly appointed from Citizen Force units.

Brig-Gen H T Lukin CMG, DSO, 1st South African Infantry Brigade commander. (Photo: Cloete-Smith Collection)

The nominal rolls of officers of the four regiments of the Brigade on its formation in Potchefstroom in August 1915 is worth putting on record. (See Appendix A).

Some details about each regiment are relevant here, particularly the 4th Regiment which was considered something of a wonder in the South African context.

The 1st Regiment was known as the Cape Regiment. Nearly half of 'A' Company (Western Province) was made up of men of the Duke of Edinburgh's Rifles;[2] 'B' Company (Eastern Province); 'C' Company (Kimberley) was recruited by Capt H H Jenkins from 1st and 2nd Bn of the Kimberley Regiment. As this latter company was full of mechanics and artisans, it became known as the Workers Company. Finally, 'D' Company (Cape Town) was composed chiefly of

---

1   *Military History Journal* Vol 7 No 3, June 1987. p124-5.
2   Orpen, N, *The Dukes* p 80.

civil servants and bank employees; it became known as the Clerical Company.

The 2nd Regiment was recruited from Natal and the Orange Free State with men from the Kaffrarian Rifles.[1]

The 3rd Regiment was known as the Transvaal Regiment but included men from Rhodesia as well. 'B' Company contained fifty-one members of the Witwatersrand Rifles with Capt R F C Medlicott as OC.[2] The whole of 'C' Company, with Captain J W Jackson, were men of the Rand Light Infantry.[3]

The raising of the 4th Regiment (South African Scottish), was largely due to Colonel William Dalrymple, honorary colonel of the Transvaal Scottish, who, after consultation with the Caledonian Societies and prominent Scotsmen throughout South Africa, approached the Union government on their behalf with an offer to raise a Scottish battalion as the 4th Regiment. Dalrymple's novel idea was accepted!

In order to make the 4th Regiment fully representative, it was decided that as far as possible 'A' Company should be recruited from the Cape Town Highlanders and the Cape generally; 'B' Company was to be from 1st Bn Transvaal Scottish; and 'C' Company from 2nd Bn Transvaal Scottish. Both were supplemented from the Transvaal as a whole. Recruits from Natal and the Orange Free State were allocated to 'D' Company.[4]

It is interesting to note that the 4th SAI (SA Scottish) adopted 'The Atholl Highlanders', the Regimental March of the Transvaal Scottish, as its Regimental March. Fourteen out of the thirty-nine officers, as well as the RSM, pipe major and drum major, were Transvaal Scottish men. The Regiment received kilts of the Transvaal Scottish tartan – the Murray of Atholl. Colonel Dalrymple was given the fullest support from Caledonian Societies throughout South Africa who encouraged their members to join. The enthusiasm for the idea is shown in one of the many telegrams received which read: 'The heather is afire'. The matter of highland dress was a great problem until Major Sir Harry Ross-Skinner, a former Transvaal Scottish officer and Col Dalrymple together approached Lt-Gen Sir John Cowans, the Quartermaster-General of the British Army, and obtained an undertaking from the British Government to equip the SA Scottish in highland dress. The kilts were issued on the Regiment's arrival in England.

As the honorary colonel of the SA Scottish, Dalrymple was a frequent caller at Potchefstroom camp to monitor progress of each successive draft and bid them farewell.

1 Tylden, Major G, *The Armed Forces of South Africa 1659-1954* p167.
2 Monick, S, *A Bugle Calls* p103.
3 Simpkins, B, *Rand Light Infantry* p41.
4 The Nominal Rolls of Officers are documented in WO1 Series Box 14 at the SADF Documentation Centre, Pretoria.

Two real Scots – Capt F McE Mitchell (2IC, B Coy) – left – and Major D M Macleod DCM (Second-in-Command). Potchefstroom, 1915, 4th SAI (SA Scottish). Both these officers had served in the Cameron Highlanders during the Anglo-Boer War and thereafter in the Transvaal Scottish Volunteers. (Photo: Transvaal Scottish Regimental Museum)

Cyril Choat, shortly before entraining for Cape Town, wrote to his parents that

> we were also given a pipe and half a pound of Transvaal tobacco, the gift of Col Dalrymple and the 'Comforts Committee'. Capt Reid, our OC, also spoke to us and told us to treasure the pipes and we then gave three cheers for Col Dalrymple.[1]

The collar badges were those of the Cape Town Highlanders except for the unit title which had been replaced by the family motto of the unit's OC, Lt-Col Jones – *Mors Lucrum Mihi*. When the Regiment embarked for England on 26 September 1915 it was 1 400 strong with four companies and a reserve company. A sixth Company, 'F', was left behind at Potchefstroom under Captain J L Reid as a Depot Company, numbering 220 strong.

No 1 South African Field Ambulance, under the command of Lt-Col G H Usmar SAMC, also assembled with the Brigade at Potchefstroom. Volunteers from the staffs of No 1 General Hospital, Wynberg and No 2 General Hospital, Maitland formed a South African Military Hospital that was to be based at Richmond in England and No 1 SA General Hospital in France. No 1 South African Field Ambulance was closely associated with the SA Brigade to the end of the war.

Other South African Units raised for service in France but not connected to the Brigade were:

A Signal Company; No 7 and No 8 SA Light Railway Operating Companies; 84th Miscellaneous Trades Company RE (South African); plus No's 2, 5, 8, 10, 11 and 22 Cape Auxiliary Horse Transport Companies ASC and 5 battalions of the SA Native Labour Contingent.

Finally, perhaps the most important of all these other units raised for service

Lt-Col F A Jones DSO, (left) OC 4th SAI, with the honorary colonel 4th SAI (right) Col William Dalrymple at Potchefstroom, August 1915. Jones's family motto was adopted by his unit. (Photo: Transvaal Scottish Regimental Museum)

1   Letter dated 22 March 1916

in France was 'The Regiment of South African Heavy Artillery' consisting of five batteries. (See Appendix F).

The necessity of keeping the 1st South African Infantry Brigade up to strength was addressed. The Brigade was required to carry an extra thirty per cent above establishment. They would be accommodated at the SA Brigade Depot in England until required. Monthly reinforcements of fifteen per cent of the Brigade establishment were to be forwarded from Potchefstroom. Later reinforcements were forwarded with officers who returned to South Africa after handing over the draft in England. Thus, as far as possible,

> no officer will be sent forward to the Brigade from this end except those originally appointed, thereby preserving the principle of promotion in the field of those most fitted to hold commissioned rank.[1]

These stipulations, desired by the Army Council, give a new significance to the nominal rolls of initial officer appointments to the Brigade, while at the same time highlighting the meritorious nature of all promotions in the Brigade.

Several final touches were now made to the Brigade before its departure. King Edward VII School, Johannesburg, presented the drums of the bugle band of its Cadet Detachment to the 3rd SAI. The hope was expressed 'that ere long they will be heard in Berlin; and that they will rattle the nails out of the wooden frame of the Von Hindenburg Colossus'.[2] The drums were later suitably emblazoned by George Potter and Co, Potter's Corner, Aldershot. After an odyssey of three years of war, only one of those drums – a side drum – found its way back to the school in 1922, with an accompanying letter from Lt-Col E Christian DSO, MC.

The 3rd SAI also had Jackie. Jackie was a baboon and had come to the unit on its formation. Until 1915, Jackie was the beloved pet of the Marr family, who lived on Cheshire Farm, Villieria, on the outskirts of Pretoria. When, as No 4927, Private Albert Marr attested at Potchefstroom on 25 August 1915, for service in the 3rd Regiment of the Brigade, he asked for and was given permission to bring Jackie along with him. At first Jackie's presence was ignored but he was so well behaved and had such an impressive beating that he was noticed. Jackie was then officially adopted as the mascot of the 3rd SAI and taken on strength as a member of the regiment. Once in England, he was provided with a special uniform and cap, complete with buttons and regimental badges.

1   Letter to Brig-Gen H T Lukin CMG, DSO from Lt-Col C R Burgess, Staff Officer Central Bureau, SA Overseas Expeditionary Force, WO1 Series SADF Documentation Centre.
2   *King Edward VII School Magazine*, December 1915 p46.

'Jackie', mascot of the 3rd SAI and Private Albert Marr (centre front) Potchefstroom, September 1915. (Author's Collection)

The only side drum presented by King Edward VII School Cadet Detachment to 3rd SAI to find its way back to the school in 1922. (Photo taken by Courtesy of King Edward VII School)

The 4th Regiment, the South African Scottish, could boast about their Nancy.

Acting on the principle that no regiment is fully equipped without a mascot, and showing a keen interest in the Scottish contingent, Mr David McLaren Kennedy, of the farm Vierfontein, OFS, presented the Regiment with a young springbok. The message sent runs as follows:

> Hey Jock! am sendin' ye ma 'Nancy'
> An' hope that she may tak' yer fancy!
> Ye're gaein' faur across the seas;
> Sae mind puir 'Dauvit' if ye please -
> that's me.
> David McLaren Kennedy,
> Vierfontein OFS.
> 20 August 1915.

No more appropriate mascot could have been found. The SA Brigade badge was a springbok head, surrounded by a circle with the motto: 'Union is Strength – Eendracht Maakt Macht'.

The regimental poet, Sergeant McVean, recorded the men's appreciation of the gift:

> Richt pleased I was tae get the beastie,
> And mony thanks is in my breastie,
> And Sir, I'll no neglect ma' duty,
> Tae praise her for her grace and beauty,
> Mete emblem o' this sunny land
> Fit pet tae grace our gallant band.
> You may be sure I'll no neglect her,
> Wi' kindly care I'll aye respect her,
> She'll be ma' first and constance care,
> And dine upon the daintiest fare
> Wee bits o' grass and heaps o' stubble,
> She'll aye hae plenty for tae nibble,
> Nae maitter whether here or France,
> We'll aye be prood o' bonny 'Nancy'.

RIGHT: Nancy, mascot of the 4th SAI with its keeper, Private A E Petersen, Potchefstroom, September 1915. (Photo: Transvaal Scottish Regimental Museum)

INSET: Cap badge worn by all members of the 1st SAI Infantry Brigade. The 4th SAI (SA Scottish) wore a circle of Murray of Atholl tartan behind the badge.

For the duration of the war, Nancy's keeper was No 186 Bugler Alfred Edmund Petersen of 'D' Company, South African Scottish.[1]

Nancy soon learnt how to walk and trot in an orderly fashion in front of the newly established Pipes and Drums of the SA Scottish under the control of Pipe-Major Donald Cameron and Drum-Major Hadfield. The band had been presented with thirteen sets of bagpipes, drums and other accessories such as horsehair sporrans by Mr William Dewar.

Nancy and all the members of the SA Brigade, in a succession of long troop trains, specials, now began the long journey south to Cape Town for the next stage of the great adventure.

We are the tango army, we are the SAI.
We cannot fight, we cannot shoot.
What blinking use are we.
And when we get to Berlin, the Kaiser he will say:
Hoch, Hoch, mein Gott, what a bally fine lot!
Are the boys of the SAI.

1   Poems extracted from the papers of the late Col Sir William Dalrymple KBE, VD in the Transvaal Scottish Regimental Museum. This information has appeared in articles by the author.

Chapter
4

Embarkation

Sometimes as the long train journey to the south drew to a close the officers persuaded the chefs to provide a last bumper breakfast. The normal economy meals for the rank and file gave way to a slap-up breakfast. The train was temporarily halted on a side line at Bellville, near Cape Town. Orders were taken and meals served by the stewards as if the dining saloon were the Ritz. Pte G Lawrence, 1st SAI wrote:

> I don't suppose they or any of us realised how few of the five thousand would return and that less than twenty per cent actually would do so. Those Port Jackson trees at Bellville give me sad nostalgic memories when I pass them by train these days en route to Cape Town.[1]

In all cases troops were moved on board immediately after they detrained at Cape Town docks. The regiment formed up, the gangway was lined to facilitate the passing of rifles to be stowed in the armoury; a last stroll along the wharf and time to send a telegram to parents before being ordered aboard. With their pipe band playing and before a cheering crowd, B and D Companies 4th SAI left Cape Town aboard the *Balmoral Castle* at 5 p.m. on Sunday, 26 September 1915. Some 300 civilian passengers, Lukin and Brigade HQ, and the two Companies of the 4th SAI travelled on this initial voyage of the *Balmoral Castle* in its new role. A number of *Union Castle* ships had been converted to be used as troop transports.

Pte A W Cloete-Smith, 2nd SAI, described his voyage in the *Balmoral Castle*.[2] This was the *Balmoral's* second voyage out, now that the original contingent had all arrived in England. A number of other descriptions enrich the narrative so that it is possible to relive the experience of a member of the SA Brigade as he sailed to war:

---

1 *Militaria* 8/1 1978 p11. Lt G G J Lawrence. wrote a four part series called *Echoes of War* which Militaria published. Sadly Lawrence died in 1978 just before the series commenced.
2 Letters of Cpl A W Cloete-Smith.

HMT *Balmoral Castle*
8-12-1915

A good many of us sleep on deck as we can't stand the heat and smell on the troop deck. What I miss most is a bath. The nearest approach we can get to one is to strip when they wash the decks down and get the sailors to turn the hose on to us. It is all right in its way but you can't get properly clean as it is only salt water which makes you feel sticky the whole day and it is useless trying to use soap with it.

I have not had my clothes off since we left Cape Town and some of the chaps haven't even taken their boots off. They simply throw themselves down at night and in the morning they give themselves a shake and are ready again. We have parade fatigues, orderlies &c, just as in camp. There are even guards and pickets. They are stationed at different parts of the ship to see that the chaps keep within the specified bounds.

The food they gave us at first was simply awful, but it has improved slightly. You should just see the gambling. The ship is like a floating Monte Carlo. The two great games are 'Banker' and 'Crown and Anchor'. Most of the

The Union Castle Line Royal Mail Steamer Balmoral Castle that was one of the ships used to transport the 1st SA Infantry Brigade from Cape Town to England. (Photo: Transvaal Scottish Regimental Museum)

Officers of Brigade HQ and 4th SAI enjoying the afternoon nap on board the *Balmoral Castle*. (Photo: Transvaal Scottish Regimental Museum)

fellows are stoney broke, while the fellows who hold these games, are absolutely coining money. I saw one man lose £5 10/- this morning, and just after dinner I saw him lose a further £4. I am told that one lunatic lost £25. We are due to arrive at St Helena on Thursday, but in any case we won't be allowed ashore. We (also) call at Ascension and Madeira.

HMT *Balmoral*
16-12-1915

We had some fearfully hot days. At dinner last Tuesday there was not a square inch of clothing being worn in our mess. Saw thousands of flying fish yesterday. They look just like streaks of silver flashing across the water. Some of the fellows thought at first they were birds. Quite a number of the Dutch chaps have never seen the sea before and I think it has been a revelation to them. Having a rotten time at present as the canteen has run out of everything. There are no cigarettes to be had on board at all.

Of the voyage out, Pte Cyril Choat, 4th SAI, wrote a diary letter to his parents between 29 March and 13 April 1916, until RMT *Walmer Castle* docked at Plymouth, England:

3 April 1916

We have had lifeboat drill and instructions for the last few days and whenever the alarm sounds we have to get on lifebelts and fall in on the boat deck.

6 April 1916

The weather near the Equator was terribly hot. My serge trousers were absolutely wet with perspiration. While eating down below the perspiration simply dripped off one and it was impossible to wear anything while sleeping. Whenever possible I sleep on deck.

The troops were crowded into two decks which had been built into the fore-hold and a wooden staircase made of rough timber descended in two flights to the top troop deck and another two to the lower troop deck. This had the appearance of a dungeon. It was inadequately illuminated by electric lights that were never turned off.

Tables run on either side (of the troop deck) each seating twenty-two men and above these tables, in the roof, which is about seven feet high, are racks for putting kit. Hooks are also fixed in the roof and hammocks are slung on these at night above the tables. Hammock racks, for stowing hammocks during the day, are also furnished. Rooms for stowing rifles, blankets, mattresses and kit bags adjoin. As there is only one porthole to each table, you can guess what it must be like with a few hundred men sleeping below. At present too, the portholes have to be kept shut, as the sea is coming in. In the well deck are washhouses, lavatories and the cookhouse which takes up most of the space. From this you will see that we are rather crowded, in fact sometimes there's hardly room to move down below with everybody doing different things at the same time. The whole of one side of the first and second class promenade decks has been given to us as an exercise deck and even then there's hardly room to sit down sometimes as 600 men take up a lot of space. Big racks of lifebelts are fixed on this deck. The orderly room and canteen are also there. At the canteen, I believe, 720 bottles of lemonade are sold each day.

The usual routine during a voyage was Reveille at 6 a.m., unless you'd been sleeping on deck. Two orderlies for the day would stow the bedding of each mess, lay tables, fetch food, wash up and clean up. Platoons took it in turn to do Swedish drill for half an hour, followed by a general parade at 10.45. Free time before and after dinner at noon, was followed by tea at 4 p.m. Blankets were drawn at 6 p.m. with 'Lights Out' at 9 p.m. After leaving Madeira, strict instructions were issued regarding a total black out at night because of the submarine threat. To relieve the monotony of the long afternoons, sports were organised with events such as bolster bar, greasy pole, tug-of-war, boxing, sack race and turtle pull.

9 April 1916

...Yesterday afternoon some more comforts were issued. Each man got a bag containing a balaclava cap, mittens, one pair of socks, some tobacco, a sulphur bag and either a muffler or cardigan jacket and in some cases boracic ointment... The weather is quite cold now especially with this strong wind blowing and everybody is wearing overcoats and wraps on deck.

12 April 1916

As we expect to reach Plymouth tomorrow morning, I am completing the letter so that it will be ready to post there. The emergency orders were put into force today and everyone has to wear lifebelts at all times and guards are mounted on each lifeboat. There are also lookout men and signallers at various posts... Plenty of ships have been passing us during the last few days and we always steer away from them until certain of their identity. I should have thought that we would have had an escort of some sort by this time but so far nothing is in sight... I will write again from Bordon as soon as I am able.

Heaps of love and kisses
Your ever loving son
Cyril

ABOVE The 'waist' of the troop-deck from the masthead of a troop transport ship during daily inspection with life boats slung outboard on the davits ready for lowering in case of submarine attack. (Photo: Cloete-Smith Collection)

RIGHT: Men of the 1st SA Infantry Brigade on sentry duty on a troopship. They mounted guard with life jackets. (Photo: Cloete-Smith Collection)

Cyril Choat's experience was certainly the exception to the rule. Cloete-Smith recorded an escort of two torpedo boat destroyers as the Balmoral Castle reached Cape Ushant. Warwick, who was part of the first contingent to leave, stated that from Madeira 'we were now in a danger zone from enemy submarines so the ship steered a zig-zag course. We were escorted for the rest of the journey by two destroyers'.[1]

To most of the SA Brigade, as their ships docked at Plymouth, a long awaited moment had arrived. England was the land of their forebears. Now they were going to see for themselves the land their parents had talked about so often. The first sight of their destination had been the Eddystone Lighthouse and then the ship had anchored in Plymouth Sound. The civilian passengers and officers were taken ashore in a tender and thereafter the troops with a company at a time. The harbour docks were often not large enough to accommodate a ship of the size they had travelled on.

In this manner draft after draft would make the same journey with varied experiences, from Cape Town to England, to keep the Overseas Brigade up to strength until the end of the war.

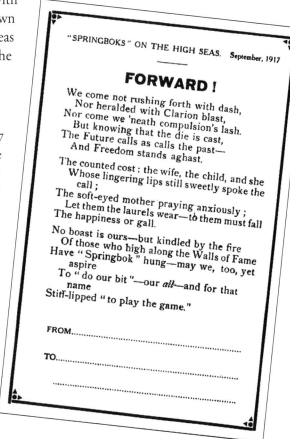

"SPRINGBOKS" ON THE HIGH SEAS.   September, 1917

FORWARD !

We come not rushing forth with dash,
    Nor heralded with Clarion blast,
Nor come we 'neath compulsion's lash.
    But knowing that the die is cast,
The Future calls as calls the past—
    And Freedom stands aghast.

The counted cost: the wife, the child, and she
    Whose lingering lips still sweetly spoke the call ;
The soft-eyed mother praying anxiously ;
    Let them the laurels wear—to them must fall
The happiness or gall.

No boast is ours—but kindled by the fire
    Of those who high along the Walls of Fame
Have " Springbok " hung—may we, too, yet aspire
    To " do our bit "—our *all*—and for that name
Stiff-lipped " to play the game."

FROM..

TO..

....

Even as late as September 1917 when men who had served in the German East African Campaign were now proceeding to France via Potchefstroom, such cards were handed to reinforcements to the 1st SA Infantry Brigade. This card was posted home by Pte E C Cloete-Smith (brother to A W). (Photo: Cloete-Smith Collection)

Chapter
5

The preparation: Bordon Camp

On the train journey to Bordon Camp, not very far from Aldershot, I was overwhelmed by the small, hedged fields, green and narrow lanes, the elms and oaks that lined the roads and made every one an avenue, the coppices and woods, the endless row upon row of lazily smoking chimney-pots above greyslate or red-tiled roofs, the tall steeples or crenellated towers of churches rising above trees that shaded some village beyond the fields, wheeling as we sped by – these and a hundred other reminders moved me so deeply that I felt that all I had suffered to come to them, and which I knew I would still have to suffer, would be supremely worthwhile.[1]

Then began the next stage – the preparation for battle. Until mid-December 1916, when the SA Brigade depot moved to Inkerman Barracks, Woking, all members of the Brigade, as well as subsequent drafts of reinforcements, journeyed to Bordon Camp in Hampshire. Between 28 August and 17 October 1915 the whole SA Brigade had arrived there consisting of 160 officers and 5 648 other ranks. The Heavy Artillery had gone to Bexhill-on-Sea and the Field Ambulance to Fleet in Hampshire.

Successive drafts recall the unfailing kindness in all weathers of the ladies of Exeter. One dear old lady remarked that the people of Devon had never forgotten how kind the South African population had been to 'The Devons' – the Devonshire Regiment when they had fought in the Anglo-Boer War.

The huts at Bordon were like those at Potchefstroom except that instead of corrugated iron, they were made from weather boards. There were thirty men to each hut, as far as possible of the same platoon. The iron beds were the same: one half of the iron bed slid under the other when not in use, and on top were stacked three 'biscuits' which formed the mattress when the bed was extended. A trunk reposed under the bed. On the wall above the head of the bed were three pegs, then a rack, and to the side a fitting to hold the soldier's rifle. The barrack-room was heated by two iron coal burners.

1   Levyns, p35.

We began route marches in light marching order for a start [wrote Pte F Addison], working up to heavy full kit later on. Our full marching order contained things something like this. On our backs was a canvas bag called a valise in which our greatcoats and blanket were carried, and then we draped about ourselves in pouches, haversacks and bottles, the following articles compiled from an official kit list which was used at every kit inspection.

One greatcoat, one blanket, one mess tin, one mess tin cover, one fork, one knife, one spoon, one shirt, one pair of socks, one soap, one towel, one housewife [not alive], one hold-all, one razor in case, one lather brush, one comb, one cardigan, one cap fatigue comforter, pay book [usually overdrawn], one identity disc, one waterproof sheet, one tin of grease [to rub on sore feet], one field service dressing, gas mask, one jack knife, water bottle, entrenching tool, toothbrush, pair of laces, 150 rounds of rifle ammunition, rifle, bayonet, oil bottle and pull through, tin helmet, iron rations, rations for the day or week, and other articles too numerous to mention.

With all this weight on the shoulder straps the arms often went numb, and I have seen men when given a ten minute break on a march sit down, and not be able to get onto their feet again without a helping hand from a pal. They broke us in gradually to carry this load, and instead of real ammunition we loaded up with two blocks of cast iron, the exact weight of 150 rounds of ammunition in our pouches. Some smart alecs, as soon as we got into the country, the blocks known as 'Kitcheners chocolates', were tossed into the hedges. On return to camp all pouches were inspected, and the culprits forfeited three days pay to repay the British tax payer, and for good measure, three days pack drill thrown in.

When we were really toughened up we had five mile platoon marching races in full kit led by an officer, who carried nothing but a walking-stick. He was the pacemaker. It was all done by stop-watch so we could run if we liked, and God help the poor devil who fell out. Our platoon never won because we had a huge chap named 'Barge Arse' being heavy in the hams. We usually arrived carrying all his kit, and he in a state of collapse. We also had a chap called 'Pull Through' because he was so thin and weedy looking, and when he arrived in camp to join up I thought he would not march across the parade ground, but we were soon put wise when told 'Pull

Quebec Barracks, Bordon Camp, Hampshire, England.
(Photo: Transvaal Scottish Regimental Museum)

> Through' was a fireman on the railway, and stoked the mail passenger train
> from Durban to Ladysmith, and handled nine tons of coal on the trip. He
> often ended a march in France carrying another man's kit.[1]

This period marked the beginning of a special friendship between the 2nd SAI
and the 4th SAI. L/Cpl G Warwick was in charge of a 4th SAI fatigue party that
prepared the barracks for the arrival of the 2nd SAI. Besides blankets, they found
a hot meal ready for them. A few months later the favour was returned when the
4th SAI arrived at Mex Camp, Egypt.

Seven days leave was granted to members of the Brigade, with a rail warrant
for a free return journey to any destination in the British Isles. A week's pay was
advanced, plus arrears and a ration allowance. Almost all had friends or relatives
they could visit.

After the leave, it was back to reality. To some, the ruthless drilling and
instruction at Bordon seemed excessive, especially if the man had seen service
before, but it gave them great confidence in themselves. Almost every man had
been trained as a cadet at school, could shoot with a rifle and may well have been
on active service in German South West Africa. The fact that many were veterans
did nothing to modify their treatment. The regular army instructors assumed they

1   Addison, *Foot* p6-7.

did not know left from right.

> So the long agony began again of learning right turn by numbers, what part of the rifle was the muzzle, and not to spit on parade. These instructors certainly had an intelligent group of men to train, but we soon found out we did not know anything. We were taught how to dig trenches and must have dug up half of England.[1]

Particular attention was given to training to prepare the soldier for the real and terrible danger of gas. To become used to wearing a gas mask, they were drilled while wearing them. The company of unfortunates donned the grey-flannel masks with the mica eyepieces. They assumed the appearance of Martians or priests of the Inquisition. The skirt of the mask had to be tucked securely under the neck of the tunic. To inspire confidence in the masks a walk through a tunnel with the real stuff – chlorine gas – was part of the training schedule. The gas was so potent that it left brightly polished brass buttons dull and tarnished. Nevertheless the soldier could breathe easily and naturally, as he walked through the swirling fumes. The strong chemical smell in the mask remained unchanged. Masks were not removed until several minutes out of the air lock, to allow the gas that had penetrated their uniforms to diffuse.

All training was conducted by grim-faced bemedalled instructors. They were members of the British Regular Army who had suffered such terrible casualties in 1914.

Bayonet instruction was always vividly remembered. Rows of dummies suspended from a wooden framework awaited mass execution. In front of them lay another row, prone on the ground. The men moved into extended order and were ordered to 'Fix bayonets'.

> 'Remember,' shouted the bayonet-fighting instructor before our first lesson, striding up and down in front of us, 'that the muscles of a man grip a bayonet thrust into his body, so it is easier to stick it in than get it out. The thrust must be upwards under the dummy's ribs into where a man's heart would be. Don't ever try to stick a man straight into his heart. His equipment and his ribs'll deflect your weapon, and he'll get you before you can recover your balance.'

> He grabbed the rifle and bayonet of one of our men to demonstrate what he had told us. Then he gave the platoon the order to charge. I felt a little

1   Addison, *Foot* p5.

sick as I stabbed the straw-filled dummy on the ground, stamped on it with my left foot, drew out the long blade, imagining it to be covered with blood, and then dashed on to spit the suspended figure behind the prone 'corpse'. But before I had got that far, I heard the instructor bawling at 'that tall man on the left' and realised that he was addressing me.

'Good God, man' he shouted 'You're not going to kiss the bastard; you're supposed to be trying to kill 'im! Put some bloody life in it! Imagine 'e's murdered your mother, and raped your sister, and you hate 'is bloody guts!'[1]

Musketry training was another integral part of the period of preparation and this skill had another set of instructors. Addison wrote:

Sergeant Major Wells was a short, cocky little man, so we called him Cock Robin. He was an ex regular, but we brought him from South Africa, so he was one of us. It was a real treat to see him handle a platoon, company or battalion of men, and also a beer mug. He used to impress upon us, to wait for the enemy until you could see the white of his eyes and then pour in the lead. I never saw him in France, but I am certain he poured in the beer down his gullet. He survived the war and I often met him in Maritzburg still pouring in the beer.

When it came to musketry we really showed these Englishmen how to shoot, in spite of the highest standard of musketry set in the British Army, after the lessons of the Boer War. We went through our musketry course from the first elementary principles of the work, but when we came to do our passing out firing practice, the War Office questioned our returns as they had never seen a supposed recruit battalion send in such a high standard of shooting. My own case was typical of dozens. I had shot for every shooting team of my age group at school, had attended three Rifle Association bisleys, and had shot twice for Natal in the school cadet Inter-Colonial Shield competition, but the trophy of which I was most proud was winning my marksman's badge in the British Army.[2]

Weekend leave to London was frequently granted. A very good bed and breakfast could be had for three shillings and sixpence. Even in wartime, London was the place for the sightseer to explore. London was full of Dominion troops. The

1   Levyns, p38-39.
2   Addison, *Foot* p6.

Australians and South Africans got on very well. 'If any Anzacs were in trouble, as they often were, a "Co'ee" would bring Dominion troops nearby, rushing to help. At that time there seemed to be a few Canadians about.'[1]

On 15 November 1915, the 4th SAI [SA Scottish] were issued with their kilts of Murray of Atholl tartan. On Tuesday 23 November, the SA Scottish was inspected by their Colonel-in-Chief, the Duke of Atholl, who later remarked that he had never seen so much of his tartan before. At the end of the war the Duke, a canny Scot, bought army surplus kilts for his 'Atholl Highlanders', the only private army in Britain. In 1973 there were still new kilts awaiting use in storage baskets in the towers of Blair Castle with the label 'Transvaal Scottish, War Department 1918'.[2]

In 1916, successive drafts of the SA Scottish that arrived at Bordon as reinforcements did not receive their kilts until many months later and those who had remained as the depot company, hired their kilts at five shillings a time to those who wished to look the part when they went up to London on leave.

Training became more practical in the form of the construction of trench systems for practice attacks. A portion of Lord Selborne's estate at Blackmoor had been placed at the SA Brigade's disposal. Movements such as flank attacks, bayonet charges and skirmishing could be practised with greater realism while Brig-Gen Lukin assessed the battle readiness of each regiment of the Brigade as they competed with each other.

On 2 December 1915, the SA Brigade was inspected by Her Majesty Queen Mary, accompanied by Prince Albert, later King George VI, and Princess Mary. Immediately after the National Anthem, Lukin gave the command 'Three cheers for Her Most Gracious Majesty the Queen'. Caps were thrown into the air during the lusty response. After a brief stand to attention while the Queen drove round the lines, there was a march past. The Queen asked particularly to see 'Nancy', the springbok mascot of the 4th. She regretted the absence of King George V who had met with an accident and could not attend the parade.

December saw training intensify. Departure for the front was imminent. All leave was cancelled. During Christmas Day 'Tim' – General Tim Lukin was always 'Tim' to his men – and other officers, looked in to wish the members of the Brigade a happy Christmas. All the bungalows at Bordon were decorated with holly and mistletoe. Each company of the 4th SAI was allowed £43 to provide Christmas fare. Pte Arthur Betteridge of 'C' Company 4th SAI recalled that RSM Cameron and the company commander, Major D R Hunt, honoured

---

1   *Militaria* Vol 8/1 1978. 2/Lt G Lawrence's reminiscences.
2   This fact was discovered by the author during his visit to Blair Castle in 1973. The label from one of these kilts now reposes in the Transvaal Scottish Regimental Museum.

On 15 November 1915 the 4th SAI (SA Scottish) were issued with kilts of Murray of Atholl tartan. This photo of No 9 Platoon at Bordon shows the men still wearing the tunics they had worn with their trousers. (Photo: Transvaal Scottish Regimental Museum)

The Officers of 4th SAI in Review Order at Bordon Camp, November 1915. (Photo: Transvaal Scottish Regimental Museum)

their bungalow with their presence for the meal. For the twenty-one men of the bungalow, the list of food was: two joints of roast beef, four geese and one stuffed turkey; green peas, mashed, boiled and roast potatoes, cabbage and cauliflower. The dessert was: jellies, blancmanges, custards, angels' food and plum pudding with sauce. Liquid refreshment consisted of seven bottles of whisky, one barrel of beer, one stout and two wine with cigars and cigarettes galore. Thereafter, in the camp drill hall the pierrots entertained an appreciative audience. The Christmas spirit continued for two days.

For many of the SA Brigade it would be their last Christmas.

Sketched in chalk by one of the men in their hut at Bordon. (Photo: H W Kinsey)

It's a long way to Tipperary, it's a long way to go;
It's a long way to Tipperary, to the sweetest girl I know.
Good-bye, Piccadilly, farewell, Leicester Square,
It's a long, long way to Tipperary, but my heart's right there.

Chapter
6

Egypt: The land of pyramids and leisure

Although it had been announced that the destination of the SA Brigade was France, plans were changed. The camp climate and the cold in England had affected many men. Several had died of pneumonia and many were sick. It was considered unwise to send a Brigade newly arrived in England to face the rigours of winter on the Western Front. Far more importantly, their expertise could be valuably employed in Egypt against the Senussi. It was well known that a large proportion of the Brigade were veterans of the German South West Africa Campaign where conditions had been similar to those they would face in Egypt.

The Brigade was issued with khaki sun helmets, shorts and new puttees, and the 4th SAI (SA Scottish) with khaki aprons to be placed over their kilts. The SA Scottish were ordered to pack away their diced blue Atholl balmorals in their kitbags. The kitbags they left behind in the QM store at Bordon would be raided after they left England to provide diced balmorals for ceremonial parades for those who stayed behind and new drafts that were to arrive in the months ahead.

The 1st and 2nd SAI were the first to leave on 28 December. The 4th, piped to the station the next day by pipers of the Royal Irish Rifles, were destined, on account of a severe storm at sea, to be delayed in Devonport docks on the *Oriana*. The 2 500 troops onboard, which included 700 Australians, were squeezed into hammocks slung three feet apart in the holds of this small ship. The Australians were sick and wounded men from Gallipoli, passed as fit to rejoin their units in Egypt.

On 2 January the *Oriana* steamed out of Devonport, now that the rough sea was calmer. The usual zig-zag course was followed.

Pte Arthur Betteridge of the 4th SAI recalled that:

> ...the night before we left, newly installed boilers were used for the first time to cook our hot dinner of rabbit. Officers and crew were fed from

the normal kitchens of the ship. Due to verdigris in our boilers all of the troops had ptomaine poisoning. This was the first experience of the ship's captain as a carrier of troops. Only sixteen covered lavatories had been erected on each side of the deck for 2 500 troops. Natural seasickness due to the high seas we had sailed into, added to the stomach poisoning, verged on the catastrophic. The 'lucky' men who reached the lavatories first, stayed there, too ill to move. The remaining 2 450 odd men couldn't hang over the sides of that rolling and pitching vessel.

Pte Arthur Betteridge 4th SAI.
(Photo: A Betteridge Papers)

Every inch of space above and below decks, on the steps leading out of the holds as well as in some of the lifeboats, was occupied by desperately ill men. The ship's supply of chlorodyne ran out at once and every scrap of paper was used within an hour. Two men died and forty were taken to hospital at Gibraltar. The state of the ship was indescribable. Crew deck hands hosed the decks and holds where men lay prostrate with stomach pains.

Many of the seriously ill chaps were taken to officers' quarters where they were given special attention, many not caring whether they lived or died. Parties of men not so seriously affected helped the eventually sympathetic sailors clear up that huge unpleasant mess.[1]

On Friday, 14 January, the *Oriana* arrived at Alexandria. The 1st, 2nd and 3rd SAI had arrived four days earlier on the *Saxonia*, a Cunarder of 16 000 tons together with a large number of Imperial officers and men on their way to join their units. There were over 4 000 men on board. The mass of humanity on deck was reminiscent of the streets of London.

1   Betteridge, A, *Combat In and Over Delville Wood* p9-10.

On landing the SA Brigade set out for Mex Camp. Mex was a fishing village on the outskirts of Alexandria, three miles from the harbour, while Mex Camp, was a mile further on.

It was while at Mex Camp that the 4th SAI (SA Scottish) received a most unpleasant shock. 'Nancy' their springbok mascot had parted her rope leash and was absent without leave. Pte A E Petersen, her keeper, scoured the lines of the surrounding tents and the sand dunes in the vain hope of locating his beloved mascot. The homes of nearby Egyptians were searched in case she had been kidnapped to be served up as dinner for an Egyptian family. Finally a 'patrol' of skirling pipers was sent out; each piper went in a different direction into the desert in the hope that the music of the bagpipe would succeed where all else had failed. As all regimental calls in the camp had been sounded on the pipes and Nancy had already learnt how to step it out in an orderly fashion in front of the pipe band when on parade. The pipe music worked like magic. Nancy re-appeared and walked nonchalantly into camp to return to her good food and comfortable bed, having forsaken 'the call of the wild'. A stout dog collar of leather and new rope, no doubt renewed at intervals, secured Nancy until the end of the War in 1918.

Mex Camp was pitched on a slope and faced a large salt pan some hundreds of yards away. To the rear the ground sloped towards a series of sand hills, 100 to 150 feet above the level of the Camp.

Betteridge had no accolades for Mex Camp.

'Nancy', the centre of attraction at Mex Camp after her return from the desert. (Photo: Transvaal Scottish Regimental Museum)

Tent pegs persisted in coming loose, mosquitoes welcomed the fresh South African blood. Egyptian flies could not be controlled by our energetic sanitary section. Sand got into everything. Hordes of Arabs loomed up from nowhere, selling dates, figs, monkeynuts and many other things, including 'dirty pictures'. We soon found these unclean, dirty-robed hawkers were a menace; in addition they were light-fingered, adept at stealing food, equipment and personal belongings. They were soon forbidden to enter the camp.[1]

There was another objection to this unpleasant camp: a smell worse than a foul pigsty or old fashioned country lavatory from a large tannery built right on the seashore. The overpowering stench wafted in whenever the wind blew from the sea.

After two weeks' training a few other ranks were allowed to visit Cairo. Betteridge wrote:

This short holiday started off in hair-raising fashion. About sixty of us walked two miles to the tram terminal where fast electric trams with open sides, started the four mile journey to Alexandria. These vehicles were driven by ambitious Arabs who regarded each journey as training for the Grand Prix. The trams were usually packed with screaming fellaheen hanging from the sides, clambering on top and anywhere else they could find a foothold.

Our crowd of happy chaps managed to overfill the inside of the tram, mostly standing room only, and some clung on to the sides like the Arabs. The fare was one piastre (1/-) in those days. By diligent manoeuvring, half of us were able to dodge the ticket collector who finally gave up the ghost. The driver seemed to grit his teeth and try hard to get the blasted tram to fly. We must have averaged forty miles an hour, swaying from left to right and bucking like a bronco over the badly kept track. It was a hair-raising trip we never forgot.

On arrival we were surrounded by a flock of filthy young and not-so-young Arab pests, screeching 'dirty pictures, Soldier' and 'you want my small sister – very cheap, one piastre'.

Here the South Africans encountered Australians and New Zealanders fresh from Gallipoli. They received 5/- a day, much to the envy of the Springboks. Their fathers had fought in the Anglo-Boer War, so they were particularly friendly and

1   Betteridge, p11-16.

soon showed how to dodge the ticket collectors at Alexandria station. Betteridge recorded that only one in four of his fifty-four paid the railway fare to Cairo. The city was thronged with soldiers – Indians of imposing physique like the impressively mounted Bengal Lancers and men of the proud well-disciplined British Regular Army.

Soon it was realised that Cairo was like the rest of Egypt: blessed with stenches from a variety of sources, be it the modern cheese factory or far worse, the untreated human excreta which fertilised the lush, green market gardens. The smell was beyond description. Nevertheless farmers paid good prices for the fertiliser. Dysentery could be contracted from unboiled vegetables or fruit that was not washed in permanganate solution. Rubbish was emptied into the Nile alongside those collecting water or engaged in washing clothes. If a soldier fell into the Nile he was immediately given a series of injections. No soldier, in spite of precautions, escaped an attack of 'gyppo tummy'. The land of the Pharaohs understandably bred an uncountable variety of flies and other bugs.

A pleasant three hours railway journey, a capital lunch *en route* and then an hour's tram journey could transport you far from the routine and aggravations of Mex Camp to the Pyramids of Gizeh. The Sphinx and the Pyramid of Cheops have been the tourist priority of visitor or soldier-cum-tourist since the turn of the century. Captain G J Miller of 1st SAI along with a lieutenant and major of his unit reserved an afternoon for this tourist priority. Their Egyptian guide, usually quite merciless in the treatment of his donkeys refused to allow the corpulent major the privilege of a donkey ride and on trying a camel all efforts failed to persuade the beast to move with its burden. In the end a twenty minute walk brought the trio to the base of the 425 foot high Cheops, near to which was an Australian camp. Miller recorded that:

> .. all around the pyramid was an unending crowd of soldiers, donkeys, camels, shrieking natives and a few sightseeing Red Cross nurses. Our guide first took us to see the Sphinx... Sand dunes hid it from view and belittled its alleged magnificence. Looking towards the great pyramid, there was an unending stream of tourists, mostly soldiers, crawling up the stereotyped tourist route. They looked like a thin stream of ants. The outer covering of the pyramid, (except) a portion near the summit, had been removed and used to build mosques. One layer of huge stone blocks had been removed and it is now comparatively easy of ascent... a matter of going up a huge staircase, the steps of which vary from three to five feet in height. If you want assistance, there are plenty of natives who will help you. They do so in parties of three, one to each hand and one pushing

The Sphinx and Pyramid of Cheops with South African sightseers in the foreground. (Photo: Transvaal Scottish Regimental Museum)

The Australian Camp referred to by Capt G J Miller, 1st SAI. (Photo: Cloete-Smith Collection)

on behind. The senior subaltern and myself declined any assistance. We climbed half way, the perspiration oozing out of every pore and waited for the major. He was a long time coming. His advent was heralded by loud screaming and fierce imprecations in Arabic. He was slowly being hauled up from one high stepping stone to another. There were six Arabs hard at work. Four of them grasped his hands and two pushed with all their might behind. The major, his tunic and helmet off, was being slowly dragged along and upwards. His heavers, hot and angry, chattered volubly. Half of them were for giving up the job and going down again, but the major grasping the gist of the conversation, seized hold of the nearest two and knocked their heads together. 'What the hell are you laughing at?' roared the major, as he caught sight of the two of us. 'I'm going to get to the top of this charnel-house, if I bust! Come on, you sons of Satan, and get a move on'. Once more the laborious ascent commenced, the natives adopting the more dignified method of hauling up their weighty customer by organised rhythmic chanting. We dared not stay longer... it would have been too much for his equanimity and ours.

We reached the top and waited patiently. At last he arrived. He had kept his word, but his assistants were in a state of collapse... even the question of 'baksheesh' seemed to have been forgotten. The descent was easy. The major came down slowly and surely. With him it was a question of sliding in a sitting position. His progress was careful and dignified! Having reached the bottom, we decided to explore the interior of the pyramid. Unfortunately for the major, the entrance was not large enough to admit his bulk. He made several attempts to enter, but it was not to be![1]

In Cairo, at the Sultan Hassam Mosque and the Coronation Mosque, the major was unable to procure a pair of slippers large enough and as Miller remarked 'the delay and subsequent admonitions in English and Dutch bestowed on the kneeling servitor of the mosque must have been extremely unpalatable to the ears of the Prophet'.

Cairo was the city where the modern and the medieval mingled. The bazaar gave you entrée into the forgotten age of the Arabian Nights – the world of money-lender and water-seller and in a quiet corner of a narrow street was the letter-writer with his quills, parchment and heap of white sand. Mosaics in the

---

1   *With the Springboks in Egypt* p66-72. The author of this anonymously published volume, the forerunner of the modern paperback, was Captain G J Miller, 1st SAI, who was killed in action at Delville Wood on 16 July 1916.

making, silks, costly carpets, amber necklaces and wares of every description invited you to bargain and haggle while the would-be buyer was regaled with coffee and cigarettes. For the officer there was dinner at one of Cairo's hotels. You dined late, then evening entertainment which began at 10.30 p.m.

The only sightseeing many private soldiers managed, was a visit to the catacombs at the foot of Pompey's Pillar in Alexandria, near Mex. Incredulous soldiers goggled at the sarcophagi and mummies of ancient Egyptian royalty of 2000 BC.

Such brief moments of leave of twenty-four to forty-eight hours, for those who could afford to exploit the opportunity on their meagre soldier's pay at British rates were enjoyed to the full. For the less fortunate there was little to break the routine. Camp life for the 1st, 3rd and 4th SAI continued with all its attendant field days, forming square, trench digging, bathing parades, bayonet and extended order drill, picket duty and fence guard.

However, life had not stood still for the 2nd SAI, who had been in action on 23 January 1916 at Halazin.

The 2nd SAI was envied by every member of the SA Brigade. Camp talk bandied reactions to the news such as 'Just our rotten luck! We shan't see a scrap now.' And then the retort of the old campaigner: 'Just hang on, you will get more fighting than even your wildest dreams could make you long for. This is not a German South West touch'.

Collar badges and shoulder flap insignia of 1st SAI (left) and 2nd SAI (right).

Chapter 7

Baptism of fire: The Battle of Halazin

On the outbreak of World War 1, Britain had withdrawn her Regular Army regiments from Egypt to fight on the Western Front, replacing them with Indian Army units. The safety of the Suez Canal, essential for a secure hold over the British Empire, was now threatened by Turkey. On 11 November 1914, the Sultan of Turkey, the religious head of most of the Moslem world declared a holy war, or jihad, against France and Britain. Egypt, in spite of British troops being stationed there since the 1880s, was still theoretically a province of the Turkish Ottoman Empire.

The Sultan's call was only heeded by the Senussi in the Western Desert. The Senussi religious order founded in 1837, had already established control over the local bedouin. This was easy as in Islamic society secular rule and religious leadership were indivisible.

Between Sollum and the Nile there was an open area of 200 000 square miles of desert, populated with bedouin and dotted with oases. It was feared that the Senussi might inflame these tribesmen to attack the Nile Valley. Initially it was uncertain whether the Senussi would take a pro-British or pro-Turkish stance, but in April 1915 Turkey had increased its influence in the area and sent money and arms. By the autumn of 1915, the Senussi could boast of a force of 5 000 men with some machine-guns and ten-pounder mountain artillery pieces with Turkish officers who had trained the force. The Grand Senussi, Sayyid Ahmed, was now persuaded to invade Egypt because his people faced starvation as a result of crop failure and the British blockade.

The British chose Mersa Matruh, 120 miles within the frontier, as a base from which they would launch their campaign against Sayyid's forces. There was a good harbour with fresh water supplies.

There was little else to recommend the choice, as reinforcements could be brought from Alexandria only in small groups by trawler or overland to a railhead at El Dab with a further seventy-five miles on foot until Mersa Matruh was

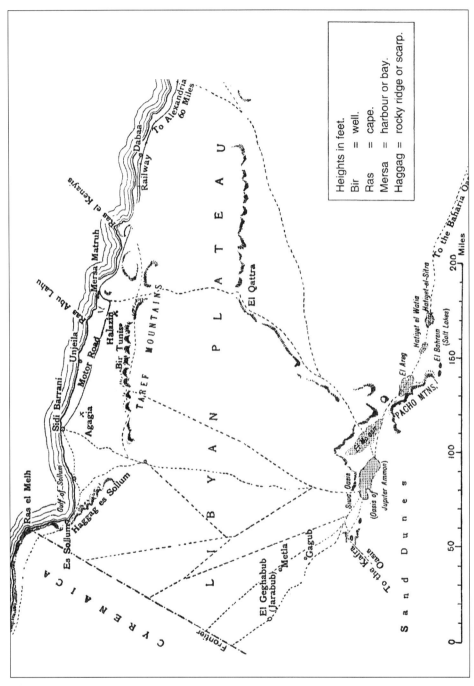

OPERATIONS ON THE WESTERN FRONTIER OF EGYPT.
(SADF Documentation Centre)

68

reached. From there to Sollum there was a coastal road which bore the grandiose title of the Khedival Motor Road. This was nothing more than a track cleared of bush that in the rainy season was reduced to the consistency of glue.

South of the Khedival Motor Road that ran along the coastal plain was a plateau of barren limestone hills. These extended to the actual desert, fifty to one hundred and fifty miles distant. Further south was a network of oases that dotted the desert. This belt of oases extended south from the Mediterranean for 500 miles to within one hundred miles west of the Nile Valley. The gateway to this network was the Siwa Oasis, 160 miles south of Sollum, and this was a main centre of Senussi influence. This whole area was now potentially exposed to bedouin raids.

The efforts of three British columns operating in the area had met with little success and no decisive blow had been struck against the Senussi.

By 11 January 1916 the 1st, 2nd and 3rd SAI had arrived at Mex Camp, Alexandria. On 19 January from his aeroplane, Capt L V Royale of the Egyptian Coastguard spotted the main Senussi camp of 300 tents at Halazin, twenty-two miles south-west of Mersa Matruh. Maj-Gen Wallace, the commander of the Western Frontier Force, decided to attack the Senussi camp. On the same day as the sighting, the SA Brigade was ordered to send a battalion by sea to Mersa Matruh. That afternoon two companies of the 2nd SAI embarked.

As there was no railway rolling stock the troops were crammed on to the HT *Borulos* and HT *Noor el Bahr*. Even with packed decks each could accommodate only 12 officers and 200 other ranks. The small trawlers bucked and rolled in heavy seas until they docked at Mersa Matruh sixteen hours later. The men staggered ashore, cold, wet and sea-sick. The next day the remainder of the regiment followed. By the evening of 21 January, the 2nd SAI under the command of Lt-Col W E C Tanner had pitched camp at Mersa Matruh and were ready for orders.

Lt-Col W E C Tanner, who was OC 2nd SAI at the battle of Halazin 23 January 1916 (later promoted to Brig-Gen). (SADF Documentation Centre)

At 3 p.m. the next afternoon, Maj-Gen Wallace's force, with the newly arrived 2nd SAI marched out of camp to bivouac at Bir Shola, some eighteen miles distant. Bir Shola takes its name from a small well which the engineers had opened up so that water for the force could be extracted by means of canvas troughs and pumps. The well was one of many along the route. Roman legionaries who had marched that way before the birth of Christ had made the narrow, circular wells, drilled through the hard rock. Their fifty to sixty foot depth was gauged by the number of puttee lengths, with dixie attached, required to reach the water.

At 6 a.m. on 23 January, Wallace's force set out. The Rev H Harris, Chaplain of the 2nd SAI, recorded in a letter that

> we had to leave some men at the well, their feet had gone in, and their stomachs too, in some cases. Others would no doubt have to fall out as well as they advanced. The cause for this had been the immediate move that the 2nd SAI had been forced to make on arrival at Mersa Matruh.[1]

Unlike the other regiments of the SA Brigade, the 2nd SAI had had no period of desert training in the hills and sand dunes west of Alexandria. That the 2nd SAI fared so well, says much for the quality of the men of the Brigade.

The force, of which the 2nd SAI formed a part, was divided into two columns by Maj-Gen Wallace and represented almost the whole British Empire. The first, which the 2nd SAI had recently reinforced, was commanded by Lt-Col J L R Gordon and also included the 15th Sikhs, 1st Bn New Zealand Rifle Brigade, a squadron of the Duke of Lancaster's Yeomanry and the Nottinghamshire [Notts] Battery, RHA. The second column, making a parallel advance on Gordon's left front, consisted of the Royal Buckinghamshire Hussars, a machine-gun section, 'A' Battery of the Honourable Artillery Company, and one squadron from each of the following: Hertfordshire Yeomanry, Dorset Yeomanry and Australian Light Horse with two troops of the Surrey Yeomanry.

The weather worked in league with the enemy lessening Wallace's mobility. The whole area was a morass. The mud exhausted the infantry and the horses. Wallace's supply train found forward progress across the wet, sloping ground almost impossible, so he had to leave them at Bir Shola with all the baggage. Next to them was parked the field ambulance. Because of the mud he had to give up the idea of utilising the detachment of the Royal Naval Armoured Car Division and sent them back to Mersa Matruh.

At 5 a.m. on Sunday, 23 January, the march was resumed after a night of little sleep caused by the piercing winter wind and the torrents of rain that greatcoats

---

1   *Militaria* 5/1 1975 p14.

Mersa Matruh, January 1916. (Photo: Transvaal Scottish Regimental Museum)

and groundsheets had done little to alleviate. Cold and wet, the 2nd SAI huddled together. Much against their will, those whose feet were too bad to march, were ordered to remain with the transport. By the time of the breakfast halt, all were feeling the effects of the unaccustomed exertions of the previous day. The New Zealanders now drew level with the South Africans and when the march was resumed at 9.30 a.m. the two colonial battalions went forward side by side. The South Africans plodded along wearily while the New Zealanders, accustomed to long desert marches, marched forward with a spring in their step.

Worn-out men never talk on the march, but the sound of a field gun far ahead had an electrifying effect. As if by magic, every Springbok leapt into a brisk step, his lethargy forgotten, and from every throat came the great war cry: 'Gobalaio Ghee! Gobalaio Ghee! Gobalaio Ghee! Wah!' On they went at a pace that would have been impossible without that stimulating sound of gunfire

That South African war cry would resound across the battlefield again and again. Those fragments are today still enshrined in the school war cries of certain great South African schools whose old boys served on those far flung battlefields of the Great War. These words are plainly audible in the war cry of King Edward VII School, Johannesburg.

As the war cries rang out the Senussi opened up at long range with machine-guns and nine-pounders. The desert mirage prevented the advancing infantry from seeing either the cavalry or the artillery although they were not far ahead Pte P Cockcroft, 2nd SAI wrote:

> The sound of the guns became louder and louder. How impatient we were! The one great fear from which we all suffered seemed to be that the artillery and cavalry would 'finish them off' before we got a chance. On, on we went,

laughing, singing, joking, until a halt was called just behind the guns. We were content to sit and watch the guns as they barked in quick succession. We were soon on our way again, but before reaching and passing the guns we were under fire. Ping! Zipp! Wheouw! Came the stray bullets all around and amongst us, each being greeted with a string of jests: 'Rotten shot!' 'Try again!' 'Missed again!' 'Hold hard, you careless devils, you will be hurting somebody!' Thus did the lads of South Africa greet those who gave them their baptism of fire. For the first time in history a South African force was in action overseas; this knowledge and the zest for battle kept away fatigue and held our spirits at high water mark.[1]

The mirage made forward observation deceptive but apparently the Senussi were defending their camp on a two-mile front where they had dug in in a semi-circle behind a low ridge. The concave shape of the ridge with flanks well forward ensured that any attack on the Senussi centre would receive fire from either side. The infantry would have to attack the centre, while the mounted troops would engage the Senussi's flank. At 10 a.m. the 15th Sikhs advanced in open order, the 2nd SAI split into companies, then into platoons and doubled out into extended order directly behind the Sikhs. The New Zealanders, covered by the Notts Battery, were in support with the 6th Bn Royal Scots and 2nd/8th Middlesex Regiment in reserve.

Because of the mirage and the undulating terrain, the Senussi were invisible to all but the men in the front line, who returned the fire. The enemy's shooting was erratic and inclined to be high, with the result that the rear lines were getting their quota of punishment without being able to return the fire. Men fell but the 2nd SAI went forward as though on parade, except that they laughed and joked and smoked their pipes and cigarettes.

So continued the fight – Wallace's force advancing and the Senussi retreating over the dead level country, quite without cover. The Senussi used their machine-guns in a masterly fashion, but the Turkish gunners with their nine pounder sent their shells in all directions causing more fun than damage. All the time the steadily advancing Sikhs and 2nd SAI moved further and further into the semi-circle of prepared positions in front of the Senussi Camp, coming under heavy rifle and maxim fire they found hard to locate.

For the next three hours Gordon had to send sections of his force to protect his flanks as the Senussi vigorously renewed their efforts to encircle the advancing column.

1   Doitsh, E, *The First Springbok Prisoner in Germany* p43-45. Private Philip Cockcroft's account of the battle of Halazin is included in this book.

In spite of the continued counterattacks of the Senussi on both flanks, Wallace knew that the continued forward movement would bear fruit. By 2.45 p.m. his persistence resulted in the 2nd SAI, the Sikhs and a company of New Zealand Rifles penetrating the Senussi entrenched centre positions. The Senussi, streamed off into the desert, deserting their flank positions and camp without making a stand. Pursuit was impossible because Wallace's yeomanry were completely exhausted, after the march before the battle and the continuous fighting to ward off the repeated flank attacks. In addition, the horses had had no water all day. The armoured cars, which would have been ideal for the pursuit, were languishing in Mersa Matruh. Although defeated, the Senussi would fight another day.

The Rev Heywood Harris, Chaplain of the 2nd SAI, wrote of the event in a letter which was printed in St Paul's Parish Magazine, Durban, April 1916.

> It was marvellous how our men stuck it out, but the spirit was excellent. Tired and hungry as they [men of the 2nd SAI] were, they would not give in. Men who fell out on Sunday morning through blistered feet, footed it into the firing line in stockinged feet; others limping up an hour or so late got into action with another regiment, aye and got wounded into the bargain.

Wallace's casualties were 21 all ranks killed and 291 all ranks wounded. Of these the South African casualties were the highest: Captain J D Walsh and 7 other ranks killed with 5 officers and 100 other ranks wounded. Senussi casualties were estimated at 200 killed and 500 wounded.

The muddy roads had kept the transport miles back so the only protection against the long, rainy, bitterly cold night ahead was the clothes the men stood up in. Shivering Springboks huddled round fires made from an inadequate grasslike substance, or paced up and down. At dawn the drizzle changed to torrential rain. At last they could satisfy their raving thirst from puddles on the ground. As the sun broke through the clouds smiles came to every face. The dead were hastily buried. Along the slow march back, ambulance and ammunition wagons, axle-deep in mud were helped forward by teams of exhausted men, who filled their cups and mess tins from the muddy water in the ruts, quaffing it with greater relish than if it had been Rhenish wine. Suddenly the mud changed to dry, sandy soil. The pace increased. Bir Shola was reached at 2 p.m. Here the men drank until satiated. Precious groundsheets and greatcoats were retrieved from the parked transport vehicles. That night the 2nd SAI, in spite of more rain, slept the sleep of the dead.

Grave of Capt J D Walsh 2nd SAI killed in action at Halazin on 23 January 1916. (Photo: Transvaal Scottish Regimental Museum)

> In a blinding sandstorm, the 2nd SAI, limping or dragging one foot after another, dirty, unshaven, as brown as the desert, but still smiling, reached their camp, [on 25 January] having in exactly seventy-two hours, marched sixty miles, fought in a six hours' action, and undergone an experience which would not be easily forgotten by those who survived in spite of the greater and more trying ordeals which lay before them in France.[1]

wrote Pte Philip Cockcroft, 2nd SAI.

Although the 2nd SAI had experienced all this, they were not to escape what the rest of the SA Brigade were receiving. In true army fashion they were condemned to spend the next six weeks at Mersa Matruh training for desert marches! There was garrison duty and they acted as convoy guard to a supply column to Ungeila, a distance of forty-five miles each way, as part of the preparations that had to be completed before the advance on Sollum began.

The GOC British Forces in Egypt, Lt-Gen Sir John Maxwell, who had been Military Governor of Pretoria during the Anglo-Boer War, wrote of the 2nd SAI in his dispatch of 1 March 1916 that they had shown 'invincible dash and resolution of their attack'. When he had inspected the Brigade shortly after their arrival at Mex Camp his statement that 'the SA Brigade is evidently fit to take its place alongside the best troops in the army' had not been misplaced.

---

1   loc. cit. p43-45.

Chapter
8

Agagia

It was all activity. The Western Frontier Force was once again reconstituted. The headquarters and remaining yeomanry units of the 2nd Mounted Brigade joined the Force along with the seventeen light armoured cars, under the command of Major the Duke of Westminster, which replaced the heavy RNAS armoured cars. The 15th Sikhs, the only regular unit of the force, returned to India and were replaced by the remainder of the SA Brigade.

SA Brigade Headquarters and 1st SAI were now ordered to Mersa Matruh. On 4 February Brig-Gen H T Lukin and his headquarters staff arrived there to find that the main Senussi force was situated near Sidi Barrani, while a smaller force was outside Sollum. A landing at Sollum Bay, commanded by heights which would be heavily defended by the Senussi, made it necessary to move the whole force along the coast road to seize Sidi Barrani. Even though this route had only a few wells to supply the advancing troops, the allocation of 2 000 camels made it possible to solve the problem of long lines of communication, more than quadrupling the load-bearing capacity of mules or pack horses. The Western Frontier Force was mobile for the first time. Now the force could conduct operations at a great distance from their base at Mersa Matruh for longer periods.

The distance between Mersa Matruh and Sidi Barrani was ninety miles. Maj-Gen W E Peyton, who had succeeded Maj-Gen Maxwell as Force Commander, established a depot at Ungeila to keep the force supplied. As it lay nearly half way between the two points and was adequately supplied with wells, it was the obvious choice.

The other units of the SA Brigade now started to arrive at Mersa Matruh and began training for desert warfare.

The main Senussi force of between 400 and 600 men, with some fifteen Turkish officers, were encamped at Agagia. This camp, situated ten miles southeast of Sidi Barrani, had been spotted from the air on 15 February. Maj-Gen Peyton now dispatched his main force to Sidi Barrani.

On 20 February, Lukin led his force out of Mersa Matruh in a dense dust storm. On 22 February the column reached Ungeila. To avoid reliance on the extended lines of communication and to prevent the Senussi from learning their adversary's strength, there was to be no delay in the advance. The men's feet blistered, and it was found that sea water was a good cure. Along the march, whenever possible, the troops were allowed to run down to the nearby beach for a refreshing swim.

On 23 February fourteen miles were covered and another fourteen miles the following day, taking the column as far as Wadi el Maktila, where they would be given a day's rest. As the Senussi were known to be in the area, Lukin took special precautions to conceal the actual strength of his column. He gave orders that his men were to keep away from the skyline along the camp perimeter. Fires and the smoking of cigarettes by those on picket duty was forbidden during the hours of darkness. Similarly the Senussi should have nothing to cause them to leave their camp at Agagia.

Lt-Col Dawson, officer commanding the 1st SAI wrote:

> We are bivouacking on the beach in a very pretty little bay, where there is an excellent bathing place. Everyone is happy and contented. It has taken the majority of them nineteen months to get near an enemy – they think they are really going to have a show at last, especially as there is now a little shooting going on at the outposts, and the Senussi put a few shots among our men drawing water just now.

Lukin's objective was to locate the Senussi so that he could destroy his forces. To locate the enemy was no easy task but at 11.20 a.m. on 25 February a BE2C reconnaissance aircraft dropped a map of the enemy position for transmission to

The Column on trek to Ungeila, February 1916.
(Photo: Transvaal Scottish Regimental Museum)

Lukin. With this lucky break he was able to have the map copied and immediately distributed to his commanders. This was supplemented by a sketch of the main features of the approach to and the positions of the Senussi encampment at Agagia. Lukin had instructed his Brigade Major, J Mitchell-Baker, to prepare the sketch. At 3.20 p.m. orders were issued for a night march to commence at 7 p.m. to be followed by a dawn attack.

However, Lukin was not to have it all his own way. The Senussi had moved up two of their ten-pounders so that at 5.30 p.m. from a point just to the south of the Khedival Road, they began to direct shells into Lukin's camp. The campsite became thereafter 'Shell Fire Beach'. Suddenly all was pandemonium.

> Shells fell thick and fast among us, while we were all huddled up on a small beach under cover of a ridge and sand hills. Being not too safe to remain on an open beach, we got round under shelter of the rugged coast. I afterwards received an order from my platoon officer to go back to the beach to see to some equipment when I came across 'Jackie' left all alone on his ownsome, and trying to pull a blanket over his head. I often wished I had had a camera to have snapped him, it was very funny.[1]

Jackie, the baboon mascot of 3rd SAI, had already become a firm favourite and comrade rather than pet of all ranks of his regiment. He drew rations just like any soldier. He drilled and marched with his company. He would entertain the men – such entertainment would become all important to relieve the boredom of the stalemate of trench warfare once the Brigade reached France. At night when on guard duty with Pte Albert Marr, his master, he was particularly useful because of his keen eyesight and acute hearing. He could give early warning of enemy movement or impending attacks with a series of short, sharp barks and tuggings at Pte Marr's tunic. Jackie wore his uniform with panache, would light up a cigarette or pipe for a pal and always saluted an officer passing on his rounds. He would stand at ease when requested, placing his feet apart and hands behind his back in regimental style. At the mess table he used a knife and fork in a proper manner and cleverly used his drinking basin. All this was forgotten when his companions were under shellfire for the first time. Pte G Lawrence, 1st SAI wrote:

> Soon the range was found and shells were bursting very close. It was a new situation for most and our first battle casualties at close quarters. There was a very tense atmosphere; to each of us, it was the moment of truth. One was aware that to keep one's balance in a moment of stark terror it was

1   *The Springbok Magazine* Oct 1918 p44.

necessary to harden one's mind against remorse for a comrade killed and mutilated beside one.[1]

The camp was evacuated and defensive positions taken up before an advance was made. The Senussi pulled out of their strong position and melted into the darkness, their shouts to each other coming through the darkness. When the evacuated Senussi positions were reached a halt was called. All the Senussi had left behind were numbers of ravenous fleas that plagued the South Africans during a night of fitful sleep. As dawn broke on 26 February it was back to camp for a hurried breakfast before setting off. Three miles out of camp the 1st SAI fixed bayonets and continued the advance in extended order in support to the 3rd SAI who were 500 yards ahead in the same formation.

Capt G J Miller, 1st SAI, wrote of the advance:

> It was a magnificent sight to see the force advancing in battle array, over the country which was perfectly flat as far as the eye could reach. The infantry platoons looked like darkish cardboard squares equidistant and moved steadily forward with now and then a brief halt. The column now left the coast road and moved inland in an almost southerly direction. Gradually the ground changed in nature and became undulating with some stony kopjes.[2]

Pte Geoffrey Lawrence, 1st SAI, continued his narrative:

> Soon the Turkish guns opened fire and we could see the black smoked shells falling amongst the men of the 3rd Regiment's advancing line. To our amazement men would fall over as the shells burst amongst them and then they all would be up again moving forward seemingly untouched. Either the shells were of poor quality or the sand took up the explosive effect. Our guns now opened fire and seemed to check the enemy battery. Bullets were coming over from the 3rd Regiment with whom we were fast closing. Going over a rise we came under direct fire and also flanking machine-gun fire, as well as shells falling around us. We had a few men wounded here. We now caught up with the 3rd SAI passing many of their killed and wounded.[3]

One of those lying among the wounded of the 3rd SAI was Pte Albert Marr with a bullet in his shoulder. Until the stretcher-bearers arrived, Jackie, the mascot

---

1   *Militaria* 8/1 1978 p14.
2   *With the Springboks in Egypt* p100.
3   *Militaria* 8/1 1978 p15-16.

baboon of the 3rd SAI, was beside himself with agitation. He attempted to do what he could to comfort the prostrate Marr, by licking the wound.

On another part of the battlefield the Dorset Yeomanry was waiting to charge the Senussi. At 10.15 a.m. their OC, Lt-Col H M W Souter, had moved forward from his first position to take a small hill about two miles from the main Senussi position.

Lukin had then ridden up to Souter on his vantage point and surveyed the Senussi positions for himself. While the infantry continued to move up, Lukin had sent the detached squadron of Dorset Yeomanry with two of the four armoured cars to the left of the infantry to protect his flank. The main body of Dorset Yeomanry was ordered to move to the left flank of the Senussi to prevent them from breaking away to the west. In executing this movement the Yeomanry came under machine-gun, rifle and artillery fire. Souter's men then occupied a strong position half a mile west of the Senussi left flank. They had dismounted and were advancing to pin down the enemy in his positions. The other two armoured cars commanded by Major the Duke of Westminster, escorted the Yeomanry and kept down the Senussi machine-gun fire. They found the soft sand heavy going for their vehicles.

By 11 a.m. Lukin's infantry was in position. He could now deploy them for the attack. The 3rd SAI was to lead, with the 1st SAI in support. On a mile front, they advanced in line with the men spaced at two pace intervals. The line of advance was covered by the machine-guns of the four flanking armoured cars. The Notts Battery of the Royal Horse Artillery galloped into position. Their guns opened up an accurate covering fire at three miles range. The infantry also came under fire. This increased in intensity as they advanced. The flat terrain gave no cover while the heat haze rendered the Senussi invisible. Gaafer Pasha, as at Halazin, attempted to outflank the infantry. Lukin was able to counter it by ordering Lt-Col Dawson to extend a company of 1st SAI to the left. So successful was this move that Dawson was not only able to deploy this company to threaten the Senussi left flank but also release the detached squadron of Dorset Yeomanry on his left. They were able to rejoin the main party of Dorset Yeomanry on his right, so strengthening Souter's pursuit capability.

Geoffrey Lawrence took part in the advance of the 1st SAI against the Senussi position.

> Bullets of all kinds were flying thickly about us – it was fortunate the Senussi were very poor marksmen. They were firing with all kinds of rifles, modern as well as old blunderbuss types, using homemade bullets that went bumbling by and some that turned over and over, said by our old soldiers to be sawn off pot legs.

RIGHT: Major the Duke of Westminster DSO, who commanded the force of 17 light armoured cars attached to the 2nd Mounted Brigade of the Western Frontier Force. (Photo: Cloete-Smith Collection)

BELOW: The Duke of Westminster's armoured cars. (Photo: Transvaal Scottish Regimental Museum)

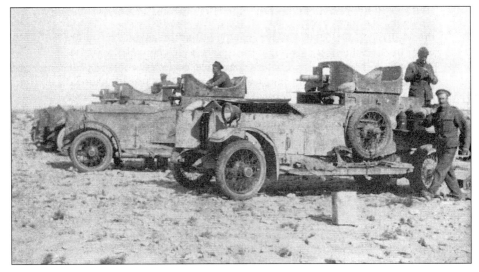

We stopped on a bushy rise overlooking a valley below and as we moved down I said to the old soldier beside me, 'There seems to be a lot of singing canaries around here'. 'Canaries be blowed', he said, 'those are bullets'. Another rise and into another valley where it seemed impossible to cross alive for bullets were nicking and spurting up the sand like raindrops on water. Still no enemy could be seen to fire at. We went down and up the next rise and at last we could see our enemy and open fire. I got off fifteen rounds rapid at white fleeting and dodging figures. We advanced no further. Here I drank my last drop of water.[1]

Since 10 a.m. Souter had noticed indications of Senussi preparations for withdrawal. He had not been idle. To cover the Senussi withdrawal, he had

1   *Militaria* 8/1 1978 p15-16.

moved his squadrons in succession along the enemy flank, parallel with their line of retreat.

By 1 p.m. Lukin's front line of infantry were within 500 yards of the Senussi positions. At the same time he warned Souter to prepare for a Senussi withdrawal. Soon afterwards a company of the 1st SAI on Lukin's left occupied part of the Senussi line and the long awaited withdrawal began in real earnest. The rest of the infantry soon followed into the Senussi lines. As these were a series of sand dunes, it was difficult to expel the defenders. The Turkish officers who commanded them had anticipated the route the advance would follow and had cunningly placed machine-guns on both flanks to direct fire on either side of the advancing 1st and 3rd SAI. Fortunately their aim was high. The Senussi fought bravely, taking up fresh positions as they gradually retreated.

Only after three hours had elapsed did the 1st and 3rd SAI finally reach the southern edge of the Senussi lines. By that time most of the enemy had escaped.

The charge of the Dorset Yeomanry which routed the Senussi after they were expelled from their lines by the infantry, was said to be one of the last cavalry charges in modern warfare. With all his squadrons closed up, under cover of machine-gun fire, Souter ordered the charge with the Senussi only fifty yards from him. His 200 horse-men streamed forward. Geoffrey Lawrence witnessed the event.

> The attack was made in two lines and was met by sturdy resistance from men accustomed to this type of fighting used for centuries past. The enemy lay flat once the horsemen were on them and shammed death whilst the swordsmen had difficulty in reaching the prostrate figures with their swords. Charging right through, the Dorsets reformed and galloped back through the Senussi again; this time the Dorset colonel's shot and dying horse landed him at the feet of the Turkish General, Gaafer Pasha. The colonel promptly put his sword through the General's right arm as he was about to fire his revolver at him. The General, his staff, machine guns-and many Senussi were taken prisoner and the rest completely scattered. A great deal of booty later fell to our forces as a result of the Senussi defeat, including fifty camels loaded with dates which represented the entire rations of the Senussi force for the next ten days. Many very interesting suits of chain mail armour were taken. These were apparently captured from the early Crusaders and handed down the centuries as heirlooms. Centuries-old long-barrelled guns were also found.[1]

1   *Militaria* 8/1 1978 p15-16.

In that mad charge, not only did Souter capture Gaafer Pasha, the Turkish general, but a number of his Turkish officers. It is interesting to note that later when the Arabs of Hejaz revolted against the Turks, Gaafer Pasha, served with Feisal, commanded his regular forces and received a CMG from the British. After World War I he became Minister of War and Prime Minister in the Iraqi Cabinet and, thereafter, Iraqi Ambassador to Britain.

For his gallantry at Agagia, Souter was awarded the DSO. He went on to command the 14th Bengal Lancers and by the end of the war he had also been awarded a CMG and French Croix de Guerre.

The Dorset Yeomanry continued their pursuit of the Senussi deep into the desert. Their losses were heavy although they killed large numbers of the enemy.

Lawrence wrote of the fate of the Dorsets when isolated after their pursuit had petered out. The next afternoon,

> ...a gruesome procession of camels and horses entered camp with thirty-six white naked bodies dangling and swaying two at a time on each camel and one to a horse. The Senussi had returned in the night and had killed and mutilated all the Dorset's wounded and stripped all of them of every stitch of clothing. The sight of these stark bodies that only yesterday had been fine soldierly men was too appalling and suddenly one had a terrifying realisation of what possibly lay before us. The bodies were identified and buried in one grave the same afternoon.[1]

Casualties were:
1st SA Infantry – 6 killed, 18 wounded;
3rd SA Infantry – 11 killed, 78 wounded, including 1 officer killed and 5 wounded.
Dorsetshire Yeomanry – 5 officers and 28 men killed and 2 officers and 25 men wounded.
The Senussi force of 1 800 had suffered about 500 dead.

The wounded of both sides were killed without mercy. As Lt-Col Dawson of the 1st SAI explained in a letter of 27 February 1916:

> All the wounded Senussi we found were finished off and prisoners were only taken when one could not very well do otherwise. It was very horrid, but the only thing to do with people of that sort, who will shoot one if able to, even when wounded.

The crushing defeat suffered by the Senussi, was to be pressed home

1   *Militaria* 8/1 1978 p15-16.

LEFT: Gaafer Pasha, Turkish Commander-in-Chief of the Senussi, immediately after his surrender, wounded and bloodstained, at Agagia. (Photo: Cloete-Smith Collection)

BELOW: Senussi prisoners in the custody of the Dorsetshire Yeomanry. (Photo: Cloete-Smith Collection)

Four hours marching with a ten minute break each hour was the order of the day for 28 February until Sidi Barrani was reached. Here the column camped. Many a shelter was made from material salvaged from ruined buildings shattered by shell-fire from British warships. A landing ground was cleared so that young Lt van Ryneveld (later Maj-Gen Sir Pierre who became Chief of the General Staff, UDF, in World War II) could land his aeroplane. His services had already proved invaluable to Lukin. A hospital ship took the wounded to Alexandria. Graves had to be dug once again for the Agagia dead as the Senussi had disinterred them to steal the uniforms the men were buried in. It was hoped they would now rest undisturbed if brought to Sidi Barrani, a permanent ganison town. The dead were reverently laid to rest, covered in blankets strewn with thousands of desert flowers, before the common grave was covered in. Each soldier placed stones on the mound. The 1st, 3rd and 4th SAI were present at the funeral service taken by Father Eustace Hill for the second time.

Hill, who had served as chaplain to the forces during the Anglo-Boer War, the Zulu Rebellion of 1906 and the German South West Africa Campaign 1914-15 was no stranger to the battlefield or what was required of him. Although attached to the 1st SAI he ministered to the whole Brigade.

From Sollum he wrote on 23 March 1916 to Canon Nash, headmaster of St John's College, Johannesburg, where he had been an assistant master until the outbreak of the war.

Machine-guns captured at the battle of Agagia by the South Africans.
(Photo: Transvaal Scottish Regimental Museum)

Brig-Gen Lukin relaxing at Sidi Barrani shortly after his return from Agagia.
(Photo: Transvaal Scottish Regimental Museum)

Lieuts J L Shenton and A M Cameron, 4th SAI, in one of the makeshift shelters erected at
Sidi Barrani. Shenton was later wounded at Bernafay Wood while Cameron suffered the
same fate at Delville Wood. (Photo: Transvaal Scottish Regimental Museum)

Dear James

I am at present moment lying on my valise with my left guarded from the sand-wind by an 8ft. by 3ft. 6in. wooden frame covered with opened-out oil-tins; my head by same only, but 3ft. by 3ft. 6in. Yesterday my batman put a few 2ft. boards over my head, so I am sheltered from sun as well as sand today. The camp resembles a very poor kaffir location. Boards, tins, sacks, basketwork, matting and any old flat stuff; all goes in as roof or walls against sun and sand.

The sea is a good absolver, and one forgets all the dirt in it. It's quite wonderful how a float in it removes all aches and pains which five minutes before seemed so horrible on the march. The pack aches one's back and boots make feet very tired, but the sea bears it all and caresses every toe in turn. We have stuck here over a week, and rumour says we may expect three more.

I have a fig tree under the branches of which Fynn and Moses (two of his former pupils) built a stone altar. I have daily Eucharist there at 7 a.m., but don't find the atmosphere of war easy of course.[1]

From Sidi Barrani, the new advanced base, further operations could be launched. To supply the whole force presented a problem, so all but a few of the mounted troops were sent back to Matruh. The day was saved when the ship HT *Borulos* arrived on 3 March with sufficient stores. Maj-Gen Peyton could now start the advance on Sollum.

---

1   *St John's College and the War 1916* p15.

Chapter 9

The last phase of the desert campaign

After the arrival of the 2nd SAI and Peyton's headquarters, on the 9 March the whole force was on the move again. This time the objective was Sollum, fifty miles west of Sidi Barrani. Sollum possessed a good harbour in the bay but approaches were difficult.

The only approach to the town, encircled by the Taref mountains, was a narrow strip of coastal land between the escarpment and sea on the east side of the bay. The Haggag el Sollum stretched from the top of the escarpment into the desert plateau westwards and southwards. At Sollum the escarpment is especially precipitous and leans over the bay from a height of 600 feet. To attack Sollum from the front would have been successful only at a cost of many casualties. If a foothold on the plateau east of Sollum could be secured, the Senussi flank would be turned once troops advanced along the plateau edge.

Once again aerial reconnaissance had kept Peyton well informed: Sollum itself and the escarpment overlooking the bay was well held. This information confirmed Peyton's resolve to ascend the plateau by the passes east of Sollum even though they were little more than steep, rocky tracks.

This plan would present new problems. The attacking force would be cut off from road and sea and the water supplies that would normally come by those routes. Known sources of water along the way could not supply the whole force. For this reason the force was split into two. Lukin would lead the one from Sidi Barrani, via Bag Bag, in a south-westerly direction to Bir el Augerin, where sufficient water was apparently available. From there he would attempt to capture the passes of Nagb Medean and Nagb el Erajib, seventeen to twenty miles south-west of Sollum. Large cisterns at Medean and Bir Siwiat, on the plateau itself should solve the water problem. The armoured cars could not negotiate these passes so they would have to ascend the plateau thirty miles further to the south-east, rendezvous with the infantry and then co-operate in the capture of the passes.

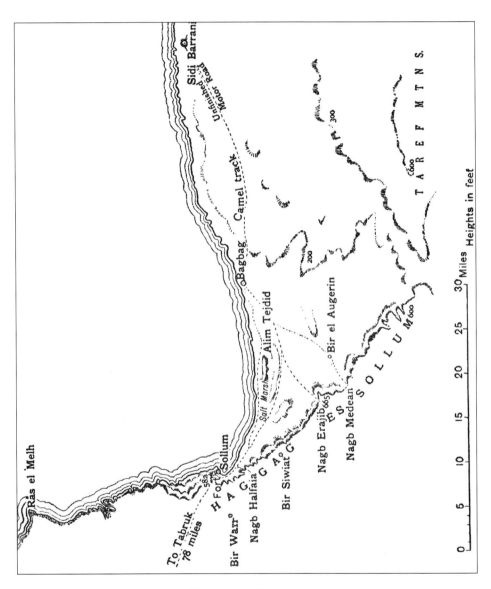

BARRANI TO SOLLUM.
(SADF Documentation Centre)

88

Lukin's force set out from Sidi Barrani as planned. No wheeled transport was included but baggage, technical equipment, ammunition, stores and precious water supplies were carried by 600 camels. Nevertheless the men were warned that in spite of the seemingly large supply train, rations would be in short supply and they should be particularly careful to conserve what they had.

On the second day Lukin's force moved off in a sandstorm. To add to the men's trials, they had very little water. The next day, 11 March, saw better weather. Lawrence wrote:

> The marching that day was quite terrific. At one time the 1st and 4th Regiments were marching in a wide plain parallel to each other, two hundred yards apart and in the centre between us was a small party of guarded prisoners including the Turkish General. At one time the 4th would gradually draw ahead and then the 1st, not to be beaten, would catch up and pass the 4th who in turn would take up the challenge. A see-saw process of marching competing columns in perfect step and long loping strides took place. Each regiment of close on a thousand infantrymen sweating it out. It was an experience and a sight seldom seen and never to be forgotten. We heard afterwards that the Turkish General was entranced by the sight and said he had never in his life seen such marching and such strapping soldiers.[1]

For the men of 'D' Company, 4th SAI (SA Scottish) the march was made less arduous by Piper Neil McNeil. He was greatly admired by one and all of his Company who marvelled how he could keep his pipes blowing for such long periods to make the marching easier for his comrades.

After four and a half hours, Bag Bag was reached. Joy of joys, although so close to the sea, any amount of beautifully fresh water was found three feet below the surface of the sand.

The march continued. Lukin's force was up at 4 a.m. the following day.

The Rev Heywood Harris wrote of the disappointment of the troops when they found the wells to be dry at Augerin after six hours of continuous marching. The 1st and 4th SAI were not allowed to rest for longer than an hour. They had to dig for water. Harris wrote:

> The water was sixty feet deep and smelt and tasted dreadfully of sulphur. Incidentally, bits of camel and goat came up into the troughs and it was reported that two Senussi had also been found, but I believe that was a libel

1 *Militaria* 8/1 1978 p18-19

One of the 600 camels that was to carry the precious stores on the advance to Sollum. (Transvaal Scottish Regimental Museum)

on the spot. In any case, there was a distinct element of truth in the saying of one man that the water had plenty of body in it!

The objective of the 1st and 4th was to seize the Medean Pass, some five miles off over some of the most difficult terrain yet encountered. They were to rendezvous with the Duke of Westminster's armoured cars.

The far distant mountains never seemed to get nearer. After two hours marching the foot of the steeply-rising escarpment was reached. Here they broke formation to scramble up the rocky side. Amongst the rocks the heat was even worse. Some men succumbed to sunstroke while others became almost deranged with thirst. Those who still had any water in their waterbottles after the twenty mile march, now drank what was left.

Only a handful of retreating Senussi were encountered and three shots were fired. This left the two regiments terribly exhausted and almost dead with thirst at the top of the escarpment or 'Thirsty Hill' as it came to be known.

The Duke, or 'Bend Or' as he was nicknamed, had just received a message by heliograph from his right: 'This is General Lukin. Left Bag Bag early this morning. General Peyton then at point four miles east. Wells dry here. Searching for water. Position serious'. The Duke signalled back that he had found no water on the plateau and his car engines were boiling water away at an alarming rate. All wells in the area had been destroyed by the Senussi, but nevertheless the Duke threatened any man under his command with a court martial if he took water from the radiator of an armoured car or from the rubber bottles filled with water to cool the Maxim guns.

> J Wentworth Day, who was with the armoured cars, related how the cars roared on across the plateau, bumping and lurching until they came to the Medean Pass (the rendezvous point). There they ran into the men of a South African battalion. They were in a shocking state. Stumbling towards the cars they gasped 'Water! Water! Water! For the love of God, Water!' 'Bend Or's' men promptly disobeyed his orders. Every drop of water they had was given to the half-dead South Africans. Long after the last bottle had been emptied still more men staggered out of the pass, along the edge of a cruel precipice, 'crying like babies and gesticulating like madmen'. One man clawed at the tunic of one of the Duke's drivers, and was just able to whisper in a croak: 'Here is my card, I'll write you an IOU for as much money as you like. See! £50 for a drop of water'.

He dragged out his paybook and pushed a frayed, dirty business card into

ABOVE: The 1st and 4th SAI file down the Medean Pass to 'Thirsty Hill'.
(Photo: Transvaal Scottish Regimental Museum)

RIGHT: A rest along the way. (Photo: Transvaal Scottish Regimental Museum)

the driver's hand. It bore his name and the address of a bank in South Africa. The driver had an old maxim bottle in his tool locker. It might still hold a drop of water. He hauled it out, unscrewed it. The water was stinking. The bank manager snatched the bottle and gulped.[1]

This account indicates the plight of the men of the 4th SAI on 'Thirsty Hill'. The thirsty camel boys slaked their thirst with the urine of the camels.

Captain Miller, 1st SAI, wrote that:

..only those who have known what it is to be really in need of water know what it is to suffer from thirst. It is when your lips have been parched black by the sun and dust, when your tongue cleaves to the roof of your mouth, when your throat feels like a hollow sandpit ...Some of our men even went so far as to drink the contents of their rifle oil bottles. Slight relief was given by digging for certain roots which contained some kind of moisture, and eating them. But it was a poor substitute for the liquid necessity.[2]

1   Warwick p41-42.
2   *With the Springboks in Egypt* p126.

Heliographing the Duke of Westminster from the Medean Pass.
(Photo: Transvaal Scottish Regimental Museum)

Camels, with a limited supply of tainted water from Augerin that tasted even worse after it had been heavily medicated with chlorine, with other supplies, finally reached the men. To them it was the most perfect drink they had ever received, but not enough.

Because of the water shortage it was no longer possible to send the whole force along the escarpment. Nevertheless Peyton had succeeded in getting some of his force on to the plateau.

To exploit the advantage to the full, Lukin was ordered to proceed along the edge of the plateau and seize Halfaya pass so that mounted troops and guns could proceed through the pass. Halfaya had been evacuated and left for the takers. Lukin's flank march had made the Senussi positions untenable. They had also abandoned their encampment along the edge of the plateau at Bir Warr that overlooked Sollum. Peyton's column now advanced along the coast towards Sollum. The Senussi retired to the south-west after destroying quantities of ammunition and supplies. At last ample water arrived.

On 13 March the Duke of Westminster's armoured cars, in hot pursuit of the Senussi, had overhauled them twenty miles from Halfaya. The Duke's machine-guns opened up and scattered the surprised tribesmen. To add to their discomfort a burst of bullets caught two of the Senussi camels loaded with ammunition, which then blew up with a tremendous explosion. Demoralisation was complete. Those not killed or captured fled into the desert. Among the many prisoners taken were three Turkish officers as well as supplies, three ten pounder quick-firing guns, nine Maxims and 300 000 rounds of ammunition.

On 15 March, the edge of the table land was reached. The area had been vacated by the Senussi shortly before, on realising the threat from the rear. Below lay the harbour of Sollum,

> the most perfect bay I have ever seen [wrote Captain G J Miller, 1st SAI]. In the harbour were several gunboats, destroyers and a large number of trawlers. Our descent from the plateau took a considerable time. We had to proceed in single file along narrow bridle paths, over loose rocks and rubble. The path wound round, in and out of a deep and precipitous gorge, and one had to be careful of one's foothold. At every turn were signs of a large camping place. Fires, rags, old tins, and innumerable snail shells marked where the enemy had had his last night's repose and early morning breakfast...[1]

The 1st SAI and then the 4th SAI were met by General Peyton. He had ridden out alone to meet them, taking the salute from each platoon and repeated 'Well done, men; you have done exceedingly well. Thank you, men, for doing the most damnable march I have ever asked men to do.' Every man stepped out with renewed spirit in spite of his heavy load and the heat.

The 4th SAI marched into Sollum at 10 a.m. The 1st and 2nd SAI had already arrived. The 2nd SAI had very kindly prepared tea for the South African Scottish, keeping up the tradition of friendship between the two units. To celebrate their entry into Sollum, Lt-Col Jones of the 4th SAI, ordered an issue of rum. On the first afternoon an impressive ceremonial parade was held for the whole Force.

It was a case of history repeating itself. As at Sidi Barrani, the members of Peyton's force made short work of the ramshackle houses of Sollum and the Arab village of miserable wood and iron shanties. Using the material to construct small bivouacs as shelters from the wind and sun, the native village was transferred piecemeal to the SA Brigade's camping area. Soon the village had disappeared and its remnants were used as firewood. At least the shelters were in orderly lines!

From now until the first week of April, the Brigade was kept occupied with a variety of tasks, one of which was the construction of a road from Sollum up to the plateau. It is interesting to note that this became a key road in World War

---

1 *With the Springboks in Egypt* p134.

II and was in constant use by South Africans and British troops fighting in the Western Desert campaign.

The Brigade still had time for other activities, recalled Lawrence.

> It was not long before a businesslike Greek sailed from Alexandria and set up a general store on the beach. The troops were disgusted when the vendor took advantage of our dependence on this one store and began overcharging. One of his sources of revenue was a large wooden cask of beer with the tap on the inside of his barricade. Some of our old regular army sweats drilled a hole in the cask on our side and fitted a tap. Whilst everyone engaged the salesman with much hoo-ha a steady stream of dixies was being filled out of sight below. When the barrel inexplicably ran dry the 'fat was in the fire'. The Greek, gesticulating wildly, ran round to discover the second tap, screaming insults and calling to high heaven for vengeance and redress. The upshot of it all was that our Colonel Dawson, a man with a sense of humour, ruled that we had had our fun and some the beer, so all must pay for it. Every man was deducted a portion of his pay and a goodly sum handed over to the disgruntled but now consoled vendor.[1]

All the time ships of various kinds were transporting companies of the SA Brigade piecemeal to Alexandria. With the SA Brigade now established at Sidi Bishr camp, it could be re-equipped for service in France. On Monday, 10 April, the Brigade was inspected by General Sir Archibald Murray, the GOC British Forces in Egypt. In his address he stated: 'I don't know what division you will go to in Flanders, but I am writing to Sir Douglas Haig, and telling him what stuff you fellows are made of. I wish you God speed and every success in your new surroundings'.

Although the occupation of Sollum marked the end of their desert campaigning, the war with the Senussi continued until February 1917. In April 1917, the Grand Senussi, signed a *modus vivendi* with Italy.

It is ironic that in the Great War troops from South Africa, Britain, India, Australia and New Zealand fought on battlegrounds close to Mersa Matruh, Sollum, Halfaya and Sidi Barrani, contributing to the Italian Empire's future existence in the area. Some twenty-four years later soldiers from those very countries would effect the destruction of that same empire.

Between the 13 and 15 April, the Brigade left Alexandria on the five-day voyage to Marseilles. The three months in Egypt had converted the Brigade into a hard-bitten, battleworthy force. A tremendous *esprit de corps* had developed

Arrival at Sollum and getting a cup of tea or something stronger from the 2nd SAI.
(Photo: Transvaal Scottish Regimental Museum)

which inter-regimental rivalry had fostered. The Brigade had received the finest possible preparation for its inclusion into the famous 9th (Scottish) Division.

The SA Brigade was on its way to what was regarded as the 'front of all fronts'. Here there was real work to be done. The Western Front was where the action was to be found.

Chapter 10

Marseilles and after

Excitement heightened as the Brigade prepared for France. The floppy, soft field service caps with their six arcs of stitches on the peak were issued. On Tuesday 11 April, the 4th SAI also had their khaki helmets replaced, but with the khaki balmoral or tam o'shanter.

Egypt had a final surprise. Over the period 13 and 15 April while the Brigade was leaving Alexandria, a thick red dust totally obscured the city from view; even the ships anchored close by were rendered invisible. This first experience of the Khamsin had to be sat out behind closed hatches and portholes. The blood red dust was like an omen of what lay ahead. For these men, toughened to the peak of condition, there was no gloom, only anticipation for the real war in France.

The Brigade was transported in the *Tintoretto, Scotian, Megantic* and *Oriana* to Marseilles. To the dismay of the 4th SAI they found the old *Oriana* waiting for them, still stinking from their last voyage in her. It was as though the ship was cursed, for a case of contagious beri-beri fever was diagnosed and the whole 4th SAI, along with 20 officers and 594 men of the 1st SAI, had to be placed in quarantine outside Marseilles at La Valentine.

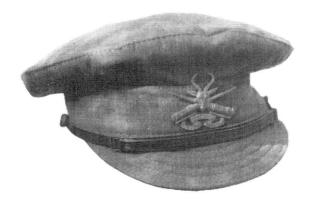

The floppy, soft field service caps issued for service in France; badge of the SA Heavy Artillery.

After disembarkation at Marseilles – 4th SAI.
(Photo: Transvaal Scottish Regimental Museum)

How different had been the voyage of the 3rd and the 2nd SAI who made the trip on the Megantic, a large White Star liner, still with cabins, saloons, lavatories and hot and cold water. It had not been converted into a troop transport ship. Except for the quality of the food those on board, for once, had nothing to complain about. After four and a half days the ship docked at Marseilles at midnight on 19 April. As L/Cpl Ernest Solomon of 3rd SAI wrote:

> France – what a wealth of signification attached to that name – was reached, and the realisation brought visions of early participation in events on that most important of all battle areas in the war, the Western Front.[1]

Solomon was given little time to study Marseilles; not that there was much to see. The 3rd SAI was soon on the march, from the quay to the station, led by bugle bands, to the approving applause of the local populace. The long circuitous journey north, finally ended at Steenwerck near Bailleul on 23 April. Wherever the train stopped the warmth of the French people was remarkable. Solomon, like his fellows, was greatly taken by the French bread, procurable at stations.

1   Solomon, E, *Potchefstroom to Delville Wood* p42.

A march of two miles brought them to small huts. All was exciting and new. Fights in the air and the antics of the flying machines provided their first thrills. On board the Megantic instruction had been given in the use of gas masks or helmets. At Steenwerck the speedy and expert fitting of this new nuisance was perfected. Every civilian, young and old, was obliged to carry a gas mask. A favourable wind could carry gas far behind the lines. A round of inspection parades took place. The new arrivals were exhibited to the top brass like a new range of products in a department store. Inspecting officers included several who had served in South Africa during the Anglo-Boer War; hence their particular interest. These included General Plumer, with ever-present monocle, and Field Marshal Sir Douglas Haig whose kindly face and manners particularly impressed Solomon and his party. Training had already begun.

Meanwhile the half Battalion of the 1st and the 4th SAI were still in quarantine at La Valentine, a beautiful semi-rural area just outside Marseilles some eight miles from the harbour. On Saturday morning, 22 April, Lt-Col F A Jones DSO of the 4th SAI addressed his men to the effect that they would be in quarantine for at least nine days. At the same time he warned them about women and informed them that inter-company competitions would be organised to keep the regiment 'out of mischief'. The next day was Easter Sunday. A church service took care of the morning and in the afternoon a route march was organised. Pte Lawrence of 1st SAI, also confined to the restrictions of quarantine, recalled how on the 4th

The inter-company competitions to keep the 4th SAI 'out of mischief' during their quarantine in Marseilles. (Photo: Transvaal Scottish Regimental Museum)

McGill tossing the caber at the Marseilles sports.
(Photo: Transvaal Scottish Regimental Museum)

The Pipes and Drums of the 4th SAI (SA Scottish) at the Marseilles sports.
(Photo: Transvaal Scottish Regimental Museum)

SAI's return they were made to enter the camp by scaling a high wall as a fitness test.

> French women turned up in force to watch the fun. The hilarity and shrieks of laughter as some of the Jocks stuck at the top with kilts over their heads could be heard from afar [answering] the recurring feminine question of what Scotties wore under their kilts.[1]

After moving to a nearby camp on the 26 April, the 4th SAI (SA Scottish) handed in their blankets, greatcoats and kilts for fumigation. The next day the kilts were returned, pleats crushed and the tartan wrinkled. This was soon rectified by placing the kilts on a waterproof sheet on the ground. After dampening them and aligning the pleats, a ground sheet was placed over them. The large garden roller in the camp was dragged across them to iron the pleats. In this way the Scottish could once again steal the limelight.

The camp fence was never without an array of French girls. The camp main gate was an area of high risk! Pleadings on their part were resisted with difficulty. George Warwick of the 4th SAI, recalled:

> One evening a sentry put his khaki balmoral and greatcoat on a woman and smuggled her into camp. Another woman was brought in in the same way. The women were taken to a stable and men visited them there, offering tins of bully beef in payment... No wonder the Colonel was worried about his men. Men were advised to go to the medical tent for treatment before going on pass, whether they intended to misbehave themselves or not, and to visit the medical tent on their return from their adventures.[2]

Finally departure day arrived, Monday, 8 May 1916. The SA Scottish had travelled by train from La Valentine to a point near the city. The local newspaper had already prepared the population of Marseilles for their departure. Special postcards were printed to commemorate the event. Never before had a kilted regiment been seen in Marseilles.

One such postcard showing the 4th SAI preparing to move off features Nancy wearing a smart tartan coat as protection against the cold. Private Petersen clutches the rope that secures his important charge.

Colonel Jones had prepared them for the ovation they were to receive, permitting his men, on this one occasion to break regulations and accept flowers

1 *Militaria* 8/2 1978 p41.
2 Warwick p52.

from the crowd. The moment the pipe band struck up, the springbok mascot leading, the crowd got out of hand. Sweets and cigarettes were pressed on the South Africans, flowers were stuck into equipment straps and into rifle muzzles.

Each Jock almost lost sight of the man in front of him because of the mass of girls jostling in between and was hugged or kissed by countless girls cn routc. Pte Arthur Betteridge estimated the crowd along the way to have been at least 200 000, mostly females. The three and a half mile march took three and a half hours! Lt-Col Jones and each mounted officer was presented with a huge bouquet. Each soldier arrived at the station with his hands full of flowers.

Long tables covered with white table-cloths, loaded with cakes and coffee, well laced with rum, had been set up at St Charles Station.

> Frenchmen were pouring champagne out of bottles and filling glasses for us to drink. The idea was that each soldier should have a glass of champagne. Actually some old soldiers contrived to get more than one. Those of us still living will never forget that send off from Marseilles.[1]

1   Warwick, p53 and 54.

One of the special postcards printed to record the day the 4th SAI departed – 8 May 1916. Never before had a kilted regiment been seen in Marseilles. Nancy, the Springbok mascot, is wearing a tartan coat. (Postcard: Transvaal Scottish Regimental Museum)

GRANDE REVUE DES TROUPES BRITANNIQUES A MARSEILLE
La Musique du Régiment des Ecossais et leur Mascotte "La Gazelle"

GRANDE REVUE DES TROUPES BRITANNIQUES A MARSEILLE
Le Regiment des Ecossais

Lt-Col Jones permitted his men on this one occasion to break regulations ancl accept flowers from the crowd, as the 4th SAI departed from Marseilles.
(Postcard: Transvaal Scottish Regimental Museum)

History repeated itself. It was a highly uncomfortable journey in the tightly-packed second and third class carriages, with attempts to sleep on the racks and floor. The discomfort had been somewhat relieved by the unfamiliar sights as the train journeyed beside the banks of the Rhone River between high hills with many castles occupying strategic positions along the way. A troop train filled with Russian soldiers was, for a while, drawn up alongside the South Africans. These big men from North Russia with their long rifles and long thin bayonets were off to reinforce the French.

After detraining at Armentières at dusk and proceeding along endless cobblestoned and gravel roads, through village after village, Le Bizet was reached. The men were too exhausted to eat the hot meal that awaited them. Their boots were pillows and their overcoats blankets. Next day they were to find that Armentières was only seven miles away and in the total blackout their guides had marched them more than double the distance.

Billets for the new arrivals had been prepared by the other units of the SA Brigade in a variety of farm buildings with a liberal supply of fresh straw.

It was remarkable to find that each trench was named and to encounter famous London thoroughfares and places in France! There before them were *Oxford Street, Regent Street, Hyde Park Corner*, etc., while *London Bridge* spanned a fearsome waterway some two or three feet wide and as many deep.

The trenches lay one and a half miles away. Pte Geoffrey Lawrence wrote:

> At night the rumble of gun fire could be heard with occasional machine-gun fire. There were the constant flashes of the guns lighting up the sky and Very lights of all colours going up, giving us newcomers this April of 1916 a foretaste of what was to be our lot at close quarters during the next two and a half years. The few weeks before taking over duty in the trenches were happy days spent in fine weather busily training for trench warfare by day and in the evening strolling to estaminets in nearby villages. The estaminets mostly very small and homely, the central feature being the stove in the middle with its horizontal pipe extending across the room for warmth and usefulness. We were most agreeably surprised to find that these Flemish people on the border of Belgium could understand our Afrikaans and we their language and newspapers.
>
> Our fortnight of peaceful existence over, we marched by platoons in cautious silence along the road leading to the entrance of our trench

An infantryman's view of the French cobbled roads – cartoon by Lt W H Kirby 4th SAI. The march from Armentières to Le Bizet to join the rest of the SAI Brigade was an introduction to French roads that no member of the 1st and 4th SAI would forget in a hurry.

A first look at No Man's Land. (Photo: SA National Museum of Military History)

system. We filed with interest through a roofless building in the little village of Ploegsteert, our gateway to the underground sand bagged defences. A long communication trench brought us to the front line. The greatest care for silence and for keeping well below trench parapets was stressed. We passed notices such as 'Hell Fire Corner', 'Keep moving, duck or die'. The opposing lines here were fifty to a hundred yards apart.

I occupied the first few nights firing at the flashes of the German rifles as they fired at us. It was too dark to see or be seen so really not risky provided one ducked quickly after each round. The enemy was probably passing the time in the same way. Every now and then we would loose off a Very light to make sure no one was creeping up on us.[1]

This was the Western Front. What had inspired the great adventure was now at hand. However, the whole spectrum of sights and sounds, so novel to begin with, would soon sink into a monotonous routine.

During this period before training for the Somme battles began, steel helmets or tin hats, as they were called, were issued for the first time, initially to frontline sentries early in 1916. The SA Brigade were among the first to wear them. They prevented wounds from light shrapnel that could penetrate the ordinary cloth caps. The delusion that the steel helmets provided protection against bullets was shattered after several fatalities. The helmet served as an excellent wash basin when required!

Gradually the men of the Brigade became familiar with the darkness being relieved at night by the periodic starshells. And how besides lighting up No Man's Land, Very lights could be used in various colour combinations to signal to the artillery in the rear. During the day the sentry used a periscope to watch enemy movements. There were also the long periods of 'standing to'. All men in a trench had to be ready to repel a German attack between 2.30 a.m. and 4.30 a.m. and 8 p.m. to 9 p.m. These were the hours during which a German attack was most likely to occur. It did not matter whether you had been on sentry duty until 1 a.m. You were up again ninety minutes later for the sacred ritual of 'stand to' and possibly on sentry duty again for an hour at 6 a.m.

A whole new routine of sleep taken in snatches, restless days and busy nights became ingrained. For the present, however, all was a novelty with the gloss of new paint.

I wore a tunic, a nice khaki tunic,
And you wore a civvy suit.
We fought and fell at Loos,
While you were on the boose
At home, while everyone knows
You stole the wenches while we were in the trenches
And facing the angry foe.
You were a-slacking while we were attacking
The Hun on the Longueval Road.

Chapter
11

A final honing

Routines become boring yet it was this routine that was constantly with the soldier on the Western Front. It was as predictable as sunrise and sunset.

The 2nd and 3rd SAI as well as the majority of the 1st SAI had been gradually acclimatised to the trenches. On 25 April their trench warfare initiation had begun when each South African battalion had sent 12 officers and 120 men for forty-eight hour tours of duty alongside well-seasoned men of the 9th Scottish Division. The SA Brigade's short period of gaining experience came to an end on 6 May. They were now considered ready to occupy the front line, independent of further assistance. They marched to Le Bizet seven miles away and two days later the 2nd and 3rd SAI relieved two battalions of Highland Light Infantry in trenches 1 000 yards from the village. There was no such consideration for the 4th SAI and remainder of the 1st SAI. On the very evening of their arrival at Le Bizet, 200 men from each Regiment were sent straight into the trenches to relieve the 2nd and 3rd SAI. Over the next few days they continued to be reliefs for the 2nd and 3rd. On the morning of their arrival in the line, a notice appeared above the German Front line trench. Chalked on a board were the words 'Welkom Afrikan Skotch' – proof of the efficiency of German intelligence.

The trenches were arranged in three lines: a front line, a support trench and a reserve trench. Their right-angled zig-zag construction lessened the potency of shell bursts. Each straight section of the trench was known as a fire bay. In each bay two men were on duty for two hours and rested for four hours while others took their turn. On the side nearest the German front line, a firestep was cut into the side of the trench. From here attacks could be repelled. The three lines that made up the trench system were linked by communication trenches. The system was entered through an access trench in the rear areas that would be well concealed from German observers. While in the line, officers and senior NCOs occupied proper rooms that led off the trench, after descending several steps. These dugouts usually provided inadequate protection for their occupants in the case of a direct hit from a shell – unlike the sophisticated dugouts deep underground, that the French and particularly the Germans, were most skilled

Aerial photograph of the trench system near Arras which illustrates the front, support and reserve trench systems. The British lines, are in the bottom half of the picture, facing the German trenches. (Photo: SA National Museum of Military History)

at constructing. In some British circles it was considered 'not cricket' to make yourself totally invulnerable! For the men in the trenches shelter was taken where it could be found – in recessed, scooped out, areas in the side of the trench or on the firestep itself.

Before first light, as explained, there was stand to. After the men had stood down and breakfast was over, sentries were posted. For the rest of the day all there was to do was sleep. However, equipment had to be worn. There was the constant

PROPRIETOR OF DUG-OUT (*politely*): "Would you mind keeping off the roof?"
(We *don't* think.)

These cartoons by Lt W H Kirby, 4th SAI, demonstrate how inadequate shelter was for the British soldier in the line. In Kirby's own words: 'The conditions at the Front are often so nearly intolerable that, if troubles were taken seriously, one would very quickly "go under".' This was his response to how he was able to keep his cheerful outlook at concert-pitch.

disturbance of men moving along the trenches on various errands. Daylight and night activities were in sharp contrast to each other. The day may have been disturbed by the odd rifle grenade or sniper's bullet but for the most part a 'live and let live' attitude prevailed on both sides. At nightfall, 'stand to' took place once more. Cpl Arthur Betteridge, 4th SAI, recalled the transformation that took place once darkness enveloped the trenches.

> Within a few miles of the front, roads were deserted in daylight, but from dusk to dawn they were chock-a-block with transport of every kind conveying rations, ammunition and supplies to dumps near the front line. Ambulances mingled with guns of all sizes, infantry regiments on their way to relieve others in the front line, squeezed to the side of the road to let the horse-drawn and motor vehicles past, none of them were allowed to show their lights. An incredible quantity of stores had to be moved every night from dumps in the rear to those near the front line, no matter how bad the weather.
>
> At the same time the communication trenches to the line itself were a hive of industry at night; depending on the flatness of the country, these seven feet deep, winding trenches, were half a mile or longer. Duckboards were frequently covered with mud and broken in places due to enemy shell fire. Every item used in the line itself had to be manhandled, usually by troops out of the line 'on rest'. Casualties were often greater during these 'rest' duties, than when on front line duty as the German shells sought to hinder the work they knew was going on, just as it was behind their own lines.[1]

This was a dirty war. For such prolonged periods, never before or since had great concentrations of humanity lived, eaten and slept in the same filthy barns, trenches and dugouts, the walls of which could sometimes literally crawl with lice. In German South West Africa or Libya, troops had been on the move. At worst they complained of fleas. In France each man provided accommodation and sustenance for his own private zoo. After their first ten days in the line, the South Africans needed assistance to rid themselves of the unwanted company. In front line conditions without a bath or shower each soldier was soon lice-ridden. Many hours were spent searching the seams of clothes and cracking lice.

At the delousing station, wrote Betteridge,

> ... the joy of our first hot bath in two weeks was unbelievable. Huge tanks

---

1   Betteridge, p24-27 (selected extracts).

'There was the constant disturbance of men moving along the trenches on various errands'; on this occasion the men's dinner is being brought up along the front line.
(Photo: SA National Museum of Military History)

> five feet deep held forty to sixty troops at a time. Soap suds were skimmed off the top of the water for the next batch to bathe. The temperature was regulated. While so occupied, our kilts and shirts were deloused in a fumigator. This with clean socks and shirt helped us feel human again.[1]

Tags were attached to clothing so that the owner would get his items returned to him after fumigation. The pleasure was short lived. After a couple of nights in a barn everyone was scratching and hunting vermin like a troop of baboons.

While out of the line, besides having to undertake the usual irk-some chores, the training of the SA Brigade was proceeding apace. During daylight instruction was given in signalling, bombing, bayonet fighting and the use of the Lewis gun. However, on 26 May, Brig-Gen Lukin issued orders that would see his brigade move thirty miles to the rear with the whole of the 9th Division to the First Army manoeuvre area at Erny St Julien. Here the Division would receive further training. This period was very short and the limited facilities made it impossible

1   Betteridge, p24-27 (selected extracts).

At the delousing station – this helped the men to 'feel human again' recorded Pte. Arthur Betteridge. In this case a brewery had been converted for the purpose.
(Photo: Cloete-Smith Collection)

for a battalion to receive any single form of training at one time. From 6 June companies and platoons received lectures from 6.00 a.m. and were drilled as well until 5.30 p.m. Rain frequently interrupted the programme that concentrated on offensive training. Preparations for a summer offensive were obviously being made.

On the fourth day of training entire regiments were put through their paces in a mock attack. Before the Division could practise as a whole, orders came which moved them to the Somme in the south. The 9th Division joined XIII Corps which fell under the command of General Rawlinson's Fourth Army.

At the time the 9th Division consisted of 26th Brigade: 8th Bn The Black Watch; 7th Bn Seaforth Highlanders; 5th Bn Cameron Highlanders; 10th Bn Argyll and Sutherland Highlanders. The 27th Brigade was made up of: 11th Bn Royal Scots; 12th Bn Royal Scots; 6th Bn King's Own Scottish Borderers and 9th Bn Cameronians (Scottish Rifles). The Pioneer Battalion was the 9th Bn Seaforth Highlanders. These thirteen battalions were only two-thirds of the complement of 19 000 men that made up the strength of a British infantry division at the time. The remaining third consisted of field artillery, engineers, medical staff (the South African Field Ambulance had rejoined the SA Brigade after receiving training, at the nearby village of La Creche, since mid-May), signallers and drivers. The latter were needed to see to the 5 000 horses of each brigade and its sixty motor vehicles. An Army Service Corps company for transporting the baggage and supplies was thus part of the SA Brigade, as was a

Royal Engineers field company. Each brigade also had a machine-gun company of 9 officers and 140 other ranks attached to it. They were armed with the Vickers medium machine-gun. It was water-cooled, required a tripod or fixed position to fire from and was twice the weight of the Lewis gun. The Vickers could be relied upon for sustained fire or short bursts of very rapid fire. It was not prone to jamming or over-heating through over-use as was the Lewis gun, which was the forerunner of the sub-machine gun.

The SA Brigade had inherited the 28th Machine-Gun Company from their predecessors in the Division. They had been the 28th Brigade who, along with the rest of the 9th Division, had been blooded at Loos, but had been cut to pieces. The SA Brigade had been chosen to replace them. The rest of the Division were not over-thrilled with the idea of losing a sister brigade, however good the replacement might be. Brevet Major John Ewing MC of the 6th Bn KOSB, which was one of the battalions of the 27th Brigade, wrote of the change.

> The inherent clannishness of the Scot revolted at the idea of friends being taken away and of strangers coming in. Nothing much was known about the South African Brigade except that they were the pick of South Africa, and that was saying a great deal. From the first it was apparent that their standard of discipline was very high and their critical Scottish comrades realised that the Division had been greatly honoured in having such a doughty brigade attached to it.[1]

As for the South Africans, they understood. Pte F Addison, 2nd SAI, joined the SA Brigade immediately after Delville Wood. He recorded:

> When we eventually did join, a chap called Cpl Gold pointed to a platoon of these Jocks and said: 'See those men over there. Their regiments were raised by Charles II and their battle honours are a yard long, and we must not let them down.'[2]

Although coming from a proud lineage, they were territorials not regulars; men of Kitchener's New Army – *The First Hundred Thousand* as Ian Hay called them in his famous book of that title. For all their enthusiasm they could not be put on a par with the British Regular Army, the 'Old Contemptibles', who had been almost wiped out at the 1st Battle of Ypres in 1914. The regulars had been experts in combining fire and movement. Their old standards of musketry, developed

1   Ewing, J, *The History of the 9th Scottish Division 1914-19*, p81-83.
2   Addison, *Foot* p9.

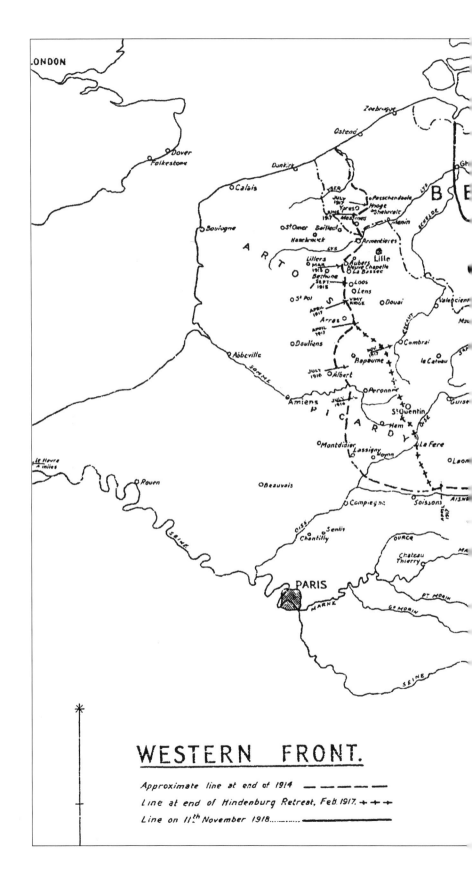

LONDON

Zeebrugge

Ostend

Dover
Folkestone

Dunkirk

Calais

YSER
JULY
1917
Ypres
JUNE
1917 Messines

Passchendaele
Hooge
Gheluvelt

Menin

Boulogne

St Omer   Bailleul
Hazebrouck

ARTO

LYS

Armentieres

Lillers
MAR
1918
Bethune
SEPT
1918

Lille
Aubers
Neuve Chapelle
La Bassée

Loos

Lens

ECHELDE

S

St Pol

VIMY
RIDGE
APRIL
1917

Douai

Valenciennes

Arras
APRIL
1917

Doullens

ESCAUT

Cambrai

la Cateau

Abbeville

SOMME

MAY
1917

Bapaume
JULY
1916 Albert

Amiens
P

Peronne
JULY
1916

St Quentin
Ham

Guise

OISE

Montdidier   Lassigny
Noyon

La Fère

Rouen

Beauvais

Compiègne

Soissons
APRIL
1917

Léon

AISNE

SEINE

OISE
Chantilly

Senlis

OURCQ

Chateau
Thierry

MA

PARIS

MARNE

PT MORIN

Gd MORIN

SEINE

BE

Ghent

Gh

Mau

Ser

WESTERN   FRONT.

Approximate line at end of 1914 — — —
Line at end of Hindenburg Retreat, Feb. 1917. + + +
Line on 11th November 1918............ ———

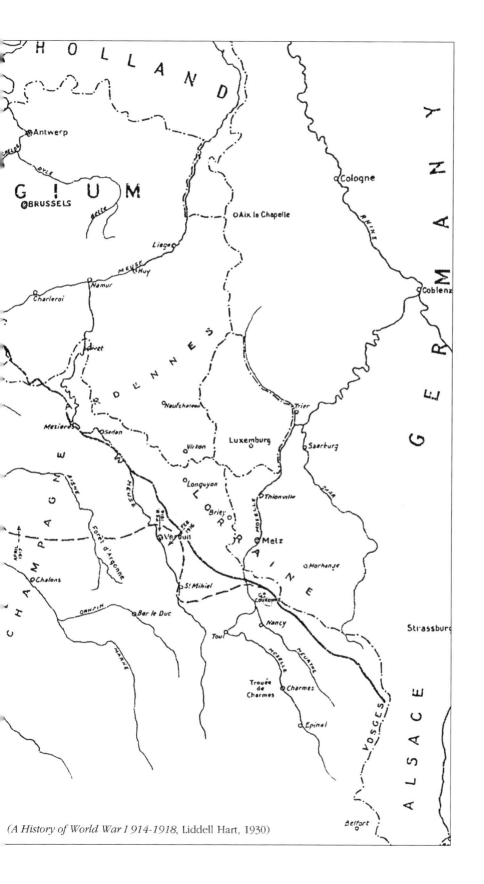

(A History of World War I 914-1918, Liddell Hart, 1930)

after the Anglo-Boer War, that had at first been mistaken by the Germans as machine-gun fire, could not be maintained in the telescoped training schedule for the 'New Army'. At least one exception to this was the marksmanship of the SA Brigade, as had been demonstrated already.

For the ordinary New Army brigades increasing reliance was placed on bomb and bayonet. The old Regular Army soldier had a military knowledge that was the product of long and expert training. In the New Army, infantry attack formations were drawn up as though an eighteenth century battle was being fought. But this was the only method infantry officers could use to keep firm control over their inexperienced troops in their original form of battalions, companies, platoons and sections during the most vital phase of any offensive. This method of control remained in force even though, during the training period before the Somme offensive, Fourth Army commanders had stressed the importance of officers and NCOs taking the initiative when the unexpected occurred.

Trench warfare had necessitated various changes. An infantry battalion consisted of approximately 1 000 men and 36 officers divided up into four rifle companies of about 240 men with a small headquarters staff. As various members of each company were assigned to specialised tasks such as that of stretcher-bearers, cooks, signallers, snipers, clerks, sanitary and transport men, the effective fighting strength of a battalion during an attack would be about 800. Of these a further 200 men or four platoons would be allocated to the task of carrying Mills bombs, wire, sandbags and large quantities of ammunition, as well as food and water. Such supplies would have to be immediately at hand after any force had advanced and attacked a German position. As for the other three rifle or attacking platoons that made up the attacking force, three out of every ten men were detailed to carry fifteen to twenty Mills bombs and probably a knobkerrie for hand-to-hand fighting. The rest of each platoon was armed with the .303 Lee Enfield rifle with eighteen-inch sword bayonet and 170 rounds of ammunition. His total load of equipment, arms and ammunition weighed 58 lbs 3 ozs according to official calculations. Lewis gun teams were attached to each platoon. Their weapon was really an automatic rifle firing a .303 cartridge. One man carried and fired the gun, but another man carried spare barrels and four men carried drums of ammunition. Its drum magazines contained either 47 or 97 rounds and fired at the rate of 450 rounds a minute.

The Germans were armed with the 7mm Mauser and the 7.2mm 98 Gewehr rifle with five-round clips of ammunition with a 37cm or 52cm bayonet – some with the notorious 'saw back'. Their machine-guns were the water-cooled 1908 Maxim model and they had the newly developed Flammenwerfer. The Germans used stick grenades as the counterpart to the Mills bomb.

Each British division in 1916 had four artillery brigades attached to it. Each artillery brigade had three batteries of four 18-pounders each and a battery of four 4.5 inch howitzers. The 18-pounder fired ten rounds a minute with a range of 3 400 yards for high explosive and 6 500 yards for shrapnel shells. The howitzers fired seven rounds a minute – 7 000 yards range for high explosive and 7 200 for shrapnel. Each infantry brigade had its own artillery component in the form of a light trench mortar battery of eight Stokes mortars, each weighing 84 lbs with a rate of fire of twenty 10 lb rounds per minute and a range of 430 yards. Its mobility and rapid rate of fire made it a most useful weapon. A good team could have ten bombs in the air at the same time. The Stokes mortar battery was operated by two officers and twenty-four other ranks. The 2-inch medium mortar weighed 320 lbs, so it could not be moved. Its bombs weighed 51 lbs and in spite of this could hit targets up to 500 yards distant. The 2-inch mortar's very high trajectory, steep angle of descent of the projectile, and localised destructive power, was ideally suited to the close barrage needed by the infantry. Like the Stokes mortars it was, for tactical reasons, under the direct command of the brigade commander.

To keep the brigade commander in touch with his higher formation commander, the division had its own Royal Engineers signals company for communication between division and corps and division and brigade; but signals between brigade and its units were its own responsibility. The wireless was too cumbersome for use in the front line. Telephone cables, buried six feet under ground, were rarely destroyed. They took many tedious hours to install. From the buried cable towards the rear, were linked the light-weight cables that ran along the side of communication trenches. These were frequently destroyed even though miles of wire were used with the duplication of lines. Ultimately visual methods in the form of signalling lamps and flags had to be used with the frequent use of runners to keep information flowing according to the shifting fortunes of the battle. Communications continued to be a problem.

All this was part of a new type of warfare and the new British Commander-in-Chief, Field Marshal Sir Douglas Haig, had to ensure that his armies were familiar with it. As John Buchan, the official historian of the SA Brigade wrote 'the whole British front became one vast seminary'.[1] One of Haig's despatches stated:

> During the periods of relief all formations are instructed and practised in all classes of warfare... to take advantage of the closer contact with actual warfare, and put the finishing touches, often after actual experience in the trenches, to the training received at home.

1   Buchan, p46.

By 15 June the SA Brigade had entered the Fourth Army's area after their long march south. The Picardy countryside had been barely touched by the war. Pte Geoffrey Lawrence, 1st SAI, described it as

> ...lovely green peaceful country far removed from the sounds of battle. It was hard to believe there was a war on....One was struck by the neat fields of ripening crops, the profusion of red poppies and deep blue cornflowers and the birds. The larks in particular were new to us – so numerous and strangely interesting with their happy singing high above, almost out of sight in the clear sky.
>
> We reached the area near the town of Corbie and were billeted at Sailly le Sec until moved quite close to the line at Welcome Wood and sheltered there safe from observation.[1]

All along the line the great bombardment of the German trenches had already commenced. The South Africans were in time to witness and listen to its progress. They wondered whether anything could survive the terrific battering. For the most part men of the Brigade were free of all parades, duties and training. They

---

1   *Militaria* 8/2 1972 p44.

could enjoy days of unclouded skies and the shade of the beautiful woods they were billeted near. The 4th SAI were the last to arrive. Lost training time through the quarantine period in Marseilles, was still being made good. The 3rd were employed in some last minute pick and shovel work. The River Somme flowed conveniently nearby and when opportunity offered the chance of a bathe, it was greatly enjoyed. An unexpected entertainment was the inspiring sight and sound of the marching and playing of the massed pipe bands of all the famous Scottish regiments of the 9th Division. They filled the whole horizon. Each piper seemed to be playing his heart out. To a man, the SA Brigade was spellbound. Always there was the distant roar of the guns.

The barbed wire was the primary target for the first two days of the bombardment which had begun on 24 June. The focus of attention was then altered so as to destroy the German batteries, communication trenches and villages. Day and night the guns roared without respite. At specific times barrages were concentrated at certain points.

Other preparations had also been made. To facilitate the offensive, about 120 miles of water pipes had been laid; new railways and roads had been constructed;

The Massed Pipes and Drums of the 9th (Scottish) Division near Corbie, June 1916. (Photo: SA National Museum of Military History)

miles of excavations to a depth of six feet had accommodated newly-laid telephone lines so that they would be protected from artillery bombardment; barbed wire cages for prisoners of war had been erected. Huge mass graves, each as large as half a football field, had been dug. Enemy strong points had been mined after they had been tunnelled under. There were tents for half a million men and 100 000 horses were on hand.

The area Field Marshal Haig had chosen for the summer offensive was a thirty mile front that ran from north-west to south-east between Amiens and Peronne at the junction of the French and British sectors. Any map of the Western Front will show that this area, which slopes up from the north bank of the River Somme to a wide plain, is dominated by a long ridge that was about 500 feet above sea level. The ridge ran from Guillemont to Fonquevillers, passing through the villages of Longueval, Bazentin le Petit, Pozieres, Thiepval, Beaucourt, Hebuterne and Gommecourt. The area consisted of cultivated farmland and cider apple orchards which also contained several large impenetrable woods such as Mametz, Bernafay, Trônes and Delville. The Germans had positioned their front line in a curve running from north to south. Some 2 000 to 5 000 yards behind this line along the dominating ridge, already mentioned, the Germans had sited their second line of trenches. The villages and woods between these two trench systems had been turned into defensive positions interspersed with fortified points or redoubts on the crest of ridges. A third line was under construction behind the second. Both the first and second German trench lines had been well wired as further protection against attack. The chalky soil was perfect for the construction of deep dugouts and in nearly two years of waiting the Germans had not been idle in constructing such shelters thirty to forty feet underground. Unbeknown to the British, this was the most strongly defended position on the Western Front. The

The British bombardment as preparation for the great Somme offensive. The guns were almost wheel to wheel and the bombardment could be heard in England.
(Photo: Cloete-Smith Collection)

Shell cases – indicating the enormous scale on which ammunition was consumed by British artillery. One of the many piles of 'empties'. (Photo: Cloete-Smith Collection)

Germans were familiar with the area because of their association with it during the Franco-Prussian War of 1870. The dugouts provided concealment and protection from the British bombardment that had continued for seven days. One and a half million shells were fired. Aerial photographs and other intelligence confirmed that the front line trenches had been completely shattered. Yet the machine-gunners and their weapons were still intact and these were carried up in time to check the British advance on 1 July 1916. When the barrage ceased and 60 000 British soldiers went over the top on a fourteen mile front, the Germans, all the time safe in deep dugouts, emerged with their machine-guns and mowed them down.

The German dugouts and trenches were a revelation: both were much deeper than their British counterparts, affording far better protection because of their very solid construction. The dugouts for officers boasted the luxury of boarded walls and wallpaper, with sheets on the beds. Underground passages from concrete dugouts which housed the trench garrisons, forty feet underground, opened into the front line. Cpl Arthur Betteridge, 4th SAI, noted that:

> Very few of our millions of shells damaged these massive underground structures. I actually saw one of these consisting of battalion headquarters, with sleeping bunks for many men, a small theatre for their entertainment

Entrance to a German officer's dug-out before and after the bombardment. (Photo: Cloete-Smith Collection)

'The dugouts for German officers boasted the luxury of boarded walls . . . with sheets on beds' and were constructed deep underground. (Photo: Cloete-Smith Collection)

Two British officers enjoy a little gramaphone music and refreshment outside their dugout. (Photo: SA National Museum of Military History)

Photographs confirmed that all along the area of the Somme offensive the German front line trenches had been completely shattered by the British bombardment. However, the entrance to where the German trench garrison was housed deep underground was unscathed and ready to disgorge its men with their machine-guns. (Photo: Cloete-Smith Collection)

A captured German front line trench at Ovillers-la-Boiselle on the Somme. It is a trench no more as a result of the British bombardment.
(Photo: Cloete-Smith Collection)

complete with piano and wardrobes for stage shows. We were astonished to find electric lights in two of these underground 'homes'. This particular sector had been held by the enemy for twelve months and they had certainly made themselves comfortable. It was (also) our first experience of German cunning. German Prussian helmets were always regarded as trophies, and some of these were found in dugouts attached to booby traps. One of our sergeants was killed as he picked up some trophy. Obviously the Hun had anticipated our arrival. We were warned not to touch anything in dugouts until engineers had inspected the place.[1]

It was Winston Churchill who subsequently remarked that the Somme was 'undoubtedly the strongest and most perfectly defended position in the world'.

So it was that this strongly-held ground was the objective of the offensive planned for 1 July. General Rawlinson's Fourth Army had the responsibility of taking a fourteen mile frontage with twenty-five British divisions. XIII Corps was part of the Fourth Army and consisted of three Divisions, one of which was the 9th (Scottish) Division. Along the Fourth Army line 1 537 guns would be evenly distributed at fifty yard intervals for the five-day bombardment of the German defences, due to begin on 24 June.

The weather changed. On 27 and 28 June, heavy rain fell. The German front line and No Man's Land already shattered and churned up by countless shells was turned into mud. The attack would now commence on Saturday, 1 July, instead of 29 June. It was across this strip of land that the British divisions would have to advance, each man overburdened with unnecessary equipment, the pace of advance limited to a slow walk. The Germans would have ample time to get themselves out of their dugouts.

It was resolved that the 9th Division of XIII Corps would be held in reserve while the 18th and 30th Divisions attacked.

Lt-Gen. Sir Henry Rawlinson KCB commanding the Fourth Army of which the 9th Division formed a part.
(Photo: Cloete-Smith Collection)

1   Betteridge, p37-38.

Chapter 12

The opening rounds of 1 July 1916

The SA Brigade moved to Grovetown, a large supply dump outside Bray, on 30 June with Headquarters at Celestine Wood. They waited.

Sixty per cent of the British divisions that made up the attacking force were volunteers – New Army troops. For the last two years they had been painstakingly trained. In the first hour 30 000 were casualties, with 58 000 being the total by the end of the first day.

Lt-Gen W N Congreve's XIII Corps were on the extreme right of the British line. Unlike the rest of the line, greater success was achieved here than at any other point. Within an hour the German front line was in British hands. Montauban village, severely battered, was found to be deserted and the vital position near Briqueterie was seized. Their right flank was firmly established on Montauban ridge. To the south the French XX Corps were advancing beyond their scheduled targets and wished to continue. Bernafay and Trônes Woods were empty of German troops. However, General Rawlinson refused to allow further advance before the captured ground had been consolidated. The delay gave the Germans time to send the 12th Reserve Division to reinforce the area. Still the SA Brigade waited in readiness.

On 2 July Rawlinson was ordered by Field Marshal Haig to resume the attack all along the line. Instead of exploiting Congreve's success of the 1 July, he was instructed to continue to consolidate his position. The Germans continued to reinforce the threatened sector. At last Haig became aware of the opportunity offered for success on his right.

On 3 July the SA Brigade moved forward. Time was spent in repairing and strengthening these front line positions.

Pte Dudley Meredith of 'C' Company, 3rd SAI, described the view from the front line.

From horizon to horizon in front of us lay a broad belt of red earth, a

'From horizon to horizon in front of us lay a broad belt of red earth, a veritable desert of death.' Pte Dudley Meredith, 3rd SAI. (Photo: Cloete-Smith Collection)

veritable desert of death, where all vegetation had been destroyed and the earth churned up by the fury of the shell fire. Tracks through this waste there were and wounded men and working parties passed up and down, but the first impression remained – a dreadful red belt of death and destruction.[1]

The 2nd SAI and 4th SAI were now to enter the fringes of the battle proper, their task being to hold the captured Bernafay Wood which was being shelled very heavily by German artillery situated on rising ground at Longueval and Guillemont which was the German second line. From this commanding position the German artillery was brought to bear on Bernafay and Trônes Woods which are virtually adjacent, being only some 500 yards apart. An understanding of what happened at Bernafay and Trônes Woods places the later developments in and around Delville Wood in better perspective.

1   Uys, I *The Battle of Delville Wood* p32.

On 8 July while the 21st and 90th Brigades were attacking Maltz Horn Trench and Trônes Wood, 'A', 'C' and the HQ Company of 2nd SAI had been sent into Bernafay Wood to relieve part of the 27th Brigade occupying the eastern perimeter of the wood. One officer was killed and nine men were wounded while making this move. A working party of 3rd SAI lost three killed and eleven wounded in the wood, so heavy was the shelling. The relief of 6th KOSBs of 27th Brigade who had lost 16 officers and 300 men during their five-day occupation of the south-eastern section of Bernafay, was now completed by 'D' Company 2nd SAI. To limit the number of casualties, Brig-Gen Lukin, the SA Brigade Commander, ordered Lt-Col Tanner, OC 2nd SAI, to withdraw from the wood. He was to leave behind only a small garrison as well as the bombing party. The latter had secured Longueval Alley Trench which linked the two woods. A wood was easier to capture than to hold.

The situation in nearby Trônes Wood was similar. Early on the morning of 8 July, the 17th Bn Manchester Regiment had taken Trônes Wood but because of heavy shelling they were authorised to withdraw. The Germans retook Trônes Wood. That same evening at 6.15 p.m. the 16th Manchesters retook the southern part of the wood. They were reinforced by 'A' Company 4th SAI. Besides a platoon of 'C' Company 4th SAI, the remainder of the 4th SAI, was held in readiness as reinforcements while the 3rd SAI occupied the positions that the 4th SAI had occupied in the vicinity of Glatz Redoubt. On the 9 July the possession of Trônes Wood fluctuated between the Germans and the British.

Meanwhile casualties were mounting in Bernafay Wood. The 2nd SAI garrison actually occupying the wood had to be kept up to full strength in case of a German counterattack. The 2nd SAI continued to lose men. Captain W F Hoptroff of 'D' Company 2nd SAI, at 12.15 p.m. reported on his desperate situation resulting from the heavy shelling on the south-east corner of the wood and the exposed position of his men:

> Many men are bordering on 'shell shock' and the loss of many NCO's makes the position very difficult. No one has had any sleep and everyone is strained to the uttermost... ....Practically all cover in front cut away by artillery fire so that if anyone moves he can be at once seen.[1]

Tanner found that his greatest problem was to keep in touch with his three companies who were covering an extensive area. Telegraph and telephone lines continued to be cut.

---

1   *Militaria* 7/2 1977 p23.

For the whole critical period Tanner noted how three signallers laboured without respite. One of the signallers, Private Eddie Fitz, related what occurred. Fitz rose to the rank of major in the Second World War but always remained rather reticent when it came to his war experiences. Of these three days with the 2nd SAI in Bernafay he wrote:

> When we went into Bernafay Wood it was our first experience of really terrific bombardment. We were in that wood for nearly sixty hours. A chap named Fred Mitchell (L/Cpl) and I were the lines-men in this telegraph 'show'. We decided to run lines to three different points; left, centre and right. The right faced Trônes Wood. By 12 o'clock that night every damn line was cut! Fred and I spent our time, night and day running new lines or going out and running along the line with your hand until you found the break, then trying to pick up the other bit and joining it. We carried on doing that. Most of the time we were drenched with lachrymatory gas and mustard and there was plenty of high explosive... They came in thick and fast! This went on the whole period we were there.[1]

With the 2nd SAI having been tried almost to their limit, 'B' and 'D' Companies of 4th SAI relieved the 2nd SAI in Bernafay on the night of 10 July. The following day offered no respite. The steady shelling of Bernafay continued. The number of casualties continued to rise.

Sergeant Wilfred Brink, aged 22, was supervising two 3rd SAI teams of stretcher-bearers whose numbers he had augmented with German prisoners of war. Capt George Cook, Wesleyan chaplain of 3rd SAI had asked Brink if he could assist. He had confided in his colleague, Padre Eustace Hill, that he had been terrified by the initial shelling in Bernafay, but now he had conquered fear. Shortly after starting out, Cook and his party of German stretcher-bearers were killed by a shell. Padre Hill was with Cook at the end. 'We were together till a shell by Bernafay,' wrote Hill, 'pierced his tin hat. I commended his soul to God'.[2]

A far greater impact was made by the death that day of Lt-Col F A Jones, the colonel of the 4th SAI (SA Scottish). The commanding officers of the four infantry units of the SA Brigade had nurtured their units until their debut on the Western Front. These men seemed indestructible, like the fathers of a large family.

To indicate the humanity of this most loved commanding officer, Pte (later Lieut) W A 'Alf' Beattie, 4th SAI, recalled an incident on the *Oriana, en route* to Egypt.

1 Uys, p41.
2 Warwick, p168.

I was warned for sentry duty outside the commanding officer's cabin. What I'd be protecting him from I couldn't imagine, but it was a lovely evening, the stars shone as never before, and there I was with rifle and bayonet ready to challenge anything on two feet. The evening was wearing on when I spied the colonel approaching. He seemed to have dined well, or it may have been the roll of the ship, but he ignored my elaborate salute and passed into his cabin. He hadn't been there many minutes when his batman came out and in a very peremptory tone said to me 'The colonel wants to see you'. In fear and trembling I entered the cabin and there was the colonel in his pyjamas sitting on the side of his bunk. He looked up and said, 'Are you the sentry here?' I replied 'Yes, Sir'. Then his next question simply bowled me over. He said 'Well I suppose you could do with a drink?' I was on the point of saying, 'You're telling me' when I remembered that colonels and privates do not swap drinks, at least on active service, so I grinned sheepishly scenting a snag. However, he told his batman to bring two whiskys and sodas and thereafter we had an amiable discussion on life in Johannesburg. At last he bid me goodnight and I returned to duty, and whether it was the whisky or the thought of the unusual honour conferred on me, I certainly felt that the incident had re-established my diminished ego. In fact I was prepared to let the war go on.

What had happened to Lt-Col 'Fatty' Jones on the 11 July 1916 shattered the equanimity of nineteen year old Private Harry Cooper of 'C' Company 3rd SAI who saw Jones lying dead as he passed by.

An ordinary soldier, yes, but not a colonel. I then began to realise that this was not going to be the fun we had expected. This was war![1]

Shortly before his death, Colonel Jones had spoken to Padre Hill in Bernafay. Pointing to the row of medal ribbons on his chest he had exclaimed 'This war is a crusade – a privilege – these past ribbons nil'. And now Jones was dead, killed on the eve of a battle for which his whole life had been a preparation.

Cpl Arthur Betteridge, 4th SAI, wrote in his autobiography of the event. He was an eyewitness of Jones's Death.

That day I had brought a message from 'C' Company in the front line to Headquarters at Bernafay Wood. The opening to this dugout naturally

1   Warwick, p166.

faced the new German front lines. Within seconds of leaving, a salvo of German shells burst a few yards away, knocking me sideways. Two men nearby were killed and one of those shells entered the dugout I had just left. Colonel Jones and an orderly were climbing up the steps at that moment. As the shell exploded, both of them were killed instantly and several in the dugout wounded and shocked.

I rushed down the dugout after the explosion and assisted in bringing the colonel's body to the road where we placed it on a stretcher and covered it with a ground sheet. I took a map of the area from the dead hand of our OC and gave it to Major Hunt. He told me to keep it as he already had one. Major Hunt there and then appointed me as his temporaty orderly and signaller.

I was sent with a message to 'C' Company in the front line and returned to find the major in a trench near headquarters, half buried. Corporal Hockey who was with him was killed and three men of a ration party all badly wounded. The major told me that a shell burst almost in front of him, killing Hockey, who was at the back of him. An astonishing escape. I had evidence that day of the several escapes from death [which] 'Dolly' Hunt, as he was affectionately known, was to experience.

Two privates of the Black Watch were about twenty feet from that shell burst, and they ran to help the major to his feet. One of them told me the shell burst almost next to the major and it was a miracle he was not blown to pieces.

A few hours after this incident I had to accompany Major Hunt on a round of the shallow trenches leading to the new front line. Most of these trenches were clearly within sight of German gunners.

I tried to get a line back to headquarters through wires which had been run along the trenches. We stopped half a dozen times to do this and were never successful.

Major Donald R Hunt, 4th SAI. 'This was a War that made a comparatively young man, prematurely old,' wrote Hunt. Photo taken in 1917.

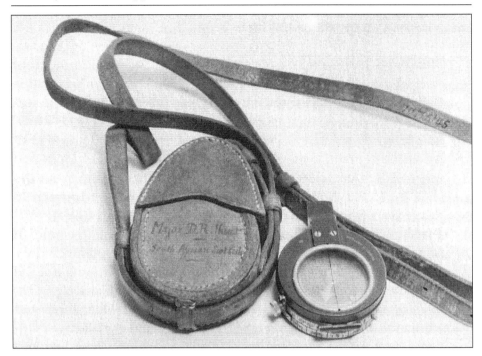

Compass and leather case used by Major D R Hunt, 4th SAI, on the Western Front. (Photo: Transvaal Scottish Regimental Museum)

Leather money belt for carrying his Company's pay, that was worn by Major D R Hunt, 4th SAI, on the Western Front. (Photo: Transvaal Scottish Regimental Museum)

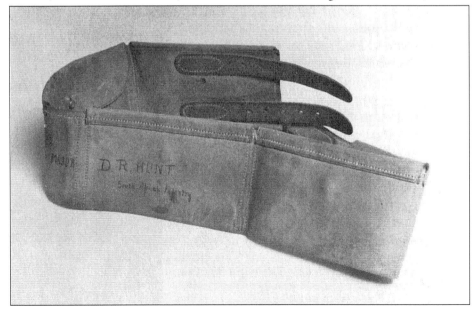

All lines of communication had been damaged by shell fire. It was most noticeable that immediately we left one of these stopping places, a salvo of whizzbangs exploded near the spot we had just left. After the fourth instance, I looked anxiously at the major when my impossible task was done, 'Yes, Betteridge', he said 'I think it's time for them to have reloaded their beastly whizzbangs – let's go'. He must have been a mind-reader because the next salvo arrived immediately we departed. I never met a luckier man, nor a braver one.[1]

Lt-Col D M Macleod DSO, MC, DCM, who succeeded Lt-Col Jones as officer commanding 4th SAI. Photo taken in 1922 when Macleod was OC of the Transvaal Scottish.
(Photo: Transvaal Scottish HQ)

Major Hunt took command of the 4th SAI until Major D M Macleod DCM arrived from Divisional Headquarters the next morning. Macleod's reputation as a soldier was considerable. He had won the DCM while serving with the 1st Bn Queen's Own Cameron Highlanders at Omdurman in 1898, in the Sudan. He had been recommended for the VC at Lake Chrissie during the Anglo-Boer War and thereafter had become RSM of the newly formed Transvaal Scottish Volunteers, rising to the rank of captain and adjutant of 1st Bn Transvaal Scottish at the start of the German South West Africa Campaign, to be appointed major and second-in-command of the 4th SAI (SA Scottish) on its formation in August 1915.

It was at this stage that the Fourth Army's offensive against the German second position was about to take place. By 13 July, the last men of the SA Brigade in Bernafay Wood were relieved. In the orders issued for the attack on the German second line, the 9th Division would be responsible for the capture of Waterlot Farm, the village of Longueval and Delville Wood. Since 1 July the SA Brigade had suffered nearly 1 000 casualties.

---

1   Betteridge, p41-42

Was the failure of 1 July to be repeated? This was the thought of some 22 000 men of XIII and XV Corps who were waiting in pitch darkness in No Man's Land, across their entire front. The time was 3.20 a.m. 14 July 1916.

Communion Cup of the South African Scottish used from August 1915 to 30 September 1916 while S Thomson was Chaplain to the Regiment. From numbering nearly 1 000 on 1 July 1916, they marched out of Delville Wood on 20 July 1916, 38 men and 4 officers strong. (Transvaal Scottish Regimental Museum)

Chapter 13

Delville Wood

To the SA Brigade all this was a mere continuation of the Somme offensive. Little did they realise what lay ahead during the next six days.

The attack was renewed at 3.25 a.m. on 14 July. The four mile stretch of the second position was taken with speed and economy because of the dash and daring tactics employed. Instead of attacking in broad daylight, as had been the case of 1 July, the troops had assembled under cover of darkness in No Man's Land. The assault took place in the pre-dawn half light. This time there was no week-long bombardment – only a barrage of five minutes duration to herald their approach. The result was complete surprise and sweeping success.

However, it was one thing to penetrate the German front line by a sudden blow on a limited front, but quite another to consolidate and extend the breach in the face of a fully-alerted enemy.

The SA Brigade was not included in the initial attack of the morning of 14 July. This was because of their scanty experience in trench warfare. It had become accepted practice not to place unseasoned troops in the vanguard of an attack.

The plan of campaign for 14 July required the 26th and 27th Brigades of the 9th Division to take Longueval village and then seize Delville Wood, with the SA Brigade in reserve for 'mopping up' operations. The two positions were seen as a strategic entity. The attack on Longueval at dawn on 14 July met with initial success. The front line garrison was surprised and quickly overwhelmed. Then resistance stiffened. The German Commander-in-Chief General Erich von Falkenhayn, had issued very definite instructions. His men were not to yield an inch. *'Nur über leichen darf der feind seinen weg vorwärts finden!'* (The enemy must not be allowed to advance except over corpses.) That these instructions were being observed to the letter is shown by the response of a small German detachment to an offer of quarter by Highlanders of the 9th Division who had completely surrounded them. 'I and my men' their officer replied, 'have orders to defend this position with our lives. German soldiers know how to obey orders. We thank you for your offer, but we die where we stand.' This they did. The alternative

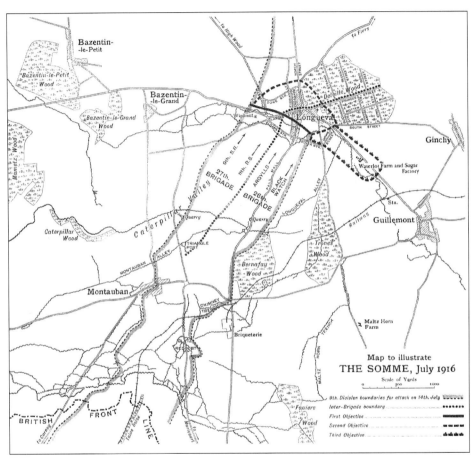

(*The History of the 9th (Scottish) Division*, John Ewing, 1921)

138

Roll call before the battle. The Black Watch before Delville Wood.
(Photo: SA National Museum of Military History)

was equally terrifying – to be shot in the back by your fellow Germans as you surrendered. Such an incident Privates J A Lawson and Breytenbach of 3rd SAI were shocked to witness.[1]

In Longueval fierce hand-to-hand fighting moved the battle from house to house. This was a costly business for the attackers. The preliminary bombardment had been insufficient. Much of the village was still standing. Nor had the network of subterranean shelters and passages that lay beneath it even been touched. In many cases all the bombardment had done was to tumble the masonry so as to provide the German defenders with further cover in the form of nooks and crannies within easy access of the underground communication tunnels from which they could harass the attackers with impunity.

By the afternoon of that first day – 14 July – Longueval still remained untaken in its entirety. This delayed the advance on Delville Wood, as unless the village was captured, no attack could be made on the wood. The unexpectedly heavy losses suffered by the Highlanders of the 26th and 27th Brigades of the 9th Division in the street fighting necessitated their reinforcement within the village and their

1   Lawson, J p4 and Uys, I, *The South Africans at Delville Wood*, Military History Journal Vol 7 No 2 p55..

replacement outside it, by the troops of the 9th Division reserve – in other words the SA Brigade.

Pte Jack Carstens, 1st SAI, recalled an episode during this phase of the battle when the SA Brigade entered Longueval.

> We spent some time in and around Longueval Village – a most unpleasant spot with continuous sniping from all quarters. On one occasion we were passing through a wrecked garden with a small gate at its end. One at a time we had to pass through and make a bolt across the road for the comparative safety of a ruined building. We had to wait for the officer's order: 'Run!' and then each made his dash. The fellow in front of me was unlucky. He was killed in mid-flight.
>
> It was now my turn. I opened the gate and was about to run when an explosion occurred uncomfortably close to my ear. A piece of the gate had been shot away and I turned to 'Moeg' Carey immediately behind clutching his face in pain. Taking his hands away I could see that his lower jaw had been blown to pieces.
>
> It was during that same episode in Longueval Village that Bill Carlson was killed. Many of the old generation must remember this great sportsman who played centre-three-quarter for Villagers and cricket for the Alma Club.
>
> Our little party were sheltering behind that ruin across the road and awaiting further orders from the officer, who so far had not appeared. We spotted the enemy in a trench not fifty yards down the road. For a handful of men, without an officer or even an NCO, to attack and possibly fall into a trap seemed out of the question. But not for Bill; and he could not resist the temptation of pitching into the enemy forthwith. I'm perfectly certain that he imagined himself back on the rugger battlefield of Newlands and he had to cross that line.
>
> I can see him now with a Mills bomb in his hand careering down the main street of Longueval. None of our shouts would stop him. On he went. On – until a machine-gunner from the top of one of the ruined buildings let fly. He was riddled with bullets and never moved again.
>
> I am happy to think that our recommendation for the Military Medal for Bill Carlson was accepted but nothing could make up for the gap that was left in our little intimate group of sportsmen who had left for the wars together.[1]

1   Carstens, Jack, *A Fortune Through My Fingers,* pp20-21

'Over the top' – the scene repeated all the way long the line.
(Photo: Cloete-Smith Collection)

The ruins of the village of Longueval after its capture. (Photo: Cloete-Smith Collection)

The SA Brigade was now called upon, first to take and then to hold the area known as Delville Wood 'at all costs'. The fighting in Longueval had delayed the attack on the wood until 5.00 a.m. on 15 July. Progress was slow. This was because of the nature of the terrain rather than the German garrison. They had been largely withdrawn from Delville Wood because of the planned bombardment of the area.

John Buchan, the official historian of the SA Brigade succinctly describes the geography of the area that was at issue. It was

> beyond doubt the most difficult in the battle-front. To begin with, we were fighting in a salient, and our attack was under fire from three sides. This enabled the enemy to embarrass seriously our communications during the action. In the second place, the actual ground of attack presented an intricate problem. The land sloped upwards from Bernafay and Trônes Wood to Longueval village, which was shaped like an inverted fan, broad at the south end, where the houses clustered about the junction of two roads, and straggling out to the north-east along the highway, to Flers. Scattered among the dwellings were many little enclosed gardens and orchards. To the east of north-east of the hamlet stretched the wood of Delville, in the shape of a blunt equilateral triangle, with an apex pointing northward. The place, like most French woods, had been seamed with grassy rides, partly obscured by scrub, and the Germans had dug lines of trenches along and athwart them.[1]

These rides were typical of most woods in the area. In Delville Wood the main one, that divided the wood in two and ran approximately east to west, had been dubbed *Princes Street*, for obvious reasons by the Highlanders of the Division. At right angles were secondary rides also appropriately named.

By midday on 15 July, the SA Brigade had cleared Delville Wood and reached the perimeter in every sector, except the north-west corner. Intense shelling began almost immediately. Counterattacks could be expected at any moment. The SA Brigade was instructed to dig themselves in. This was easier said than done. The chalky soil, matted with roots and tangled with branches, offered resistance to the most resolute spade. Machine-gun and rifle fire from the German intermediate trenches, less than seventy yards away, also hampered these efforts.

All digging was stopped by a succession of German counterattacks at battalion strength during the course of the afternoon. This delayed the positioning of machine-guns to hold the perimeter of the wood. Because of this the men in the line could not be dispersed but had to be concentrated along the 1 800 yards of

1   Buchan, p56-57.

the perimeter of the wood. For lack of alternative cover, because of roots that hampered the digging of trenches, many took refuge in the abandoned German trenches, whose exact location was well known by the German artillery.

Vividly recalled is that dawn on the 16 July when the SA Brigade was ordered to move deeper into the dense and beautiful forest. The closely set trees towered to a great height, their branches forming a roof of foliage overhead that was so thick that the sky was almost obscured. After hastily digging in, at best scratching out three feet of soil, providing enough room in which to squat, there was time to look around. Birds still flitted from tree to tree. The men crouched among the thick undergrowth of bracken and brambles, undisturbed for centuries. The previous night's fighting had left the bodies of many young dead and wounded Bavarians in the vicinity. Pte Geoffrey Lawrence wrote:

> The sun shone and everywhere great spider webs glistened with dew. The noise in the wood was terrific though in our area no shells were falling at the time.
>
> Standing up and keeping a good lookout for an enemy attack, I noticed the tree leaves close above our heads dropping steadily every now and then. It suddenly struck me that it was not yet autumn – those leaves should not be falling – they were being cut down by bullets. We got down very quickly and soon machine-guns were raking us from two sides. The fresh earth on our parapet came tumbling down on us as the bullets swept along it. Two men close by were wounded by this fire, one very badly.[1];

Pte Jack Carstens, also of the 1st SAI, recalled:

> ...arriving at the end of the Wood, a ploughed field in front of us, our orders (being) to dig in on its fringe. We carried picks and shovels for that purpose but I was never much good at that game and found the ground unbelievably hard and myself desperately tired. I noticed that one of the fellows had already finished his funk hole – a husky fellow with obviously a lot of pick and shovel work in his history. 'Robbie,' I cried, 'dig me a funk hole and I'll give you five francs.' That hole was dug, and I was in it, in a matter of minutes.
>
> Some years later, after I had retired from the Indian Army I took my fiancée to the old Tivoli in Darling Street, Cape Town and who should I meet but Robbie. He was all dressed up in Commissionaire's uniform complete with medals. He greeted me with 'By Gawd Sir, do you remember when I dug

1 *Militaria* 8/2 1978 p46.

that funk hole for you in Delville Wood?'

Shortly after, little hell was let loose. It seemed as though the Germans had brought every available gun from the whole Western Front for the express purpose of blasting the South Africans out of Delville Wood.[1]

These efforts on the part of the Germans were indicative of the determination of the German commander of this sector, General Sixt von Armin, to recapture the lost salient. He ordered further attacks for that night. Reinforcements were hurriedly assembled. Despite the protests of German battalion commanders that there was insufficient time for adequate preparations, the attacks were scheduled for midnight, on completion of a three-hour artillery bombardment.

Major John Ewing, official historian of the 9th Division, referred to 'a hurricane of shells that swept Delville Wood.' The Germans then attacked the wood three times, with great determination. Each attack was proceeded by artillery fire coming from a different direction. The South Africans repulsed these attacks with rifle and machine-gun fire. The attacks could be beaten back, but of far greater annoyance were the lachrymatory shells sent over by the German artillery. A South African soldier wrote:

> Before attacking they sent over tear shells, which blind your eyes with tears, tears streaming down your face. The pain is awful. One can hardly breathe, and there is a terrible burning in the nose, throat and lungs. The idea is to interfere with one's shooting, since one cannot see the sights on the rifle in front of one's face. Unfortunately, our tear shell goggles are useless, and only make things more unpleasant, becoming quite opaque with tears so that it is quite impossible to see.

The Germans began the shelling of Delville Wood in earnest on 16 July. That morning 'B' and 'C' Companies of the 4th SAI, moved into the wood led by Major Hunt who recalled:

> ...big chunks of trees were coming down with the shell fire. Young Angus Murdoch-Keith,[2] the youngest of my company laughed at these and seemed to think it great fun.[3]
>
> As the bombardment increased the ground behind and before us became littered with shell holes. Bushes and small trees were torn up, large trees

1 Carstens, pp22-23.
2 Major A M Keith, MC died in Johannesburg in 1988.
3 Major D R Hunt's diary, *The Springbok Magazine*, September 1933

uprooted. Many a grand monarch of the wood, lifted from its roots and projected forward, was seen to crash through the branches of other trees and settle down full length to earth. Others borne up by neighbourly branches rested in that position like so many tired giants.[1]

Within twenty four hours all of the hundreds of trees in the wood were reduced to a tangle of greenery and stumps. Not one tree was intact. The whole area was a shambles. Under this unbelievable rain of shells we had to clear paths and small communication trenches of rubble to bring up ammunition and what replacements we could find for the casualties.[2]

To move in a wood in such chaos was vividly described by Pte J Simpson, 4th SAI:

Shells whistled through the trees and burst with awful cracks all around. Men were falling fast, and everyone was calling for the stretcher-bearers. To add to the confusion all the fellows were carrying extra loads of ammunition boxes, rolls of barbed wire, tins of water and a hundred and one other things. We in the gun section each had to carry two canvas buckets of Lewis gun magazines besides our rifle and equipment and I can tell you every time we trekked the perspiration simply ran off me and then came the shivers when we halted. We struggled through the wood, being tripped up almost every step by the thick undergrowth, barbed wire, and falls into shell-holes or else our equipment would get entangled in the brambles. The boys were falling right and left.[3]

The wounded could not be evacuated for hours at a time. A first aid post had been set up in a house on the outskirts of Longueval. The so-called secure and sandbagged dressing station in nearby Bernafay Wood was frequently shelled by the Germans.

An unknown private in the SAMC wrote how he was detailed to one of the party to go to Longueval to collect the wounded.

It was a horrible job removing the patients, as the roads were one mass of shell craters, at a distance of only about 2 feet apart in a large number of places; and as it had been raining for nearly five days these were mostly half-full of water and we were constantly falling into them, patient and

1   Solomon, p65.
2   Betteridge, p44-45.
3   *The Battle of Delville Wood Told in Letters From the Front* p38.

all. Our greatcoats and equipment we had disposed of long before, and we were all wet through to the skin. We were knocked down twice owing to the concussion of shells bursting quite near us and it was a miracle that we were not all blown to pieces. Three trips we managed safely, but on the fourth a shell burst very close to us – we were carrying the stretcher on our shoulders, one man to each handle – and we were all flung down again. The patient was killed, the three other bearers wounded, while I escaped with a piece of shrapnel through my coat and my steel helmet being knocked off. I patched up the other bearers as best I could and we managed to get safely to Bernafay. It was about 2 a.m. by now and I was sent up to the village to see if I could be of any help. As I was nearing Longueval, I saw a walking patient coming down and when about 20 yards from me a shell burst almost next to him. Seeing him fall I ran up and found that his left foot had been taken clean off, so I tied up the artery and as there was nobody in sight to give me a hand I managed to get him on my back. I had not gone more than ten yards when a big shell burst under me and I was picked up and flung about ten feet away into a shell crater, landing on the side of my head. I just remember coming round again and starting to climb out, when I heard a terrific explosion and the earth seemed to hit me in the face. When I came round again I had a splitting headache, and was bleeding from my nose, ear and mouth. The second shell had completely buried me, but luckily some Camerons saw me getting up and they dug me out as quickly as possible. At first I thought part of my head had been blown off, but I found that everything was all right, with the exception of my one ear, which was quite deaf. On remembering my patient, we went to look for him, but found him smashed to pieces. They then helped me down to Bernafay, and as I was feeling pretty bad I was sent to hospital at Rouen.[1]

On that same day, 16 July, an attempt was made to wrest the yet uncaptured north-west corner from the Germans, who were holding it with dogged determination. No artillery preparation could be expected as the German and South African positions were too closely situated. Trench mortars were the only support possible. Great gallantry was displayed but it was not enough. The fixed bayonet could not compete against the German machine-guns. The heavy losses caused the attempt to be abandoned.

The SA Brigade's first Victoria Cross was won by Pte W F Faulds 1st SAI, that Sunday. Under intense fire, Faulds led a party of three men to bring in Lt A W

---

1   *The Battle of Delville Wood Told in Letters from the Front*, p28.

Craig who was lying wounded in the open after an abortive bombing raid.

For that and carrying in another wounded man under similar circumstances two days later, Faulds was awarded his 'Cross'.

The next day, 17 July, saw the Germans make yet another attempt – once again without artillery support – to dislodge the South Africans. Again there was nothing to show for their efforts except casualties. The pattern of events was repeated again and again: shelling followed by German counterattacks, followed by further shelling. Conditions in the Wood deteriorated steadily. Rain alternated with parching heat. Sleep was impossible. Men were without blankets or greatcoats from 4 to 20 July.

Snipers were a growing hazard for those awake as well as for those asleep with fatigue. The unwary ended up with a bullet in the centre of the head.

Brig-Gen 'Tim' Lukin was among the shells near the front line on numerous occasions, seeing at first hand what his men were up against, giving new heart to all those who saw him.

During the 17 July, the wood's garrison commander, Lt-Col Tanner, OC 2nd SAI, was wounded in the thigh. He was very reluctant to leave the front line.

Fortunately there was Lt-Col E F Thackeray, OC of the 3rd SAI, to replace Tanner in controlling operations in the Wood. With ever mounting casualties, it was undoubtedly Thackeray's courage and leadership that saved the day as these two statements by fellow officers on the spot confirm.[1] The frst was Capt and Adjutant Claude Browne of the 4th SAI, who spent the whole of 18 July lying on the floor of the Brigade HQ dugout in *Buchanan Street*, waiting to be sent down to the dressing station at Longueval after being wounded in the right thigh.

> Colonel Thackeray got four stretcher-bearers and sent me away. We had hardly gone a few yards when one of the stretcher-bearers was shot by a German sniper. The other stretcher-bearers dropped me and took shelter in shell holes. In the meantime, the sniper was still firing at me. Thackeray crept out and pulled me into safety. On the following day I was lying on the parados of the trench when two shells, luckily duds, fell within a very short distance of me and partly covered me with earth. Thackeray again pulled me into safety and carried me into the dug-out used by him as Headquarters; while he was doing this another shell fell within a few feet of me. During the whole of the day I lay in close proximity to Colonel Thackeray's Headquarters, and he continually by his example kept the men fighting till the very last, although the odds were very heavily against us.

1   Document in Transvaal Scottish Regimental Museum.

We were bombed and fired at from both sides of the trench at the same time by the Germans who had managed to creep through places where the men had been entirely wiped out. I heard Colonel Thackeray tell the men that he would not leave the trench unless relieved, and the men were encouraged to hang on until the very end.

Thackeray had miraculously escaped unscathed after being hit six times by bullets and having been knocked down three times twice by shells and once by a bomb.

What Captain Browne had survived with Thackeray was the climax of the shelling of Delville Wood. The bombardment that had gone before paled into insignificance. The new intensified bombardment began at sunset on the evening of 17 July. It continued throughout the night, and then from 8 a.m. on 18 July, it suddenly reached and sustained a rapidity of fire rarely equalled elsewhere. From an examination of German regimental histories it is clear that altogether 116 field guns and upwards of seventy medium and heavy guns, not to mention howitzers of every calibre, were used for the bombardment of an area roughly 1 000 by 1 200 yards.

For seven and a half hours shells rained on the defenders, often at the rate of 400 to the minute. The earth trembled and shook. The sky became quite dark with the smoke of burning branches and the debris from the explosions. The noise was deafening – the crash of falling trees mingling with the scream of shells and the heavy concussion of high explosive. The sand and stones hurled into the air, showered down on the men, clattering on their steel helmets as they cowered in the bottom of their improvised trenches or 'funk holes'. Death was all around and reaped a lavish harvest. Terrible and awful fear accompanied the hiss of each approaching shell and the brief speculation as to whose turn would be next. Shell after shell fell. Seconds, minutes, hours, filled with the all-consuming inferno, dragged on. At times it was noted that there were seven explosions per second. On the 18 July, 20 000 shells fell in the area held by the SA Brigade which amounted to less than a square mile.

All prayed for an instantaneous death. The sufferings of the wounded all around were most unnerving. With friends dying on every side, no one expected to emerge from the wood alive. Yet men went unscathed, some without even a scratch.

Thackeray was now superseded by Lt-Col F S Dawson, OC 1st SAI, who had brought up some meagre reinforcements, numbering only 150.

Meanwhile, nine crack German battalions were being massed on the perimeter for a determined thrust the moment the bombardment ended. These troops marvelled at the destruction before them, and doubted whether anyone could have survived such a storm.

At 3.30 p.m. on 18 July the bombardment suddenly stopped. To the astonishment of the attacking German infantry, a handful of South Africans had not only survived, but, fatigued and shaken though they were, were clearly determined to let no one pass. The official German history described the fight that followed as 'extremely terrible'. With rifle fire alone the South Africans repulsed attack after attack, and, when their ammunition gave out, they charged to their deaths with bayonets fixed. A German officer, described the scene after the perimeter had been taken. In his diary he noted:

> The wood was a wasteland of shattered trees, charred and burning stumps, craters thick with mud and blood, and corpses, corpses, everywhere. In places they were piled four deep. Worst of all was the lowing of the wounded. It sounded like a cattle ring at the spring fair.

As dusk gathered, the chaos in the wood increased. Isolated individuals and small parties of Germans and South Africans found themselves hopelessly lost amid the tangle of wreckage and smoke. The historian of the German 52nd Infantry Regiment depicted the scene as one of 'indescribable confusion'.

The South African Brigade fighting with bomb and bayonet in Delville Wood. (Photo: Transvaal Scottish Regimental Museum)

As many South Africans as were able filtered back to the centre of the wood where Lt-Col Thackeray had established a strong-point at the intersection of two rides, named *Rotten Row* and *Buchanan Street*. Here they combined to make a stand, and, shoulder to shoulder fought throughout the long hours of 19 and 20 July to prevent the German infantry from consolidating their hold on the wood.

To make matters worse, the British counter-battery fire was not always accurate, shells often landing in the South African positions.

On 19 July at 1.15 p.m. Thackeray sent a message detailing his desperate need of relief:

> Our heavy artillery shelled our Buchanan trench for some two hours and ground on either side east and west – injured several of our men and buried several. This... is becoming beyond endurance... I do not feel that we can hope to hold the trench in the face of any determined attack. The enemy attacked last night and this morning snipers and artillery casualties are continuing. I cannot evacuate my critically wounded or bury my dead on account of snipers. Four men have been hit helping one casualty... My MO (Capt S Liebson) is completely exhausted. Will you manage his relief together with ours as soon as possible... So far the SAI have held on but I feel the strain is becoming too much...[1]

The only other officer, besides the wounded Capt Browne, with Thackeray was Lt E J Phillips who provided the second account of Thackeray's bravery on the desperate days of the 19 and 20 July.

> On the night of 19 July, when the enemy massed and assaulted our lines of trenches, Lt-Col Thackeray jumped on to the parados and threw hand grenades, and when enemy's grenades exploded, throwing him into the trenches he immediately got up and continued throwing grenades until the enemy's attacks were repelled. In my opinion had Lt-Col Thackeray not shewn [sic] his total disregard of danger, our men would never have fought the way they did in Delville Wood. Even when the situation was at a most critical stage, Lt-Col Thackeray issued orders to hold the line at all costs, and when the men were absolutely beat by fatigue, he went up and down the trenches encouraging the men. On the second attack early on the morning of 20 July, he grabbed a rifle and fought with the utmost

1   'The South Africans at Delville Wood', Uys I, *Military History Journal* Vol 7, No 2, December 1986, p56.

gallantry, by his acts inspiring the men to do their utmost.[1]

Lt-Col Dawson had ordered the withdrawal of the reinforcements he had brought up the day before as well as other remnants of the SA Brigade. At 7.00 a.m. on 19 July, Major Hunt, acting OC of the 4th SAI received an order timed 3.40 a.m. from Dawson to retire to Talus Boise. He handed over to the Norfolks and then followed 'B' and 'C' Companies of his unit, or rather what was left of them. As Hunt reached Brigade HQ, death once again brushed by. A shell nearly killed him, throwing him upside down. He came to rest

Lt-Col E F Thackeray, OC 3rd SAI, who held on at Delville Wood.
(Photo: Transvaal Scottish Regimental Museum)

at the foot of the dugout steps – uniform and tartan once again thickly browned with powdered earth.

He found General Lukin sitting on a tree stump. 'You know, Thackeray is still in there, in the Wood. Are you and your men ready to go in and get Thackeray out?'

'Yes Sir!' Hunt replied, but in his heart he knew all his lot were done in after six days and five nights of holding the Wood or its surrounds.

Lukin then asked: 'What is your strength?'

Hunt told him: ' "C" Company 21; "B" Company 19; and "A" Company, lying down there, 6.'

'No!' Lukin retorted immediately. 'That would be no use. Stop where you are.'

The following day, Captain Mitchell of the Scottish, who had been seconded to Highland Brigade Staff, came to see them. Hunt showed him what was left. He wept. It was this pathetic remnant of the 4th SAI that Pipe Major Sandy Grieve and his pipe band led from Talus Boise – four officers and thirty-eight other ranks strong.

1   Document in Transvaal Scottish Regimental Museum.

A corner of Delville Wood in September 1916.
(Photo: SA National Museum of Military History)

At 1.00 p.m on 20 July, Thackeray sent a last desperate message to Lukin.

> Urgent. My men are on their last legs. I cannot keep some of them awake.
> They drop with their rifles in hand asleep in spite of heavy shelling... Food
> and water has not reached us for two days – though we have managed
> on rations of those killed...but must have water. I am alone with Phillips
> who is wounded and only a couple of Sgts. Please relieve these men today
> without fail as I fear they have come to the end of their endurance.[1]

At last Thackeray's request bore fruit. After six days and five nights without sleep,
he and two remaining officers, 2/Lt E J Phillips and 2/Lt Garnet G Green, both
wounded, and 120 men left the wood. He heard at 4.15 p.m. that they could
depart as soon as their relief arrived.

Thackeray was the only officer in the 3rd SAI Mess, the night after Delville
Wood.

The measure of the achievement of the SA Brigade is highlighted by the fact
that it took six weeks for British units to recapture the whole of 'Devils Wood', as

---

1   Uys *loc cit*. p57 – quoted by Uys.

Delville Wood, September 1916. (Photo: SA National Museum of Military History)

All that was left of the village of Longueval - September 1916.
(Photo: SA National Museum of Military History)

it came to be known by both sides. When the dead were buried only 151 bodies of the many South Africans who had fallen there, were found. Of these only 81 could be identified. The SA Brigade had not been found wanting. As untried troops they had stood their ground against the flower of the German army.

The stand made by the SA Brigade ensured that the ground that had been gained so expensively was held. The second stage of the Somme offensive in this section of the front was secure.

Reduced to matchwood – Delville Wood, September 1916.
(Photo: SA National Museum of Military History)

Chapter 14

Reflections

With the passage of time Delville Wood has become the only battle on the Western Front associated with South Africa that is remembered – more so since the recent opening of the Delville Wood Museum.

The Battle of Delville Wood is viewed by South Africans with special pride and reverence because it was the first major action of the SA Brigade on the Western Front. Casualties were extremely high and almost every white South African family was touched in some way. The Brigade had hung on in the Wood without reinforcement or relief for an incredibly long time – six days and five nights, standing firm against impossible odds. This had also been the first occasion of any significance that South Africans, whether of British or Dutch descent, had fought and died together. Yet if this had not happened at this precise point of time there would have been another place in France, another Delville Wood, that would have the same significance today.

Because it is a first in so many ways, Delville Wood has been written about more than any other battle that South Africans were involved in during the twentieth century. Let us remember that the SA Brigade fought other battles on the Western Front. Some of these verge on the impossible in terms of achievement. Yet having said all this, the name of Delville Wood will remain uppermost, for it was here that the horror and stark reality of the Western Front experience was brought home to South Africa, just as Gallipoli stunned Australia.

Through all the horror that was Delville Wood there shone one beacon of light. A promise of a future. Hope. A conviction that there was still a God. For it was as though Christ walked with Captain The Rev Eustace St Clair Hill, Chaplain to the Forces.

In Longueval, when the bombardment of the 17 and 18 July was at its worst,

> at the first-aid station was Father Hill, Chaplain to the 3rd (SAI), sitting over a fire in the open making coffee for the wounded, quite regardless of his own personal safety,

wrote L/Cpl Ernest Solomon of 3rd SAI.

> The artillery officers objected to his fire as it was too conspicuous and told
> him to extinguish it, but he ignored them. Many a wounded man blessed
> him for his untiring and unselfish efforts on their behalf.

Although nominally attached to the 3rd SAI, Hill was always up with what ever
regiment of the SA Brigade was in closest contact with the Germans; in trenches
that were under fire. He did not know the meaning of fear. He counselled and
encouraged men, helped the wounded and buried the dead.

Hill's record has survived in letter form in a publication called *St John's
College and the War* of February 1917. Hill's activities centred around the
dressing stations at Longueval, where Dr Taylor of 1st SAI and Dr Leibson, 3rd
SAI, had established themselves in a well-shelled house and cellar, with Major
Power, MO of the 4th SAI in a barn next door. The following extracts speak for
themselves.

16th July (Sunday)

> After spending the night in Bernafay Wood dressing station cooking Oxo, I
> left my servant Waigel and walked into Longueval through a mass of fallen
> houses. I found Capt Miller, 1st SAI Battalion. I sat in his trench for a bit,
> then left him and found a dressing station in a half ruined house, where Dr
> Bates, of the Black Watch, was MO. Cooked Oxo in the yard until a shell
> brought the roof on to my pot and a brick on to my helmet, and another
> fired a house near us, which set two other houses on fire, causing them
> to blow up. I reported the fire to Capt Miller, and said the well should
> be cleared of wood and its iron cover put on to prevent its being filled by
> debris, and recommended all to fill water bottles.
> Kept Oxo and tea going for wounded. An order came for us to evacuate, as
> the town was going to be shelled by our guns. I was asked to clear a cellar
> full of wounded men. I found the steps blocked by a man hit badly in the
> stomach, who refused to move or be moved. Below him was a captain hit
> in the arm and leg. I got him past and then got the rest up. I asked all to
> commit themselves to God's protection, and carried the captain, with other
> stretcher-bearers, to Bernafay Wood, through fairly heavy shell fire. All got
> through safely, despite mud and rain. Returned to Longueval. Put a badly
> wounded patient in a bed I found in a house near by, but that night we
> were ordered to clear out. Dr. Laurie, SAMC, helped me carry this bed-

patient. Rain and mud awful. Some Highlanders helped us, and we finally got them to Bernafay Wood. I got to bed 5 a.m.

17th July

I walked to Longueval, Pte Waigel carrying my Oxo, etc. He left and I started Oxo and coffee, a German bag of which I had found, and also I found sacks of tea and sugar and bacon and biscuits. Gave drinks to wounded while Leibson and Laurie dressed them. Returned to Maricourt 6 p.m. I left Maricourt with Cook and Waigel, 1st SAI. Buried Trotter by railway as we passed.

July 18th, 1916

Walked to Longueval. Intense bombardment of village and our trenches in Delville Wood. Looted clothing for wounded with Stuart, 3rd SAI, and when men's kit was gone I got women's clothes and baby mattresses, etc. I kept hot drinks going until shell fire got too hot and my larder was badly hit and my equipment cut to bits. I got all patients who could be moved down into the cellar and barricaded the door and both windows looking towards street, where snipers kept firing and shells bursting. Our house was hit at an angle twice. Burmester, Gordon, Sansom (of 3rd) and two others couldn't be moved to the cellar, so I gave the three named the Holy Communion and put bags around the other three. Now we saw the Camerons retiring and all who could hobble of ours left. Dr Leibson took a sergeant, and Dr Laurie remained. At last stretcher-bearers came and took all off. I helped carry Bailey (3rd SAI) to Bernafay Wood.

5 a.m. bed, Maricourt, 19th July

I returned (to Longueval) and found water short, so watched my opportunity and filled all cans, escaping snipers.

This unadorned statement is more fully expanded by Sir Philip Gibbs in *Realities of War* published in 1944:

There was no water except at a well at Longueval, under fire of German snipers, who picked off our men when they crawled down like wild dogs with their tongues lolling out. There was one German officer there in a shell hole not far from the well, who sat with his revolver handy, and he was a dead shot. But he did not shoot the padre. Something in the face and figure of that Chaplain, his disregard of the bullets snapping about him, the upright fearless way in which he crossed that way of death, held back the trigger-finger of the German officer, and he let him pass. He passed many times, untouched by bullets or machine-gun fire and he went into bad places, pits of horror, carrying hot tea which he made from the well-water for men in agony. The padre in question was Father Eustace Hill CR, of St John's College (Johannesburg).

In the bombardment of the 18 July it was nothing short of a miracle that the Regimental Aid Post where Hill was ministering to the wounded, was practically the only place that did not get a direct hit.

Hill continued his narrative:

> I brewed tea, etc., and later on about 30 stretcher-bearers came up, all of SAMC. Dr Laurie and Welch came to the wood and returned with Capt Browne (4th SAI) and another. The Germans made an attack on the town, so I advised all unarmed stretcher bearers to clear with the stretchers. They did and I was left alone. I waited in our hospital for more wounded.

> 5 a.m., July 20th

> We brewed tea, etc. I sent off stretcher cases and remained and buried three more corpses in the same crater in which I had buried nine or ten the night before. I could get no help to carry in more corpses because of snipers, so about noon I returned to Maricourt and rested till 7 p.m. Then I joined 1st SAI at Happy Valley, about four miles behind Maricourt.

For those who had died at the Longueval dressing station, Hill had erected a wooden shield made by L/Cpl R O Sanders, 4th SAI on 19 July. He wrote:

> While wondering how to dig a grave to hold all the twelve lying about the aid post, a terrific shell fell in the garden amidst the rose trees. Clods of earth went up and left a cavern into which I easily pulled all, and took the Burial Service throwing in rose leaves at 'ashes to ashes'. (So in the huge shell hole by the SAI Dressing Station were buried the 12.) 50 yards from the Big Church and Cemetery, just by a red brick coach house with rose garden... This cross replaced my first and was put up by me on return to

same area in 1918. (It was) knocked down and discovered in grass after armistice. No trace of church or houses by 1918 – just sand and later on grass.[1]

In a later letter to Canon Nash, the Headmaster of St John's College, Hill wrote:

I own I felt great spiritual elevation at it (Delville), and rejoiced at being able to prove God's protecting love.. . I hope this war goes on until men loathe war and determine for ever to give it up as an unChristian damnable method of settling disputes.[2]

Father Hill's attitude to honours is made plain in an unpublished manuscript in St John's College archives.

Father Eustace Hill's courage and spirit in Delville Wood won him the MC. There were persistent rumours that he had been awarded a VC. Indeed the men he served thought that he had deserved it on many occasions. He would not have refused a VC but in his humility thought it too personal an award for him. It is safe to say that he discouraged any attempt to get it for him. He did not mind the Military Cross for it was a more general award and many had it.

Hill's chief concern had been the care of the wounded. From his advanced position near the front line, the wounded were passed on down the line. Major C M Murray DSO recalled the arrangements for dealing with the wounded.

If a man was wounded in the front line, he was conveyed by the regimental stretcher-bearers to the reg. MO, who dressed him. This meant a distance of anything from a few hundred yards to half a mile. From the reg. MO, the ambulance stretcher-bearers formed a chain through the shell swept area – a distance of nearly 4 – 5 miles, the last mile or so being accomplished in horse drawn ambulances. From this point to the main dressing station they were taken in the French ambulance motors. Quite a number of these motors were blown up by shells at distances of nearly 9 miles behind the front line. At the main dressing station where I worked we redressed the cases, amputated shattered limbs, tied arteries and generally made the patient fit to travel to the casualty clearing station. As the wounded were

1   Warwick, p164.
2   Lawson KC, p127.

Capt The Rev. Eustace Hill, Chaplain to 3rd SAI. Photograph taken in the 1920s when he was Headmaster of St. John's College, Johannesburg.
(Photo: St. John's College Archives)

The cross and shield Eustace Hill erected at Delville Wood on 19 July 1916. The cross was re-erected in 1918 by Hill and was still standing in place in 1925.
(Photo: St. John's College Archives)

always very dirty and covered in mud or dust as the case might be, we also gave them a dose of anti-tetanic serum. We arranged ourselves in 8 hours shifts and the station thus never ceased working day or night. From the main dressing station a convoy of fifty motor cars plied incessantly carrying the wounded to the CCS (Casualty Clearing Station). Owing to the awfulness of the fire nearly all the reg(imental) stretcher-bearers were killed or wounded in the first day or two (of the Delville Wood battle) in spite of only going out when 'things were more or less quiet', and so our men had to go right up to the line as well.[1]

Matters could go wrong as they did for Pte Bob Grimsdell, 4th SAI, who was wounded in the neck in Delville Wood and was left for dead.

I regained consciousness to find myself among assorted dead bodies including a German sergeant-major wearing a tasselled sword bayonet.

1　*Chronicle of the Family*, December 1916 Vol 4 Privately published.

His helmet with the gold eagle was in good condition except for the bullet hole in front. I don't know how long I'd been lying there and in my dazed state I tied helmet and bayonet on to me. I then crawled away from shellhole to shellhole. A British soldier, one of the walking wounded, gave me a hand in finding a 1st Field Dressing Station. At the end of the war I returned to Johannesburg and looked up an old comrade – Foreman Carpenter, Johannesburg Municipality. I had grown a moustache and had filled out a bit. 'What's your name?' he asked. 'Bob Grimsdell, surely you know that', I replied. 'Now look', said my old comrade, 'I'm sick and tired of you bums coming the old soldier trick and trying to make an easy quid, you just f... off before I throw you out – it happens that I was next to Bob Grimsdell when he was killed at Delville.' So I just went. Our family joke – 'Were you in Delville Wood?' 'Yes, I was killed there.'[1]

Grimsdell was one of the lucky ones. The casualty list for Delville Wood shows that when the SA Brigade went into the Wood on 15 July it numbered 3 155 all ranks and six days and five nights later it numbered 18 officers and 702 other ranks. Total casualties of 2 536 consisted of 763 dead – 457 killed in action, 186 missing death assumed and 120 who died of wounds. For the rest, 1 476 had been wounded and 297 taken prisoner.

There were also many unsung, unrecognised acts of heroism that far exceed the number of decorations actually awarded. Pte George Sturgeon, 3rd SAI, while in hospital heard of the circumstances of his brother's death in Delville Wood on 17 July.

A fellow told me about dear old Norman. This man was wounded and Norman was just going to give him a drink of water when he was shot through the heart and died instantaneously. He lay on the wounded man for fourteen hours before being moved.[2]

How many of the SA Brigade had emerged unscathed from the Delville Wood experience after the six days and five nights was not immediately apparent. In the heat of battle men had been separated from their units or had been detached for various reasons.

One was Major F H Heal whose duties as transport officer had prevented him from actually entering Delville Wood, but his work during the battle had been

1   Manuscript in Transvaal Scottish Regimental Museum.
2   *St John's College and the War*, February 1917, p18.

Pencil sketch by GAM, an unknown officer of the 9th Division, of Delville Wood, drawn in July 1916. (Author's Collection)

of vital importance. He expressed his feelings about the losses the Brigade had suffered in a letter.

> Poor old 'D' (Company 1st SAI). I cried when they formed up after the battle – only 36 left. If ever the CPR[1] (Company of 1st SAI) march through Cape Town every man should take off his hat. I told you they were sound – I trained those boys and I know.
>
> Delville Wood is written in letters of blood, but if we were wiped out, the Germans lay in a thick carpet of grey, in places piled up over the whole of the wood. Our poor old Brigade is nearly gone, but we have others coming in, and they will do well, but they are not the old crowd – they never will be until they have passed through their Delville and proved themselves.[2]

1   Cape Peninsula Rifles.
2   *The Story of Delville Wood told in Letters from the Front* p13.

Some of those who survived the ordeal had not been through the full experience, but had been a draft of raw recruits straight from Bordon Camp, who had been rushed into battle only to become almost immediate casualties. This was nearly the experience of Pte F Addison, 2nd SAI, who with another draft straight from Bordon had arrived at the Brigade wagon lines on 16 July near Bray-sur-Somme. The new draft had been quickly surrounded by some of the original Brigade men who gave the latest news of the battle and the casualties suffered.

The next morning, the 17 July, Major Gee, second-in-command of 2nd SAI inspected the new draft, made them welcome and told them that at sunset he would lead them into Delville Wood where reinforcements were badly needed. Early that afternoon, Lt-Col Tanner was wounded, so Major Gee left at once to take command of 2nd SAI. Gee was killed soon after his arrival. As Gee had left no orders for the draft moving into the Wood they remained where they were and missed the battle. 'So we consoled ourselves by going to a vantage point and watching the wood spouting great columns of earth and smoke from shell fire and the trees disintegrating before our eyes.'[1]

On 20 July when the remnant of the SA Brigade still in the Wood, 143 strong staggered back to Talus Bois, Addison and other members of his draft went out to meet them

> and there were no heroics, just hand-shaking and anxious questions of some friend or relation. I am glad I saw this gallant band of survivors come out of that dreadful slaughter house, and actually took a photo of them on the quiet, but lost it later from shell fire. To own a camera was a court martial offence...
>
> Next morning we had an early church parade, which was most moving and impressive. We had it in the open field under the sky, ammunition boxes as an altar, and the boom of guns for the music.
>
> By this time quite a number of missing men had found their way back to the Brigade. General Lukin had a parade but it was obvious he had lost his brigade, and when he took the salute he uncovered his head and tears were running down his cheeks. He could not have paid the Brigade a higher compliment.[2]

On the final count, out of the 3 155 all ranks, 18 officers and 702 other ranks had emerged unscathed, but exactly how many men marched past Brig-Gen Lukin in

---

1   Addison, *Foot* p12.
2   Addison, loc. cit.

All that was left of them – men of the SA Brigade cleaning Lewis Guns at Carnoy Valley, the day after coming out of Delville Wood.
(Photo: SA National Museum of Military History)

Happy Valley near the village of Bray-sur-Somme a few hundred yards away from the Somme River, will never be known.

'You see,' Lukin said, when he spoke afterwards of that day, 'I know the fathers and mothers of those lads. They're not just cannon fodder to me: I feel responsible for them to their parents.'[1]

1   Johnstone, RE, *Ulundi to Delville Wood* p150.

Chapter 15

A new preparation

For those at Bordon the wait had been long. There had been calls for a few small drafts, however. This was after the campaign in Libya. Especially for those who had arrived a week after the Brigade's departure for Egypt, the period of inaction had been particularly frustrating. Admittedly the mud, rain, cold and misery of winter had been replaced by the budding of spring and an English summer.

Long columns of men tramped steadily through the beautiful English countryside. They sang songs – some well known. Others concerned army life, pungent and to the point, composed very often by those on the spot. The men were fully trained and fit for battle. In the lanes and roads round Bordon their coming and going was a familiar sight as were their songs:

> There are styles that show the ankle
> There are styles that show the knee
> There are styles that make a man's eyes wander
> To a place they never ought to be
> There are styles that have a saucy meaning
> That the eyes of man may only see;
> But the style that Eve wore in the garden
> Is the style that appeals to me.
>
> Good-bye-ee! Good-bye-ee!
> Wipe the tear, baby dear, from your eye-ee
> Tho' it's hard to part, I know,
> I'll be tickled to death to go
> Don't cry-ee! Don't sigh-ee!
> There's a silver lining in the sky-ee.
> Bon soir, old thing! Cheerio! Chin-chin!
> Nah-poo; Too-dle-oo! Good-bye-ee![1]

1 1st SAI Brigade Association Hymn Sheet.

Month had followed month: six long months of inaction. The route marches and repetitive training had helped to pass the time.

Now all was action. During July 1916, drafts totalling 40 officers and 2 826 other ranks had been sent from Bordon. The absence of significant casualties had made it possible for reinforcements to be available on such a scale.

The usual route was from Southampton or Dover by sea to Le Havre; a small episode in the transmigration of men that had been taking place since August 1914. Embarkation in the evening meant arrival early the next morning. From Le Havre it was up the River Seine to Rouen, fifty miles upstream. Pte F Addison, 2nd SAI, wrote:

> Rouen was a main base through which thousands of men were sorted out to go to their various units in the line, and also it was a testing out ground. Before any draft was allowed to proceed to the front it had to pass out in the Bull Ring which was famous throughout the Western Front. It consisted of a large open sandy piece of ground, acres in area, fitted up with all the appliances to test the skill and endurance of a soldier. So far the instructors we had encountered we considered fierce, but they were lambs compared with the tigers we met in the Bull Ring. Our individual greeted us with the remark that no squad of his went back to camp without their shirts sticking to their back with sweat. We all survived and passed our tests with great credit, creating a sensation with our shooting returns. Believe it or not, our draft also beat the local cricket champions among the base wallah cricketers, and because Ernest Addison could bowl a cunning off break, he was offered a job as instructor.[1]

If a man had been wounded, the Bull Ring was still his lot before he could rejoin his unit. A plus factor was the probable issue of a new rifle, still in its coating of factory grease. Warwick remembered being exposed to the full gamut of thorough and strenuous training for trench warfare.

> For all the rough language in which the talks were given, they contained shrewd advice and sound common-sense.
> Sometimes tins of pork and beans appeared among the rations. The beans were there all right, but the pork, if at all present, consisted of a minute cube of pork fat. This led an instructor to say,

1   Addison, *Foot* p9-10.

Collar badges and shoulder flap insignia of 3rd SAI (left) and 4th SAI (right).

'If I can teach you men to take cover like that pork does in the beans no German will ever shoot you!'[1]

The remnants of the SA Brigade had left the Somme on 23 July and arrived in an area north-west of Arras. The 2nd SAI were billeted in a barn in a village called Estree Gauchy which the men immediately re-named Extra Cushy. The new drafts for the various regiments of the Brigade rendezvoused there. In these pleasant surroundings the Brigade rested and besides some training, meandered through the cornfields by day and spent the evenings in the many estaminets. By the middle of August the SA Brigade was considered to be ready to go into the line again. The Vimy Ridge sector, assigned to the Brigade, was a quiet one as all the activity was still centred in the south on the Somme. The area was ideal to break in the Brigade to the realities of trench warfare as so many of its members were freshly arrived in France. Addison wrote:

1   Warwick, p91-92.

The crest [of Vimy Ridge] was no higher than the Durban Bluff, but had no trees on it, and in this flat featureless country it commanded a very extensive area, on which thousands of men had died.

The Vimy Ridge sector made an indelible impression on me principally through my nose.

The smell of quick lime or chloride of lime takes me straight back to the trenches where these chemicals were extensively used to counter the sickly smell of rotting Frenchmen and Germans, who were buried shallow in the parapets and at the bottom of the trenches, and if any new digging had to be done it was like working in a cemetery, which the place really was. The whiff of hessian and burnt gun powder also bring back the sight of thousands of sand bags used in the line, and the exciting feeling of fear, and the anticipation of further shell fire.

Because of the closeness of the trenches sniping was almost deadly, and the Germans had a sniper whom we called Cuthbert who was a dead shot. He killed and wounded several men and delighted in smashing our trench periscopes. One day I was in the front line on the Black Watch sector, and close by was a Jock who was throwing out earth from the bottom of the trench, and every time the spade came over the parapet Cuthbert put a bullet through it which made the Jock so hopping mad that he stood on the fire step in full view and shouted out 'Gang away and f... yourself.' Cuthbert must have been surprised. I was with Lt Garnet Green when he shot Cuthbert who had got careless and exposed himself.[1]

While in the Vimy area the men of the SA Brigade were frequently called upon to undertake tunnelling as a fatigue duty. The idea was to mine the whole ridge and the German front line would go up in a series of explosions. The Brigade was full of gold miners from the Witwatersrand. Used to the flint-hard rock of the Rand, they found the chalk sub-strata under the trenches like cheese. Their progress was regarded as phenomenal by the Royal Engineers Tunnelling Company responsible for the work. Tons of high explosive and thousands of pine pit-props were carried for the miners and many tons of excavated soil on the return journeys. Sometimes by placing an ear to the ground the subterranean pick work could be heard quite clearly. The following year the mines under the ridge were blown and the Canadians took the crest. Addison wrote:

The holding of the Vimy Ridge had done us a world of good, We had all shaken down into our places, knew each other and our officers, in fact had

1   Addison, *Foot* p14-16.

become a regiment and not a mob of men.

The love a soldier feels for his regiment is something I cannot explain. It just happens. His friend is just behind him on his heels. This close proximity creates the feeling of belonging, even if you do number a thousand. And when that thousand acts as one man; and when at the command of one man goes over the top almost shoulder to shoulder, that is what it means to belong to a regiment.[1]

2/Lt Addison in the RFA, 1917.
(Photo: W Addison)

Before the 9th Division left the Vimy sector on 25 September 1916, General Plumer, commanding the 1st Army, inspected the SA Brigade. The billets of 'Extra Cushy' with their lice were left behind without regret. The long week's trek on foot in gloriously fine weather through the back areas of the beautiful French countryside led to new adventures. But first a three day pause so the 9th Division could rest.

Addison described the time the 2nd SAI was in the village of Lingernel.

> We certainly had a quiet time, but so long as we did not hear the scream of a shell or gun fire we were content. While in these back areas various regiments of the 9th Division came through our village on a route march, and no regiment ever went past a village without marching at attention; and what a sight it was as the battalion came past. We all used to line the road to see how they looked and marched, and what a joy it was to see the men clean shaven, and their uniforms and equipment all spick and span.
> The Jocks of course with their kilts, pipes and drums always stole the thunder.[2]

---

1 Addison, *Foot* p17-19.
2 Addison, *Foot* p17-19.

This idyllic interlude had to end. The units of the SA Brigade packed up, fell in and marched away from this forested area where they had been billeted. Soon they were marching down one of those typically French poplar-lined roads that disappear out of sight in the far distance, as straight as a die all the way.

Chapter 16

The Butte de Warlencourt

On 7 October 1916 the appointed place of departure was reached. As far as the eye could see were waiting soldiers who had been given the order to fall out at the side of the road. The whole 9th Division was there. Hundreds of motor buses rumbled up. They were provided by the French Army and were driven and conducted by French coloured troops, well-built and proud natives very similar to Zulus. For the South Africans it was a new sensation to be detailed, directed and looked after by black men and they seemed to enjoy the novelty.

As the buses travelled on hour after hour, the route and direction indicated one certainty. It was obvious that the SA Brigade was returning to the Somme. That name had a sinister sound to every soldier. As they debussed the distant roar of the guns could be heard. The area was that of Mametz Wood, torn and desolate in appearance, the mud and the rain adding to the depressing scene. The German positions that had been taken on 1 July, the first day of the Battle of the Somme, were crossed at the village of Fricourt, shallow depressions marking what once had been well constructed trenches.

Pte F Addison, 2nd SAI, recorded that:

> ...the surrounding country beggars description, and it is impossible to convey it to the eye or mind of one who has not actually seen it, because nothing since the world began has occurred to form a basis of comparison. The village of Fricourt was 'non est' save for a few bricks lying about, and a notice board telling all that this spot was Fricourt or had been, and I defy anyone without that notice board to point out where the village once stood. The rest of the country as far as the eye could see was in exactly the same state, just a featureless waste, not a tree, house, or road, the ground churned up and shell holes so closely fitted that their craters touched.[1]

---

1   Addison, *Foot* p20.

The roar of battle had not stopped on the Somme since 1 July and now it was October. From Ypres to Bapaume, along the road to Albert, there was utter devastation. Nearly a million men had been killed. The debris of war lay everywhere. It was hard to believe that the trenches across this earth-torn desolation were still occupied by both sides.

On 9 October the SA Brigade moved into High Wood notable for the attempted break through by the British Cavalry Division, still armed with lances and swords. They had come to an abrupt halt in the face of barbed wire and machine-guns. It was the machine-gun and trench warfare that had made the cavalry charge suicide. Unfortunately the majority of those at British High Command, in charge of operations, were cavalry men. They could not face the reality of this new type of war. It took them too long to realise that the day of their beloved cavalry was over. Many thousands of wonderful horses were slaughtered in bringing that lesson home. Cpl Arthur Betteridge, 4th SAI, remembered later seeing a mine crater in which over a thousand dead horses had been thrown for burial. Addison wrote:

> High Wood had been captured a few days previously by the most bloody fighting and sacrifice of life on both sides. The trenches (were) blown almost flat, the trees gone, the dead lay about in heaps, both British and German, and these bloated mangled heaps of dead had a quietening effect on us, and all conversation ceased, silenced by the overpowering presence of death.
>
> It was not a very cheering prospect for men who had yet to go on to where this carnage was actually taking place. Here we saw what had been done, but in a short time we would be among dead men who were still warm.
>
> We waited in High Wood (it really was not there) until it was sun-down, and watched our artillery in action.[1]

From the time the SA Brigade had left the Somme in late July the British advance had slowly dragged forward. The third German position had been largely incomplete at the time of the battle of Delville Wood but during September it had been strongly fortified. By now there was even a fourth line slightly west of the Bapaume-Peronne road. This was the final German prepared position. In mid-September Field Marshal Haig had put into operation his plans to break through the German third line. With the use of tanks for the first time, the British advance on a six mile front had penetrated a mile in depth, followed on 25 September by a similar success which had pushed the Germans behind their fourth line. All

1   Addison, *Foot* p22.

the advantages of the high ground they had previously occupied were now lost. It seemed that the Allies were set to shatter the whole German front between Arras and Peronne. These high expectations depended on fine weather but on 26 October gales accompanied by drenching rain lashed the front line. The Allies were immediately faced with a new problem.

Fifty square miles of much fought over battlefield, the product of the Allied effort during the past three months since the Somme offensive had started, was now turned into a sea of mud. The chalky soil, so disturbed by the constant shelling, had lost all cohesion. John Buchan, the official historian of the SA Brigade wrote:

> The consequence was, that there were now two No Man's Lands – one between the front lines, and one between the old enemy front and the front we had won. The second was the bigger problem, for across it must be brought the supplies of a great army. Every road became a watercourse, and in the hollows the mud was as deep as a man's thighs.
> The army must be fed, troops must be relieved, guns must be supplied, so there could be no slackening of the traffic. Off the roads the ground was one vast bog, dugouts crumbled in, and communication trenches ceased to be. Behind the British front lay six miles of sponge, varied by mud torrents. It was into such miserable warfare, under persistent rain in a decomposing land, that the South African Brigade was now flung.[1]

Although the German third line and the Thiepval-Morval Ridge was in British hands, a number of spurs descended from the ridge into the valley. These intermediate positions, although not part of the German fourth line, shielded it and blocked the British advance to the fourth line. The Germans had taken full advantage of this by strongly fortifying these positions, utilising dead ground, ruins and sunken roads. General Sir Henry Rawlinson's Fourth Army, which held this section of the line, had to clear these fortifed spurs before a general assault on the whole front could take place. Attempts made to achieve these objectives had been largely successful except for the spur between Eaucourt l'Abbaye and Le Sars, known as the Butte de Warlencourt. On 7 October the 47th Division had been almost wiped out in making an unsuccessful attack on this front, but before being relieved, they had managed to occupy and establish some forward strong points in No Man's Land. The 9th Division now took the place of the 47th Division with orders to take the Butte de Warlencourt and the intermediate line it helped to form. The Butte, as men who were there described

---

1   Buchan, p89.

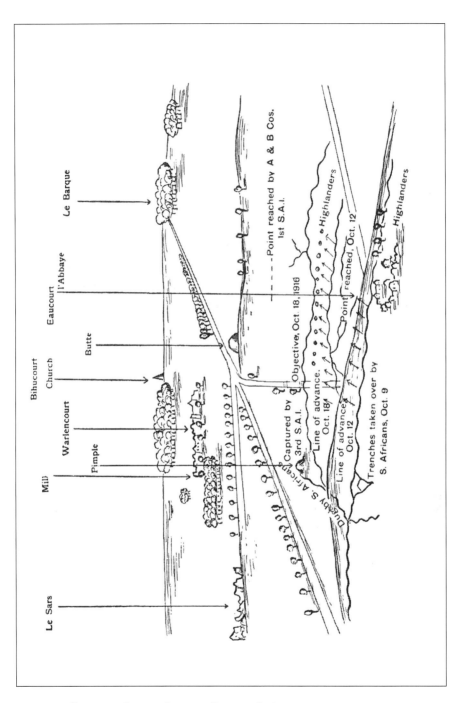

SCENE OF SOUTH AFRICAN BRIGADE'S ADVANCE AGAINST THE
BUTTE DE WARLENCOURT POSITION
(SADF Documentation Centre)

Trench inspection by the Commanding Officer. In the words of the official photograph:
'Showing very little of the mud we had in the trenches.'
(Photo: SA National Museum of Military History)

Moving a field gun in the mud to a new position on the Somme front.
(Photo: SA National Museum of Military History)

it, had the bare appearance of a Witwatersrand gold mine dump in shape, size and colour. Its stark, forbidding eminence dominated the surrounding countryside and the Germans had not been slow in turning it into a concrete strong point, bristling with machine-guns.

On 9 October, the units of the SA Brigade were allotted positions. The actual SA Brigade front was occupied by 2nd SAI whose strength at the time was 20 officers and 578 other ranks – a far cry from when they had first landed in France. All the units of the Brigade would have their turn. John Buchan described the front line area that the 2nd SAI occupied.

> 'B' and 'C' Companies of the 2nd Regiment held the front line, ...together with two strong posts, Nos. 58 and 77, on their left and right fronts respectively. 'A' and 'D' Companies were in the support trenches of the old Flers line running along the south-west side of Eaucourt l'Abbaye. The German front trenches, known to us as Snag and Tail, lay about 1 000 yards from our front line, and conformed roughly to its shape. Beyond them, running through the Butte de Warlencourt, was the enemy main intermediate position, cutting the Albert-Bapaume road beyond Le Sars. The confused fighting of the past weeks and the constant rains had made the whole front on both sides indeterminate.'[1]

The confusion mentioned by Buchan is borne out by the difficulty the two companies of the 2nd SAI had in finding the front line.

Pte Addison was one of the 200 men of 'C' Company, 2nd SAI, who wandered down a shallow valley, like a lost sheep with no landmarks to give a bearing. They expected to be mown down by machine-gun bullets at any moment or collect a 5.9-inch shell. Shelter was found in a well defined sunken road that also featured on maps of the area, and so it was frequently shelled by both sides. The British and German dead that littered its length were ghastly to see, but by this time, such sights had begun to make the South Africans indifferent to the horrors of war. The officers and guides eventually got their bearings and brought the two companies to the trench they were to occupy, but not without casualties from vigilant machine-guns.

> The trench we came to was the front line to be held by 'C' Company 2nd SAI, and it was blasted almost flat and in places hardly knee deep. We relieved the 22nd London Regiment or what was left of them. They had

PHOTO No. 22 N 1724. TAKEN AT ABOUT M 29 CENTRAL AT ABOUT 1000 FEET, 9-11-16.

Aerial photograph of the pulverised, featureless countryside in the vicinity of the Butte de Warlencourt 9.11.1916 as taken by the Royal Flying Corps.
(Photo: SA National Museum of Military History)

been under shell fire for four days, gone over the top, been wiped out, counterattacked, and all the stuffing, both mental and physical, had been knocked out of them. They lost no time in showing us the local beauty spots, and left us their wounded and dead. Sergeant Vivian Addison and Capt (B E) Burne, our company commander, had a fearful argument about the position of the front line, and Vivian could not believe that this depression was the only protection between us and the German Army. However, it was the front line but the whole layout was so complicated and confused we really did not know where we were. Feeling weary and sad I sat down on the upturned face of a dead man. I soon got up. Our stretcher-bearers to their everlasting credit, by working all night, cleared the trench of the abandoned wounded Londoners. We had heard shouts and cries from (the wounded) in No Man's Land, but we spent all that night digging like hell to get some cover before daylight revealed us to the Hun. We tried to make them understand we could get them at nightfall.

Our mess of four at once begun to deepen our portion of the trench and we scooped out funk holes in the sides so as to get protection from overhead shrapnel, but against high explosive they were quite useless.

During certain times of the day and night the Germans shelled us continuously, and it is hard to describe being shelled for a long period, say for three hours with a shell arriving near you at the rate of one a minute, sometimes faster, and sometimes as slow as ten minute intervals or more.

There was no relief in being able to hit back so one just had to stick it out. As soon as the first shell was on the way we would dive into our funk holes, squeeze ourselves up as small as possible, and wait for it. Meanwhile we could hear the shell coming; that whining, screaming, shrill tearing sound, coming closer and closer, increasing in sound and seemingly in anger. One would brace the body muscles, shut the eyes, bow the head and wait with every nerve at breaking point until the deafening roar and shock of explosion was over. Then came the acrid smell of high explosive, and the thuds and patterings of the lumps of earth blown into the air falling around you. Often after a burst the cry would go up for stretcher-bearers, and you would know some poor chap had caught it.

The worst affair close to us was when a shell fell into the next bay, and we were all badly shaken. Norman Dixon and the survivors ran round to us absolutely white with shock, saying several men were hit.[1] We went round to help and found four dead, and poor old [Pte S S] Symons had his arms and legs blown off, and an unfortunate Londoner who had been rescued from No Man's Land that night with a shattered knee was blown to bits. We removed him with a spade.[2]

For the four days in the front line the only food was bully beef, biscuits and cold water.

At midday on the fourth day in the line, 12 October 1916, all NCOs were

1   Pte N C Dixon died of wounds 15.11.1916.
2   Addison, *Foot* p23-27: edited extracts.

The Butte de Warlencourt – looking from the Albert-Bapaume Road *circa* September 1917. (Photo: Cape Archives)

called to company headquarters. Certain that it was to receive instructions for their relief that night, 'B' and 'C' Companies, 2nd SAI, were shocked to hear they were not to be relieved. Instead it was 'over the top' at 2.05 p.m. that afternoon in battle order. 'A' and 'D' Companies would be in support.

> Here we waited for zero hour, each with his own thoughts which must have been rather grim, because one peep over the parapet revealed a gentle bare slope down to the bed of the valley, parallel to our front and then the ground rose to the crest about half a mile away. This ridge, strongly held by the enemy, was our objective. They could see every movement we made. On our left, over-towering and overpowering the entire landscape was the ever menacing Butte, which could enfilade the whole valley and the approaches to the crest. We knew Fritz had machine-gun posts out in front, which in theory would be smothered by shell fire. Dotted over the landscape, just to emphasise the reality of war, were pathetic bundles of khaki: the bodies of British soldiers killed in the previous attack. Here we were waiting for the whistle to blow, and Fritz also waiting to shoot with piles of ammunition next to him. My own thoughts, as I looked at the sun shining and the blue sky, was of anger, and the utter foolishness of the whole set-up, and what a damn silly way to go out of this life. My heart was beating nineteen to the dozen.

I was on Capt Burne's left and Percy Gold on his right. On the tick of 2.05 p.m. he blew his whistle and over we went. At the very same second our shells screamed overhead, exploding in front of us.

The empty landscape was suddenly full of hundreds of men in long lines walking towards the enemy. Away on our right we could see the Seaforth Highlanders and Argyll and Sutherland Highlanders advancing on their front.

At once the German machine-guns opened fire and the bullets fairly crackled around us, and his counter barrage came down on us in front and behind like a thunder clap. So in a few seconds all hell was let loose.

We had hardly got moving when Capt Burne dropped dead and so did Percy Gold, and I could see fellows dropping to the right and left of me along our line.

In front the ground was heaving and spouting earth, smoke and dust, and we had to walk behind this creeping barrage, and into the German counter one. Our line was rapidly thinning out and I wondered when I would be hit.

I remember reaching the bottom of the valley and started up the opposite slope, and I seemed to be the only man above ground, which proved too much for me and so I dived into a shell hole, and looked around, but could not see a soul. Our attack had failed.

I felt I had to join the men in front so I jumped up and ran, and every Hun seemed to have a shot at me, and something like a blow from a sledge-hammer hit me on the right thigh and I fell sideways into a shell hole.

To my joy I found the leg was not broken, the bullet just missing the bone, otherwise I would very likely have died in No Man's Land because the Butte and ridge were not captured for weeks afterwards.

So I lay in my shell hole with the German counter barrage spouting up columns of earth all around me, and often the clods fell on me, and every now and then I had a peep above ground but saw no human movement of any kind.

The sun slowly went down which I thought it would never do, and when I judged it was dark enough not to be picked off by a sniper I began to crawl back to our lines, dragging my leg which had become as stiff as a poker.[1]

The attack had been a failure because the German forward positions and machine-gun nests had not been located and obliterated by the British barrage.

1   Addison, *Foot* p23-27, (edited extracts).

The Germans had been waiting for the South Africans and had caught them as they started down the first slope. They stumbled forward through the haze of drizzle and smoke with cloying grey clay weighing down their army boots. Here the horror of every soldier's disturbed dreams had become a reality: that useless frontal attack where most were scythed down by machine-gun fire while still a long way off from the enemy.

The 2nd SAI had disappeared down the slope into an area that was one mass of churned up grey clay. The poor visibility, because of the drizzle, was aggravated by the British smoke barrage drifting back towards the British front line. The fortunes of the 2nd SAI were screened from view. For this reason the first reports misled SA Brigade HQ into believing that the advance was proceeding rapidly and successfully. The German barrage that had come down one minute after zero hour had cut all communications.

The 4th SAI, who were supposed to go over the top with the 2nd SAI as a second wave of attack, were severely pounded by the German barrage in the packed communication trench before they could reach the front line assembly area. In places their dead lay in piles.

Those of the 4th SAI who had not been caught in the communication trench met a similar fate to the 2nd SAI while crossing No Man's Land.

Reports came through indicating the true state of affairs. One company of 3rd SAI was thus ordered to occupy the original front line from where the attack had been launched. Patrols were sent out. Despite the total failure of the 2nd SAI's attack, Lt T F Pearse and a party of men had succeeded in digging in, some 150 yards from the nearest German trench.

Soon after occupying the positions in the front line, Lt-Col Thackeray, OC 3rd SAI, had received a message from Lt Pearse, saying that his position was critical as many of the seventy other ranks who had dug in with him were wounded and he was exposed simultaneously to artillery, machine-gun and rifle fire. Relief was impossible until dark. Pearse managed to hold on until he and 2/Lt D J Donaldson with some men of 4th SAI could be relieved. It took time to find them.

Just how confused the situation was in the featureless landscape of churned clay is illustrated by the report Brig-Gen Lukin had received from Captain T H Ross MC, of 4th SAI, at 4.00 p.m. on the 12 October. Ross thought 'A' Company of 4th SAI was in front of him at the first objective and believed the 2nd SAI was in front of them again. Reconnaissance that evening established that this was not so and that nowhere had the first objective been reached. No advance could survive the long-range concentrated fire from the German machine-guns in the prepared positions on the Butte.

Because of the heavy casualties sustained by the 2nd and 4th, they were withdrawn to High Wood and relieved by 3rd SAI under cover of darkness. The 1st SAA was now moved up in support. Before dawn large working parties had completed the deepening of the communication trenches and the digging of a new communication trench from the left of the British line to a strong-point. This was a mound close to the German main line trenches. It was sixty feet long and from twelve to fifteen feet high. It became known as the Pimple.

Brig-Gen Lukin, who regarded the occupation of the Pimple as essential, ordered its capture and occupation at nightfall on 14 October, after hearing of the expulsion of a few snipers from its top. It was the lot of 'B' Company, 2nd SAI, under Capt L F Sprenger to capture and consolidate the Pimple, plus as much of the German trench as possible. Running east to west this 300 yard section of trench linked the Pimple with two other German trenches that met at this point. The Tail Trench angled in from a north-westerly direction on the left, while the Snag Trench, doing the same from north-east on the right, was a continuation of the 300 yard section of trench and linked up with the main German trench lines to the north. Second Lieutenant S Mallett led the assault for 400 yards and rushed the mound which 2/Lt G H Medlicon, 2nd SAI, and his party now proceeded to garrison. Mallett then entered the German trench that linked the Pimple with the junction of Snag and Tail Trenches and bombed the Germans out of this section until he and his men were driven back by heavy machine-gun fire and bombs. Mallen was mortally wounded and died soon afterwards. Capt Sprenger was also wounded with thirty-five other ranks killed, wounded or missing; 2/Lt Medlicott was killed. The dead were buried where they had fallen.

On the night of 16 and 17 October, the 1st SAI now had its turn. It took over from the 3rd SAI who moved into support trenches.

During the 17 October Brig-Gen Lukin visited the front line and discussed the position with Lt-Col F S Dawson, OC 1st SAI, who then took his officers round the whole trench system to be sure there would be no mistakes in recognising objectives in a landscape that was growing more featureless by the hour. Later orders were received that he was to organise an attack by his regiment for 3.40 the next morning, the objective being the same as that attacked without success on the 12 October. Rain continued to fall. Divisional Headquarters had learnt nothing from the experiences of previous divisions or the more recent experience of the 2nd SAI in their vain attempt to take the Butte de Warlencourt. The suicide of the 12 October was to be repeated.

To make matters worse, during the night of 17 October, soaking rain fell making the trenches heavy and the parapet slippery. The condition of the sea of grey clay that had to be crossed was now beyond description.

What it felt like fighting round the Butte de Warlencourt.
Cartoon: 'Two different points of view' by Lt W H Kirby, 4th SAI.

'Been looking round here for "Five Tall Willows" all day, 'ave yer? Well, there they are right under yer bloomin' nose.' – Lt W H Kirby.

At zero hour, 3.40 a.m. on the 18 October, the attacking companies were already formed up in No Man's Land and moved off on time, keeping as close as possible to the British barrage as it crept forward towards the German positions.

The left company, 'C' under Captain H H Jenkins, was blocked by wire. Captain Jenkins was soon wounded and he withdrew what was left of 'C' Company to the original line. Of the one hundred men who had gone over the top with him at zero hour, sixty-nine were casualties.

'A' and 'B' Companies, 1st SAI, were under the command of Major H Woodhead and Captain E Whiting respectively. Halfway between the front line and the Snag Trench which was the objective, Captain Whiting was mortally wounded.

During this period Father Hill was constantly ministering to the many wounded and dying in No Man's Land. He went out often, looking for wounded in that featureless maze of abandoned trenches and waterfilled shell holes. He always used to walk erect and fearlessly, wearing his surplice with a red cross, over his uniform, when everyone else hugged the ground or any cover that was available. He had been unscathed in his rescue missions.

But Hill was not to go untouched this time. He heard that Captain Whiting was lying seriously wounded, so he went out to find him.

A wounded soldier warned Hill of a sniper lying inwait. For the first time on such a mission, Hill dropped to his knees. As he did so, a sniper's bullet caught him in the wrist and heel. He crawled with his injured arm over his back to try to keep dirt out of the wound. He became delirious; after losing all sense of direction he finally lapsed into unconsciousness as he reached the South African front line trench. The wound he had tried to protect was filthy. By the time he was admitted to the hospital at Rouen, his whole forearm was gangrenous. He had begged the surgeon not to amputate. 'You don't know what it is to lose a right hand.'

Hill's divisional commander, Maj-Gen Sir W T Furse, wrote to his brother the Bishop of Pretoria of his visit to Hill in hospital. He related how Hill, just out of the anaesthetic, apologised for getting wounded seeing that he had brought in thirty wounded men the night before and fifty the night before that with impunity. He continued: 'I don't know why it should have happened. But I'll be back very soon.'[1]

By the end of November Padre Hill's foot had healed and he was making plans to have an artificial forearm and hand fitted in February. By then he had also learned to write with his left hand and to make himself as independent as possible. He could do everything except tie his shoelaces. He even wrote to the Army Pensions Board suggesting that they stopped paying him a disability pension as he could now manage with one arm!

Neither Hill's sortie into No Man's Land or a search party shed any light on the riddle of Whiting's and Woodhead's companies that had disappeared so mysteriously into the 'blue' at dawn that morning through a heavy curtain of rain.

Later when the 6th KOSBs advanced after the SA Brigade was withdrawn they saw

> a large party of South Africans at full stretch with bayonets at the charge – all dead; but even in death they seemed to have the battle ardour stamped on their faces. They were led by their officer, a magnificent specimen of manhood.[2]

But that was not the full account of what happened to 'A' and 'B' Companies, 1st SAI. One officer and one man survived to return to tell the story. Lieut P R Stapleton, 1st SAI, who had been promoted to subaltern's rank on the eve of Delville Wood wrote to his mother of the episode.

> The contents of my haversack saved me; bits of shell penetrated the bag, a much-folded groundsheet and a packet of biscuits. By the time we reached

1   *St John's College and the War*, February 1917, p24.
2   Croft, Lt-Col W D, *Three Years with the 9th Division*, p84.

our front line I had lost nearly half my platoon. We then started attacking in pitch dark and pouring rain; a storm of small shells, bombs and bullets broke over us. The trench my company was to capture, was so flattened by our guns as to be almost unrecognisable, so when I found that our men on my right and left were advancing further, I thought I had mistaken the trench, so proceeded to overtake them, but found them all at sea, so I left them to dig in while I went to the left to see what was happening there. I reached a trench packed with Germans, so knew our left had been held up. I then returned to rejoin my own men but found none. Then I picked up some stragglers and took them to an unoccupied trench.

At day-break I found we were completely surrounded by Germans, who were also at sea as to the position. With my revolver and the only two rifles not clogged with mud, we had great sport sniping enemy stragglers – up to ten – and took nineteen prisoners. As it got lighter and our ammunition nearly done, I decided to rush my party about 400 yards towards our trenches. Only one man, who was leading the prisoners, was left to me as the few others still alive, had taken shelter in shell holes.

We gained our lines, but what an escape and how lucky the prisoners did not know we had only two rounds left in my revolver. I was the only officer to come out whole. The colonel (Lt-Col F S Dawson) had been good enough to tell me he was quite pleased with what I did and intends reporting it to the general.[1]

Stapleton was awarded an MC for this action and went to Buckingham Palace to receive it. He was killed in action at Gouzeaucourt on 8 December 1917.

Somewhat later, at dawn on the 18 October, after the disappearance of the two companies, Major Ormiston, 1st SAI, commanding the troops on the Pimple had launched a separate attack. This was along the trench leading from the Pimple to the Nose which was the name given to the point where the Tail and Snag Trenches met. Machine-gun fire stopped the attempt. A block was established fifty yards up the trench in the direction of the Nose.

Capt G H Langdale's company of the 3rd SAI, now reinforced the 1st SAI, or what was left of it. During the afternoon of the 18 October, Dawson was ordered to renew the attack at 5.45 p.m. Owing to the shocking condition of the trenches, which were now practically impassable because of the incessant rain, Capt Langdale advanced only with one platoon and two Lewis gun teams. He

1   When war broke out in 1914 he served as adjutant to his partner in a legal firm. The partner had become officer commanding of the Carnarvon Commando. Stapleton had joined the 1st SAI as a private in 1915.

moved in skirmishing order across to the Snag Trench, apparently unobserved, in spite of heavy shell fire. He entered the trench without opposition and proceeded along it in an easterly direction for about 200 yards, hoping to encounter the missing companies of 1st SAI. At that point he blocked the trench and left a Lewis gun team there. He continued for a further twenty-five yards from the Nose, but noticed three German machine-guns waiting for him. This was a well-prepared trap. Fortunately Langdale was not enticed any further. After an hour's deliberation he withdrew his men to the original front line, reporting his action to Lt-Col Dawson. He was ordered to immediately re-occupy the Snag Trench which he had just vacated! This he did between 12 and 1 a.m. on the morning of 19 October.

Brig-Gen Lukin now ordered Major Hunt, OC 4th SAI, to dispatch a company of 120 men to be placed at the disposal of Lt-Col Dawson. They were to attack the Snag Trench with various remnants of 1st SAI. Although the company of the 4th under Captain T H Ross reached the Snag Trench at 4 a.m. on the 19 October without mishap, they were faced with a heavy German counterattack in which *flammenwerfers* and grenades drove Ross and Langdale's men back along the trench. Ross was wounded and Lieut Sandy Young VC was killed. Young, who had won the Victoria Cross serving with the Scottish Horse at Ruiterkraal on 13 August 1901 during the Anglo-Boer War, had assisted the Germans in quelling an Herero uprising while on detached duty from the Cape Mounted Police in 1906. He had captured the Herero leader.

In spite of this failure to take and hold Snag Trench, Lukin decided to make yet another attempt that day with a company of 3rd SAI, but to no avail.

Although Snag and Tail Trenches were once again held in force by the Germans and the SA Brigade was back in its old front line positions, Major Ormiston, garrisoning the Pimple, continued to enfilade the German trenches with two machine-guns. The Pimple gave its garrison a commanding view of the German trenches. John Buchan wrote:

> It often happened that small bodies of Germans, unable to stand the strain, would leave cover and bolt across the open towards the Butte, making an excellent target for our snipers and machine-gunners. When the Nose was finally occupied by the 6th KOSBs, they found over 250 Germans dead lying around it.[1]

Dawson now realised the situation was hopeless. Besides his adjutant, he did not have a single man capable of making another attack on the Snag Trench.

---

1   Buchan, p100.

Close-up view of the Butte de Warlencourt showing the memorial crosses that had been erected. The soil shows evidence of the litter of battle. (Photo: Cape Archives)

The ground seemed to have no bottom. Men battled waist deep in mud in the trenches. Any man who was wounded sank below the surface and suffocated, unless he was rescued quickly. The men who walked across the area often did not realise that the welcome firmness of the ground was the body of a drowning comrade. Each yard seemed a mile. When a man paused for a breather he rested his elbows on the sides of the trench to prevent himself from being engulfed in the mud. Parties with ropes and spades rescued stranded men. One Lewis gunner of the 6th KOSBs next to the 1st SAI position was so firmly embedded in the mud that when he was finally extricated through the use of ropes, both his ankles were broken. The men were utterly exhausted.

By the time the last of the 1st SAI was relieved by the 6th KOSBs on the night of the 19 and 20 October, conditions were so bad that the men could not even clean their weapons. On the night of the relief, Major Ormiston's party holding the Pimple, did not have a single rifle that could be fired. Because of the mud a stretcher required eight bearers and took four to six hours to cover the thousand yards between the front line and battalion headquarters.

As Cpl A W Cloete-Smith, 2nd SAI, wrote in his diary: 'Four divisions have been cut up trying to take it (the Butte). It is the strongest position on the front.'

Cross on the Butte de Warlencourt in memory of the 2nd SAI.
(Photo: SA National Museum of Military History)

The Colours of the 4th SAI (SA Scottish) in 1983 before their removal to the RHQ of the Transvaal Scottish. The central cross is from the Butte de Warlencourt and commemorates the men of 4th SAI who were killed in action there. The cross is still to be seen in St Andrew's Presbyterian Church, Pretoria. (Photo: Martin Gibbs)

The whole operation had been a fiasco from the start. In a letter to his parents dated 22 August 1917, he wrote of the Butte de Warlencourt:

> Old Furse (Maj-Gen Furse, the Divisional Commander) was deprived of his command for making a mess of things at Warlencourt. It appears now that (on 12 October) instead of going over the top at 2 p.m. as we did, we should not have gone over until 2 a.m. the following morning. I should have thought that by this time they would have got rid of men who do not know their work but apparently there are still some of them knocking about.

The SA Brigade had little to show for their efforts in trying to gain minor objectives. Often these were not much more than a string of mud-filled shell holes tenuously linked. However, the period 9 to 19 October had cost the Brigade approximately 1 150 casualties, including 45 officers.

On 3 September 1917, nearly a year later, Cpl A W Cloete-Smith, 2nd SAI, marched to the area while billeted close by and described the scene to his mother in a letter dated 8 September 1917:

> I had no difficulty in finding the old trench in what at that time was No Man's Land, where we were lying for four days. The ground in front of the Butte is simply a huge graveyard. Nothing but little wooden crosses wherever you look. I managed to find the graves of some of the men I knew. There are still quite a number of skeletons knocking about but they are mostly Germans. Although it is over a year since the Somme advance the place is still a mass of wreckage, etc. There is enough ammunition and shells lying about to start another war. England will never know what the Somme cost her both in lives and money. It makes one perfectly sick to see the hundreds and thousands of little crosses...

The Butte de Warlencourt was never captured during the Battle of the Somme. Yet another attempt was made by the 50th Division in November 1916 with equally futile results and many casualties. In February 1917 the Germans abandoned the position after falling back to straighten their front line. Only then was the Butte de Warlencourt occupied by British Forces without a shot being fired.

> *Take me back to dear old Tempe: put me on a train for Bloemfontein.*
> *Take me over there, drop me anywhere:*
> *Bethlehem, Vrede or Theunissen, well, I don't care.*
> *I should like to see my best girl.*
> *Cuddling up again we soon shall be; Whoa!*
> *Tiddley, iddley, ighty— to H— with France and Blighty.*
> *Africa's the place for me.*

Chapter 17

Waiting on winter

By 22 October 1916, the SA Brigade was in reserve. A week later they reached the Arras area south of the Doullens-Arras Road. After the Butte de Warlencourt there were many new faces in the Brigade. Gradually those who had been wounded during the disastrous interlude on the Somme would recover and return.

The 9th Division had become part of Maj-Gen Aylmer Haldane's IV Corps in General Sir Edmund Allenby's Third Army. Both generals were veterans of the Anglo-Boer War. Haldane, while a captain in the Gordon Highlanders, had been captured by the Boers along with Winston Churchill during the armoured train ambush on 15 November 1899 at Chieveley near Colenso. He with two other officers had made a dramatic escape from the officers' prison at the Staats Model School in Pretoria.

It was strange to think that a mere fourteen years before Boer and Briton had been at each others throats and now the SA Brigade was constituted of elements of erstwhile enemies. At this period the proportion of those of British descent to those of Dutch descent was approximately eighty per cent to twenty per cent, although the latter percentage increased to about thirty per cent towards the end of the war.

The SA Brigade was spread out, in villages, with the 4th SAI billeted in Arras itself where it was involved

Lt-Gen Sir E H Allenby KCB, the Third Army Commander.
(Photo: Cloete-Smith Collection)

in the improvement of the city defences. The other three regiments spent their time in constructing telephone cable trenches, new roads and other preparations for the offensive that was planned for the spring. Maj-Gen Furse was eased out of his position as OC of the 9th Division into the backwater appointment of Master-General of Ordnance. His replacement was Brig-Gen Lukin with the rank of Temporary Major-General. Lt-Col F S Dawson, OC 1st SAI, now became Brig-Gen F S Dawson commanding the SA Brigade. Major F H Heal succeeded him as OC 1st SAI.

The SA Brigade front line was a stretch of trenches 1 800 yards long, east of the town of Arras. This was on the extreme right of the 9th Division front with Canon Street Trench on the left flank and the River Scarpe on the right flank. Here duck shooting could be enjoyed 800 yards from the German trenches. The four regiments of the SA Brigade spent their time in and out of the front line, support or reserve. The cobbled streets of the old town were littered with debris and broken glass from periodic bombardment. Most of the buildings were damaged with the cathedral and town hall in ruins. From the exposed streets a cellar town was entered where comparative safety was enjoyed. The flinty chalk consistency of the ground had made it possible to cut out deep trenches and dugouts. The line had been quiet in this sector since the failure of the 1915 French offensive. The French had settled into the area, making comfortable, deep, well revetted dugouts. These were often only refinements to the subterranean world of Arras that had been hewn out of the chalk and rock and used down the centuries. Large caverns and wide drives that had probably sheltered Romans, Spaniards and English, in bygone European wars, now accommodated South Africans under similar circumstances. Arras had been the centre of the wool industry dating from the 4th Century, while it had been the last of the chief Gallic towns to surrender to Julius Ceasar.

Fires were made on the paved floors for it was bitterly cold underground in these chambers. Pte Geoffrey Lawrence, 1st SAI, recorded how, when these fires died down,

> the rats came out in their hundreds. They were the largest imaginable, and quite unafraid. I could only sleep by covering my head completely for they ran over us all night. Several sat and scratched themselves on my blanket-covered face. My companion next to me woke in the middle of the night cursing and spitting. He had slept on his back snoring with his mouth open – a rat had slipped on its way across his face and put its foot in his mouth! It is reported he never snored again.[1]

1 *Militaria* 8/2 1978 p51.

LEFT: Lt-Col F H Heal DSO who replaced Lt-Col Dawson as OC 1st SAI. RIGHT: Brig-Gen F S Dawson CMG, DSO who replaced Brig-Gen Lukin as the SA Infantry Brigade Commander, after being OC of the 1st SAI. (Photos: SADF Documentation Centre)

Pte Cyril Choat, 4th SAI, related in a letter to his parents dated 9 November 1916 how he

> had some cheese between two army biscuits wrapped in paper and in my gas helmet satchel which I put near me while at work. On looking at the food later I found that a rat had eaten through the gas helmet bag and paper and had taken out the cheese from between the biscuits without touching the latter!

Driven out from destroyed buildings, the rats flourished in the trenches where food and shelter were in abundance. They swarmed everywhere and grew to the size of cane rats

If the billets were in the part of Arras that was constantly shelled, the SA Brigade would be in cellars. Otherwise it was above ground, perhaps in a convent. Some nuns who wore a peculiar winged head-dress occupied part of the building. A few members of the civilian population remained in Arras. Some shops were open.

Because the opposing front line trenches were so close, the Trench Mortar Battery was very active. They were most unpopular with men of the Brigade because they had to carry up the huge 'plum puddings' the mortars needed, recalled Cpl George Warwick.

Arras in ruins – the roofless cathedral. The city was a frequent target for German artillery. (Photo: SA National Museum of Military History)

Heavy things they were, a huge steel ball with a steel handle. These handles used usually to fly back into our lines when they had been fired by the TMB into the German trenches. The Trench Mortar Battery bombarded the German front line with these 'plum-puddings' then packed up and got out. We poor infantry in the line had to bear the brunt of the shelling when the Germans retaliated, and retaliate they always did, either with whizz-bangs (small shells from field guns) or from heavier guns or by their own trench mortars known as *Minenwerfers* or, as we called them, 'Minnies'. You would hear the minnie gun go off. One of our men on minnie guard would blow one blast on a whistle if the minnie was coming straight for

Cpl. George Warwick, 4th SAI, whose experiences of World War I are recorded in his book *We Band of Brothers*. The photograph shows him aged 18 years and 8 months at Bordon Camp. (Photo: SA National Museum of Military History)

him; two blasts if it was falling on his right, and three on his left. You would see the minnie go right up in the air and apparently come down

Cpl. George Warwick's group of World War I medals (L to R): British War Medal 1914-1918; Bilingual Victory Medal; Somme Medal. (From the Author's Collection)

'Minnies' – cartoon by Lt W H Kirby. 'Unlucky – a superstitious soldier seeing five minnies coming straight at him on a Friday.'

straight for you. You ran to the right and looked up and it seemed still to be descending on you. You ran back and by this time the minnie would have reached our line and gone off with the most nerve-shattering detonation. The minnie was just as terrifying at night, for it lit up its path through the air with a fiery trail.[1]

Inevitably during this period of static warfare men were killed during the daily bombardments and trenches blown in. In the icy weather the work to repair the damage with pick and shovel was difficult. The frozen ground was unbelievably hard. At night sparks would fly off a pick driven into newly-frozen ground from

1   Warwick, p96.

earth blown into a trench shortly before.

With No Man's Land snowbound, large scale attacks were impossible. However, there were frequent bombing raids with an officer, NCOs and a few men all dressed in white overalls for concealment. Prisoners and information were brought back. These excursions were not without mishap. There were also clashes between opposing patrols in No Man's Land at night. A fight in the dark would ensue.

Periods of 'rest' out of the line, in Arras or while in support or reserve trenches saw the men of the Brigade called upon to do additional tasks.

The infantryman was nothing but a glorified navvy, day and night digging trenches, filling sandbags and lugging them along to where they were heaved into position; carrying projectiles and ammunition for the array of artillery as well as steel girders, planks and heavy wooden supports. All had to be negotiated along the twisting convolutions of narrow trenches. Pte J E P Levyns, 4th SAI, noted how he and his companion Byrne

> carried hundreds of 'plum pudding' mortar bombs up to dumps in the trenches, rolls of barbed wire, carried between the two of us on steel stakes supported on our aching shoulders, up to the front line and worst of all

In camouflage white overalls going over the top to a snowbound No Man's Land for a daylight patrol from the Arras trenches. (Photo: SA National Museum of Military History)

A ration party going up to the front line during winter.
(Photo: SA National Museum of Military History)

sheets of corrugated iron, which cut our chapped hands. Byrne and I
carried numbers of these through miles of communication trenches to a
spot where the engineers were digging a mine.[1]

The three months that the SA Brigade spent in the trenches before Arras were the
coldest winter experienced in nearly seventy-five years. Levyns recalled that

the worst hardship was the shortage of water caused by the continued frost.
Washing was impossible in the line, and we had to save a little of our
tea to shave with. The Brigade had a high reputation for smartness and
cleanliness, which officers and enlisted men seemed determined to uphold
even in these Arctic conditions.[2]

In the back areas when the units of the SA Brigade were out of the line the troops
suffered just as much if not more as they were without the protection against the

1   Levyns, J E P, *The Disciplines of War*, p65-66.
2   Loc. cit. p66.

During periods of 'rest' the infantryman was nothing but a glorified navvy: taking up a trench support through a communication trench in winter.
(Photo: SA National Museum of Military History)

cold that the dugouts in the forward areas afforded. Cpl A W Cloete-Smith, 2nd SAI, in a letter to his mother dated 16 November 1916 wrote:

> The sooner we are moved into decent winter quarters, the better. The great thing here, is to get wood for our fires, and the fellows have pulled half the village to pieces. There have been several rows over the mysterious disappearance of all the wood-work of ploughs, etc., but of course none of us have ever seen a plough, much less taken anything off one. The other day a large gate vanished and all the information they could get out of us was that *Allemande*[1] must have taken it. The old woman to whom it belonged, put in a claim for 150 francs, but was I believe quite satisfied with the five which she received... I am now able to buy a few extras such as tinned fruit etc. and am really quite comfortable. The prices out here are something wicked and these French people must be fairly coining money. Simply every house you come to is either a store or an estaminet. I have

1   The Germans.

Cpl A W Cloete-Smith 2nd SAI, whose letters from the front 1915 to 1918, have survived intact and which have been quoted from extensively. During World War II Cloete-Smith served as a captain in the Native Military Corps.
(Photo: King Edward VII School Museum)

become quite used to drinking coffee without milk as they very seldom have the latter. In the village we are in at present, Agnez-lez-Duisans,[1] there is only one place, where you can get 'cafe-au-lait' and we very seldom take the trouble to go there. One thing I do know and that is that their coffee is the best I have yet tasted.

1   The name was gleaned from Cloete-Smith's diary as no place names were permitted in letters by the strict censorship that was imposed. Very often the most interesting letters were those written from England during periods of leave or hospitalisation.

On 22 December 1916, Pte Cyril Choat, 4th SAI, wrote to his parents:

> I wish you could see me now, up in the front line trenches in a small shelter 5ft x 5ft by 3ft high, with the rain dripping through the roof and down the sandbagged walls, endeavouring to write you a letter. My hands are filthy, clothes wet and muddy and my boots hardly recognisable.
>
> 30 December 1916
>
> I slept one night on guard in our little shelter, just a covering over the trench, with the rain and occasionally a bit of earth falling on my shoulders, in a sitting up position and in a soaking wet great-coat, and strange to say I slept well...At about 12 a.m. on Christmas morning, a pouring wet night, I stood on duty and sang Christmas carols and songs and wished every one who passed a merry Christmas... We had a bit of a celebration on Christmas day on stuff we could buy from the canteen. The Huns got an extra special strafe from us as a Christmas present. We were paid yesterday so champagne is floating around, there is plenty of the cheap variety to be bought here. I shall have a glass to toast your health.

For those in the trenches, the nights were the most dreaded. In sub-zero temperatures to sleep in the shelters cut into the side of the trench traverses was

'Every house you come to is either a store or an estaminet' – AW Cloete-Smith letters. Frenchwoman selling eggs to Tommies. (Photo: SA National Museum of Military History)

'So severe was the cold that five times a day hot drinks would be served to men in the front line, transported in a large container strapped to a man's back' – Choat letters. (Photo: SA National Museum of Military History)

a fitful experience. To all intents and purposes a week in the front line meant a week without sleep. This more than anything else sapped the men's strength. No blankets were issued in the front line and there were no dugouts either. Greatcoats and sheep-skin leather jackets were protection against the cold. The SA Scottish found that the thick pleats of their kilts under their greatcoats kept them very warm, unlike the other three regiments of the SA Brigade. Cold penetrated through their boots in spite of the sandbags tied round them. In theory stretcher-bearers should have rubbed their feet regularly with whale oil as protection against frostbite and trench-feet. Feet were always aching and numb. So severe was the cold that five times in twenty-four hours hot drinks would be served to front line soldiers. These would be transported in a large container strapped to a man's back

– hot soup, tea or cocoa.

The snow and frost caused much damage to the front line defensive works and the communication trenches. Time and time again these had to be reconstructed. When there was a thaw, long sections of the trench would collapse. The debris would have to be dug out. The mud and slush intensified the discomfort. In the support and reserve trenches each man received two blankets. Some of the men inevitably died of exposure while others were asphyxiated through having taken a brazier of coals into a dugout.

On 6 January 1917, Choat wrote:

> My feet have not yet recovered from the wet and cold and (they) have kept me off duty since we came out, and I am supposed to do no walking, so have hardly been out at all. They trouble me most when warm and at night especially, so that I cannot sleep well and sometimes can barely walk, but I hope they will soon recover.

Choat's trench feet necessitated his having a spell in hospital like thousands of others who succumbed to the effects of wet boots and socks for days on end without the opportunity of a change of footwear.

On 3 January, in spite of the cold, the 3rd SAI had carried out a very successful

An illegal photograph taken by Pte. Cyril Choat of Neil Johnson (left) and another in the support line at Arras, December 1917. (Photo: Transvaal Scottish Regimental Museum) Unofficial photographs were a court martial offence.

raid on the German front line trenches. The operation was under the command of Lieuts B W Goodwin and W F G Thomas. Picked volunteers constituted the raiding party. During the expedition all the men of the 3rd SAI had blackened their faces. Only Zulu was used as the means of communication. Concrete machine-gun emplacements were destroyed, and several occupied dugouts were blown in and set on fire. The German's suffered a number of casualties.

During this lull before the spring 2/Lt Jack Carstens, 1st SAI, recalled how in the front line before Arras

> it was the last shift of the night and as the dawn broke the sentry pointed out to me a young German soldier peering over his parapet – probably a new recruit who had come into the line during the night. The distance between our trenches at this particular part of the sector was not more than thirty yards and there was this young fellow – I can see him now with his rosy cheeks surveying the surrounding country.
>
> 'Shoot him, Sir,' said the sentry, handing me his rifle. I put the rifle over the parapet, took careful aim at the innocent face but dropped the rifle the least little bit and shot into the sand bags below it.
>
> 'Jove, that was a rotten shot, Sir,' the sentry said. But as I turned away I spotted a wild duck swimming in a marsh to my right. It was over 100 yards away and, as I called the sentry's attention to it I said: 'Watch me bowl him over!'
>
> I rested the rifle between two sand bags, again took careful aim, pulled the trigger and the duck flopped over on to its side and floated away. I was vindicated.[1]

In March Pte Geoffrey Lawrence, also of 1st SAI, welcomed signs of the coming spring but not without a certain degree of foreboding:

> As I made my way one morning along a communication trench I saw the unusual sight of a number of little sparrows chirping happily and I suddenly realised this must be Spring and felt a lightening of the heart in tune with the singing of the birds. The thought of Spring after the long bitter winter seemed wonderful and then came the sobering thought that Spring meant a Spring offensive.[2]

This was the longest period the Brigade had so far spent in any one spot since its arrival in France.

1   Carstens, p26-27.
2   *Militaria* Ibid p54.

Chapter 18

Arras

While the winter had prevented active operations, preparations for a Spring offensive had continued without interruption. Diaries and letters home all confirm that no one was spared in the accomplishment of this work. Cpl George Warwick asserted that they worked twenty-five hours out of twenty-four.

The SA Brigade had been occupying front line trenches round Arras for close on five months. Although there had been little real action the very nature of this static trench warfare had taken its toll. From December to early March, the Brigade had suffered two officers and 49 other ranks killed and five officers and 166 other ranks wounded. In spite of the severe winter the Brigade had enjoyed remarkably good health.

Early in March the SA Brigade was relieved so that it could be moved to villages well back from the line where intensive battle training was to take place.

Once again battle flashes were sewn on the sleeve near the shoulder. Throughout the three Brigades – 26th and 27th Scottish Brigades and the SA Brigade – that comprised the 9th (Scottish) Division, the colour for 'A' Company was red; for 'B' yellow; for 'C' blue; and for 'D' green. These flashes were worn to facilitate identification between members of the four companies in the heat of battle and had been worn for the first time during the Butte de Warlencourt action, the previous October.[1]

Each of the four platoons of a company was reorganised for the new type of fighting. A platoon going into battle would now consist of four nine-men sections – I. bayonet II. Lewis Gun III. rifle grenade IV. bombing. The remaining twenty men would not go into battle, but form the nucleus around which new drafts would be added. In this way even if every man were killed, a regiment would persist.

This was training with a difference. From aerial photographs an exact replica of the opposing trench systems had been constructed, although not as deep. The attack was rehearsed again and again over this training area. A smaller scale model of the German trenches was then used so that all ranks would know what to do

1   Letter from Cpl A W Cloete-Smith, 2nd SAI, dated 16 June 1917 records this fact.

Training with a difference – the exact replica of the German trench systems to instruct troops for the forthcoming spring offensive. The model was true in every detail of contour. (Photo: Cloete-Smith Collection)

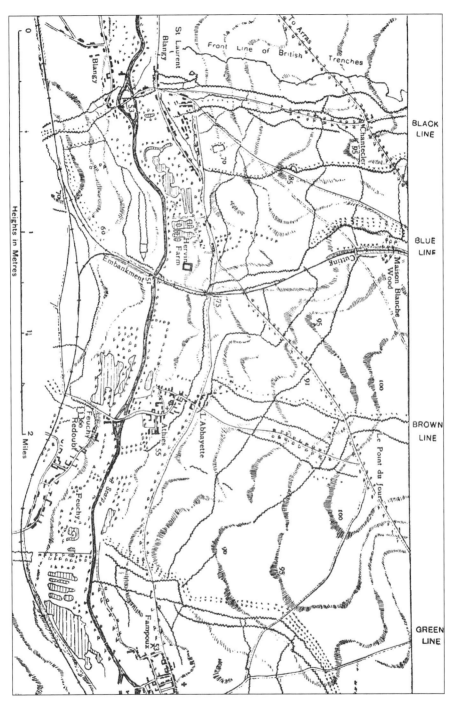

SOUTH AFRICAN BRIGADE AT BATTLE OF ARRAS. FIRST STAGE OF ADVANCE.
(Union of South Africa and the Great War 1914-1918, Official History, 1924)

208

even if all the members of the leader group were casualties. The ordinary soldier appreciated being informed so fully and became very enthusiastic about the part he was to play in the battle ahead. However, there would still be a preparatory bombardment of several days duration. The men would advance in two waves five yards apart, in extended order. They would follow hot on the heels of a creeping barrage, keeping to a distance of fifty yards behind it.

The British would be on top of the Germans before they could emerge from their dugouts and get their machine-guns in position. What had gone wrong on the Somme the previous year would not be repeated.

This was mere detail. The grand strategy had been decided by the French and British general staffs. The Arras battle was to be British responsibility, subsidiary to the great French attack on the Aisne. All depended on the success of the French. If they failed then the British, in the larger strategic sense, would fail as well. The British front, which stretched from Givenchy-en-Gohelle in the north to just short of Croisilles in the south, was more than twelve miles long. The German position consisted of three trench systems; each system had four parallel lines of trenches, studded with redoubts.

The main British attack would be the responsibility of the Third Army under General Sir Edmund Allenby. The Germans had recently retired to the newly-constructed Hindenburg Line. If Allenby could break through the old German defences north of where the Hindenburg Line ended, he would be able to occupy the flank and rear of this line. To prevent this, the Germans had begun the construction of what could be considered a fourth trench system – the Drocourt-Queánt Switch. This infamous five and a half mile long switch line extended from Queant near the northern extremity of the Hindenburg Line to Drocourt south-east of Lens. The success of the offensive depended on the penetration of the Drocourt-Queánt Switch, some six miles behind the German front line.

By the end of March the SA Brigade was back at Y Huts. This encampment was sited on a rise not far from Duisans on the Arras-St Pol road. The troops were warned not to show themselves unduly, otherwise German observation balloons and aeroplanes would observe the large troop concentrations. In this way the German staff would be alerted and they could make preparations to meet the expected atrack. The element of surprise was an all-important issue, yet the British plan of action completely contradicted the orders for caution that had been passed on to the men on the ground.

There was to be a five-day bombardment, preceded by a three week period of 'wire cutting' to prepare the way for success. The artillery preparation came from 2 879 guns – 989 of them were heavy artillery. There was a gun every nine yards.

Allenby had wanted the shortest possible bombardment – a mere forty-eight hours (which was later to be rated, in the last months of the war, as forty hours too long) making a determined yet hesitant step towards surprise. General Headquarters blocked his demands.

If this were the British idea of surprise, the Germans were not taken in for a moment. A German account of the counter-preparations they were able to make during the very convenient period of 'notice' makes interesting reading:

> Innumerable crowds of working parties laboured day and night...in unbroken sequence trains from the Homeland laden with material and munitions reached the main depots...Mountains of shells were piled up in the ammunition dumps...The construction of the defences and the organisation of the troops was completed...The enemy could come...[1]

In the light of all this, what occurred on the first day of the battle of Arras was a triumph.

During this period the SA Brigade waited. The routine of war ran its relentless course. While at Y Huts waiting to replace the 1st SAA who were in the front line, Cpl Arthur Betteridge, 4th SAI, recalled how

> Captain Ross of 'C' Company was killed by a direct hit of a whizzbang, not five yards from where two of us were standing, or more precisely, ducking down. We heard the shell fired and the consequent whizz. Long practice had taught us to guess and duck when one of these unpleasant shells was about to land close by. We had a nasty job finding some parts of the Captain's body which we took back for burial in the St Nicholas cemetery.[2]

Ross had been one of the four officers of the 4th SAI to emerge unscathed after five nightmare days in Delville Wood. Death decreed its own timetable.

The weather worsened. Bitterly cold weather and rain were the lot of the 2nd, 3rd and 4th SAI during their four hour wait for Lt-Gen the Right Hon J C Smuts, accompanied by Brig-Gen J J Collyer, both fresh from their success in the German East African Campaign. Led by the Divisional Band, the three regiments marched past in column of route. Before that the General had made the welcome announcement that private soldiers would now be paid South African instead of British rates of pay – a jump from one shilling to three shillings per day. That evening all the estaminets were filled with celebrating South Africans.

After such a send-off into battle from Jan Smuts, albeit in the rain, the focus of

---

1   Liddell-Hart, *A History of the World War* p411.
2   Betteridge, p90.

The South African Scottish Memorial Joubert Park, Johannesburg. The face of the figure is modelled on that of Capt T H Ross MC, OC 'B' Company 4th SAI who was killed on the eve of the Arras offensive by a direct hit from a German 'whizzbang'.
(Photo: Author's Collection)

the following day's activity was to determine which German troops were holding the line opposite to the 9th Division's front.

The 1st SAI, who were in the line, were detailed to conduct a daylight raid to ascertain the required identification. Under cover of a barrage, 5 officers and 50 other ranks under the immediate command of Capt T Roffe reached the German trenches without a casualty shortly after 3 p.m.

Brig-Gen F S Dawson wrote of the episode as follows:

Captain T H Ross MC, 4th SAI, killed in action, Arras, 4 April, 1917. (Photo: R. Cook)

> The official cinema man was up in the front line and took the whole thing. Some four or five Germans, including an officer, were shot in the trenches and a number must have been killed in the dugouts. In fact when one was blown up, a man's leg and boot were blown out of the entrance into the trench. Maj-Gen Lukin and a lot of other senior officers watched the whole show through telescopes from a distant observation post and they all said the behaviour of Roffe and Scheepers was magnificent. General Lukin came up and congratulated me and said the above officers must be recommended for awards.[1]

Both were awarded the Military Cross. Roffe received a bar to his MC in 1918. Capt J C Scheepers was killed in action on 20 July 1918.

Three Germans belonging to the 8th Bavarian Regiment were taken prisoner. Roffe now ordered a retirement as he considered that the object of the raid had been accomplished. Casualties were one killed and three wounded.

At 2 a.m. on Easter Monday, 9 April, the two battalions of the SA Brigade

1   GSWA Series Box 125 SADF Documentation Centre

that were to lead the attack, took up prepared positions in twenty-six craters in advance of the front line. These craters had been blown by the 64th Field Company, Royal Engineers, two nights previously. The 9th Division front was 1 800 yards from the Scarpe River to a point just north of the Bailleul Road. The Springboks were in the centre with the 26th (Highland) Brigade on the right and the 27th (Lowland) Brigade on the left. Packs and blankets had been left at Y Huts. A skeleton pack, rifle, extra rounds of ammunition and two Mills bombs, a smoke bomb to make a smoke screen, empty sand bags, wire cutters, a small box-respirator and P H helmet made up 'battle order'. Steel helmets were worn.

Although the preparatory bombardment had warned the Germans of the impending attack, they did not know the precise area of front from which it would be launched, or the precise date and time. Apparently they never expected it to begin exactly when it did because of the unusually severe weather of the first two weeks of April 1917.

The 9th Division had been detailed to take three objectives, code named the Black, Blue and Brown Lines. The Black Line was 800 yards from the British front line. To reach this objective two, and in places three, trench lines had to be captured and crossed. The Blue Line was to the immediate rear and east of the German second trench system – some 900 yards from the Black Line and it was situated astride the Arras-Lens railway. Once again several trenches had to be taken and crossed and strongpoints outflanked before this second objective could be reached. The Brown Line was the third German trench system, 800 to 1 000 yards from Blue Line, and ran from Point du Jour to the village of Athies. Once the Brown Line was taken Maj-Gen Lambton's 4th Division would pass through the 9th and capture the Green Line, which included the village of Fampoux. Beyond that lay the Drocourt-Quéant Switch. The SA Brigade would have 2 700 yards to cover before reaching its final objective.

Each trench system was heavily and densely wired. For days a systematic cutting of the wire had been carried out. The first system had been heavily shelled by British field artillery and trench mortars that not only destroyed the wire but almost obliterated the trenches. Heavy artillery was employed in cutting wire entanglements that protected the second and third German trench systems.

The SA Brigade was allocated a two-battalion frontage of 600 yards, each with a two-company frontage and each company with a two-platoon frontage. Each battalion, company and platoon would have its equivalent in support. The first two objectives – the Black and Blue Lines – would be assaulted by the 3rd SAI on the right with a strength of 21 officers and 585 other ranks under the command of Lt-Col E F Thackeray, with the 4th SAI (SA Scottish) occupying the left of the Brigade frontage under the command of Lt-Col E Christian with 22

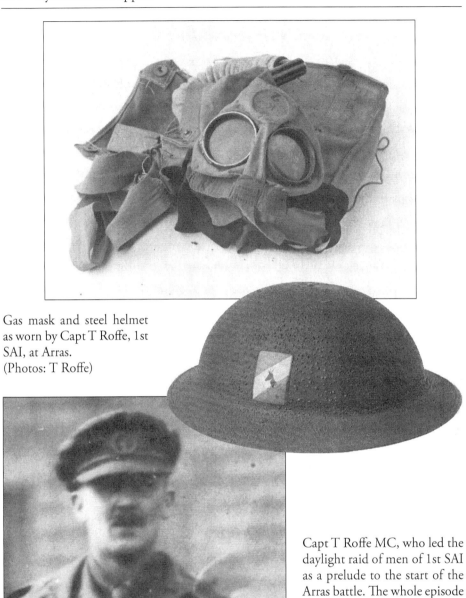

Gas mask and steel helmet
as worn by Capt T Roffe, 1st
SAI, at Arras.
(Photos: T Roffe)

Capt T Roffe MC, who led the
daylight raid of men of 1st SAI
as a prelude to the start of the
Arras battle. The whole episode
was filmed. Roffe wrote his
report in a shell hole with the
wounded man he had rescued,
while a stretcher was procured.
(Photo: T Roffe)

officers and 587 other ranks.

Punctually at 5.30 a.m. the British artillery barrage opened up fifty yards in front of the German front line and the advance began. Every now and then a shot would drop among the advancing line of South Africans and throw a man high into the sky!

Pte Leslie Moses, 4th SAI, in a letter he wrote to St John's College dated 9 August 1917, described those anxious moments from 5.24 a.m. on the morning of 9 April 1917.

The guns which had been firing intermittently all night now ceased. In that one moment of silence, how many minds were searched by the one question: 'How will I carry myself today?'
It is terrible to be afraid that you might be afraid....
5.25 – Nearly loosened my grip on the ladder as the signal mine went up and pandemonium was freed.
Though we had been told much of and had experienced a fair amount of the barrage during practices, we were appalled by the intensity and suddenness of the onslaught... The roll of a thousand kettle drums in a tin shanty, the roar of a stamp battery, the noise of the angry sea beating on the reefs in a storm – all had their counterparts in it, and yet the intensity of sound needs something else to describe it.
The noise of the discharge of thousands of guns, it seemed in one's ears, was supplemented by the lazy whine of the 'lousy lizzies' 12-inch shells, the drone of the 8-inch howitzers, the roar of the 6-inch 60-pounders, our best gun, and the shrill scream of the 18-pounders like the safety-valve of a locomotive letting off steam in a confined space. These 18-pounder shells were not more than three feet above our heads, and yet I never saw a person duck on that account, such was our confidence in the artillery. We were told the gunners would put them three feet above our heads, and that is where we expected them, not at 2ft 9in or 3ft 3in.
The barrage was like a big brother to us, metaphorically taking us by the hand. Defeat was not thought of.
The space which a moment before was like a desert now presented an amazing spectacle. Out of the very earth itself rose thousands of men, and in a moment the space between our front line and wire was a seething, struggling mass of humanity...The whole scene savoured of unreality. Like a wall, between us and Fritz the high explosive, shrapnel, and flame, and smoke shells, threw up their masses of smoke, flame, splinters and dirt...
(While moving) slowly and irresistibly forward.

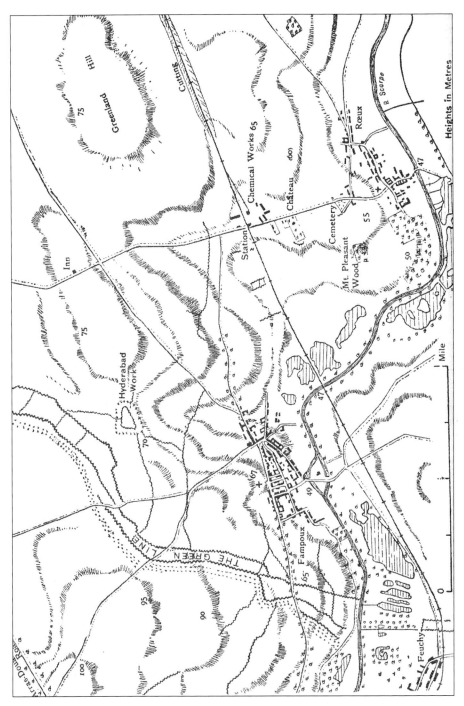

SOUTH AFRICAN BRIGADE AT BATTLE OF ARRAS. FINAL STAGE OF ADVANCE.
(Union of South Africa and the Great War 1914-1918, Official History, 1924)

I turned and helped my section up the ladder...(At) his front line we were supposed to wait four minutes, but alas! we were too keen, and after about three minutes advanced – into our barrage. – Thud!! the earth reeled and my knees shook – a pause and then a flash as the drums of my ears seem to be pierced by a thunderous noise. I wondered why two men close by fell bleeding to the ground, and then as I looked down saw my left foot on the edge of a crater still exuding gases and smoke. Then began a hail of mud and muck, which but for my tin hat must have laid me out completely. From all around the crater men rose, dusted themselves, felt themselves, and carried on, but some twenty yards away two or three men fell never to rise. Such eccentricities of the high explosive make it all the more frightful.

Not once, nor twice, but many a time did I have such escapes, and no wonder with a gun firing to every yard of the front.

After years, it seemed, of waiting, the barrage lifted, and we moved on slowly until we reached his front line. It was a lifeless ditch... The deepest part was about three feet. I was quite fed up at such a bloodless capture of his line, but it served to give one confidence in the barrage.

It started drizzling... The going here was awful, and the ground was churned up to such an extent that my feet went up to the ankles, and to keep up with the barrage, even though it only went fifty yards a minute, was quite an effort. Ever so slowly we neared the first objective – a sunken road. We were on him before he could get out of his dugouts, whence he had fled to get out of the barrage. A smoke bomb down one entrance, a couple of Mills shrapnel bombs down the other, and if there were any survivors they soon rushed up and were captured... Down I crouched. Fritz looked round the door of a dugout, and before he could fire I was up to him. 'Kamerade!' should I??? I am too tender-hearted to be a good soldier... I let him buzz off to our lines. Time, 6 a.m.[1]

Cpl George Warwick described the further progress of the advance of the 4th SAI on the left, which unlike Pte Moses's company on the right, failed to find their first objective.

...At last from high ground, looking across a small gently sloping valley, we saw a railway embankment which disappeared into the hill opposite. There, we concluded, must be the Railway Cutting, our Second Objective – the 'Blue Line', so we halted for the forty minutes during which the

1   *St John's College and the War* October 1918 p19.

barrage was to lift and subject the back areas of the German trench system to a terrific bombardment…(At last) the creeping, bouncing barrage took up its flaming position to lead us on to our second objective. But alas, we had advanced too far beyond our first objective, because we could not find the sunken road, and now we found ourselves between our own barrage and the enemy. We flattened down in an old shallow German trench as our barrage overtook us. Most of the casualties we suffered that day were through running into our own barrage. Among those wounded was Captain Reid. I offered a prayer that God would see me safely through the battle.[1]

The strong German position on the railway embankment now seemed likely to bring the South African advance to a halt and turn the initial success into a costly failure.

It was 2/Lt Hugh Boustead, 4th SAI, who saved the situation. From this dominating position German machine-gunners kept up a steady fire in spite of the barrage. Practically all the officers had been killed or wounded. Boustead had seen Captain Browne fall, shot in the knee. As he passed, Browne said 'I'm afraid I can't get on'.

Boustead passed other officers either dying or wounded. Now Boustead's insistence for his snipers and himself to be involved paid off. His commanding officer, Lt-Col Christian, had wanted him to remain at his HQ during the action. Boustead wrote:

It was clear, that the left hand company must push on quickly if we were to make the objective and take full advantage of the barrage. I moved the snipers round to where some form of covered approach gave us a chance to get forward on to the left of the enemy machine-guns.

The German gunners (in their concrete machine-gun nests) were so engaged that only their officer noticed us. I suddenly saw by my side an officer of the Royal Scots with his pistol raised but the German officer got him first, and I in turn got the German officer with my pistol at some thirty yards. In the meantime the snipers with me had got two of (Captain) Browne's Lewis gunners forward where we were able to enfilade the vital German machine-guns that were holding up the attack of the SA Brigade. Presently the whole line came forward and the Blue Line, and the great railway cutting was ours with God knows how many prisoners.[2]

1   Warwick, p113-115.
2   Boustead, p40-42.

These Germans had fallen an easy prey to the 3rd and 4th SAI. When the South Africans moved into position on the railway embankment after Boustead had eliminated the machine-gun threat, they looked down on an array of entrances to many dugouts and soldiers still sheltering from the British creeping barrage. The Germans were quite unaware of the changed circumstances above them.

For his initiative and courageous action in taking command at a critical time when all the officers of Captain Browne's company were casualties, Boustead was awarded the Military Cross.

The Germans were cleared from the area. Now the 3rd and 4th SAI could survey their prize. One side of the cutting was tunnelled and lined with dugouts lit by electric light, much to their astonishment. For the Germans, surprise had been complete, because the lights continued to burn for forty minutes after the cutting had been taken. The 2nd and 1st SAI now swept through the 3rd and 4th SAI to capture the third objective, the Brown Line.

Back at SA Brigade Headquarters, Brig-Gen Dawson was in a state of suspense and agitation. His diary reflects this in the entries for 9 April. He began writing these at 6 a.m., yet it was two hours after the first objective, the Black Line, had been taken that he received concrete information. Only then could he jubilantly record:

> 8 a.m. First objective captured with very few casualties at just before 6 a.m. We were due to start for the second at 7.30 and are probably well on the way by now – a lot of prisoners have come past.[1]

The 'few casualties' was true of the 4th SAI but the 3rd SAI had not been so fortunate in its advance. Heavy machine-gun fire from the railway cutting had caught their right flank and among the officer complement alone 2/Lt M Burrow had been killed and T/Lts G Elliott, A G Money and 2/Lts S E G Gray, R K Hyde, F C Lee and T V van Ryneveld were among the wounded.

An hour and a half later Dawson received further information and he noted a flood of details just to hand.

> 9.35 a.m. The whole of this Division has now got its second objective. A lot of prisoners are coming down. A wounded officer of the 2nd Regiment says there are a lot of German dead. In one dugout they got eleven officers. Our casualties are still light. We still have the 1st and 2nd Regiments untouched to tackle the 3rd objective. The men are absolutely on their toes and the wounded do not want to leave the fighting line. Have just got a message from Christian saying he has captured guns, MGs [machine-guns] and many

---

1   GSWA Series Box 125 SADF Documentation Centre.

prisoners. One bunch of 150 prisoners has just been brought back by three men of the 1st Regiment. The men say they are having a regular picnic. There have been several cases of Germans coming out of their dugouts after our men had passed and firing at our men from behind. In one case they brought out a MG and shot a good many pioneers who were digging a trench. In each case our men have killed the lot. A [German] Regimental Commander, i.e., full Colonel commanding three battalions, is in my dugout now with

At zero hour, 'out of the very earth rose thousands of men' – the battle of Arras, Easter Monday, 9 April 1917. (Photo: Cloete-Smith Collection)

his staff and has just had a cup of tea. He has been weeping but I cannot say that I felt much sympathy for him. The German Commander had an Iron Cross. I am just going to have a walk up to the front line.

12 Noon. Just back, it is very interesting up in front. The Germans are firing about one shell to every one hundred of ours. I only went a few hundred yards beyond the old German front line. There are very few of our dead about. The 1st and 2nd Regiments will have started now,[1] [for the third objective – the Brown Line.]

1   GSWA Series Box 125 SADF Documentation Centre.

The SA Brigade had pushed forward somewhat ahead of the 26th Brigade that was advancing to the right of the South Africans. The 3rd and 4th SAI had now reached their final objective on schedule as has been described. The Blue Line was occupied and consolidated. Approximately 200 prisoners were taken.

The taking of the Brown Line had been allotted to the 1st SAI, on the right under the command of Lt-Col F H Heal, with a strength of 20 officers and 488 other ranks. The 3rd SAI was in support. On the left was the 2nd SAI, 20 officers and 480 other ranks strong, with Lt-Col W E C Tanner in command and the 4th SAI in support. Punctually at 12.45 p.m. the two regiments moved forward behind the shielding artillery barrage.

Brig-Gen Dawson described the attack on the Brown Line in a letter he penned the day after.

> I had not time to finish my letter yesterday as Brigade HQ had to move forward....When the Germans saw them coming they got out of their trenches, threw away their arms and equipment and bolted like rabbits. We only took forty or fifty prisoners, but after we had got these a number of them came back – half a mile or so – and gave themselves up.
>
> The position was an exceedingly strong one and when the infantry arrived at the wire, they found it uncut by our artillery and so thick that they could not cut it. They had to stop and look about for the passages which the Germans used and eventually found two, one for each regiment. If the position had been held those two regiments [1st and 2nd SAI] would have been wiped out. Then some other troops [4th Division] passed through [the 9th Division] and took the next and first properly prepared line of trenches – also without opposition. Our men saw the Germans streaking away with several batteries galloping away for all they were worth. The cavalry then came through with what result we do not know. I do not know how many prisoners this Brigade took but we got one gun, ten or more MGs and several Trench Mortars. This Division took sixty officers and 2 000 men prisoners, which is more than were taken by any other Division and also we got further. We got through about two miles and the other troops did nearly a mile. Our casualties were very light for this war, less than the number of prisoners we took... Everyone is full of buck. The Germans appear to be absolutely demoralised. Among our prisoners were Bavarians, Prussians, Pomeranians and Wurtembergers. One regimental commander taken by one of our Brigades refused to go back without an officer escort. He was promptly shot.[1]

1   GSWA Series Box 125 SADF Documentation Centre.

In fact the 9th Division took the strength of a brigade in prisoners.

Now that the 4th Division had passed through the Brown Line and taken the fourth objective, the Green Line, the SA Brigade withdrew to the Blue and Black Lines. The next day, 10 April, was spent cleaning rifles and equipment and replenishing ammunition. The Brigade could also count the cost of the previous day's success. Casualties were as follows:

1st SAI – 15 other ranks killed; four officers and 63 other ranks wounded; two missing.

2nd SAI – two officers and 18 other ranks killed; five officers and 64 other ranks wounded.

3rd SAI – two officers and 40 other ranks killed; 10 officers and 215 other ranks wounded and 12 missing.

4th SAI – two officers and 55 other ranks killed; nine officers and 176 other ranks wounded with 1 missing.

In spite of these casualties, the officers and men of the SA Brigade had been in the highest of spirits and confidence. The Germans had been surprised and demoralised, firstly by the rapid advance on the fringe of the creeping barrage and secondly by the steady progress forward.

For the achievement of 9 April the 9th (Scottish) Division was awarded the DCM: every man of the Division was entitled to wear a circular black patch with white metal thistle in the centre, just below the shoulder on each sleeve.

On Wednesday, 11 April snow fell. The troops had no blankets with them, only their greatcoats. It was bitterly cold but what did it matter? Relief was expected. However, their expectations were shattered. The 4th Division had been held up so the 9th Division was to be moved forward and flung back into the battle. A change of plan to meet the new circumstances was not only the whim but the prerogative of General Headquarters.

Chapter 19

The Fampoux fiasco

Early on 11 April the SA Brigade had the intentions of General Headquarters revealed to them. They were to relieve 10th Brigade on Brown Line and were attached to the 4th Division to participate in the attack that was scheduled for noon.

The 1st SAI and 2nd SAI now moved forward to behind a ridge 500 yards to the rear of the Green Line in support to the 4th Division. At nightfall the 1st, 2nd and 4th SAI positioned themselves in a line north-west of Fampoux called the Effie Trench. The 3rd SAI was in reserve.

On the first day of Arras all the German positions had been breached on a two and half mile front with no defensive works of any consequence short of the Drocourt-Quéant line, but the rain and snow gave the Germans time to prepare while the British brought up their artillery across the marshy ground. The infantry had to wait for the arrival of the guns. As an interim measure captured German guns were actually utilised by the British! Nevertheless the vital advantage of 9 April had been lost. The Germans had brought up two fresh divisions, artillery and a special machine-gun section.

The Germans now occupied a line running north to south from the Inn near the Hyderabad Redoubt along the Gavrelle road past a railway station and then through the Roeux chemical works. The 9th Division was ordered to attack and capture this line. The SA Brigade and 27th Brigade were detailed to capture the road from the Inn to the station.

At 4.30 p.m. two companies of the 4th SAI and two companies of 2nd SAI went marching past to the main road through Fampoux. This village, west of the objective, consisted of approximately 200 houses with a few shops. It was virtually undamaged because of the rapidity of the British advance. A few shallow trenches had been hastily dug half a mile south-east of the village facing the railway embankment some twenty feet high and five hundred yards long.

It was late afternoon. All was still. The four companies, numbering about 800, were now concentrated in the main street of Fampoux.

One platoon had passed through the village to enter a shallow trench. At that point a Very light was fired from a house. Cpl Arthur Betteridge, 4th SAI, described how

> instantly the most incredible barrage of shells fell on the men massed in the main road. Within minutes, half of them were casualties. We eventually found that only hours before we arrived, eight German light gun batteries had dug themselves in just behind the embankment which was an excellent observation point for them. I must truthfully say this brief bombardment was worse than any in Delville Wood while it lasted. In the midst of it, Major Clerk of 'D' Company calmly directed our chaps to take cover in doorways, up alleys and anywhere out of the main road. But the damage had been done in the first few minutes when we had more casualties than during the previous two days advance. It was shocking that practically a whole regiment of men had been allowed to fill a main road in full formation within clear sight of the enemy observation posts on the embankment.[1]

The shells bursting on the stone 'pave' of the road and the splintering stone had been responsible for many of the casualties.

Cpl Victor Bowes, 2nd SAI, recalled that while

> marching up the hard cobbled road I had the extraordinary, almost unique, experience of looking up and seeing a 9.2 shell coming straight at me. There was no time to shout a word of warning. I fell flat on my stomach as the shell burst in the midst of my section. When I found my feet, I looked upon the shocking sight of my comrades' mangled bodies. It was worse than a shambles. One, in a sitting position, and still clutching his equipment was headless. I was the only survivor, without so much as a scratch.[2]

John Buchan, who was on the staff at General Headquarters at the time, attempts to make excuses for this gross carelessness on the part of those directing operations there. He wrote in *The South African Forces in France* that

> there was no chance of an adequate bombardment and there was no time to reconnoitre the ground. The country between Fampoux and Roeux Station was perfectly open, and was commanded in the south by a high railway embankment and three woods, all of them held by the enemy; while

1   Betteridge, p97.
2   The Daily Representative, Tuesday 4 August 1964.

in the north it sloped gradually to the Inn around which the Germans had organised strong-points. It was impossible, therefore, to prevent the movement of troops being observed by the enemy.[1]

In spite of this failure to reconnoitre the position, the SA Brigade was now ordered to deploy from the shelter of the houses on the east side of Fampoux. Shells were still falling. The 300 yards that the Brigade had to cross between Fampoux and the line held by the 4th Division was open ground in full view of dozens of German machine-guns. The 1st SAI was on the left and 2nd SAI on the right. Each was supported by two companies of 4th SAI. To compound what had already gone wrong, before zero hour there had been no artillery preparation.

> At zero hour, about 5 p.m., [wrote Cpl George Warwick, 4th SAI], the order was given: "'A' and 'C' Company, ready!" This was followed by the signal for 'A' and 'C' Company to advance. And away in extended order charged a line of kilties. The German machine-guns rattled, but nothing seemed able to stop these determined men. Then came the order from Major Clerk: 'B' and 'D' Company, ready!' and the signal was given to advance. The Germans had got the range beautifully. A wounded man dropped a bucket with Lewis gun drums and ammunition. I picked it up and carried it forward with me. Something hit me a terrific blow in the stomach.
>
> We jumped into a trench held by men of the Royal Irish Rifles, where 'B' and 'D' Companies were ordered to halt. Meanwhile 'A' and 'C' Companies had disappeared into the blue. Our sausage observation balloons reported that our kilties – the men of 'A' and 'C' Companies – were seen advancing as far as the chemical works at Roeux. Our own Brigade Headquarters said this was impossible for the strong German machine-gun posts must have mowed down our men long before they got anywhere near Roeux.
>
> But three months later, when Roeux was captured, the bodies of men of the South African Scottish were found near the chemical works. These brave men had done the impossible.
>
> So accurate was the German machine-gun fire that all the wounds were waist-high. Major Clerk was wounded in the hand. His other hand had been put out of action years ago by a Zulu assegai during the Zulu Rebellion. Now that both his hands were out of action, he passed it off with a joke.
>
> Once in the trench I was able to examine myself to see what had caused the terrific blow I had received while advancing in the open I found that a bullet had struck and pierced the satchel of my PH gas helmet, gone

1 Buchan p124.

The village of Fampoux. (Photo: SA National Museum of Military History)

> through my leather jerkin, my tunic and the top fold of my kilt and out on
> the right 'Hard lines' said I. 'It might have been a blighty!'[1]

The disaster was complete. Taken as a whole, casualties were heavy. The 1st SAI
on the left had suffered least with two officers and 163 other ranks wounded and
19 missing with 21 other ranks killed. The 2nd SAI, living up to its reputation
as the 'suicide regiment' had one officer and 29 other ranks killed, two officers
and 49 other ranks missing, 13 officers and 207 other ranks wounded, after going
into action 400 strong. The 3rd SAI, in reserve, had sustained one officer and
two other ranks killed and five wounded. The 4th SAI had two officers and 22
other ranks killed, four officers and 172 other ranks wounded with six missing.
In general, except for the few men of the 4th SAI, the advance had not reached
more than 150 to 200 yards from the starting point on the outskirts of Fampoux.

The artillery, such as it was, had missed its target and dropped its barrage
of shells 500 yards east of the 4th Division's line on the reverse side of the railway
embankment and beyond the first enemy line of defence. This had left the
German machine-guns intact to mow down the South Africans as they attempted
to cross the 800 yards of open ground before they could come up to where the
barrage was falling.

1   Warwick, p118.

At 8.15 p.m. on the 12 April, the remnants of the SA Brigade were withdrawn to the Green Line. Brig-Gen Dawson, the Brigade Commander, in a letter dated 13 April wrote:

> It is a very different story I have to tell today. After the men had been without sleep for four nights – for three of which they had been lying in the snow without blankets and many without greatcoats – we were yesterday given a job which everyone recognised as impossible without a heavy bombardment. There was no bombardment worthy of the name and the result was what we expected. We are not strong enough for another fight... I went down to see the Regiments this morning; they have been badly shaken up and are completely exhausted, but were very cheery and did not appear demoralised... very few officers got through.[1]

On 13 May 1917 the Third Army Commander, General Sir E H Allenby, had inspected the remainder of the Brigade and congratulated them. Brig-Gen Dawson wrote of the visit in a letter dated the same day.

> We were inspected by the Army Commander this morning and he could not possibly have been nicer. He complimented me on the turn out, which was incidentally much worse than usual and told [the men] that they had done what had never before been done in this or any other war – namely that they had fought their way through three fortified systems of German trenches [at Arras]. He also told them that they had behaved exceedingly well in the second attack [at Fampoux] and that no troops could have done better. I appreciated that rather more than anything else he said – especially as he seldom bestows praise and the majority of his remarks are the reverse of complimentary.[2]

Allenby's success at Arras had been marred by the fiasco at Fampoux, after his delay in pressing home his initial success.

Allenby believed this was the reason why he had been recalled to England early in June and given the command of the Egyptian Expeditionary Force, which he regarded as an unimportant appointment. Nevertheless, at the time of Arras, relations between Haig and Allenby were not cordial.

Whatever the reason – whether it was Fampoux or Allenby's disagreements with Field Marshal Haig, the following extract from a letter home on 22 August

---

1   GSWA Series Box 125 SADF Documentation Centre.
2   loc cit.

View from the railway line embankment of the ruins of the Roeux Chemical Works. (Photo: Cape Archives)

After the battle, men of the 1st SAA Infantry Brigade relax, at Blangy near Arras on 3 May 1917. (Photo: SA National Museum of Military History)

1917, written by Cpl A W Cloete-Smith, 2nd SAI, is worth recording.

> General Allenby was in charge of our Army Corps but he got the sack
> for messing up the Fampoux business. The Colonel [W E C Tanner] took
> us into action under protest and when the remains of the regiment came
> out he turned to General Lukin (the 9th Division Commander) and said:
> 'Look at my regiment, Lukin, what did I tell Allenby.' One of the runners
> who was close by heard him say this. This is the second time we have been
> let down by our generals. Old Furse was deprived of his command for
> making a mess of things at Warlencourt.

I want to go home,
I want to go home–
I don't want to go to the trenches no more,
Where Jack Johnsons tumble and whizzbangs galore.
Carry me over the sea...
Where the Alimans can't snipe at me!...
Oh, my! I'm too young to die–
I just want to go home!

For the achievements of the 9th Division at Arras every man was granted the privilege of
wearing a circular black patch with white metal thistle in the centre, on the upper arm
of his tunic.

Chapter 20

The 'three-bob-a-day' men

After the action at Fampoux the SA Brigade was a shadow of its former self. As a brigade it was no longer an effective force, so in order to utilise the remnants, all four units supplied companies to form composite battalions to act as Divisional Reserve troops until 6 June.

If the SA Brigade was to preserve its identity in the light of the casualties suffered on the Western Front, reinforcements would have to come forward in far larger numbers. In spite of the 1 448 men of all ranks who had been sent from the SA Brigade Depot at Woking between the end of April and the end of June to repair the damage done to the Brigade at Arras and Fampoux as well as the usual wastage from sickness, disease and active service conditions, the SA Brigade was still under strength. On 30 June 1917, the situation was as follows:

1st SAI – 38 Officers and 680 other ranks.
2nd SAI – 37 Officers and 601 other ranks.
3rd SAI – 35 Officers and 691 other ranks.
4th SAI – 39 Officers and 818 other ranks.

From 10 June to 6 July the SA Brigade was billeted outside Arras at Y Huts and then moved to a new training area near Simencourt and Berneville.

While at Simencourt Cpl A W Cloete-Smith, 2nd SAI, in a letter home dated 13 July 1917 wrote:

> Our billets are in a ripping place at present. The huts are in a large orchard which contains a number of cherry trees simply loaded with fruit. The officers bought these trees for us and we spend a good deal of our time in them eating cherries until we are nearly bursting. Yesterday we were out on field manoeuvres near Wailly. We had some Tanks operating with us and I am afraid we paid more attention to them than we did to the manoeuvres. You would think it simply impossible for them to get over the different obstacles. I do not think there is anything that can stop them except a direct hit from a heavy gun or the mud.

'Behind the British lines lay six miles of sponge...' Hanging up clothes to dry after washing under impossible conditions. (Photo: SA National Museum of Military History)

Serving stew in the frontline trench. (Photo: SA National Museum of Military History)

And then on 25 July

> we are going into the trenches again worse luck...Last night we were out
> on manoeuvres and had a great time instructing the new men in trench
> routine. Some of them have perfectly wonderful ideas about the trenches
> and we stuff them with the most appalling yarns about trench life. We told
> one chap that if he did anything wrong while in the line that he would
> be taken out into No Man's Land and chained to the barbed-wire and
> that Very lights (star-shells) would then be fired at him. I simply collapsed
> with laughter on hearing him relating this yarn to a circle of awe-stricken
> and gaping compatriots. The best of it is that they firrmly believe all these
> stories.[1]

> In the 4th SAI the arrival of new drafts was always a matter of great interest
> from more points of view than one. Major D Hunt was popular. No matter
> when and in the most unlikely places, he would come out with: 'Ha! Ha!
> Get your hair cut!' His way of greeting new drafts was in this fashion:–
> 'How many men, Sergeant-Major?'
> 'Sixty men, Sir!'
> 'Ha! Ha! One shell and you'll all be dead. Ha! Ha! Get your hair cut.'
> A weary draft of the South African Scottish, in full marching order, was
> resting for a moment. A passerby asked for the meaning of the Dutch
> words on the Springbok badge, 'Eendracht maakt macht', and was told
> that it meant, 'Load not to exceed three tons!'[2]

The 1st SAI had a company detached from them during July. Pte (now 2/Lt)
Geoffrey Lawrence, 1st SAI, recorded how the men of the company had returned
dispirited and disturbed from a task that should never have been given to fighting
soldiers.

> The men had returned from burying the many thousands killed in the
> Somme battles in a number of enormous graves behind High Wood and
> Mametz Wood. Some sources estimate the number at 35 000. Our men
> had to deal with the bodies of men in every stage of decomposition, take
> identity discs from every corpse, where possible, also any personal papers
> for recording in each case. This gruesome task went on for three weeks
> and dealt with South African, Allied and German soldiers. With deflated

1 Cloete-Smith, letters.
2 Warwick, p106.

morale, these men, sick at heart and with the reek of death still in their nostrils, were to be called on not many weeks hence to go into one of the sternest of the Third Ypres battles. To go into battle with these memories would be disturbing to even the hardest. It had been bad enough previously to advance into battle over the dead bodies of comrades we had known only days before. But this misuse of fighting troops was cruel and senseless.[1]

Padre Hill[2] had officiated at several of the mass burials, wearing his conspicuous white surplice.

By 3 April, having recovered from his wounds, Hill had returned to France. He wrote to Canon Nash, his colleague and headmaster at St John's College, Johannesburg from 32 Casualty Clearing Station.

> Every three days we receive all the casualties from the front – say 400 and evacuate by third day and receive again. Private communions (or rather carrying It round), preparing men for It, or writing letters for serious cases, and collecting dead and taking funerals fill up a busy day. I can do this job with one arm, and a slightly game foot...I told the DCG (Deputy Chaplain General) you wanted me back if I were not at the fighting front. (This is out of gunshot.) He said: 'Well, stay on a bit, and see if a vacancy in SAI occurs – anyway English troops want your services.' It's great and solemn work – the concentration of the carnage of a bigger than a brigade front. The doctors are awfully kind, and a good servant sees to my tent and me, though there is nothing I can't do in dressing.[3]

As Cloete-Smith had predicted, on 27 July, there was another move. The SA Brigade took over part of the front line at Trescault. This was north of Havrincourt Wood along the Canal du Nord. Cloete-Smith, in a letter to his mother dated 22 August 1917, wrote:

> This is the quietest front I have been on...In our part of the line his trenches are about twelve hundred yards away so we have a nice little stretch of No Man's Land to play about in – at night... We are doing eight days in and eight out, so are having a fairly easy time. At present we are billeted in a place called Metz. It must have been quite a nice little village once, but all that now remains are a few heaps of bricks and stones. I do not think

---

1   *Militaria* Vol 8/2 1978 p55.
2   Chaplain to the Forces.
3   *St John's College and the War* October 1918, p20.

One of the villages devastated by the Germans when they withdrew to straighten their line. Entire orchards were felled to eliminate future crops or to block roads. Large trees were cut down in the vicinity of buildings to destroy them. Otherwise they were blown up. (Photo: Cloete-Smith Collection)

there is a single house standing between here and Bapaume which is about ten miles away. Fritz must have blown up every house as he retreated, (to straighten his line) and here and there he has sent up mines just to make a really nice mess of things....All the wells too have been blown up and as a rule there is only one place in each village where we can get water. Where we are now the water point is about a quarter of a mile away....

We are actually over strength now, a thing which we have not been since the Brigade came over to France. They are nearly all new men however, and it makes one quite sick to think of all the splendid men one knew who have 'gone west'. The new fellows are quite a decent lot on the whole but they are not fit to clean the boots of the old 'bob-a-day' crowd. It is only the three shillings a day that has brought them over.[1] A finer set of men than the original 1st SAI Brigade could not have been found anywhere.

I have not yet seen anything of the Americans but there were some of their medical people at Rouen when I was there. From what I have heard I do not think our troops will get on too well with them. One of them came into a canteen at Rouen where there were a lot of our chaps, Imperials and

---

1   These new arrivals were not popular because the old hands who had volunteered for one shilling a day felt that the increase of pay to three shillings that General Smuts had announced before Arras had been their inducement to volunteer.

Australians. After holding forth for some time about the American Army he said, 'You people have been messing about with this war for three years and now we have got to come over and finish it for you.' This was too much for one of the Australians, and with the remark, 'Well, here goes for the first b.... American casualty,' he picked up a bottle and hit Mr Yank over the head, killing him. He was up for Court Martial about it but got off. I believe the Canadians, too, have had some pretty decent rows with them. They are making a great mistake if they think they are coming over here to teach us how to fight.

Now that the SA Brigade was over strength, swelled for the action that was to come or to put it less euphemistically, fattened for the slaughter, it was relieved so that it could begin the final preparation for what would become known as the Third Battle of Ypres.

All too soon this period ended. While it lasted it seemed to go on forever. Cloete-Smith, on 17 September in his last letter home, before the battle, echoed the feelings of every man of the Brigade. 'We are going into action again very soon so anything may happen to me. I hope to come out safely this trip but still one never knows what will happen...'

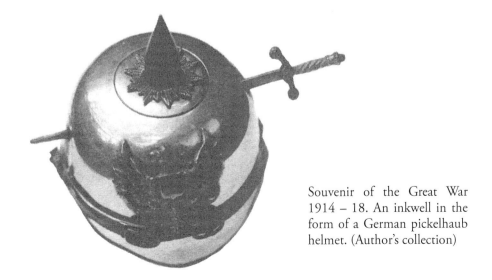

Souvenir of the Great War 1914 – 18. An inkwell in the form of a German pickelhaub helmet. (Author's collection)

Chapter 21

Memories of Menin Road

Once again the weather proved to be Germany's ally. This factor more than German tactics had shattered Field Marshal Haig's expectations. July and August had brought gales and deluges of rain. To add to this, with the Revolution in Russia, large numbers of troops would be released for service on the Western Front. The war on two fronts was over and each week of delay meant the further strengthening of the German forces in France and Flanders.

Before the bad weather had begun, Haig had enjoyed success in taking the Messines-Wytschaete Ridge. The new target was the high ground east of the Ypres Salient which had been contracted, by constant pressure over three years, to a half circle of low hills. With this obstacle out of the way, Haig could move against the German bases in West Flanders and take the coast line.

Time was of the essence. The low ground west of the ridges occupied by the Germans had been transformed. Constant shelling had blocked or diverted streams and completely disturbed the natural drainage of the area. Any rain would make it a marsh. The use of tanks would be impossible and the misery imposed on the troops and their transport would bring any offensive to a standstill.

Von Armin, the German general commanding their IV Army, a tactician of note, was not unaware of these problems. He could only succeed with prepared defences. John Buchan succinctly outlined Von Armin's appreciation of the problem and his solution.

> In Flanders the nature of the ground did not permit a second Siegfried Line. Deep dugouts and concreted trenches were impossible because of the waterlogged soil, and he was compelled to find new tactics. His solution was the 'pill-box'. These were small concrete forts, sited among the ruins of a farm or in some derelict piece of woodland, often raised only a yard or two above the ground level, and bristling with machine-guns. The low entrance was at the rear, and the 'pill-box' could hold from eight to forty men. It was easy to make, for the wooden or steel framework could be brought up on any dark night and filled with concrete. They were echeloned in

depth with great skill, and, in the wiring, alleys were left so that an unwary advance would be trapped among them and exposed to enfilading fire. Their small size made them a difficult mark for heavy guns, and since they were protected by concrete at least three feet thick, they were impregnable to the ordinary barrage of field artillery.

Von Armin's plan was to hold his first line – which was often a mere string of shell craters – with few men, who would fall back before an assault. He had his guns well behind, so that they should not be captured in the first rush, and would be available for a barrage if his opponents became entangled in the 'pill-box' zone. Finally, he had his reserves in the second line, ready for the counterstroke before the attack could secure its position. It will be seen that these tactics were admirably suited for the exposed and contorted ground of the Salient. Any attack would be allowed to make some advance; but if the German plan worked well, this advance would be short-lived and would be dearly paid for. Instead of the cast-iron front of the Siegfried area, the Flanders line would be highly elastic, but it would spring back into position after pressure with a deadly rebound.[1]

The offensive had begun at the end of July with deceptive success for the British, but rain caused a delay of two weeks while the country dried out. The second stage brought the British advance face to face with the pill-box system of defence. The British Fifth Army's fine brigades were sacrificed in succession as they were thrown fruitlessly against this concrete wall. There was another lull, to wait for the weather to improve and the Salient to dry out.

It was for the fourth stage that the 9th Division, which included the SA Brigade, was brought from the Somme area. On 12 September they had left Achiet-le-Petit and by Saturday 15 September they were at Eyre Camp, near Poperinghe. Here the Brigade received intensive and thorough training, using clay models of the ground, with the involvement of all ranks in the briefing as had been done before the battle of Arras, in case of heavy casualties.

Maj-Gen Lukin, the 9th Division Commander, had made an in-depth study on the pill-box problem with his brigadiers: Brig-Gens Dawson of the SA Brigade and Frank Maxwell of the 27th Brigade. Their brigades were to lead the coming attack – the fourth attempt by the British. There would be no repetition of the three months of fruit-less failures of other divisions. Lukin and his brigadiers had observed what had gone awry previously. Once the attacking wave had passed, the Germans had emerged from dugouts or trench, focused their fire from pill-boxes, isolated the first wave and held up the second. The two brigades were schooled to

1   Buchan, p131-132.

stop at all these strong points and eliminate their occupants, while the second line of the advance would leapfrog through the first line and continue the attack. The irregular and non-continuous line and the likelihood of a delay in front that could hold up the entire advance if this method were followed, had to be accepted. This was the only course of action that offered a reasonable chance of success. Each pill-box or strongpoint in front of the 9th Division was carefully reconnoitred and located. Field gun barrages would use the easier-to-follow high explosive and not shrapnel shells. The barrage would pause on either side of a pill-box so that the advancing troops, following close behind, could move to the unprotected rear of the pill-box and neutralise its garrison.

On the afternoon of 17 September the SA Brigade was transported in open trucks from a railway line near Poperinghe. The 4th SAI received a particularly rousing send-off with their pipe band playing their regimental march 'The Atholl Highlanders' as the regiment steamed away from them at a snail's pace to detrain at Ypres – a battered and ruined shell of a once beautiful city – to occupy deep dugouts along the canal bank west of the town.

The rains of July 1917 had brought the new advance to a standstill. There was a delay while the British waited for the country to dry out.
(Photo: SA National Museum of Military History)

LEFT. General Sixt von Armin, commanding the German IVth Army. (Photo: Cloete-Smith Collection)

RIGHT. Diagram of Von Armin's defensive organisation to make the British advance impossible. *(Times History of the War)*

BELOW. Plan and elevation of a German 'Pill-Box'. Successive heavy concussions of high explosive shells on the concrete structures, especially in the smaller structures, stunned the garrison. They could be taken from the rear but attacking troops had to first get into position! *(Times History of the War)*

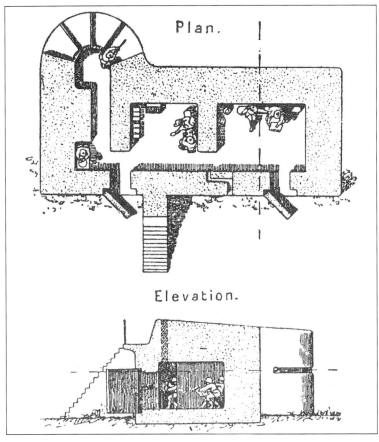

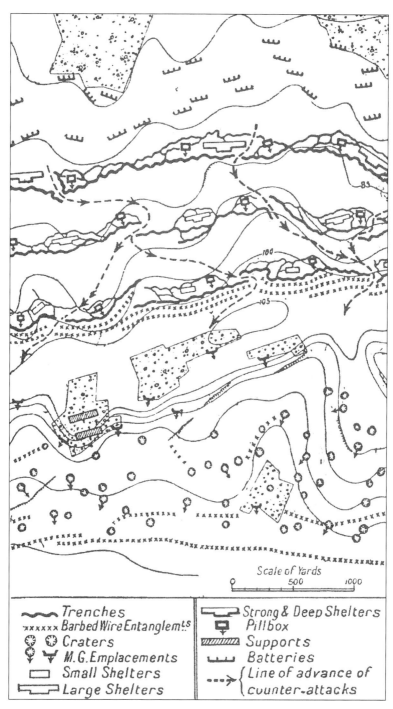

Scale of Yards

	Trenches		Strong & Deep Shelters
xxxxxx	Barbed Wire Entanglem.ts		Pillbox
	Craters		Supports
	M.G.Emplacements		Batteries
	Small Shelters		Line of advance of
	Large Shelters		counter-attacks

DETAILED PLAN OF GERMAN DEFENSIVE ORGANISATION
(The Times History of the War)

241

On the nights of 17 and 18 September the routes that had been selected from the reserve trenches to the assembly area were thoroughly reconnoitred. The attack was to be spearheaded by the 4th SAI on the left and 3rd SAI on the right. Arrangements were made to have available sufficient rolls of wide white tape. These were to clearly mark the assembly position and the route to it, from the duckboard tracks that each platoon would use. In that featureless landscape the tape was essential to keep the advancing troops on course. Notice boards were erected on one or other of the platoon flanks to indicate the exact position each platoon was to occupy. The 3rd and 4th SAI who were to advance, each with three companies in front with one in support, would be given the use of the track until 11 p.m. Brig-Gen Dawson expressed his apprehension about these arrangements. 'The night was very dark and the country was quite unknown to the majority of the officers and men. I could not but feel exceedingly anxious as to the ability of the battalions to get into position.'[1]

The 2nd and 1st SAI, in support of the 3rd and 4th SAI, assembled close behind the two attacking battalions, in order to be clear of the front line trench as soon after zero hour as was possible. In this way they would avoid the German barrage that usually came down on the British front line as soon as the alarm was given that an attack was in progress. This bitter lesson had been learnt through heavy casualties at Butte de Warlencourt.

Major C M Murray, SA Field Ambulance, described the area:

> We had to go under cover of dark and early morning mist as the ground was low lying and marshy and no trenches existed in consequence. It was a curious experience walking up in the dark with no light but the flares from the various signals and the flashes from the guns. I must confess our first glimpses of the ground over which the attack was to take place, seemed in every way to come up to and even surpass the gloomy descriptions we had already had. The ground was of deep rich soil, in which the water level was so high that all the shell holes were filled with water and evil-smelling slime. New ones would remain empty at first, but slowly fill up in the course of a day or two. So long had fighting been going on in this area, that the face of the earth was blasted and upheaved beyond description.[2]

Second Lieutenant Geoffrey Lawrence, 1st SAI, remembered how it began to rain as the 1st SAI moved up into position at 10 p.m. on 19 September, in support to the 3rd SAI. The blackness of the night under a shroud of cloud and the slippery

1   GSWA Series Box 125 SADF Documentation Centre.
2   *Chronicles of the Family* December 1917 p55.

ground, added to the problems of moving forward to the attacking positions that Lawrence had taped out the night before. Except for the occasional crash of a heavy shell, progress through the ghostly town of Ypres, along a slow and devious route with many halts, was unusually easy. There were wide gaps between sections and platoons. The lesson of Fampoux had been heeded. At last the specially-trained guides completed their journey through Ypres and brought them to the start of the duckboards leading to the front line. Shelling was fortunately light. Lawrence recorded the activity leading up to zero hour.

> With the company commander bringing up the rear I led the company along the slippery duckboards to our assembly position. Poor Captain A W H McDonald had slipped into a shell hole on the way up. I showed Captain McDonald where I had arranged for his company headquarters. He was wet and shivering with cold and nerves.
>
> He said 'Lawrence, will you put the company in position for me?' I was only too pleased to take over his job and keep occupied until zero hour. I put each platoon on their starting tapes and gave as best I could their right and left flanks and general bearings. With muddy shell holes and few salient points to be seen in the pitch blackness of the night this was no easy matter. At about 3 a.m. I reported to Captain McDonald that the whole company was in position on their attacking line. I was then asked to supervise the issuing of the rum to each man. So with the sergeant major carrying a jar of rum and I with an empty shaving stick container, we went all along the line and gave each man half a tin of rum, just enough to steady his nerves. We finished this job at 5 o'clock and I returned to company headquarters a few yards behind the centre platoon and said a few words of parting to Captain McDonald. He thanked me profusely and said goodbye. Poor Captain McDonald, he was in a terrible state of nerves and fear which he seemed unable to fight down. He appeared to dread the coming of the dawn and was apparently convinced that he would fall.[1]
>
> I could do nothing to comfort him as one so much younger and junior in rank and having the same fears, I expect, as all of us. What deep thoughts there were in those tense waiting moments of life that were ticking away so fast towards zero hour!
>
> Fortunately the rain stopped at 4 o'clock and the stars peeped out. From now on no more rain fell until we were relieved on the 22 September.[2]

1 Captain McDonald was in fact one of the first to be killed by machine-gun fire a short distance from the start line when the attack began.
2 *Militaria* Vol 8/3 1978 p38-40.

The ghostly town of Ypres through which the 1st SA Infantry Brigade moved at intervals to Menin Road for zero hour. (Photo: Cloete-Smith Collection)

There was no front line in the true sense of the word. Besides being safely ensconced in their pill-boxes, the Germans occupied one series of shell holes while the British another series. If the digging of a trench was begun in the swampy ground it would immediately fill with water. Warwick recorded in his autobiography how he led his section of nine men forward at zero hour, 5 a.m. on 29 September.[1]

> It was not yet daylight. The flashes of bursting shells lit up the ground a little around the explosions. We attacked in file, my nine men following behind me. Section leaders on my right and left were advancing in the same way. I saw a German lying on the ground. He might be alive. I fired at him. The mud and dirt thrown up by a bursting shell clogged up the bolt-mechanism of my rifle. I withdrew the bolt and cleaned it with my handkerchief. As we advanced I saw another German lying down who might be alive and again I fired. The ground was wet and muddy and covered with shell holes, many waterlogged. We appeared to be advancing too fast, so I called my nine men to a halt behind me.
>
> After the sections on my right and left appeared to have caught up, I ordered the men to continue to advance. Private W Pinder, who was immediately behind me, made no move, I cursed him roundly only to discover that he

1   Warwick, p140-148.

and seven others of my section had been killed... It was a gamble whether a machine-gun burst caught the whole of the file or missed all of the file. My section was unfortunate.

Only Pte Thomson was left and he followed me forward. (The earth was damp and I suppose that was why I had not seen any spurts from the German machine-gun bullets.) Our objective was the Steenbeck Stream, but the ground was so thoroughly ploughed up by shell fire that the stream existed no longer as a stream, but was distributed over a large area and in many shell holes. Among the pill-boxes we had to attack was one 'Borry Farm'. The men on our right were to attack another pill-box called 'Vampir'. Thomson and I ran across a hole in the ground, concreted, which appeared to lead by an underground passage into a pill-box some distance away.

I called down into it to the Germans to come out and surrender. No one came. I hurled a smoke bomb into the opening...Again I called... Nothing happened, so this time I drew the pin from a Mills bomb and threw it into the opening... We had not moved forward more than fifteen yards when a

The men of the SA Infantry Brigade filed forward to positions in near pitch darkness, reflected dimly in the water of innumerable shell holes, to be in position. (Photo: Cloete-Smith Collection)

shell burst overhead and a fragment of shrapnel struck me in the spine. I collapsed in a heap, the lower half of my body paralysed from the waistline downwards. Thomson came over and said: 'Where are you hit, Corporal?' 'I think it's the spine,' I said, 'for my legs are paralysed.' Thomson removed my equipment, my tunic and even my kilt. He took my field-dressing and smeared the wound with iodine and attempted to bandage it... Thomson did his best. He left me as comfortable as possible lying on my back in a small depression almost naked. And Thomson moved forward to continue the advance. The mud and dirt thrown up by shells bursting around me came down upon me. I wondered whether the next shell would land right on me and finish me off.

The 2nd SAI swept forward to pass through ground that the South African Scottish had captured, to capture the second objective. One man of the 2nd Regiment must have thought I looked uncomfortable. He propped me up more comfortably, put a cigarette in my mouth, struck a match and lit it and threw down a packet of cigarettes for me to smoke. He waved a cheery farewell and rushed forward to catch up with his comrades.

As Warwick lay there paralysed from his wound, he was most concerned as to the outcome of the German counterattack. Over the last three months it had always been the counterattack, made at this juncture, that had unseated determined attempts of British divisions to take the heights of St Julien. Intensified shelling with rifle and machine-gun fire now indicated that this crucial stage was in progress. With great difficulty Warwick managed to lift himself slightly. To his infinite satisfaction he saw the counter-attack repulsed.

For Warwick the war was over. Although he recovered from his wound he suffered from its legacy for the rest of his life. He bore his discomfort with fortitude and through part-time study became a Presbyterian minister in Durban.

In the mud and flooded shell holes of Third Ypres the wounded such as Warwick were the lot of stretcher-bearers, supplemented by German prisoners. No 10584 Pte Y E Slaney of Warwick's company vividly recalled how he was dragooned into this most unpopular of tasks. His account also shows how different were the experiences of men even of the same company.

First there was the journey forward:

Our guide was instructed to proceed... We daren't move off the duck board, as close by was mud, in places like quicksand. We stumbled along... I witnessed a Lewis Gun member who had slipped off the duckboard, sinking, and saved by his companions, who threw off ammunition magazines and pulled him out of the mud... On the night prior to the attack instructions were received that we should go in single file... The Pioneers had already taped the course, dug a ditch...and left an indication at the ditch for us to realise we were to occupy that spot until the attack started...In the ditch we had to sit back to back as the depth was about two feet and the width sufficient to take our bodies in that position. The main difficulty was the flow of water which used the ditch as a drain. We sat in running water. It is amusing to relate that our Regiment wore kilts, without underpants. We slept and woke up as the barrage started. The artillery centralised on a certain portion of Jerry's line, and at a stipulated time they increased their range. When this happened the officers rose and shouted indicating we were to advance... We, the stretcher bearers, held up slightly, and attended to wounded. The job got so heavy we had to find a station to bring the wounded so far, attend to them, and send them on their way if they could walk. Stretcher cases took time.

We had found a small pill-box which had been evacuated by Jerry, which gave us good protection from Jerry's counter-shelling – Jerry's artillery was excellent – I was attending to a wounded man when a runner practically fell into our station. I thought he had been shot. When he recovered slightly he said in a shaky voice 'I've seen a ghost!'... I eventually said 'Where?' He

SA Scottish stretcher-bearers at the Battle of Menin Road.
(Photo: Cloete-Smith Collection)

indicated which way we had to go... We crept around the corner of our pill-box and my guide indicated a passage to enter the box and promptly left me. I poked my nose into the passage and nearly ran myself. The ghost was standing there. When I was able to speak, I very shakily, questioned him. It appears he was a member of the Royal Irish Fusiliers – I trust my memory is correct – who attacked in that area during August 1917, slightly more than a month prior to our attack. Something went wrong with the advance and they were driven back. He got lost in the action and was left between the lines. My question 'What did you eat?' His reply, which was very faint, was 'Dead men's rations and drank shell hole water!' I could understand the rations as we all carried emergency rations which were to last us three days, but shell hole water I could not appreciate. We wouldn't even use it to wash in. It is very difficult to describe what that water looked like. Due to the constant shelling and our inability to properly bury the dead, the remains of some of their bodies was naturally mixed with the mud and water. Our chap in charge, L/Corp Adelard instructed me to accompany the man to the post where our doctor was in charge. It was a very slow trip as the patient was very weak...Jerry was very active, particularly with his artillery... I delivered the case to the doctor and returned to our base.

The trip from Borry Farm to the doctor's depot, was the only route we could take and we knew every angle of it. At one spot the stump of a tree stood... On another spot reclined a body with his finger pointing at me when I came within range. He was a member of our 2nd Regiment as I found out when I searched him. At first I thought that he was still alive. My examination did not reveal any wounds. The blast of a shell must have killed him. I dreaded walking along that patch, but had to do it many times. Somebody eventually rolled him over. Further on was one of the early tanks, with the dead crew still inside. Jerry's artillery used that tank as a sighter – with it they had perfect range. During that action there was a constant drizzle of rain. Everything was damp. Two days after the attack I was resting in the doctor's section of a pill-box when a message was received that a seriously wounded man had to be brought in from somewhere close to 'C' Company... I took my stretcher – I had to first locate the wounded man, a sergeant, who had been hit in the stomach. I now had to obtain carriers to assist me... I eventually obtained three volunteers. We loaded the wounded man on to the stretcher. We could only carry him by hand. It was impossible to use our shoulders. I don't know how long that trip took us and we had to use a U-turn to cover the area where a stream originally ran. I was amazed and grateful to see a man

Pte Y E Slaney 4th SAI in recent years laying a wreath on Remembrance Sunday. In 1947 he was presented to the Royal Family in Durban. The legacy of his wound is clearly visible on the left side of his head. (Photo: Y E Slaney)

directing us as to how we could avoid the softer patches. This was done under fire. I don't suppose that that man's bravery was recognised. On passing I saw that he was a parson... Don't imagine that we just went on walking. We had to break regularly, change position, listen to our histories as voiced by the sergeant and carry on. It's hard to believe, but after that action my hands and shoulders were blistered.

The way I have portrayed some of my experiences during that action any one would imagine that it all happened in a day. My adventures lasted six days continually active. I saw many things: some I was unable to forget. For instance we wore the kilt. If a man was killed in the attack, he fell forward and his kilt carried on and left his backside bare. This happened in other attacks.

News circulated that we were to be relieved. I was more than ready and we eventually wended our way back to the outskirts of Ypres. There we were met by some reserves who had prepared a meal for us. A roll call was held. I do not know how many we lost, but I was given a treble helping of bacon and bread. The cooks had cooked too much. Then the officer who had brought up the reserves and in the company of L/Corp Thompson inspected us – in those days I did not drink – but Snowy Thompson insisted that I should have my share. The officer agreed, and I was told to swallow more than a double tot of rum. Much to the amusement of the Company it affected both my head and legs, but they treated me very well. I was then an Old Soldier at the age of seventeen years and one month.[1]

---

1   Pte Y E Slaney specially prepared these reminiscences which were typed by his daughter after an interview in May 1990.

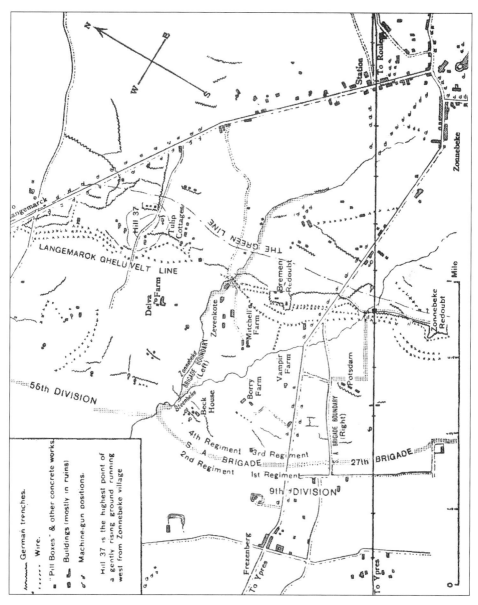

The South African's Attack at the Third Battle of Ypres.
(*Union of South Africa and the Great War 1914-18*, Official History, 1924.)

251

Chapter
22

Those who dare win

As a stretcher-bearer, Private Slaney would have had little time or opportunity to ascertain the progress of the battle. Individuals could not hope to grasp the full picture of what was taking place.

The 4th SAI had begun the action on 20 September with a strength of 21 officers and 511 other ranks. The three-company left front of the attack comprised of Capt T Farrell with 'A' on the left; Capt J McCubbin with 'B' in the centre and 'C' under Major C M Browne on the right. In support was Capt A Gemmell with 'D'. The 4th SAI had reached its first objective – Beck House and Borry Farm by 6.30 a.m. without difficulty. As Mitchell Farm was to their immediate front a number of men braved the British high explosive barrage and moved through it. Not only did they capture Mitchell Farm, but killed a large number of the Germans who garrisoned it.

A particularly troublesome enemy post across the north bank of the Zonnebeke Stream was captured by 2/Lt M Saphir and his platoon. Twenty Germans were killed, a similar number taken prisoner and a machine-gun brought back as a trophy.

The right front which was the responsibility of the 3rd SAI, under the command of Lt-Col E F Thackeray CMG, was made up of Capt E V Vivian with 'A' on the right; Capt L F Sprenger with 'B' in the centre and 'C' under Capt P H Ellis on the left. Capt L W Tomlinson with 'D' was in support. Their strength was 20 officers and 656 other ranks.[1] The 3rd SAI had met with equal success. They had cleared all strongpoints, including Bit Works, various dugouts and works north of Potsdam and south of Borry Farm as well as capturing Vampir, their main objective. Like the 4th SAI they had completely surprised the Germans by advancing hot on the heels of the barrage and in many cases through it, so the enemy could be bombed, shot, bayoneted or captured in their pill-boxes before they knew what was upon them.

So fast had the SA Brigade's advance on the left progressed that the 3rd SAI was now being enfiladed by heavy machine-gun fire from the German-held Potsdam Redoubt on the right. The 27th Brigade, on the South African right,

1   GSWA Series Box 146 SADF Documentation Centre.

Gateway to the battlefield – the Zonnebeke road. (Photo: Cloete-Smith Collection)

had been held up by this substantial defensive work which also embraced three pill-boxes. Noticing this development Lt-Col Heal, OC 1st SA, went forward himself to direct operations. Captain Vivian of 'A' Company, 3rd SAI, was killed while leading the attack on Potsdam. Heal now ordered Captains Sprenger and Tomlinson with men of 'A', 'B' and 'D' Companies 3rd SAI, with some men of the 1st SAI, to form a defensive flank and press home the attack. This was made by rushes from shell hole to shell hole under covering fire from Lewis guns and machine-guns. The attack on Potsdam was resumed at 6.55 a.m. Once again the South Africans pushed through their own barrage, crossed the Zonnebeke Stream, captured the buildings the Germans had been using as a dressing station at the crossroad, bombed other buildings and killed and captured the Potsdam garrison. Some seven machine-guns and thirty-seven prisoners were taken. Captain Sprenger handed over the position to a second lieutenant and party of 12th Bn Royal Scots who had arrived on the scene.

The Germans fled precipitately to the south in the direction of the Ypres-Roulers railway line. Now that Potsdam was taken, the advance halted for an hour before the move on the second objective began. Brig-Gen Dawson had arranged with his opposite number of the 27th Brigade, Brig-Gen Maxwell, that the SA Brigade would extend its area to the right so as to include the northern embankment of the railway. This area had to be cleared and 2/Lt Geoffrey Lawrence, 1st SAI, and half a platoon was ordered to push forward and take the area. Lawrence recorded:

> We all moved off into the dark hell of rattling machine-guns, sparks and whining splinters. I found myself followed by a section of Lewis gunners and
>
> we charged on until we came to a blast of concentrated machine-guns. Several men fell. I took cover in a shell hole and signalled to those behind me to follow.
> I decided to work round the pill-box and so we jumped from shell hole to shell hole to the right. I was the first one up and down again and each time the man behind, who was a bit slower, was hit. However, we kept on and the fire slackened.
> I went on and came to a dugout on the railway embankment. Here twenty

2/Lt Geoffrey G J Lawrence, 1st SAI.
(Photo: J. Lawrence)

Germans put up their hands frantically in surrender, whilst about ten or more others ran up the line in escape. I was firing with my revolver at these whilst at the same time motioning to the others to get back. With the prisoners we took three machine-guns and I had these marked with chalk '1st SAI'.

Our tempers were up with our losses and I had to restrain my men from shooting the enemy as they came out. We had heard of cases where some would surrender in front whilst those behind would take advantage and open fire. I felt sorry for the poor devils and had them sent back.[1]

Lawrence now persuaded a party of 12th Bn Royal Scots to close the gap on the south side of the railway line between the SA Brigade and the 27th Brigade and then he returned to his regiment with his main intention now accomplished.

The advance on the second objective was due to commence at 7 a.m. but ten minutes before that time a group of men from 1st and 3rd SAI led by Sgt H H Frohbus advanced through the British barrage on their immediate front to eliminate a large pill-box structure that would have blocked the advance that was about to begin on the second objective. Lt-Col Heal, OC 1st SAI, joined the group and took over command.

John Buchan in *South African Forces in France* expanded on this incident.

On calling on the inmates of the pill-box to surrender, some thirty or forty came out, but the remainder declined to move. All the loopholes and openings of the structure were closed, but a certain 'Mike' Fennessy of the 3rd Regiment, a Johannesburger whose past career had been largely outside the confines of the law, managed to get a bomb either through a ventilator in the roof or through a window which had been blown open by a grenade. This set fire to the wood lining, and the garrison broke out and were shot down. Four machine-guns were captured in the place. The doings of this Johannesburger are a comment on the value of the scallawag in war. Twice in former battles he had gone over with the first wave, and when their work was done managed to continue with their successors. At Arras he actually finished the day with a wholly different division, which he found had the farthest to go.[2]

It was now the turn of the 1st SAI on the right under Lt-Col Heal with 20 officers and 546 other ranks and the 2nd SAI on the left under the temporary command of Major F E Cochran with 20 officers and 566 other ranks to leap frog through

1   *Militaria* 8/3 1978 p40.
2   Buchan, p140.

the 3rd and 4th SAI while the latter consolidated the first objective which they had just taken.

Second Lieutenant Lawrence, who had had little opportunity for a breather after securing the right flank of the SA Brigade, now took part in the advance on the second objective with the 1st SAI

Pte 'Mike' Fennessy MM, 3rd SAI, after the disbandment of his unit in 1918. Although wearing the uniform of 4th SAI he is still wearing his old collar badges! (Photo: Transvaal Scottish Regimental Museum)

> I went forward again on the right of the embankment which was also the extreme flank of the 27th Brigade. I had a number of my own men and a few of the Royal Scots. Carrying on in this sector working up the embankment and firing with my pistol at the running Germans, but getting down quickly when they replied with machine-gun fire, I crossed over the bank to the 1st Regiment sector and carried on until our objective was reached. This was difficult going on account of very swampy ground that had been churned up by our heavy artillery fire and three times I sank up to my waist and higher and would have stayed there if it had not been for the hand my men gave me. Whilst working up the left bank I was amazed to see a very senior officer of the Royal Scots keeping pace with me on the right side of the embankment. He was wearing a cap with a red staff band instead of the usual tin hat. I heard afterwards that it was Brig-Gen Maxwell VC, the commander of the 27th Brigade. We were sorry to hear later that he had been killed next day by a sniper's bullet.
>
> On reaching our objective the first thing was to dig in and reorganise our men for the inevitable counterattack by the enemy. Here I met 2/Lt D C Mackie and hearing of our company commander's death we set out plans for running the company. We settled on a shell hole for our headquarters and then ran in different directions to see that all was in order. We were

the right flank of the whole SA Brigade and it was important that we should keep touch with the Royal Scots. Actually they failed to reach their objective at this point and there was a hundred yard gap between our right flank and their left. A heavy enemy barrage opened on us and when Mackie got back to our shell hole headquarters it had disappeared with all our kit, the result of a direct hit. Mackie thought I had gone up too and we were both surprised to meet in the middle of what can only be described as a downpour of shells. We both thought the other dead. The shelling was extremely heavy but we were saved to a great extent by the soft ploughed up soil. One shell, a heavy six-inch, fell beside me and jammed the back of the trench up against me; I could feel the trembling of the earth as it went down. Most fortunately it was a dud.

After an hour of this the barrage stopped to some extent and we knew a counterattack was coming. I ran down the line and gave the order for every other man to take out and clean and oil his rifle bolt and when finished man the fire step whilst his half section did the same. All rifles were clogged with the flying dust and mud.

The 1st SAI reached their objective without difficulty but on the left, the 2nd SAI ran into difficulties. Heavy machine-gun fire was directed on them from the high ground of Hill 37 and Tulip Cottage as well as Waterend Farm across the main Zonnebeke stream. These three strong-points had not yet been taken by the 165th Brigade on the left of the 2nd SAI, but the right front of the 2nd moved forward in a northerly direction and took the Bremen Redoubt plus the fortified village of Zevenkote as well as Waterend Farm. Seventy prisoners and one machine-gun was taken. Until the 165th Brigade captured Hill 37 late on the afternoon of 20 September, the 2nd SAI had set up a defensive flank to protect its exposed left.

It was during the advance that L/Cpl W H Hewitt, 2nd

Brig-Gen F A Maxwell VC, CSI, DSO, OC 27th Brigade, killed by a sniper's bullet shortly after his encounter with 2/Lt Lawrence at Zonnebeke.

4th SAI in support trenches, east of Frezenberg Ridge, Battle of Menin Road, 22 September 1917. (Photo: SA National Museum of Military History)

SAI, won his Victoria Cross. Hewitt wrote an account of what happened for his daughter, Jill, in 1952.[1] It was phrased in the humorous style that was typical of the man:

> We have seen a model of our front so we know just where we are and what we've got to do. My section has two pill-boxes to take; the first a small one, but the second, doesn't look so funny. The Jerries came out of the first with their hands up before we can reach it, five of them.
>
> We go a bit farther and then something seems to have happened as nobody is advancing any more; everyone seems to have got into shell holes. The platoon commander's (Lt Walsh) runner says I'm wanted. I duck over and he says, 'That pill-box has got us in enfilade and is holding up the Australians on your left and we can't move this side. Go and take it.' I duck back to my section – only to find disaster. A blasted shell had scored a direct hit.
>
> Well, there's no time to do anything for them so I make for the pill-box which has a sort of doorway low down on the right hand side. I heave a grenade down it and shout, 'Come out you so-and-sos'. They do, two of them and fire with rifles at me at about ten yards range and miss. Then some stinkpot throws a jampot on a stick bomb, which hits me on the chest and explodes. But the mutt who made it forgot to fill it with the odd bolts and

1   Quoted by Uys, I in *For Valour*, pp249-255

nuts, so apart from blowing off my gas mask and half my clothes, knocking out four teeth, breaking my nose, giving me a couple of black eyes, with a lot of little cuts here and there and knocking me backwards into a convenient shell hole, it didn't really do any damage – only made me damn mad.

Well, this is the pay-off. So rather gingerly I got up, picked up my rifle and made a dash for the back of the pill-box which was a real haven of refuge, as the barrage was away ahead and all was peace. I peered round the other side, and there was a jolly loop-hole with a machine-gun firing nineteen to the dozen.

I thought this is where the old bomb comes in. I still had two, so as it looked easy, I lobbed one at the loophole; but it wasn't so easy as it looked and I missed and had to duck back behind the pill-box while it exploded. As I had only one bomb left I decided to make sure, so I crept right underneath, pulled out the pin, let the lever fly up, counted two and pushed it through the loophole. Some stinker shot me through the hand, but not too badly, and I heard the bomb explode and ran round to the door as I thought there would be some fun and games in that direction – there was.

You went down three steps inside that doorway, and as I was running in with rifle and bayonet at the ready a Hun was running out with his hands up. It was my first effort with a bayonet, and though I'd been told hundreds of times, 'If you can't pull your bayonet out, fire a round, that will do the trick', I forgot all about it and with my foot on the poor bloke, I was trying to pull it out when somebody grabbed me by the throat.

I got in a nice kick where I thought it would hurt him most, and presumably I was right, but then honestly I don't remember anything more till I was standing outside, leaning against a Cameron Highlander officer (they were in support of us), looking at three Huns with

L/Cpl (later 2/Lt) W H Hewitt VC, 2nd SAI. (Photo: SADF Documentation Centre)

their hands up and a sergeant coming out of the pill-box saying, 'There's fifteen in there, sir, and they've all had it.'

The officer told me that when he got there he saw a small Hun come running out with his hands up, and me behind him, kicking him up the bottom, but I don't remember a thing about it. I got a bloke to tie my hand up, retrieved my tin hat from the pill-box which was certainly a bit of a shambles as there were bits of Hun all over the place, and started to look for my company.

When I got there I found they had taken our objective (Walsh was wounded and had gone back) and some other officer had taken charge, and as soon as he saw me he started shouting, 'Come on, come and help with these sandbags.' The next thing I remember is being poked by a walking stick, and the second-in-command saying, 'You don't look as though you're much good for anything. You'd better get back to the dressing station.' I thought this sounded sense, so I started off and came across a perfectly fit private escorting forty-eight German POWs to the rear.

Hewitt sent the private up the line, delivered the prisoners and found himself outside his old HQ, a battered German pill-box, where a few days before he and his sergeant had handed in three large earthenware jars of rum for safekeeping. After his experiences of the day he was feeling rather poorly and remembering the rum and its restorative powers wondered if there was any still there. In the doorway of the pill-box stood a Cameron Highlanders captain. There was little by now that could unnerve Hewitt. The captain spoke first:

He said, 'This is not the dressing station, my boy, it's over there', pointing. I said 'I know, sir, but I want some rum.' He said, 'Rum, rum, what do you mean?' I told him about the jars, and while I was talking, a rather elderly colonel came from inside and said: 'What's this chap want?', and the captain said in a rather surprised voice: 'He says he wants some rum, sir.' And the dear old boy said, 'Well, give him some.' So, you know those very large enamel mugs, the sort from which naval ratings drink tea. The captain brought one of those and damn near filled it.

The effect on me, who had only had about half a tin of bully and a couple of biscuits in twenty-four hours was stupendous, and I was torn between going back and taking on the German army single-handed, and a desire for sleep. Eventually I compromised and decided to look for something to eat.

The official citation for Hewitt's Victoria Cross reads as follows in the *London Gazette*, 26 November 1917:

Trench with pill-boxes in the distance, captured by the 9th Division in the Battle of Menin Road, 20 September 1917. (SA National Museum of Military History)

German pill-box after capture. The concrete walls were six feet thick.
(Photo: Cloete-Smith Collection)

No 8162, William Henry Hewitt, L-Corpl., 2nd Battn., South African Light (*sic*) Infantry. For most conspicuous bravery during operations. L-Corpl. Hewitt attacked a 'pill-box' with his section, and tried to rush the doorway. The garrison, however, proved very stubborn, and in the attempt this non-commissioned officer received a severe wound. Nevertheless, he proceeded to the loophole of the 'pill-box' where, in his attempts to put a bomb into it, he was again wounded in the arm. Undeterred, however, he eventually managed to get the bomb inside, which caused the occupants to dislodge and they were successfully and speedily dealt with by the remainder of the section.

There were many acts of bravery during the fighting over those four days. Cpl A W Cloete-Smith, 2nd SAI, whose letters have already provided much information about the SA Brigade at war, wrote at the tail end of a letter dated 28 October 1917 to his mother:

Now for it. I have left till the last what to you will probably be the most exciting bit of news. I have been awarded the 'Military Medal'. It came out in orders this morning. I am supposed to have done good work on the 20th of last month but as a matter of fact it was nothing out of the ordinary. There are men who have done far more and have got nothing for it. I had the luck to be spotted by the skipper with the above result. As soon as I get the medal I will send it to Aunt Margie and when they have seen it I will get them to send it on to you.

The official recommendation for the award, dated 26 September 1917, reads as follows:

For conspicuous bravery during operations east of Ypres on 20th September 1917. This man occupied an advanced Lewis gun post in front of an objective and though twice blown up and partially buried by enemy artillery, reorganised and held his post throughout the period, showing magnificent courage and devotion to duty.

The SA Brigade had now to hold its gains. A German counter-attack between 9.45 and 10.00 a.m. on 20 September was easily crushed by rifle, Lewis gun and artillery fire. Whenever the Germans tried to mass, concentrated fire dispersed them. Cloete-Smith, in a letter home recorded that

our aeroplanes invariably spotted him massing, and gave our artillery the tip with the result that he was blown to pieces. We saw our artillery open out on a wood where Fritz had been assembling all day. It was one of the most awful sights I have ever seen. For about a quarter of an hour you could see nothing but bodies and bits of bodies, equipments, and trees flying up into the air. How many Germans were in the wood I do not know but I am sure that very very few ever got out of it. We had some very decent sniping and it was a part that I really enjoyed. We were firing at a range of seven hundred yards and I think Fritz thought he was fairly safe at that distance from rifle fire as he did not worry about keeping under cover. He soon found, however, that he had men who could shoot straight facing him and after that took more care. I think I managed to bring two or three down but of course cannot be absolutely certain. One game they started with us was carrying machine-guns about under cover of a Red Cross flag. Fortunately we had glasses with us and soon put an end to that performance. After that we fired at anything that moved whether they were carrying Red Cross flags or not.

That night was a restless one for the SA Brigade. The following day was one of inaction, except for shelling. The Germans had been taken unawares by the very accurate British artillery barrage and the skill in which pill-box after pill-box had been captured.

The SA Brigade had gone into action on the night of 19/20 September with 91 officers and 2 485 other ranks. When they were relieved on the night of 21/22 September by the 5th Camerons and 7th Seaforth Highlanders, the casualties were: wounded – 34 officers and 903 other ranks; missing – one officer and 64 other ranks; killed or died of wounds – 16 officers and 237 other ranks. Yet these anonymous figures conceal the fact that behind each statistic was a person. One of these statistics was Pte Ernest Charles Lambourn Batten, 4th SAI – killed in action on 21 September. He had served in East Africa and four days after being discharged at Potchefstroom in October 1916 he embarked for England on the *Balmoral Castle*. Although promoted L/Cpl he requested to revert to the rank of private, joining the 4th SAI in the field in February 1917. Batten was forty years old and had been a professor of music.

To Brig-Gen Dawson, the SA Brigade Commander, his men were more than just statistics. During the battle every man, be he officer or private soldier who came into his headquarters was given a cup of tea complete with tot of rum dutifully dispensed by his staff of one cook and a waiter. By the night of the 21 September when the SA Brigade was relieved in the front line, his Brigade HQ mess had supplied 690 cups of tea with the aid of one teapot and eight teacups!

In spite of the casualties the SA Brigade was euphoric. Major C M Murray, SA Field Ambulance, wrote:

The objectives had been captured all along and everyone, including the wounded, were in high spirits. Men came down badly wounded but quite oblivious to their condition, in the elation of success and success in the face of what looked so impossible.[1]

The 9th Division had taken 3 000 prisoners and the contribution of the SA Brigade had been not inconsiderable.

Let John Buchan, the SA Brigade Official Historian, put in perspective the true nature of this success.

That day's battle cracked the kernel of the German defence in the Salient. It showed only a limited advance, and the total of 3 000 prisoners had been often exceeded in a day's fighting; but every inch of the ground won was vital. Few struggles in the campaign were more desperate or carried out in a more gruesome battlefield. The mass of quagmires, splintered woods, ruined husks of 'pill-boxes', water-filled shell holes, and foul creeks which made up the land on both sides of the Menin Road was a sight which, to the recollection of most men, must seem like a fevered nightmare. It was the classic soil on which, during the First Battle of Ypres, the 1st and 2nd Divisions had stayed the German rush for the Channel. Then it had been a battered but still recognisable and featured countryside; now the elements seemed to have blended with each other to make of it a limbo outside mortal experience and almost beyond human imagining. Only on some of the tortured hills of Verdun could a parallel be found.

Delville Wood was still for the Brigade the most heroic episode in the War. But its advance on 20 September must without doubt be reckoned its most successful achievement up to that date in the campaign. It carried one of the strongest parts of the enemy's position, and assisted the brigades both on its right and left to take two forts which blocked their way. The day was full of gallant individual exploits. The regimental commanders led their men not only with skill, but with the utmost dash and fearlessness. Heal was struck by shrapnel, and once buried by a shell; Thackeray was twice buried; Cochran was knocked down, but rose unhurt, though all thought him killed. 'The regimental officers,' wrote Dawson on the 22nd, 'were an awful sight this morning, haggard and drawn, unwashed and unshaven for four days, covered with mud and utterly tired, but very happy, and exceedingly proud of their men.[2]

1   *Chronicles of the Family*, December 1917 p56.
2   Buchan, p143.

Bronze plaque issued to next of kin of those in the British forces who died in the Great War. Pte E C L Batten 4th SAI, killed in action, 21 September 1917. (Diameter 12 cm) (Author's Collection)

YPRES

The thunder of the drums of death
Is hushed, the autumn air
No longer blights with poisoned breath
The City of Despair

The dolorous road is desolate
No longer swept by shell
That leadeth from Menin Gate
Unto the Ridge of Hell

In No Man's Land the lav'rocks rest
And sing their matin-song
Where once at zero-hour went west
The stripling and the strong

And poppies in the shell-holes blaze
Where England's bravest bled.

Extracted from the poem by Pte H L Shaw 'D' Company SA Scottish dedicated to Lieut Gordon Leighton.

Chapter 23

Marking time

On 24 September the SA Brigade left the Ypres battlefront after two days' rest. It was back to the idyllic, unspoilt countryside round Houlle. All was fresh and green with streams to bathe in. It was unbelievable to be living once again in clean, civilised surroundings, well out of the earshot of even the faintest rumble of the sounds of war. Billets were in tents or in barns filled with clean, fragrant straw. To compensate for the previous weeks, the weather was fine.

Between 10 and 12 October the SA Brigade moved to east of Ypres by motor transport to occupy trenches held by elements of the 26th and 27th Brigades that had been involved in the attack of 12 October which shocking weather had made an impossibility. If conditions had been considered bad during the previous month's fighting they were mild compared to what now faced the soldier on the ground.

The men of the SA Brigade looked over the strange scene of a battlefield 'the day after'. A vast expanse of mud was disfigured with darkshell holes that had become lakes of liquid mud. All was a dreary, pitiless nothingness, except for a few trunks of shattered trees, a pile of broken bricks, or barbed wire lolling drunkenly from stakes here and there. All was silence except for the occasional whine of a long-distance shell or the electric crack of the sniper's rifle. There was no sign of human beings except the bodies lying so motionless in the mud that they seemed part of it, or quivered gently at times as if stirred by the breeze. Many a man must have speculated on the purpose of it all, in this nightmare that was the Passchendaele battlefield.

In moving forward to the front line there were only two approaches, and these were duck board tracks that progressed all the way from the canal bank to beyond St Julien. Lt-Col W D Croft CMG, DSO in *Three Years with the 9th (Scottish) Division* recalled how when his unit was moving forward along this duck board track he encountered, Maj-Gen Lukin:

> We met the divisional commander, who, like all our divisional commanders of the 9th Division, spent most of his time near the front line.

'Lakes of liquid mud' – devastated area near Zonnebeke, October 1917.
(Photo: SA National Museum of Military History)

Drowned in the mud. (Photo: Cloete-Smith Collection)

He was on his way back, and this good old regimental officer insisted on getting off the track and standing up to his knees in mud while the men went by, saying, 'I have a comfortable dugout to go back to,' when we offered to make way for him.[1]

Cpl A W Cloete-Smith, 2nd SAI, writing home on 28 October 1917, thought that the Somme in winter had been the limit but that this place was a thousand times worse.

1   Croft, p159.

If you dig more than two feet down you strike water and in many places you cannot dig even as far as that. Imagine trying to make trenches in a place like that with the rain coming down steadily all the time. We were in water up to our knees all the time so you can imagine what it was like. I think we should all have gone mad if we had stayed there much longer. How it is that we are not all down with pneumonia or something like that I do not know.

The explosion of each shell on that tortured landscape caused sheets of slimy mud to rain down. Machine-guns and rifles were rendered useless by the cloying mud that coated everything. For the previous month's fighting at the Menin Road, the SA Brigade had developed the habit of using waterproof covers or old socks pulled back to the small of the butt and kept there to cover the rifle bolts. The 2nd SAI utilised waterproof covers to go over the Lewis gun with drum in position, thus eliminating stoppages from mud. These covers were soon used throughout the Brigade.

Rain and mud had brought any prospect of a further advance to a complete standstill. Forward progress was limited to a snail's pace. The country ahead was unrecognisable. Landmarks could not be identified or had been obliterated. Trying to operate in such conditions caused total exhaustion without any effort from the Germans. Communications failed. Many artillery pieces were bogged down in the mud. Only light railways kept supplies moving. Major John Ewing MC, 6th King's Own Scottish Borderers also of the 9th Division commented on the fighting over this period.

Possibly heroism on a grander scale has never been shown than in the brutal fighting on the foul quagmires of Flanders. Often neck-deep in mud, the men floundered forward until their over-taxed limbs could no longer support them, and to wrest victory under such appalling conditions was a task beyond the power of man.[1]

During this time the main burden fell on the shoulders of the RAMC as well as the Royal Engineers. The latter had to maintain the duck board tracks that were shelled to splinters as fast as they were repaired. Plank roads had to be constructed as well as shelters and light railway lines. If a man strayed off a prepared way he would be fast in the mud. To evacuate the wounded, three hundred infantry were attached to the RAMC as stretcher-bearers.

Lt Geoffrey Lawrence, 1st SAI, was detached to assist the RAMC in their work with the wounded. Lawrence was comforted during the night when the

1   Ewing, J, *The History of the 9th (Scottish) Division*, p244.

Passchendaele, Third Battle of Ypres, October 1917. The nature of the ground in which troops lived, fought and died. (Aerial Photograph: Cloete-Smith Collection)

officers' marquee was blown down and steady rain fell. He was convinced that the attack would be postponed. Yet at dawn, in a howling wind and drenching rain, each platoon moved forward along the duckboard track.

> It seemed the war machine was geared up and just could not stop... No one dared step off the duckboard track to avoid the shell fire. Many poor fellows further up lost their lives trying to attack and drowning in the muddy shell holes.

Being in support to the front line troops for the time being, my platoon job for the first few days was to carry out the wounded…I had to see to wounded taken to a dressing station run by our South African field ambulance.

On about the third day of fatigue work, as we were passing another dressing station, an officer called to me and asked if I was a South African for he said, 'We have a dying man whom we can hardly understand. Will you come and do what you can for him?' I went in and there was poor Loubser, one of our staunchest company stretcher-bearers with a terrible wound in his left shoulder and going fast from loss of blood and shock. I stayed with him awhile and comforted him, speaking in Afrikaans until he lost consciousness and died a short while later.

The doctor in charge told me that this man told him how he was hit when caught in very heavy shell fire in the front line and had dragged himself to a first aid post where a doctor took one look at his wound, gave him a morphia injection and told him to sit down outside in the shelter of a wall. Loubser knew when no more was done for him what this meant, so he got going again to the next dressing station down the line. Here he got the same treatment of a hopeless case and he finally made his way to where I found him. The doctor said he did not know how it was humanly possible for anyone to do what he did with such a grievous wound… A great strapping Afrikaans-speaking lad from the Western Province, Loubser had been with us from the very start. When he signed on in early 1915 he could barely speak a word of English. He had won his Distinguished Conduct Medal in Delville Wood the previous year (Private A J Loubser DCM). Afterwards he was telling some new drafts who had come to fill the gaps how he had won the coveted decoration. He said, 'Man, you know we were carrying with our stretchers backwards and forwards through that heavy shell fire in Delville Wood, and in the late afternoon we just had to sit down and rest awhile. An officer whom I did not know came up and said "What's your name?" He wrote it down and went off. I said come on, chaps, we're for it and we carried all that night and in the morning another officer also took my name, so off we went again, but the shelling got so awful my mates said, No, it is certain death to go into that wood. So I went in alone and carried men out on my back until I could carry no more! Soon after we were relieved I was told to report to the Colonel and he said I had won the Distinguished Conduct Medal'…

After four days of assisting the RAMC all platoons rejoined their companies to move up and relieve the front line troops.

...The front line [wrote Lawrence] was a series of waterlogged shell holes connected above the water level by shallow trenches. The Germans were fifty to one hundred yards distant in the same indescribably miserable conditions – indeed so miserable that quite a number came over cold and dejected to surrender, several days running. The others stuck it out. We all watched each other with the great caution and any exposure was fatal.

Three or four of us officers formed a company headquarters in the largest shell hole about the centre of our frontal area and made the best of the impossible conditions... The first morning we were basking in the sun having breakfast on bully beef and biscuits and some hot tea sent up from the rear. I was sitting comfortably on a kind of bench watching the steam rising from our sodden clothing, when, glancing down I noticed a red stripe running down the length of my bench. On looking carefully I found I was sitting on a German corpse. He was still fresh so we used him regularly as part of our amenities and furnishings....

On about our second night the early morning ration of hot soup failed to reach us as usual between 1 and 2 a.m. Under those bitter conditions of existence in that sea of mud and waterlogged shell holes, a steaming supply of soup was almost a necessity of life and undoubtedly a great morale booster. Our soup carrier had safely made his way up the duckboards from a sheltered kitchen in the rear, but on reaching the shell hole area had lost his way in the dark and stumbled through a morass of mud into Jerry's line.[1]

It was a blessing that the SA Brigade had not been called upon to go into action, but had been held in reserve.

After ten days of static trench warfare in that churned up morass of Passchendaele, the SA Brigade was withdrawn, having suffered 261 casualties. Most casualties occurred during front line reliefs. Observers in balloons or aeroplanes informed the German artillery when these took place. They then shelled the duckboard track that could not be left because of the bottomless quagmire on either side. Known junctions and assembly points were also regularly open to a barrage of gas and high explosive shells.

Meanwhile the third battle of Ypres dragged on until the 6 November when the last section of the Passchendaele Ridge was in British hands. At last the salient was eliminated. From the salient the British lines had been at the mercy of the German artillery for three years. This was progress, but Field Marshal Haig's grand strategy of penetrating through to the Belgian coast had been cheated once again by the weather.

1   *Militaria* 8/3 1978 p46.

The weather and actual conditions at the front had been largely ignored by the gilded staff in the safety and ease of General Headquarters far to the rear. This is revealed in the remorse of one who was largely responsible for condemning thousands to death in the bloody wasteland of mud.

This highly placed officer[1] from General Headquarters was on his first visit to the battle front – at the end of the four month's battle. Growing

1   Lt-Gen Sir Launcelot Kiggell, Field Marshal Haig's Chief of Staff

The only lines of approach to St. Julien – the duckboard tracks.
(Photo: Cloete-Smith Collection)

increasingly uneasy as the car approached the swamplike edges of the battle area, he eventually burst into tears, crying: 'Good God, did we really send men to fight in that?' To which his companion replied that the ground was far worse ahead. If the exclamation was a credit to his heart it revealed on what a foundation of delusion and inexcusable ignorance his indomitable 'offensive' has been based.[1]

After leaving the front line, rest billets had been the order of the day for the SA Brigade in the Fruges area west of Dunkirk until 1 December, when they began a

1   Liddell Hart – *A History of the World War* p434.

'... he eventually burst into tears crying "Good God, did we really send men to fight in that?"' so exclaimed Lt-Gen Sir Launcelot Kiggell, Haig's Chief of Staff. (Photo: Cloete-Smith Collection)

long march to the south, making for Cambrai where a big battle had taken place the day before. When making such marches the South Africans found themselves well received by the French population because they were known and liked for their orderly discipline. A good supply of army rations was always left behind for the householder or farmer.

Every day's march ended with foot inspection. From the continuous soggy conditions over the past month, the men's feet had become very tender and blistered easily. Each man had to be watched to ensure that his feet were in fact washed and any blisters treated with iodine. Bitter wind and rain was a constant companion during the second and third day. Then snow took over. Because of the scorched earth policy of the Germans when straightening their line, no shelter was to be found. On the fourth day the SA Brigade relieved the 2nd Guards Brigade at Gouzeaucourt, when the 9th Division took over that portion of the line. A battle had just ended. The fortunes of both sides had fluctuated over the past two weeks. Initially the British had made a surprise breakthrough deep into the German defences, capturing tens of thousands of prisoners and hundreds of artillery pieces of different calibre, only to be pushed back by a German counterattack. Because of a lack of reinforcements, most of the gains had been lost. It was to a hastily dug trench line, where the German counterattack had been finally halted, that the South Africans came. The sights here were different. This had been almost open warfare.

Little did the British realise at the time that the tactics employed so spectacularly by the Germans in winning back all the ground they had lost at Cambrai, and which had necessitated the SA Brigade's early return to the front, were part of an experiment that would result in a German breakthrough during their forthcoming March offensive.

The area the SA Brigade took over consisted of a newly dug trench of the most rudimentary nature on the forward slope of Quentin Ridge, extending from Gauche Wood on the right to Flag Ravine on the left. No communication trenches existed so on the right, all approaches to the front line were fully exposed

'I think we should all have gone mad if we had stayed there much longer' – Cpl A W Cloete-Smith 2nd SAI – the only safe way: the corduroy track near Zonnebeke, 15 October 1917. (Photo: SA National Museum of Military History)

during daylight hours. The front line trenches were without firesteps, dugouts or shelters nor had they been revetted, so recently had they been dug. Very little wire existed in front and salvage parties were sent out to collect wire, pickets, timber and other material – the debris of battle – which was fortunately scattered about the area. For a time no supplies were forthcoming from Royal Engineer Stores. Much had to be done to construct a proper front line trench and for a month the SA Brigade laboured morning, noon and night.

However, the first task was the burying of large numbers of British and German dead which were testimony of the ferocity of the struggle around Gouzeaucourt. These lay unburied throughout the entire sector. In one place an Indian lancer was lying dead beside a German infantry-man, the latter still pinned to the ground by the trooper's lance which had impaled him, but not before he had shot his charging adversary at close range. Lt Lawrence remembered seeing a huge Prussian guardsman who had been run over by a tank and rolled flat like a pressed flower in a book. In a corner of Gouzeaucourt lay a heap of dead Guardsmen marking the place where a German machine-gun had put up a stout fight. Broken guns and several derelict tanks which stood in the open offered excellent registering marks for German artillery. These were removed but not before a very considerable number of new Lewis guns had been salvaged from them and from an abandoned ordnance depot at Gouzeaucourt. The units of the SA Brigade were able to make up their deficiencies and replace old guns.

Initially casualties were approximately thirty per day. Throughout December there was heavy shelling. For the 1st SAI, Christmas was marred by the destruction of their Nissen hut well behind the front line where Christmas dinner was about to begin. The cook's efforts to save up rations to make special puddings and provide decorations all came to naught. He lay dead with both legs severed. He was due to go on leave to England the next day. The enemy was no respecter of the festive season.

In January 1918 the temperature plummeted to the lowest ever known. It was too cold to sleep at night. Patrols into No Man's Land wore white hooded snowsuits. To prevent feet from freezing, sandbags were tied around the men's legs and boots. Even so, many toes suffered from frostbite. If gumboots were worn continuously, the humidity caused trenchfeet. Many of the new drafts joining the SA Brigade after Ypres were fresh from the German East Africa Campaign. The harsh conditions of the trenches brought on a recurrence of the malaria they had contracted during that campaign and they had to be hospitalised. Conditions were worse than those experienced at Arras the previous year.

Special pumps were installed to extract the water and slush which was knee deep in the front line trenches and even deeper in the communication trenches,

Mark IV British tank, abandoned on the Gouzeaucourt front.
(Photo taken by Major C M Browne MC, 4th SAI)

as the snow began to thaw. Shaving water as well as soup was brought to the front line in ten gallon thermos containers strapped to a man's back. In January, before the thaw, shaving had to be abandoned for a while as the soap froze on the men's faces before they could begin shaving.

After a brief ten day respite in villages to the rear, the SA Brigade was back in the line by 23 January. At the start of December, when the Brigade moved into the line, it had numbered 148 officers and 3 621 other ranks. During this spell in the front line, particularly December, sickness returns had been the highest ever. That and casualties had whittled away the strength of the Brigade to 79 officers and 1 661 other ranks when all four battalions of the Brigade were withdrawn to a back area for a much-needed month's rest on 31 January 1918. Some were able to go on leave. One Springbok told how an English lady heard that he was from South Africa. Being somewhat confused regarding the various countries of the Empire she said, 'Then you must belong to the Anzacs?' 'No madam' was the answer, 'we are the Voetzacs.' 'Ah! I see,' she replied, 'the infantry section.'

The month of 'rest' was spent preparing for the German offensive which was expected in March. During this period it was decided that all British divisions would be reduced to ten battalions from the previous thirteen battalion strength. Each of the three brigades of a division would lose one battalion. Maj-Gen Lukin, on consultation with Brig-Gen Dawson, decided that the 3rd SAI would be disbanded in terms of this decision. For the past year this regiment had received the least number of recruits. On 8 February, Dawson visited Lt-Col Thackeray and his unit to explain the reasoning behind the decision. The officers and other ranks of the 3rd SAI were transferred to the other three units of the SA Brigade, forming complete companies or platoons.

In order that all ranks could transfer to units for which they had a preference, lists reflecting their particular choice were drawn up. Such a choice could not be guaranteed but as far as possible applications were given the greatest consideration by Brigade HQ. The final transfer was as follows: 3 officers and 86 other ranks to 1st SAI; 5 officers and 150 other ranks to 2nd SAI and 8 officers and 200 other ranks to 4th SAI. Eight officers and 24 other ranks were detached for other duties.

On Sunday 17 February 1918 it had been decided to hold a memorial service at Delville Wood as the SA Brigade was encamped within marching distance. It was estimated that some forty per cent of those on parade were veterans of Delville Wood. To many this memorial service meant much. Some sixty shattered tree stumps along the lonely ridge of Delville Wood were silhouetted starkly on the skyline. The foundations of Longueval village were dimly discernable. Although the area had been fought over since the South Africans had withdrawn in July 1916, little was changed except the tree stumps were fewer, the grass longer and to the left were many little crosses half hidden among the shell holes in which grew rank grass and tufts of broom. This wilderness was deserted except for grey rats of extraordinary size. Their burrows honeycombed the sides of shell holes. The ground still bore fragments of uniform, equipment, with lengths of wire and other material.

The memorial service commenced at 1 p.m. The SA Brigade was drawn up in the form of a square in close column of companies. In addition, the SA Light Trench Mortar Battery, SA Field Ambulance and 63rd Field Company RE were present. The units of the Brigade had begun their march to Delville Wood at 8.30 a.m. on a crisp, blue morning with halts on the hour. Even though the transfer of personnel to 3rd SAI had taken place by this date, all ranks of the 3rd were paraded as a unit for the purpose of this service under the command of Lt-Col B Young.

At 11.30 a.m. all units had lunch from the field kitchens that had set out earlier. Veterans swopped memories as they stood in subdued groups among the blackened stumps of the wood. Steel helmets were worn by those on parade with belts, side arms and slung haversacks with mess tins. Three rounds of ammunition were carried by each man of the 3rd SAI.

Maj-Gen Lukin, the commander of the 9th (Scottish) Division, and Brig-Gen Dawson, commander of the SA Brigade, along with a large party of officers and nurses were grouped near the piled drums of the SA Brigade which formed

Some sixty shattered tree stumps along the lonely ridge of Delville Wood were silhouetted starkly on the skyline. February 1918.
(Photo: Transvaal Scottish Regimental Museum)

an altar for the drumhead service. Close by was the memorial cross which had been erected in the southern part of the wood. This was a simple wooden cross of Byzantine pattern, inscribed 'In memory of the officers and men of the 1st SA Brigade who fell in action in the Battle of the Somme, 1916'. Three chaplains attached to the Brigade officiated: Father Eustace Hill, back with the Brigade after his loss of an arm, was clad in Church of England vestments, with two of his colleagues in uniform. In the background there was the rumble of distant guns and now and again the drone of aeroplanes.

Nancy was there. She, along with her 'buck major', Private Petersen, watched timorously from the background. the delicate springbok had not gone unscathed. While the SA Brigade had been near Armentières, a shell had exploded in the transport lines where she had been tethered close to the Quarter Master's Store. In fright she had bolted and broken her left horn against a wall. This horn was permanently out of alignment and started to grow downwards at an angle. No doctor wished to attempt to set the broken horn. When worn her special coat of Murray of Atholl tartan, made from a kilt, with green securing-tapes, now displayed a gold wound stripe.

Commemorative Memorial Service at Delville Wood, 17 February 1918, by 1st SA Infantry Brigade. Father Hill in the white surplice.
(Photo: Transvaal Scottish Regimental Museum)

The original Byzantine cross to the Memory of the 1st South African Infantry Brigade, 17 February 1918 at Delville Wood. (Photo: Transvaal Scottish Regimental Museum)

The Brigade was formed up on three sides of a square. The service before the memorial cross began with a lament called 'Delville Wood' played by its composer the Pipe-Major of the 4th SAI (SA Scottish), 'Sandy' Grieve. As the notes died away, Father Hill was called upon to deliver a prayer which he concluded with a moving address and then the hymn 'Now the Labourer's Task is O'er' to the accompaniment of a military band. After further prayers and hymn 'For all the Saints', the 3rd SAI, for the last time together as a regiment, discharged three volleys. After the third volley the massed buglers of the SA Brigade sounded the Last Post. One of the bugles, that was played by Cpl Drummer R Q 'Jock' Greggor of 4th SAI is preserved in the Transvaal Scottish Regimental Museum. After the hymn 'Jesus Christ is Risen' and an oration by the Dutch chaplain in High Dutch to the glory of the fallen, came the singing of the Dutch version of the 'Old Hundreth' (All People) 'Juicht Aard'. The parade came smartly to attention while the band played 'God Save the King'. Father Hill then called down a blessing and the service was over.

Maj-Gen Lukin, the Divisional Commander, read a letter he had received from Field Marshal Haig. Thereafter a presentation of medal ribbons for bravery

'Nancy' and Private Petersen, 4th SAI at the Delville Wood Service, February 1918. (Photo: Transvaal Scottish Regimental Museum)

Delville Wood, 17 February 1918. (Photo: Transvaal Scottish Regimental Museum)

awards took place: 1 Bar to MC; 4 MCs; 2 DCMs; 33 MMs. The Brigade marched back to camp, their steel helmets flashing in the sunlight. The officers and men who had been honoured received the salute of the Brigade as it marched past the spot where they were assembled. In the words of John Buchan:

> That ceremony was something more than a commemoration of a great thing in the past. It was a sacrament taken in preparation for a still greater test of manhood now impending. For before the next month had closed, the enemy flood had once again poured over the wastes of Delville, and the flower of the South Africans had fallen in a new Thermopylae.

Chapter 24

Backs to the wall: Gauche Wood

For the SA Brigade the period of rest, preparation and commemoration was over. It was back to the area south of the village of Gouzeaucourt, ten miles from Cambrai. It would be these positions which the SA Brigade had improved throughout December that would bear the full onslaught of the German March offensive.

The intensive training that the SA Brigade had received for the forthcoming battle was a new experience. It had always been attack, attack and attack and now it was training in defensive warfare. The British had their backs to the wall.

On the night of 12 March 1918 the SA Brigade at full strength of about 1 700 men moved up to the front line along with the other two brigades of the 9th Division, now under the command of Maj-Gen H H Tudor who had taken over from Maj-Gen Lukin while the latter went on leave to England. Much to the regret of the SA Brigade, Lukin now opted for a period of duty in England because his wife had been seriously ill. He did not return.

It is important to understand exactly why Germany was on the offensive and the Fifth Army of which the 9th Division formed a part would receive the brunt of the attack. Late in 1917 after the end of the fighting in the bloodied mud of the nightmare that was Passchendaele, German High Command held a series of conferences. The shrewd and realistic conclusions that were reached came from the man who wielded the power and not from any figurehead. It was General Erich von Ludendorff, the German Quartermaster General, who had pondered over the weighty problem and made the decision. The Italians had been shattered. The French had suffered defeat and their morale was poor. Peace had been signed between, Roumania, Bolshevik Russia and Germany. This left only the British undefeated, though somewhat weakened by their losses at Passchendaele.

Now that America had entered the war on the side of Britain, thousands of American soldiers would soon be arriving in France. While Germany still held such a great advantage in numbers, with all the well-trained and tried German divisions released from the fighting on the Eastern Russian front, the British armies must be destroyed. This would secure a definite decision. Then a peace

Just after occupation, December 1917. The original frontline trench on the forward slope, Quentin Ridge, Gouzeaucourt. This rare photograph was taken illegally by Major C M Browne MC, 4th SAI. (Photo: Transvaal Scottish Regimental Museum)

favourable to Germany could be concluded, reasoned Ludendorff.

The Allied Command on the Western Front realised that the changed circumstances on the Russian front would allow the Germans to assume the offensive whenever they wished. Until the Americans arrived, the Germans would be numerically superior. Between November 1917 and March 1918 the German fighting strength increased by thirty per cent while the British fell by twenty-five per cent on the Western Front.

From the Belgian coast at Nieuport all the way to Switzerland the Allied front ran without a break. The centre of the British line, running approximately parallel to the English channel from north to south, was Arras. Here the distance from the coast was fifty miles while further south on the River Somme this had narrowed to less than forty miles. The Germans planned to pierce the centre of this 140-mile line so that the main British forces would be cordoned off in a small area with the sea in their rear. With the British defeated, Ludendorff hoped that the French would agree to a separate peace with Germany. (As matters did not turn out as Ludendorff had expected, this is mere speculation, but in 1940 such a situation did develop with the outcome Ludendorff had hoped for in 1918!)

In January 1918, the French line as far as Barisis, south of the Oise, had been taken over by the British. Haig now had a front of 125 miles to defend without the necessary reinforcements for the task. Lloyd George, the British Prime Minister, distrustful of Haig's judgement after Passchendaele, placed firm control over the flow of reinforcements to the Western Front to prevent another wasteful offensive.

For this reason Haig kept his north and central portions of the line unaltered in case of an attack, which if successful would give him no room to manoeuvre. It was not this area that the Germans had chosen to attack, but that extending from Arras in the north to La Fére in the south. The portion south of Arras to Beaucamp Ridge, just north of Gouzeaucourt was held by General Sir Julian Byng's Third Army of fourteen divisions with six further divisions in reserve. The remaining two thirds of the line on which the German offensive would strike was held by the same number of divisions as the Third Army, but with only three divisions in reserve.[1] Here General Sir Hugh Gough's Fifth Army, holding the major portion of this front was stretched to its limit. The three divisions on his right flank along a seventeen mile section to where it joined the French Sixth Army could muster only one bayonet to every yard. The Germans would attack that area with four times that number. The 9th Division, of which the SA Brigade formed the right, was positioned on the extreme left of the Fifth Army.

To compensate for this weakness, the 'forward zone' in front of the Third and Fifth Armies had been carefully organised into two sections: first a series of outposts to give the alarm if the Germans were seen to be advancing. These would then fall back to the second section: a thickly wired area of resistance. Dotted within this 'forward zone' were strategically-positioned redoubts, occupied by platoons of thirty or forty men heavily defended, with machine-guns to cover the area from every angle. This would prevent a German advance taking place in an unbroken line. Before the advancing Germans realised what was happening they would find themselves between these redoubts from where the interlocking fields of fire from the machine-guns would catch them in a devastating crossfire. The gaps between the redoubts would be protected by the British barrage from an array of field and heavy artillery sited for this purpose.

The main defensive positions occupied by the SA Brigade in the 'forward or outpost zone' were the Quentin Redoubt and Gauche Wood. They fronted a line of 2 000 yards extending from just north of the former to south of the latter. Not only did the SA Brigade hold this line but were responsible for all trench lines to a depth of nearly a mile.

On the evening of 20 March a company of 1st SAI was holding the SA Brigade's left at Quentin Redoubt. Gauche Wood to the south on the South African right was held by 'B' Company of 2nd SAI under Captain Garnet Green, who had been presented with a bar to his Military Cross after the recent Service of Remembrance at Delville Wood. The 4th SAI was in 'reserve' stationed in the 'battle zone'. The SA Brigade 'battle zone' was also well wired with a similar system of strongpoints. The main line of resistance or 'battle zone' began at a

1   Liddell Hart, *A History of the World War* p503.

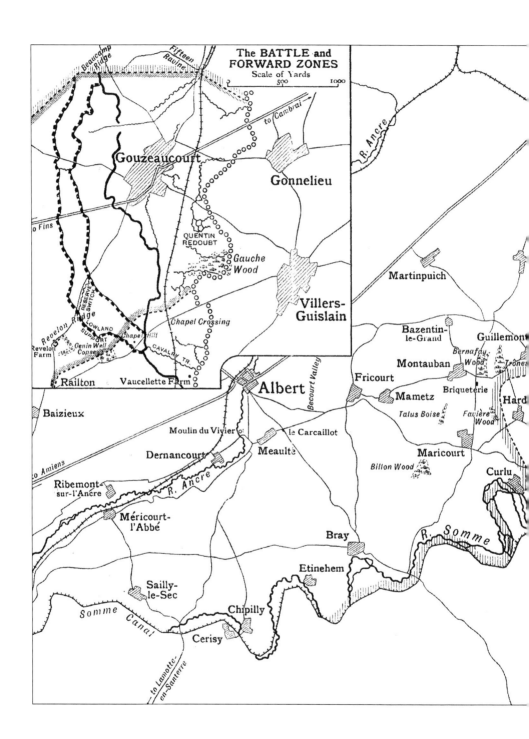

The BATTLE and FORWARD ZONES

Scale of Yards
500   1000

Beaucamp Ridge

Fifteen Ravine

to Cambrai

Gouzeaucourt

Gonnelieu

to Fins

QUENTIN REDOUBT

Gauche Wood

Villers-Guislain

RESERVE SWITCH

LOWLAND

SUPPORT

Revelon Ridge

Chapel Crossing

Chapel Hill

Revelon Farm

Genin Well Copse

CAVALRY TR.

Railton

Vaucellette Farm

Albert

Becourt Valley

Martinpuich

Bazentin-le-Grand

Guillemon

Bernafay Wood

Trône

Montauban

Fricourt

Briqueterie

Hard

Mametz

Talus Boise

Favière Wood

Baizieux

Moulin du Vivier

le Carcaillot

Maricourt

Dernancourt

Meaulte

Billon Wood

Curlu

to Amiens

R. Ancre

Ribemont-sur-l'Ancre

R. Somme

Méricourt-l'Abbé

Bray

Etinehem

R. Ancre

Sailly-le-Sec

Somme Canal

Chipilly

Cerisy

to Lamotte-en-Santerre

R. Ancre

R. Ancre

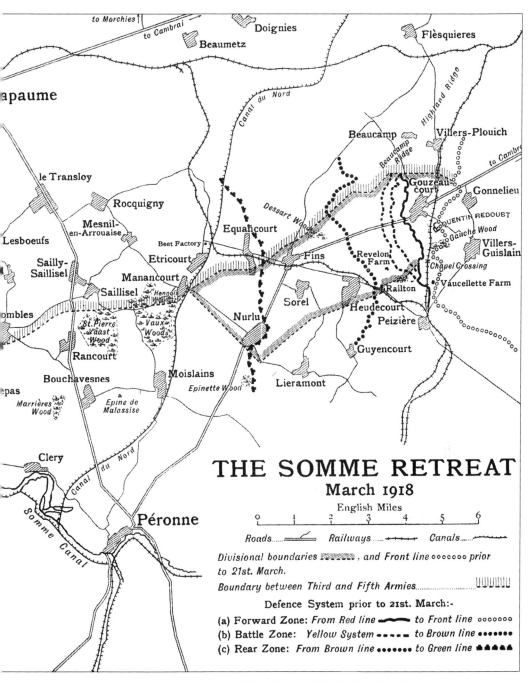

THE SOMME RETREAT
March 1918

English Miles

| 0 | 1 | 2 | 3 | 4 | 5 | 6 |

Roads————— Railways—+—+— Canals——~—

Divisional boundaries ▨▨▨▨ , and Front line ∘∘∘∘∘∘∘ prior
to 21st. March.

Boundary between Third and Fifth Armies.............. ⊔⊔⊔⊔⊔⊔

Defence System prior to 21st. March:-

(a) Forward Zone: From Red line ▬▬▬ to Front line ∘∘∘∘∘∘∘
(b) Battle Zone: Yellow System ▬ ▬ ▬ ▬ to Brown line •••••••
(c) Rear Zone: From Brown line ••••••• to Green line ▲▲▲▲▲

(*The History of the 9th (Scottish) Division*, Ewing, 1921)

287

point called Chapel Crossing on the railway to Gouzeaucourt, along the western face of the Gouzeaucourt valley following the high ground that was held until the line curved round the western perimeter of the ruins of Gouzeaucourt to include the rising ground west of Gouzeaucourt.

Just west of Chapel Crossing was Chapel Hill, a slight eminence on the SA Brigade right flank which commanded the full extent of the 'Yellow' or reserve position of the 'battle zone'. This ran from Chapel Hill along the eastern slope of the ridges north of Revlon Farm. The final line of the 'battle zone', a few hundred yards to the rear along the western slopes of these same ridges was the Brown Line. The so-called Green Line, three miles further to the rear, was supposed to represent a third zone of defence, but existed only in name. The only fortified positions near this area, as far as the SA Brigade was concerned, were Revlon Farm and beyond that the village of Heudicourt.

In spite of reports from air reconnaissance that there were large concentrations of German troops well back from the front line behind the German lines that faced the Third and Fifth Armies, the eight days prior to the 21 March had been the quietest ever in the front line experience of the SA Brigade. Trench raids on the German front line had given no indication of German strength except that their offensive was due to begin on Thursday 21 March. Yet this did not seem possible.

Throughout Wednesday not a sound came from the German front line which was shrouded in a thick mist that had been drawn from the ground after the

Field Marshall von Hindenburg (left) and his chief of staff (right) Lt-Gen. von Ludendorff, planning the German offensive of March 1918. (Photo: Cloete-Smith Collection)

LEFT: Lt-Gen Sir Hugh Gough KCB, Fifth Army Commander.
(Photo: The Great War, H W Wilson)
RIGHT: Lt-Gen Sir Julian Byng, KCB, KCMG, MVO, Third Army Commander.
(Photo: Cloete-Smith Collection)

drizzle of Tuesday 19 March. Had Ludendorff the power to order weather to suit his plan of action, he could not have succeeded better. There was no wind to disperse the mist which became even more impenetrable on the morning of 21 March. At 2 a.m. the men in the 'forward zone' were warned to expect an attack. At 4.30 a.m. the order came to man the 'battle zone'. At 4.48 a.m. the might of the massed German artillery was unleashed simultaneously on the British forward zones, battle zones, headquarters, artillery positions and back areas. The shells used were a combination of high explosive and gas. For the next four hours the bombardment raged backwards and forwards over these areas. In turn the British artillery replied, adding to the unspeakable din.

Lt G Lawrence, 1st SAI, whom Lt-Col Heal had confined to the reserve lines because of his recent prolonged spell of front line service, recalled just how severe the shelling was of the back areas. Waiting for the storm to break, he was sleeping uneasily with the other officers of the reserve in a Nissen hut. In total the reserve – officers, NCOs and men – numbered about 650 and were under the command of Lt-Col B Young. The other ranks were occupying canvas shelters. There was no cover. The bombardment of the area continued throughout that day.

The German barrage came down with a thunderous crash...(the heaviest bombardment known on the Western Front). We lit our candles and burrowed as close as we could get to the ground. First a shell blew one door in and then the other near me. The candles went out and we groped for our gas helmets in the dark. Splinters of metal were making sparks as they fell through just above us. The din was quite indescribable. Soon, amongst the high explosive shells falling all around, we heard the unmistakable plop, plop, as gas shells fell mixed with the others and the burnt potato or onion smell warned us it was time to put on our gas helmets.

One poor chap could not find his helmet, another had his torn across his face by a flying piece of shrapnel. We waited apprehensively for a direct hit any moment but luckily none came and the barrage lifted back to the front line and also to the artillery lines. We then all staggered out to find our battle positions, trying as best we could to see through helmet eye pieces and the dense fog. We were making very slow progress when Sergeant Major Alex Smith did a very brave thing by pulling off his gas helmet fully aware of the grave risk, and led us through the thick gas to our allotted posts. I was quite aghast at Smith's selfless act deliberately inviting a cruel death... death we had witnessed so graphically in our reserve line – the terrible sight of gassed men caught by the mixed gas and high explosive shell fire, probably newcomers. They were carried past on stretchers in what seemed an endless procession, each man in *extremis* frothing at the mouth and blowing bubbles. A frightful and unnerving sight seen by us all.[1]

For the Germans all was going exactly according to plan; even better with the weather as any ally. The tactics employed had been rehearsed and also tried on a limited front at Caporetto in Italy and at Cambrai. Certain of their success, they had invited foreign correspondents of neutral newspapers to witness the German victory.

In front of Gough's Fifth Army of fourteen infantry and three cavalry divisions, were ranged forty German divisions with a further forty in close reserve.

The new tactics involved the quick forward movement of massed artillery close to the front line in concealment. Without previous registration of shots and the adjustment of ranges, batteries would immediately open up on carefully pre-determined, ranged targets. Surprise would be coupled to an endless procession of advancing troops. Neither would the bombardment be long enough to alarm the British or render their front impassable to advancing troops.

The German infantry had received training in infiltration. The advance

1   *Militaria* 8/4 1978 p56-7.

would be spearheaded by 'storm troops' who would feel for weak areas and then penetrate them while reserves would pour through the breaches, backing up success, not wasting valuable time over obstacles of resistance. The 'storm troop' groups that were in advance of the ordinary attacking lines of infantry were armed with automatic rifles, light mortars and machine-guns. They could force their way through any opening leaving behind the defenders to be out-flanked and surrounded by the successive lines of advancing troops. The divisions that were to launch the offensive had been brought up under cover of darkness so the British had no way of gauging German strength at any particular point. A second line of divisions was simultaneously brought into position a mile behind the first line of divisions. Both the first and second lines of divisions moved forward when the bombardment began at zero hour. The second line of divisions would be on hand immediately and fall under the command of the first line divisional commander who was in touch with reality instead of High Command many miles away.

To keep those in the rear informed of the most recent progress, special reconnaissance groups were detailed for this specific task. Rapid advance was the order of the day. There would be no attempt at keeping a uniform alignment in the advance. Flares and rockets alerted the advancing lines as to where a breach had been made by the 'storm troops'. Field artillery would be moved forward hot on the heels of the infantry to give them support. The German divisions had been issued with iron rations for several days as their objectives were unlimited. A division would move forward until its strength was dissipated rather than stop on reaching a specific objective. Then a fresh division would leap frog through the expended one and continue the forward movement. The infiltration would cause dislocation and then disintegration. The fast forward movement would cause the British artillery to be captured before it could extricate itself. The advance would increase in momentum once the unprotected back areas were reached. Any delays would be fatal to Ludendorff's plans.

The German bombardment did not seem so severe at first but later its intensity increased as it was reinforced by mortar fire. Along the British front practically all telephone cables were severed and wireless sets destroyed. The thick mist ruled out visual signalling. There was a complete breakdown in communications but those between the three battalions of the SA Brigade held throughout the day. Initially front line battalions reported that all was quiet. The thick mist limited vision to between twenty-five and fifty yards. The forward movement of the Germans and their systematic cutting of wire went unobserved. Casualties for the Germans were lessened by the storm troopers' success in breaking up barbed wire entanglements with their mortars. They came through in open order. Then followed the serried masses of grey.

Throughout 21 March no attempts were made on the Quentin Redoubt held by the 1st SAI company. On the right between 8 and 9 a.m. the 2nd SAI company in Gauche Wood under Capt Garnet Green came under attack. This developed from the south-east corner of the wood as the 21st Division on the right was receiving the full force of the attack. Their front line was very soon in German hands. This included Vaucellette Farm half a mile south of Chapel Crossing. The cluster of ruined buildings was used from 3.30 p.m. as a German assembly point for the repeated attacks on Gauche Wood and on Chapel Hill. The crumbling of the 21st Division front line exposed the whole right flank of Gauche Wood. Possession of the Wood was fiercely contested by Capt Green and his company. Lt T Bancroft and most of his No 8 platoon in one of the posts on the east side of the wood were killed in hand-to-hand fighting. 2/Lt M Beviss and his men fought valiantly from the other post there. Bancroft, when last seen, was heard shouting 'Now then, boys. No surrender. Charge!' Only one of his men made it back to Brigade Headquarters. Beviss and half his platoon battled their way out and rejoined Capt Green and the rest of his company in Gauche Alley and Chapel Trench.

Because of the thick mist the Germans had managed to enter the wood from the east side to get between the outposts north of the wood, and so surround the two posts held by Bancroft and Beviss. In the same movement personnel of the machine-gun and light trench mortars were overwhelmed after a desperate fight.

Acting L/Cpl A F Lilford and Pte R W Harrison, 2nd SAI, were the only two men out of two trench mortar crews to survive. L/Cpl Lilford wrote:

> I make no excuses but to say that the effect of our trench mortar shells fired by my two gun crews kept the enemy from advancing on our trenches. We gave up all hope of ever coming out alive and threw caution

L/Cpl A F Lilford DCM, 2nd SAI, a hero of Gauche Wood.
(Photo: FVA Lilford)

to the winds in firing 400 mortar shells – 200 per gun.

Lilford then went to another emplacement for extra ammunition. When all mortar shells were expended, German mortar fire partially buried both his trench mortars. Assisted by Pte Harrison, he dismantled his mortars under the noses of the advancing Germans. He removed them safely to where two other mortars were in support, then withdrew all the mortars. Lilford was awarded the DCM and Harrison the MM.

Capt Green found the Germans on three sides in incredible strength, so he slowly withdrew his garrison from the third post in the wood to the fourth post in the trenches south west of the wood. Every yard was fiercely contested. The on-coming, massed German advance was unable to hasten Capt Green's retirement. A Zulu war cry rallied the exhausted men and stirred them to renewed efforts. At first the Germans exposed themselves recklessly. As they were within fifty yards range, exceedingly heavy casualties were caused by Lewis gun and rifle fire. Many German officers fell.

Cpl A W Cloete-Smith, 2nd SAI, in a letter to his mother dated 7 April 1918 described his part in the fighting to hold Gauche Wood. He was one of Capt Green's 118 who held three German divisions at bay for twenty-four hours. Since 12 March he and the rest of his company had occupied the important position on the ridge at Gauche Wood overlooking the village of Villers-Guislain and the Ranteaux Valley. That morning, exhausted from their front line stint, they had been due to come out of the line.

> Jerry's troops on the other hand were as fresh as paint. They had new uniforms and everything about them seemed to be brand new. They made quite a parade of the affair. [They] came over in platoons with their officers on horseback riding in front. My platoon was absolutely blotted out... When the 21st [Division] gave way, Jerry got in behind them. The last that was seen of them they were standing back to back fighting with Germans all round them. Our 'A' Company did some very fine work. They were detached from us and sent to give two battalions of the 21st Division, who were getting rather a hot time, a hand. As soon as our fellows got into their trenches they cleared off with the result that 'A' Company was left to hold what had been a brigade front. And what is more they held it until they were all either blotted out or wounded.

Capt Green had organised the reinforcement of the 21st Division before returning to carry on his own defence. Cloete-Smith continued:

Captain Garnet Green, MC and Bar, 2nd SAI, defender of Gauche Wood.
(Photo: BK Thomas)

Our chief difficulty when the Germans broke through on the right and we had to swing our flank round, was the lack of artillery support as our own guns (i.e. divisional artillery) were of course firing on their original front and we could not get into communication with them. It was not until about 4 o'clock in the afternoon that the guns of the 39th Division came into action in our left rear and began to support us. They were firing at a pretty long range as it was and started off by strafing us.

Nearly two hours elapsed before we could get into touch with them and give them the right range. They made a beautiful mess of Jerry when they did get on to him as he was just getting ready for another attack. He did advance a little way but the rifle and machine-gun fire was too hot for him and he had to go back. None too soon for us either as our rifles were just about red hot. There was no question about aiming. It was simply pulling your trigger as fast as you could work your bolt. It was just like firing into a grey wall and I think each bullet must have found two or three victims. The ground was thick with their dead and wounded after they had gone back. I have seldom enjoyed myself so much as I did that evening although I was feeling pretty rotten at the time. They were just tumbling down in rows under the fire of the machine-guns.

The skipper [Capt Green] of our Company also distinguished himself. He got hold of anyone he could lay hands on and at one place kept Jerry back for over twenty-four hours. I am sorry to say he was killed when the Division was withdrawing. We were compelled to withdraw in the end as the people on our right had been driven back so far that we were very nearly cut off.

Cpl Cloete-Smith had been feeling progressively worse. After wearing his gas mask for five hours, he had been compelled to remove it. The eye pieces had become so blurred that it was impossible to see through them. Then he had inhaled the fumes from a gas shell. This forced him to leave the line at 9.30 p.m. on 21 March. The effects of this mustard gas were only felt several hours afterwards in the form of sickness and loss of voice. By 9 p.m. Cloete-Smith had begun vomiting and his throat had closed up until he could scarcely breathe. He arrived at the dressing station more dead than alive with a temperature of 102.6 °F. Many other members of the SA Brigade suffered similarly from the delayed effects of the gas, sometimes as long as forty-eight hours after inhalation.[1] During the offensive

1   Cloete-Smith was hospitalised as a result of being gassed. Although he recovered, he had not yet been posted back to France for active service from the SA Brigade Depot at Woking, England, when the war ended in November.

the Germans had used different smelling, non-poisonous gas mixed with lethal gas to give the British a false sense of security.

Throughout the day there had been some fighting at close quarters, but soon a routine of the continued massacre of Germans by machine-gun and rifle fire was established. They came towards the British lines in compact formations all along the battle front. In dense masses they died. When attacking they looked neither to the left nor to the right but walked straight into the storm of rifle, Lewis gun, machine-gun and artillery fire. Line after line of grey-clad Germans were literally wiped out. All day they came on, often singing as they died. They emerged out of the mist, only visible at twenty-five yards. The target was point blank. Theirs was a monotonous, mechanical heroism. A high pile of corpses was banked up before the South African position, but fresh troops from the rear climbed over and came on looking straight ahead. Similar slaughter took place over the greater part of the front. Cpl Williams, 2nd SAI, spoke to a reporter in hospital: 'I was at Delville Wood, but....I have never seen such blood-shed as that among the Germans, nor could I have imagined such losses....The din was such that we could not hear each other speak a few yards away.'[1] Only by sheer weight of numbers had Green's company been forced to retreat to the line of trenches just west of the wood.

So heavy were the German losses that they did not attempt to advance beyond the edge of the wood, but began to dig in. As they were in full view of the trench line Green was now occupying, a heavy fire from all arms caused them to give up the idea immediately. As the wood was now unoccupied by South African troops, and the news had been conveyed to Brigade HQ, Brig-Gen Dawson ordered all the field guns at his disposal to give the wood a thorough pasting with gas, high explosive and shrapnel. With the lifting of the mist, the 1st SAI garrison of Quentin Redoubt so far unmolested, plainly observed numbers of Germans in Gauche Wood into which they now directed heavy rifle and Lewis gun fire. Considerable losses were inflicted by this combined effort.

Capt Green's company had been steadily reduced until by evening they numbered about forty.

The German attack had met with greater success to the right of the SA Brigade in the area held by the 21st Division. Here Chapel Hill, which commanded the entire 'Yellow Line' trenches of the SA Brigade was in danger of capture, so deep was the German penetration on the South African right flank. By afternoon the Germans had occupied the south-east side of this slight eminence about a mile away from South African forward posts. This deep penetration also put at risk Capt Green's company and the 1st SAI holding Quentin Redoubt.

News was then received that the Germans were also attacking Genin Well

---

Copse held by the 21st Division, even further to the rear, south-west of Chapel Hill. Although not in his area, Dawson was ordered to retake Chapel Hill. 'A' Company of 2nd SAI, held in reserve for counterattack purposes, failed to make any progress, so at 5.30 p.m. Lt-Col D M Macleod, OC 4th SAI (SA Scottish) was ordered to retake the whole of Chapel Hill. 'A' Company of the 4th SAI under Capt H Bunce led a bold attack with dash and the summit was retaken as well as the trenches on the south and south-east slopes, with an added bonus of 150 yards of Cavalry Trench. In this way the link with Genin Well Copse had been re-established.

In *The Kaiser's Battle* by Martin Middlebrook special mention is made of this feat.

> The South Africans counterattacked at once, and retook the hill. The Germans had to give up for the day then. A member of the 123rd Grenadier Regiment, a famous Württemberg regiment with a high reputation, says that, that night, his company was back where it had started in the morning. 'For us grenadiers, it was a miserable situation. We felt ashamed and shattered.'[1]

This was certainly a contrast to what was happening all around. Except for Gauche Wood, the SA Brigade had lost no ground during that first day. Cpl Cloete-Smith of 2nd SAI aptly summed up the achievement when he wrote: 'If the 21st and 16th Divisions had only fought like that, Jerry would never have got through not if he had gone on attacking for months.'

---

1   Published 1978.

Chapter 25

To fight another day

It was the crumbling of the divisions on either side of the 9th Division that was responsible for the order on the night of 21 March for the withdrawal of all units of the SA Brigade to the Yellow Line and to hold Brown Line. This was carried out under cover of darkness by 5 a.m. on the morning of 22 March.

The new positions of the SA Brigade were distributed as follows: The 4th SAI was on the right holding Chapel Hill and Yellow Line as far as the sunken road with HQ at Revlon Farm; the 1st SAI were in Yellow Line as far as the Fins-Gouzeaucourt Road with HQ in a dugout south of this road. The 2nd SAI were now the support battalion with one company in Brown Line in front of the Quarry. The remainder were in Heudicourt with Battalion HQ in Heudicourt Catacombs.

At first light on the 22 March it was evident that yet again the weather was made to order in favouring the relentless German advance. A thick fog blanketed the ground. Under this convenient cover the Germans had brought forward a great number of light trench mortars. Chapel Hill was heavily bombarded. Simultaneously other areas on the right came in for considerable punishment from the same source, as well as heavy artillery fire. These included Revlon Farm, Genin Well Copse and Railton. All were attacked with great determination. The 4th SAI came under tremendous pressure. The defence weakened. Chapel Hill was lost once again after a desperate struggle.

Cpl A W Philip, 'D' Company 4th SAI, recorded the last hours of the SA Scottish defence of the area before the order to retire was received.

> The German guns opened fire... One man just in front of me was hit. A shell burst between Lieut Leighton's legs. Instead of blowing them to pieces it only dazed him. The Germans began to come over in earnest, and we had to fire as soon as they showed themselves on the ridge opposite. Just at this time the only gun of ours in action began enfilading our trench. The enemy aeroplanes were all over us and not one of our own to be seen anywhere. On the right the Germans could be seen advancing past in artillery formation.

Very rare photograph of the 1st SA Infantry Brigade headquarters area, in the quarry near Heudicourt, taken by Major C M Browne MC, 4th SAI.
(Photo: Transvaal Scottish Regimental Museum)

> One of our machine-gun sections retiring over the ridge was taken for the enemy in the excitement of the moment. Every man was killed except one officer who, wounded, managed to crawl back to the trench. Things were getting very serious. The Germans had their heavy artillery trained on our position. A dog with a message tied to his collar, found his way into our lines. The message was from the enemy infantry to the artillery, telling them to 'straf' our position as it was a strong point. At dusk (we) were ordered to retire. Just in time.[1]

Covering fire for the retirement was provided by 2nd SAI.

Pte R J Grimsdell, 4th SAI, remembered passing through some men of the Black Watch during that period of confusion and smelt frying bacon. He shouted 'Get going Jocks or you'll get caught.' 'What,' they replied, 'And waste all this fine bacon.' They waited until it was almost too late and then moved off. At the Nurlu salient during the rearguard action he saw the astonishing spectacle of British

1   Diary of Cpl A W Philip, 4th SAI (SA Scottish) Transvaal Scottish Regimental Museum.

4th SAI Headquarters
Back Row: Left to Right: Lt L R Johnston (Transport); 2/Lt F Peacock (Lewis Guns) – captured at Marrières Wood; 2/Lt T A Stevenson (Snipers); 2/Lt V N Pougnet MC (Bombs) – wounded 17-10-18; Lt R B Marshall (Assistant Adjutant) – won the MC at River Selle. Bottom: Left to Right: Capt W Menzies (Chaplain); Major D R Hunt (2IC); Lt-Col D M Macleod DSO, MC, DCM (Officer Commanding) – wounded at Revlon Farm; Capt F McE Mitchell MC (Adjutant) – wounded at Revlon Farm; Capt H R Lawrence MC (Medical Officer) – won MC at Le Cateau. (Photo: Transvaal Scottish Regimental Museum)

The Medals of Captain Thomas Girdwood MacFie DSO, MC 4th SAI
Left to Right: Distinguished Service Order; Military Cross; 1914/15 Star; British War Medal 1914-18; Allied Victory Medal with Mid oakleaf; Russian Order of St. Anne Breast Badge (3rd Class with Swords). (Photo: Mike Taylor)
MacFie joined the 4th SAI on 12/1/1917; L/Cpl 29/5/1917; Cpl 18/7/1917; Sgt 17/1/1918 and 2/Lt 23/1/1918; Capt 30/4/1918. His citation for the Military Cross reads (in part) as follows: 'For conspicuous gallantry and devotion to duty. On March 23rd at Nurlu, during evacuation of the portion of the line held by his Regiment, this officer displayed great courage and devotion to duty, going from position to position in full view of the enemy under heavy artillery and machine-gun fire, encouraging his men and keeping them under his personal control. He was largely responsible for the orderly nature of the retirement, and for the slight casualties incurred. It was entirely due to his initiative and foresight that the documents and records of his Regiment were saved from falling into enemy hands during this action. On March 27th at DERNACOURT, although already wounded, he again showed outstanding gallantry, rallying stragglers from his own and other Units and taking them forward, in view of the enemy through heavy barrage... and secure the flank position...'

field guns in front of the infantry firing over open sights at the singing horde of relentlessly advancing Germans, with their rifle muzzles depressed. The field guns were soon captured and the untenable situation could be solved only by further retirement.

Here during the evacuation of this portion of the line 2/Lt T G MacFie, 4th SAI, went from position to position in full view of the enemy under heavy artillery fire, encouraging his men and keeping them under his personal control. He was largely responsible for the orderly nature of the retirement and for the slight casualties incurred. However, an expensive loss to the SA Scottish had taken place earlier, in the withdrawal to Nurlu from Revlon Farm. Here the 4th SAI had been so hard pressed that members of the pipe band had been issued with rifles. All the horse-hair sporrans, sets of bagpipes and drums and officers' mess furniture had been stored in a building at Heudicourt. A 5.9 shell totally destroyed them when it landed on the store.

Because of the move to the new SA Brigade HQ in Sorel without telephones, it was very difficult to keep in touch with swiftly moving events. Artillery fire could not be so promptly directed on to concentrations of advancing Germans as on the previous day. The pace of events further accelerated. All documents and records not required at Brigade HQ were dispatched to the Transport Lines.

Shortly after noon, orders were received for the SA Brigade to evacuate Yellow Line and retire to the area on Brown Line extending to Green Line, three miles in the rear. Dawson sent Acting Brigade Major R Beverley to tell the battalions of the SA Brigade to be ready to move to Green Line because of the seriousness of the situation. In the south, on the right flank of the SA Brigade, the German advance had broken through the Brown Line south of Railton in the sector of the 21st Division. Their advance now changed direction, moving north to roll up the line held by the SA Brigade. All three of its battalions were now in the greatest danger of being cut off and surrounded. Everything depended on whether the German advance could be stemmed until darkness to aid the safe withdrawal of the units before being enveloped by the advancing field-grey tide.

Major Beverley had to move fast if he were to alert the SA Brigade to the danger before it was too late. As Dawson wrote in his diary: 'He had a most thrilling ride, his horse being shot under him, but he did his job.'

Beverley's account of his ride does not do justice to the epic, but makes interesting reading nevertheless.

> At 6.30 p.m. 22 March, acting under orders of the Brigadier General Commanding (Dawson), I left Sorel for the purpose of gaining touch with the 26th Bde at their Hd.Qrs. near Desart (*sic*) Wood on the Fins-

Gouzeaucourt Road. On arrival there I found that the H.Qrs. had removed to Mannacourt and that the Battalions in the line had already commenced their retirement.

I then rode across in the direction of Heudicourt to ascertain the situation in the vicinity of the Brown Line. Rifle and MG fire could be heard from the direction of Heudicourt and it was evident that the enemy was pressing on that flank. On my way I met Lt-Col Christian and 2/Lt Cragg, the former told me that the enemy had occupied Heudicourt and were closely pressing on Sorel. Col Christian then sent me back to inform Col Heal, 1st Regt, of the situation and tell him that it would be impossible for him to retire through Sorel.

About 300 yds further towards the Brown Line I met Col Heal with his regiment and gave him this information. He asked me to go back and inform his officers and collect any stragglers and put them on the right route. This I did and then rode towards the Brown Line to ascertain if all our troops were clear. On nearing this line I was fired on by a MG and my horse was killed. The MG appeared to be about seventy to eighty yards away and it was evident that the enemy had occupied a portion of the Brown Line. By this time it was almost dark. Under cover of the ridge I went towards the Fins-Gouzeaucourt Road, on reaching which I turned towards Gouzeaucourt and very shortly afterwards met Capt Bunce, 4th SAI, with the remnants of that Regiment. I explained the situation to Capt Bunce and he proceeded in the direction of Fins, having informed me that there were some men of the 1st and 2nd Regs. behind him. I then went forward to the Brown Line Trench where I met several men of the 2nd Regt. and a few of the 1st Regt. The 2nd Regt. men were mostly of 'B' Coy. A Sgt. with the party told me that he believed Capt Green had been killed and the remainder of the

Lt-Col EC Christian DSO, MC, OC 2nd SAI, March 1918. (Photo: Transvaal Scottish Regimental Museum)

company either killed or captured.

After a short search and enquiries from these men it was evident that this trench was now clear. I then formed up the party and marched back towards Fins.

The huts and buildings had been fired by our retiring troops and the blaze lighted up the whole country in the vicinity, and by this light the enemy could be seen advancing in column of route along the main road some two hundred yards distant...Shortly afterwards a mounted man arrived from the direction of Fins and informed me that the enemy were in full possession of that village...I ordered the Sergeant I/C (in charge) of the 2nd Regt. party to Equancourt and then (to) take the road to Nurlu to join his regiment. About half a mile N. of Fins I (took) a short cut up the valley to Nurlu. As I reached the Fins-Equancourt road Very lights went up from the former village and a MG fired from one of the houses. I saw troops, evidently those of the enemy, well in advance of the village. This was about 9 p.m.

I eventually reached Mannacourt and found the HQ of the 26th Bde about 12 midnight. I reported to the Brig-General commanding and gave him what information I had.

Next morning after several attempts to find my Brigade I eventually rejoined about 12 noon.

Beverley's account underlines the rapidity of the German advance and the precarious position of the SA Brigade throughout its retirement. Between six and seven hundred men of the SA Brigade managed to escape to the north and then turned west through Fins just before it was taken – indeed as the South Africans were moving out of Fins the Germans were already entering the village from the opposite end! The losses suffered by the SA Brigade were estimated to have been some 900 all ranks.

In addition, two weak companies of 1st SAI, one under Capt E J Burgess and 'A' under Capt A E Ward became detached in the confusion and darkness from the main body and found themselves surrounded by Germans.[1] They succeeded in breaking through and made for Dessart Wood. They searched in vain for the rest of the SA Brigade for the next two days. On 24 March they managed to locate Lt-Col B Young and the SA Brigade details at Bray.

During the retreat of the SA Brigade, officer casualties had been high. Capt S Liebson MC, medical officer 4th SAI, had been killed at Revlon Farm. Lt-Col D M Macleod DSO DCM, OC of the 4th, had been wounded there along with

---

1   A full account of Capt E J Burgess' movements after being detached from the SA Brigade is to be found in WWI Diverse Series Box 32 SADF Documentation Centre.

Majors E G Clerk and C M Browne and the Adjutant, Capt F McE Mitchell. Of the 1st, Captains H H Jenkins, T F Pearse and L F Sprenger had been wounded. The 2nd SAI had suffered further losses. Capt S E Rogers and C J Stein were both wounded and captured. Lt H W S Terry had been killed as had been Capt Garnet Green MC. Green had been worshipped by his men. Universally popular, he was set up as an example to emulate by junior officers of the SA Brigade. Yet in all he did he was unobtrusive and unpretentious. He had died fighting with some remnants of his company, along with a company of 27th Brigade and a few details of 21st Division in front of Heudicourt Quarry.

In each case one company of a unit had been detailed to cover the retreat of its battalion. Communications had broken down completely, yet the withdrawal had been conducted with the most stubborn resistance. In his official report dated 23 January 1919 Dawson praised his junior commanders for

> putting out defensive flanks and fighting rearguard actions in a manner which could not have been surpassed by the most highly trained officers. It was entirely due to the behaviour and skill of the junior ranks that any portion of the Brigade was enabled to withdraw.

This was indeed lavish praise but Dawson says nothing of his own part in the withdrawal, which was no mean feat either. He recorded this on 22 March in his diary:

> It was fast getting dark, however, and I was in great hopes that darkness would save us – I didn't see what else could.
>
> Throughout the later afternoon, the gunners were taking their guns out, and troops of all kinds were streaming through Sorel. I saw twenty-three low flying aeroplanes swooping down, firing along the roads and at the retiring guns. There seemed to be none of ours in the sky. I stood on the top of a mound in Sorel and watched the men and guns streaming by. Heudicourt, less than one mile to the east, was enveloped in a cloud of smoke from bursting shells, and less than a mile to the north, I could see line after line of Germans advancing rapidly to the west.
>
> Fires were burning everywhere, being caused by our people burning huts and stores – the whole countryside seemed buried with fires and the flashes of bursting shells. Sorel was burning fiercely. I saw the enemy pass Heudicourt and advance towards Sorel, and as our guns were still coming through, I formed up the BHQ staff and put them into the trenches east of Sorel to give the guns and fugitives time to get clear.

As soon as the road was clear, I gave BHQ orders to retire to Nurlu which they succeeded in doing. Before this, however, the advanced parties of the enemy had approached Sorel, and it being just dark, the HQ staff were not certain who they were and challenged. The Germans replied: 'Second South Africans,' whereupon, 2/Lt M Webb – a son of Captain Webb who swam the channel – stood up and was at once shot dead. Our men at once opened a heavy fire with rifles and Lewis guns, which from all indications appeared to be exceedingly effective... Having ordered the retirement, I got on my horse and with Cochran, who had that afternoon returned from leave, rode away to the west towards the Green Line. The enemy had got so far ahead in the south, that I thought it quite probable we should be cut off and was much relieved when we passed the Green Line without incident. I went back to Division HQ at Moislans, where they gave me some dinner, but I could hardly touch it. I slept for a few hours on the floor in General Tudor's room.[1]

The SA Brigade details, numbering about 650 in camp at Heudicourt had been ordered on the afternoon of 22 March to move to Nurlu to cover the withdrawal of the rest of the SA Brigade and occupy the section of the Green Line from the Fins-Nurlu Road to a point about 500 yards south east of Nurlu.

The story of this rearguard action is unknown. It is fortunate that Lt Lawrence saw fit to place it on record. Lawrence takes up the story as he was moving back to the position that was to be held to cover the withdrawal.

...[In] dense fog, Sergeant-Major Alex Smith, with his pistol in hand saw someone in the fog in front of him going the same way as ourselves, holding an open map with both hands and marching calmly on. To his surprise when the fog lifted a little he saw it was a German officer. He had no option but to step forward a few paces and finish him with a bullet in his back. On reaching our battle post in the Green Line on the Fins-Nurlu road we got moving to improve our trench and siting our machine and Lewis guns. We hunted around for extra ammunition and were able to pile up a goodly supply for all arms.

During the early morning of the 22/23 March the 1st Regiment with Colonel Heal bringing up the rear passed through our lines to take up

1   Mrs W Winter, a daughter of Brig-Gen Dawson, has in her possession the original diary in an exercise book which she showed me. She loaned me a typewritten copy of the diary which was carefully transcribed by Brig-Gen Dawson's family. An identical copy of the diary also exists in the SADF Archives, Pretoria.

The remnants of the 4th SAI marching to Nurlu, 22 March 1918.
(Photo: Transvaal Scottish Regimental Museum)

positions at Marrières Wood behind us. The whole column of dazed and utterly weary men halted for a few minutes. I went to the rear to see Colonel Heal. He told me how his men had fought the enemy to a standstill. When surrounded, due to the enemy break-through on the right, they had fought their way back...He was so gentle, understanding and informal...He wished me luck and said goodbye before ordering the column to move on. We now became the rear guard to the Brigade and part of the adjoining Division on our right. Early on the morning of the 23 March Major Ormiston came up and gave the officers our orders. He said 'You are now the rear guard to the whole of this front and you are to hold this line. You will fight to the last man and the last round. There will be no surrender and no retreat. All forward troops of ours retiring, will be stopped on this line, if necessary, with your revolvers and you will shoot any man who refuses to stand.'

When he left we set about further improving our defences and awaited the approaching enemy...This was to be our final sacrifice...We few were safeguarding our weary Brigade – here we stand and here we die.

Shortly after midday we could see troops of our adjoining division streaming back on our extreme right and later nearer to us. Bursting shells falling everywhere, dumps of ammunition going up and burning food supplies emitting great clouds of black smoke.

The enemy was following closely behind the retreating troops and were soon close to our line hoping to break through. We stopped many men of all Divisions with our revolvers in our hands but were never required to use them.

I stopped a young corporal of the Northumberland Fusiliers in charge of a Lewis gun team who spiritedly said at once that he was quite prepared to make a stand and only too pleased to be given definite orders by an officer. Between us we sited his gun to bear with enfilading fire across our front. Just then a terrific racket broke out on our right with heavy enemy shelling and machine-gun and rifle fire from our troops. I suggested to Captain Hallack that we go down to the trench to see what was happening. As we were making our way along a grenade exploded in the trench and Captain Hallack, close behind me, was severely wounded in the back and lungs. Stretcher-bearers came forward at once and attended to him.

I went on down to the trouble area and found our men were holding well and doing a lot of execution amongst the attackers. The enemy was halted by our accurate fire and their infantry was clustering behind a series of square-shaped manure heaps left by the French peasant farmers...I could see that the enemy infantry, well protected by the manure dumps here on the right, were vulnerable to fire from our position on the left. I got back as fast as I could and told the Northumberland Fusilier and his team to follow me. We climbed out of our low trench and crept up to some Nissen huts divided by a sandbag wall. Peeping over, as I expected, I could see that I had a clear view of about ten of the enemy closely grouped behind their manure heap less than fifty yards distant. I said 'Give me the gun'. I let loose with a half drum of murderous fire into the bunch. There was only one survivor who staggered away in the mist to report back. I then raised my fire to the groups sheltering further down.

Things were getting very critical with the enemy in our wire nearby and once again in the distance the division to our right was moving back and leaving us all but surrounded. Major Ormiston came at this time and ordered me to get all my men away in sections to our reserve line at Moislains and to stay until the last with the final section for cover. I did this in relays, meanwhile having all remaining ranks giving rapid fire at anything or everything they could see to hide our very real weakness. I then got the last section of ten men...We hopped out of the trench with the Hun infantry in our wire firing wildly. I put on a sharp pace and led at right angles to our trench. The enemy by this time had got his field guns in our wire on a rise and started firing point blank over open sights at us. They were so close and apparently excited that their aim was poor. One shell flew just over our heads, the wind of it lifting our helmets, and burst in front of us.

As soon as they had our range I took a sharp left incline to put off their aim. My squad followed closely. When I thought they had made their new correction I switched quickly to a right incline. I was right for their next shells burst where I had been. I repeated these tactics until our little squad reached a fold in the ground and out of sight of the gunners. I followed the low valley and was soon clear of artillery and rifle fire.

Soon after I caught up with our four stretcher-bearers carrying Captain Hallack... My job was to get my stretcher party back with as many fighting men as possible...The enemy following up were close behind us and firing as they came...We were too weary to do anything but just stand. Luckily one of our planes, seeing our plight, dived down and shot up our pursuers and soon quietened them. We again picked up the wounded man and moved on slowly in peace. We crossed a small running stream with difficulty, and moved up over a slight rise. Here at last we found the casualty clearing station we were looking for.

Handing over my casualty to the colonel in charge I asked him to direct me to Bouchavesnes Ridge. He said, 'It is nearly sunset; you will not reach it tonight. You must stop here'. I said, 'I am sorry, sir, I have orders to report to our Brigade Headquarters at Bouchavesnes Ridge'. I must have looked pretty gone in for he said, 'My orders are that you stay here tonight'. I had no option but to stay, much against my will. I was fortunate, for being very keen to rejoin I would very probably have reached them that night only to be surrounded and cut off the next day when the Brigade made their famous stand and fought to a finish.[1]

Whether it was hospital orderly, clerk or officer, all had contributed in achieving the impossible. The SA Brigade had escaped to fight another day. As the SA Brigade's divisional commander said. 'None but the best could have got through on the 22nd from the Yellow Line with Heudicourt in the hands of the enemy'.

1   Militaria 8/4 1978 p58-60.

Chapter 26

No monument at Marrières

After the strain of the past two days the SA Brigade went into Divisional Reserve. It was a sadly diminished band that dug in during the small hours of 23 March along the Nurlu-Peronne Road, south-east of Moislans on the right flank of the 27th Brigade.

The SA Brigade details with the transport under Lt-Col B Young, which included Lt G Lawrence, were fighting the rearguard action just described. The base details of other brigades along the line were likewise employed. Cooks, convalescents, lightly wounded, and sick were sent forward – anyone who could shoot a rifle. Casualties were heavy.

It was the intention that the SA Brigade would fall back slowly to the high ground east of Bouchavesnes. Although successfully achieved, the Brigade found itself in the front line again because of the wide front the 9th Division was attempting to cover. All the time the 21st Division on the right was withdrawing very much faster than the SA Brigade, in order to keep in line with the units on its own right. By mid-afternoon, the 21st Division had lost all contact with the SA Brigade, leaving a yawning gap of two miles towards the west on the SA Brigade's right flank.

In the entry to his diary dated 23 March 1918 Dawson expressed his growing irritation because of the rapid retreat of the 21st Division.

During the morning he went out with General Tudor to look over the ground the SA Brigade would retire to – as a retirement had been ordered. Dawson wrote in his diary:

> In the evening, I got orders to withdraw after dark to a position a mile or so further back getting in touch with the 27th Brigade on the left and also with the people on my right. I told General Tudor who came up to see me, that it was impossible to keep touch with a hare. He told me this position had to be held 'at all costs' and if the enemy took any part of it, he presumed we should counterattack.

309

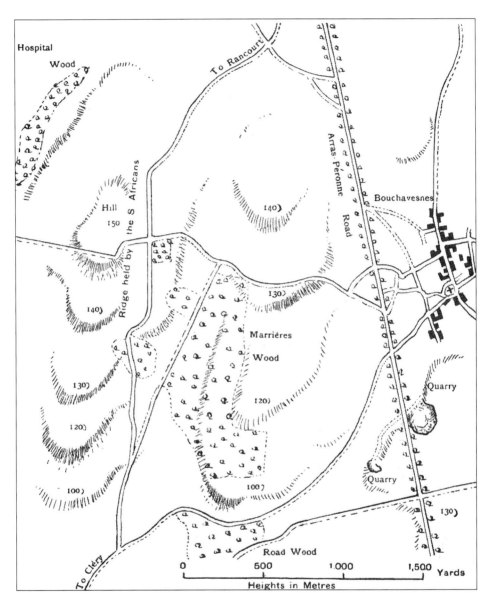

THE FIGHT AT MARRIÈRES WOOD.
(Union of South Africa and the Great War 1914-1918. Official History, 1924)

310

The move was effected without the knowledge of the Germans. That night they had heavily bombarded the area, by which time the SA Brigade was already a mile distant on their way to the Marrières Wood position.

By 3 a.m. on the morning of 24 March the move was complete. Dawson lay down in a trench and snatched about two hours' sleep, but was awakened by the cold and went round the position at dawn. Dawson wrote:

> It was quite a good one for holding on to, but not good for retiring from, I notified Division HQ where I was and said I was going to stay there whether the people on my right retired or not.

As the light improved, Dawson knew that he was no longer in touch with the left and right flank brigades of the divisions on either side of him. This would be a fight to the finish unless he was relieved or he could hold off the Germans until darkness descended that night.

Dawson realised that he must take the initiative. Although the 9th Division had been ordered to retire to a line that straddled the Bouchavesnes-Moislains Road on the ridge just east of Bouchavesnes, Dawson moved the SA Brigade further back. By bending his front he hoped that the problem of the exposed right flank would be solved or at least considerably reduced. The new position was on

The ravine at Marrières Wood that was at one time choked with German dead. (Photo: Cape Archives)

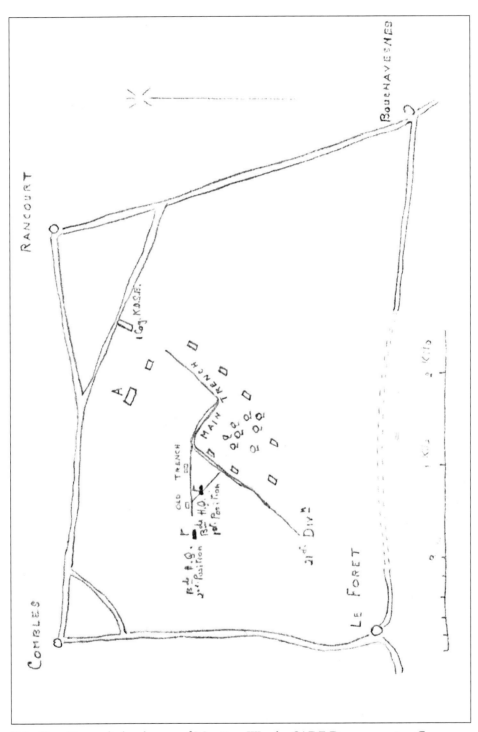

Brig-Gen. Dawson's sketch map of Marrières Wood – SADF Documentation Centre.

a ridge two miles west of Bouchavesnes just behind Marrières Wood. Before dark on the previous evening while he and his Brigade retired to this new position, the Germans had pushed across the Peronne-Nurlu road down a slope. Moislains and Heute-Allains had been taken by their advance troops as darkness fell.

It was Palm Sunday. Dawson visited Lieut-Colonels Heal and Christian, commanding the 1st SAI and 2nd SAI respectively, the remnants of the 4th SAI under Captain Bunce being attached to the 2nd. They were all told of Tudor's final instruction that the position had to be held 'at all costs'. Dawson explained the meaning of the expression. Without orders, definite orders, whatever was happening to the divisions on either flank of the SA Brigade, there was to be no retirement.

The South African position embraced an old line of disused trenches: one good trench and two bad ones and a considerable number of shell craters. The ground sloped downwards toward the east then rose to another ridge about 1 000 yards from the SA Brigade front line. This ridge provided the Germans with an excellent view as well as machine-gun positions. Brigade strength was 478. The total strength of 500 came through the addition of some men from Brigade HQ and a detachment of the 9th Machine-Gun Battalion attached to the SA Brigade. The machine-gunners would have been more numerous, but Dawson found that although there was a reasonable supply of Lewis gun drums, one section of the Machine-Gun Battalion only had four belts of ammunition between three guns, so they and their personnel were sent back to the transport lines. In certain cases officers had joined their battalions from the transport lines the previous day and the number of officers was out of proportion to other ranks. The 2nd SAI, for instance, had 14 officers with 110 other ranks. If the shortage of ammunition was not enough to confound the situation, there was no road to the position held by the SA Brigade, no communication with Divisional HQ and artillery except by runner and all 500 men were in a state of exhaustion from the stress and strain of three days without sleep. All rations were cold. Since the morning of the 21 March no hot food or tea had reached the Brigade.

In military parlance, to be selected for some desperately dangerous task that offered little chance of survival or ultimate success was known as a 'forlorn hope'. The SA Brigade had been selected for just such a task. They filled the breach between General Gough's Fifth Army and General Byng's Third Army. It was at this point that German General Von der Marwitz intended to drive a wedge between the two armies by continuing his flank advance. There could be no reinforcement from the remainder of the 9th Division as they had been detached to fight in the Third Army sector.

At about 9 a.m. Von der Marwitt's grey tide moved forward. Over the crest

The last boxes of ammunition to get through to Marrières, 23 March 1918.
(Photo: Cloete-Smith Collection)

of the ridge to the east they flowed, a mass of blurred figures becoming visible through the early morning mist. They occupied a line 750 yards from the South African position. Having learnt from the previous days' casualties, the Germans were more prudent. There was to be no massed rush across the narrow valley floor followed by a climb up the other side. Their frontal attack was held up.

The Germans contented themselves with raking the SA Brigade with machine-gun fire, followed by artillery. At about 9.30 a.m. a British plane came over. The South Africans waved. They were not completely isolated. At 10 a.m. the British artillery opened up. The badly needed artillery support did not fall on the Germans but instead on the South African trenches! A messenger was sent back on the Brigade's last horse at 10.20 a.m. and at twenty minute intervals an officer was sent to tell the artillery that if they could not stop shelling them, would they stop firing altogether. When they did stop, the artillery did not resume so they had probably retired. The Brigade HQ trench was made quite untenable by the bombardment, so Dawson moved into a shell hole where he remained until the end. Whether or not the lone British aeroplane had mistaken the waving troops for Germans will never be known.

Miraculously, the very accurate artillery fire from the direction of the 21st Division caused no casualties. German artillery and mortar fire continued to harass the Brigade throughout the day with varying degrees of intensity while machine-gun fire swept the top of their trenches. An attack from the south was shot to a standstill at 11.30 a.m.

At about 1 p.m. the Germans launched a very heavy attack on the South African left front and flank from the north-east. Using incendiary shells, the German artillery had set fire to the tinder-dry grass. Under cover of this smoke screen and a very skilful combination of fire and movement the Germans worked their advance to between 100 and 200 yards of the South African line. For some hours all attempts to cross those few yards were frustrated by accurate and measured rifle fire. Because of the shortage of ammunition after the previous three days of fighting and no likelihood of replenishment, Dawson instructed all members of the Brigade to husband their ammunition and only fire at obvious targets. The Lewis guns were employed only when their use would prove decisive.

Soon after the commencement of the attack, a German field gun was wheeled forward by hand and the Germans attempted to bring the gun into action at a range of 1 000 yards. Such cool cheek incensed the defenders at first. Then the tension relaxed. The greater situation was forgotten for the moment. Entertainment was at hand. The battlefield was the boxing ring. The rifles of the South Africans were silent. Major Ormiston gave orders to Lewis Gunner J W S Jeffrey, 1st SAI. The German gunners were about to open fire, when a sharp rat-tat-tat-tat broke the silence. All the German gunners were casualties. A muffled 'Ah!' came from throats parched with dust and fatigue and then cheers.

There was a second round. Some time later, the Germans made another attempt. This time the action was more dramatic: a full team of fine horses at full gallop. The gunners and their gun bounced over the uneven ground. Lewis Gunner Jeffrey was waiting. His finger steadied. His aim was unerring. He fired. The team got out of hand. The .77 field gun overturned. Horses and men went down in a struggling mass. This sight greatly heartened the SA Brigade and cheers of jubilation once again rang through the South African line. For his efforts Jeffrey received nothing but Ormiston was awarded the DSO!

During this time the spirits of the exhausted men were given another tremendous fillip. A messenger from General Tudor at Division HQ arrived with the news that an Australian Division and some tanks had been ordered to take up a position 500 to 700 yards to their rear. Encouraged by the news, Dawson sent a message back, that as his men had so far repulsed all attacks he was going to hang on.

The Germans tried repeatedly to advance, but accurate rifle fire drove them back each time. All through this the bravest of the brave was Padre Hill. Only that morning had he come from the rear, sensing instinctively his place during this time of trial.

Sgt W Wilson, 1st SAI, wrote:

> He calmly walked up and down the ranks, offering men cigarettes, mouthing words of good cheer, and encouraging everyone to still greater efforts. He told them what was happening. He had faced an ordeal few men would have volunteered to undertake, so great were the odds against him coming out alive.[1]

At one time in the front trench where the artillery bombardment was at its heaviest, only two men were left alive: Padre Hill and a private of the 1st SAI. Two shells burst on the parapet as if to preface the third that must land in the trench. The man said: 'I have been praying hard for the last four hours.' Padre Hill answered, 'Then you have beaten me at it.' Like Hill the man's prayers did not fall on deaf ears.

Although making no headway in front or to the north or south, the Germans were gradually working round the SA Brigade flanks. Machine-guns were directing their fire into the South African position from three sides and for the first time rifle fire was heard from the rear. Dawson recorded his personal situation at the time, while firing a rifle alongside his men.

1   St John's College Archives.

All the afternoon the shell fire was very heavy. The 5.9-inch batteries searched up and down our trenches and shells kept bursting so close to my shell hole that they positively hurt my ears. A wounded man who was crawling into my shell hole was hit by a bullet fired from the west and falling into the shell hole died there. One bullet went through the stock of my rifle.

The whole position was enveloped by smothering fumes of high explosive accompanied by clouds of choking dust.

Twice before 2 p.m. the Battalion commanders had visited Dawson and reported that the men were behaving magnificently, but the shortage of ammunition was becoming serious. The bodies of the dead were stripped of ammunition. The wounded passed forward what rounds they carried. Men not in the front line or not having occasion to use their rifles handed their ammunition to those who were in need of it. A man with both legs shattered, sat in the trench and refused to allow his wounds to be bound up. With a smile on his face he passed up his ammunition, clip by clip until his supply was in safe hands. The old trench which led to the shell hole in which Brigade HQ was situated, was used by the wounded to leave the battlefield. All those, however, who were not too badly wounded to use a rifle, Dawson stopped and sent back to the front line. No man showed reluctance to comply.

By 2.30 p.m. the German efforts elsewhere had borne fruit. Combles to the north with Clery and Peronne in the south were now in their hands. The 21st Division had disappeared from the scene and now the two other brigades of the 9th Division in the Third Army sector on the South African left were in full retreat. A South African officer and twenty-five men on the SA Brigade left, assuming that a general retirement had been ordered, started to withdraw at the double. This took place about 150 yards from Dawson's shell hole, in which Brigade HQ was situated. Recognising the danger, Dawson sent Major Cochran, Brigade Major Beverley and RSM P Keith, 4th SAI, to stop the movement. The activity in the area brought down a hail of fire from the German positions. All three men behaved in a conspicuously brave manner. Regardless of the concentrated machine-gun fire, they stopped these men and directed them into a position facing north, one hundred yards from Brigade HQ.

That was Dawson's view of the episode, but Cpl A W Philip, 4th SAI, in a support position on the left front took part in that withdrawal which was stopped and he observed Major Cochran's death.

The Germans came within rifle range under cover of a smoke barrage. We opened fire. They began outflanking us on our left. The order was given to retire 200 yards to the left. We made a dash for it four at a time. Several were hit. In the middle of all this I had an unpleasant encounter with a mad major. The two of us, obeying orders, dashed out across the open and reached a shell hole a few yards behind the rest. Major Cochran suddenly came upon us brandishing his revolver. To our great surprise and chagrin he accused us of cowardice; did we consider ourselves worthy South Africans running away from the fight; who gave us the order to retreat; he meant to shoot us there and then, it was what we deserved; I tried to explain, but realised that he

Cpl A W Philip, 4th SAI. (Photo: Transvaal Scottish Regimental Museum).

was quite mad. At this point, fortunately for us, he decided to find the officer who gave the order to retire and shoot him. He strode off. Thousands of bullets were whizzing round. Within a minute of his leaving us, we saw him fall, shot through the head (fatally wounded). We were [then] scattered about in shell holes, firing at any German who showed his head.[1]

Major Ormiston, realising the danger on the left flank, took forward twenty-five men to protect the area marked 'A' on Dawson's rough sketch of the South African position (see page 312). While making this move Ormiston was dangerously wounded and lay in the open for two hours until brought in.

The defenders still held the superiority of fire enabling them to show their heads while the Germans dared not expose themselves.

A new threat had developed at the time of Ormiston's forward move. Numbers of Germans were within 200 yards of Brigade HQ. Dawson sent Lt A E Cooper, 2nd SAI, and twenty men to take up a position one hundred yards north of Brigade HQ where, from a series of shell holes, an effective fire could be brought to bear on the Germans. Cooper's casualties were heavy and he was

1   Diary of Cpl A W Philip, 4th SAI, in possession of the Transvaal Scottish Regimental Museum.

frequently reinforced. Dawson related how some while afterwards Cooper had reappeared,

> looking as white as a sheet, and saying he had been hit in the chest. It was found that the bullet had hit his box respirator and given him a heavy blow in the chest, but had not gone through. Cooper sat down till the colour returned to his face, when he said 'Now I'm going back.' Out he went over the open and rejoined his men. Almost ten minutes later a man came in and said: 'Lieutenant Cooper is killed. A piece of the last big shell hit him.'[1]

Protecting the front on the reverse side of the South African position were the 4th SAI. 'A' and 'B' Companies were in support under Capt B H L Dougherty, who had been sent from Brigade Transport lines to command the remnants of the Scottish. On the reverse right was Lt H W Backeberg with 'C' Company; 2/Lt C G Mason with 'D', and some snipers and other odd men, was on the left. Both officers were soon wounded and on their way back to the rear. This was Backeberg's fifth wound. He thus escaped capture and survived only to be killed by a striker's dum-dum bullet while serving as a company commander with the Transvaal Scottish at Dunswart, Benoni, east of Johannesburg during the 1922 Revolt. Capt Fred Peacock, 4th SAI, with 2/Lt G A Leighton saw Mason and Backeberg pass. Peacock recorded the event in his diary kept during the battle. His brief pencilled notes say it all.

> We are being outflanked under cover of a smoke barrage and are preparing to fight to a finish. 4 p.m. This is hell. Being heavily shelled and MG fire is terrific. My men are falling fast all round me. Am still quite cool and confident. (Lt R J) Read joined me at 4.30 p.m. Says I am being reinforced.[2]

The Brigade was surrounded, yet it seemed relief was at hand. Dawson had been growing more despondent, but his gloom was suddenly dispelled. His diary recorded how, just before 3 p.m,

> ...some of the men on this side got up and ran back saying. 'The Germans are retiring! We can see some of them surrendering. Our men are coming up!' The revulsion of feeling was tremendous, and I at once sent more men

1   Document provided by Mrs W Winter.
2   Diary of Capt F Peacock in possession of the Transvaal Scottish Regimental Museum. Peacock had never applied for his war medals. This I persuaded him to do. They were mailed directly to the Transvaal Scottish Regimental Museum as Peacock returned to Britain shortly after presenting the diaries to the Museum.

out on the north side (of my HQ) to fire at the retreating enemy, who presented an excellent target. The report was, to some extent, corroborated by the fact that the enemy artillery suddenly lengthened its range and put down a heavy barrage some five hundred to seven hundred yards to the west of us.

Then Dawson's hopes were dashed. The German retirement had been caused by misdirected fire from their own men on the west side being mistaken for British reinforcements by the Germans in the east! The barrage had resulted from the same misconception. The men seen surrendering were actually South African wounded caught on their way to the rear.

Lt-Col Heal, commanding the 1st SAI was killed. He had been twice wounded already, but had refused to leave his men. One of his officers wrote:

> By this time, it was evident to all that we were bound to go under, but even then Colonel Heal refused to be depressed. God knows how he kept as cheery all through that hell; but right up to when I last saw him, about five minutes before he was killed, he had a smile on his face and a pleasant word for us all.[1]

In a report prepared by Dawson and submitted on 8 January 1919 he wrote:

> I did not see Lt-Col Heal again, but about 4 p.m. Lt-Col Christian came to my Bde. HQ and told me he was afraid we could not hold out much longer. The strain was beginning to tell and the ammunition was all but exhausted. The MGs and all the Lewis guns were out of action. The artillery fire had been incessant since 9 a.m. and exceedingly heavy. It was of sufficient intensity in all parts of the field to necessitate the frequent cleaning of rifles, on account of the falling dirt and dust. Batteries of 7.7cm, 10.5cm and 15cm were in action against us. Some of them were in full view and their fire was very accurate. A number of light trench mortars were also in action against the NE portion of our position, causing us heavy losses. Our casualties had been very high and the position was now only held by a few isolated groups of men. Control was impossible.
> I had no further hope of relief, but thought it possible that we might hold on till dark and then fight our way back. At 4.30 p.m., however, the enemy came into sight to the ENE of Bde. HQ, carrying out the final stage of the attack, in great strength and thick formation. From personal

1　Buchan, p186.

observation and subsequent investigation the number of our effectives at that time was approximately one hundred (of the original 500 early that morning), scattered over a large area. Had we had ammunition we could have stopped the attack, but under existing circumstances we could only fire a few scattered shots. The final rush was carried out by three battalions of fresh German troops evidently brought up for the purpose.

To assemble the remnants of the SA Brigade for a final bayonet charge was impossible without any assembly trench or communication trench. The unwounded men were dotted far and wide with dead and wounded around them, three to one.

Dawson's diary recorded his dilemma as to whether or not his men had reached the limit of human endurance.

> I kept wondering was I right to stay?...Anyhow, General Tudor had told me the line had to be held 'at all costs', and I had no other orders to retire...I quite realise that I shall probably be blamed for getting the remnants of the Brigade wiped out, by SA as well as by Division. That does not matter; I am confident that I did the right thing.

While these thoughts were coursing through his mind, Dawson was looking over the top of his shell hole. Suddenly he observed a white flag 500 yards to the east-north-east.

> I pointed it out to Christian and Beverley and they thought it was in our front line. I thought it was a German artillery mark as I did not see how our men could have got hold of any white material. A few minutes afterwards, I saw two flags.
> While we were looking, some twenty of our men got out of the trenches without arms and ran towards the flags, some of them with their hands up. At that moment large numbers of the enemy infantry appeared from the direction of the flags and some fifty or sixty of our men at once got out of the trenches and ran towards the west. It was out of the question to stop them, besides I realised that our power of resistance was at an end. We had held up the enemy for some seven hours, under a continuous and very heavy MG and artillery fire, without artillery or MGs of our own. The ammunition of the men in front was finished, and those behind had only some twenty rounds left.

Padre Hill also saw:

> ...the white flag tintacked on a ten-foot pole moving up our trench. It was a signal to the German gunners not to shell the German bombers who followed this white flag. Few (men of the SA Brigade) had the quickness to realise at once that the SAI had no such outfit. This ended whatever hope there was of a last set-to with bayonets against bombs, rifles and shells. Thus, on Palm Sunday, what was left of our Brigade suffered the worst experience that can ever befall a soldier.[1]

Dawson for a moment was at a loss.

> I was undecided whether to take up my rifle and run; to open fire on the enemy; or to await their approach and surrender. The first course was infra dig, the second would only have resulted in a large slaughter of prisoners, so I decided to take the third. Christian and Beverley were with me and about ten men. I walked out in front of them and felt no fear whatever.
> The first one that approached said something in German and went on. Many of them were firing their rifles as they advanced, probably at the men running away. One man came up to me – he was excited – said something in German and covered me with his rifle. I had no idea what he was talking about, but another pointed to my revolver and started unbuckling my belt. I then gathered what he wanted and took my equipment off which appeared to satisfy the truculent individual.
> I looked round at the men running away...In all my life I have never seen a more rotten sight – a crowd of fugitives without arms or equipment being mown down by MG fire...These men had borne the strain and fought as bravely as any troops have ever fought; but there is a limit to human endurance.
> Beverley and I got separated from Christian. We were told to go east but found an officer and asked him if we could look for Cochran's body to get his papers etc. He told us we could and sent a man with us. Several men told us to go back but we took no notice and the man with us explained matters to them. We soon found it and took his ring, papers, etc., including his will. We then went back to our own shell hole to look for two bottles of whisky we had left there, but it was gone. Cochran's cap was there, but I

1   Extract from the address delivered from the pulpit, St Alban's Cathedral, Pretoria, by the Rev Father Eustace Hill at the memorial service for the late General Dawson, on Sunday morning, 19 December 1920. *The Nongqai* February 1921 p73.

had not sense enough to take it in place of my steel helmet.

Several Germans who passed spoke to us. Two said: 'Why have you shot so many of us?' One said: 'Why have you kept us here so long? Why did you not surrender sooner?' A fourth said 'Now we will soon have peace,' to which I replied: 'Nein!'

What struck me about their attitude was that they no longer regarded us as enemies. They addressed one as 'Kamerad'.

The end had come suddenly all along the South African positions. On the reverse of the front line Capt Fred Peacock recorded in his diary: 'It's all up. I am surrounded by the Germans.' Pte R W Cruikshank, 4th SAI, witnessed the end.

> Andrew (Campbell) and I were still together in a shell hole near a quarry. Our ammunition was almost finished and we had fixed our bayonets for a final go, when suddenly a white flag appeared on a stick from the edge of the quarry. We wondered what this was for. After a short time a German officer stood up. I did not know we had a single officer left and he happened to be in a shell hole not far from us. He got up. I knew him quite well, Fred Peacock, and he walked towards the German who also walked towards him. He must have been able to talk a bit of English because the two men had a conversation. Fred handed over his pistol to the German officer and then came back to us and said that Jerry was prepared to take us prisoner provided we packed up now. Fred said he thought we should give up. We were finished in every way, completely played out and another ten minutes we would be wiped out. Our job had been completed and no more could possibly be expected of us. It was now 4.30 p.m. The white flag event is something I have never heard of before. It was the vanquished who might put up the white flag, not the victor. When it was decided we were giving up, I took my rifle and plunged it into the earth and walked away. The last I saw of my rifle was it swaying in the air as the bayonet was a foot into the ground and it was springy.[1]

Lt R J Read, 4th SAI, verified for himself the correctness of the surrender. He came to the conclusion that 'a bayonet charge was out of the question as we should have at once been swept down by machine-gun fire... I saw no less than ten machine-guns trained on us from one position.'[2]

News of Brig-Gen Dawson's surrender influenced the actions of others. Sgt W

1   From Pte R W Cruikshank's memoirs, supplied by his widow, Mrs Con Cruikshank.
2   WW1 Diverse Series, Box 32 SADF Documentation Centre.

Wilson, 1st SAI, wrote:

> The time came when we had no ammunition left and we stood helplessly facing the Germans without being able to resist them. Our end was near and there was nothing more we could do. At this moment a rush of men came into our section of the trench saying that General Dawson had been compelled to surrender. All told there were now only fifty of us left (in that sector). I put the matter to them that we had little hope of survival but that there was a wood not far behind us and that if we got to it we stood a chance of escaping.
>
> The men with me were all for attempting to escape rather than surrender... At a signal from me we started at a run for the wood. As though they had anticipated our move all hell burst out around us and within a few minutes the German artillery had blasted the life out of all but five of our party. It was a terrifying experience seeing our comrades torn and thrown high into the air, along with helmets and other equipment they were carrying. The five who reached the wood safely lay there exhausted.

After regaining their breath, Wilson and his four companions reached the edge of the wood. To their dismay they found a thousand yards of open ground had to be crossed before possible safety could be reached. This was in full view of the Germans. Wilson fell into a shell hole and was taken prisoner. He wrote:

> My four companions, had continued to run, but three had been shot and only one effected his escape. I saw him running, while riflemen and machine-gunners all around were trying deliberately to shoot him down as he tried to pass over a bare hill, it was dreadful to see.[1]

The only one to escape was none other than Lewis Gunner J W S Jeffrey, 1st SAI. The man who had knocked out two German field guns had no intention of being taken prisoner! On 30 November 1918 he returned to France after the Armistice, on successfully completing an Officers' Course in England.

Of those taken prisoner, Padre Hill was given the option of being released, but he refused. He felt he was needed in the prisoner of war camp. Earlier that day he had accompanied one of the officers who had made a journey through a storm of machine-gun bullets to inform the British artillery that they were firing on their own men. Then he had returned unharmed through even heavier fire only to see the surrender some while later. He was taken prisoner along with his batman who

1   St John's College Archives.

Back row (left): Lt R J Read and (right) Capt Fred Peacock who were taken prisoner at Marrières Wood. Photo taken at Maintz POW Camp. (Photo: F Peacock)

was carrying his artificial arm. The next months were spent in Upper Silesia at the Schweidntz prison camp. There he suffered great privations. He had found his imprisonment the most worthwhile experience of his whole life, as he was given the great opportunity for the apostolic work he had always put above all else. Nor would he accept offers of parole as he felt it was his duty to assist any prisoner with plans for escape. Hill was one of the first to be repatriated after the Armistice.

A senior German officer, Herr Rudolf Binding, also wrote of the surrender.[1]

> There was the corner of a little wood where the English put up a desperate stand... When the defence was broken down out from the lines of our advancing infantry, which I was following appeared an English General, accompanied by a single officer.[2] He was an extraordinary sight. About thirty-five years old, excellently – one can almost say wonderfully – dressed and equipped, he looked as if he had just stepped out of a Turkish bath in Jermyn Street. Brushed and shaved, with his short khaki overcoat on his arm, in breeches of the best cut and magnificent high lace-boots, such as only the English bootmakers make to order, he came to meet me easily and without the slightest embarrassment. The sight of all this English cloth and leather made me more conscious than ever of the shortcomings of my own outfit, and I felt an inward temptation to call out to him, 'Kindly undress at once,' for a desire for an English General's equipment, with tunic, breeches, and boots, had arisen in me, shameless and patent.
>
> I said 'Good morning,' and he came to a stop with his companion. By way of being polite, I said with intention: 'You have given us a lot of trouble; you stuck it for a long time.' To which he (jokingly) replied: 'Trouble! Why, we have been running for five days and five nights!'[3] I asked for his name, to remind me of our meeting, and he gave it. He was General Dawson, an Equerry of the King.

The ignominy of incarceration as a prisoner of war until hostilities ended was now Dawson's lot.

It is sad to relate that a career of so much promise was destined to be prematurely cut short. Always a man of action, Dawson took three months leave to go big game shooting in East Africa in 1920, while his wife was on a visit to England.

It was the call for action and adventure that prevented him from remaining inactive. During his enforced sojourn as a prisoner of war in Germany he was always planning to escape. He secured a compass with this object in view. A German search was ordered. Dawson asked permission to make tea and plunged the compass into a teapot, so avoiding detection. The big game shoot in East

1   *I Was There* Vol IV p1547.
2   Major Beverley.
3   I have inserted the word 'jokingly' as it retains the sense that Dawson later said he was attempting to convey to the German. Binding was too straightlaced to see that Dawson was 'having him on'.

South African Prisoners of War taken at Marrières Wood. Padre Eustace Hill is seated in the front row centre, Schweidntz Camp 1918. (Photo: M L Hill)

Africa was to provide him with a period of rest and recuperation from his long spell in a German prison camp, to restore his enfeebled health after experiencing the hardships inflicted on all prisoners.

Dawson enjoyed every minute of his hunting expedition until almost the end. Then there were the first indications that all was not well. Dawson refused to admit illness. Between periods of rest he attempted to carry on as normal.

As Major G H Kirkham, a fellow officer, expressed it:

'His spirit was too great for his physical strength and in a climate such as this he could scarcely hope to avoid disaster.' Dawson succumbed to enteric fever and malaria at Iringa on 26 October 1920. The garrison of King's African Rifles stationed there, buried him with full military honours.

Dawson, a product of Sandhurst, was only forty-seven years old and still had much to contribute when he died.

Brave, resourceful, cool and determined in the field: off the battlefield, he was courteous, considerate and a friend in times of pleasure and peril. A tribute written in 1920 referred to him as a 'prince of friends'. His men loved him. Only such leaders can hold a brigade, an army, together in times of death and defeat. He held Marrières not because he was told to – for he was great enough soldier to interpret always his orders with discretion but through his knowledge of the science of war he realised the indescribable importance of this point to the army at that moment.

With successes such as the destruction of the SA Brigade, Dawson's capture and the taking of thousands of other prisoners along the entire British front where the German offensive had pressed home, it seemed that Germany had won the war.

> The supreme features of this great offensive are, first, the immensity of its outward results compared with those of any previous offensive in the west; second, its ineffectiveness to attain decisive results.

wrote Liddell Hart in his *A History of the World War 1914-18*.

The psychological and physical effect on undernourished, deprived German soldiers, victims of the British naval blockade, was devastating. When they broke into the back areas they saw that the British were infinitely better fed and equipped.

Discipline disintegrated. Officers were powerless to move their troops forward once towns like Albert were entered. The German army began an unparalleled spree of drinking and looting. Useless trifles were seized and crammed into their packs. Madness and stupidity reigned supreme. What couldn't be carried away was destroyed. Sources of supply invaluable for the German advance were wrecked, such as a waterworks for the sake of brass taps. The success of the whole offensive depended on keeping to a very strict timetable. Once the intoxication for loot began to abate, the advance was resumed, but the precious hours squandered could never be regained. The Germans lost their chance of reaching Amiens before resistance to their advance could stiffen. When the chance of military success faded, a far more serious disintegration of German morale would start. The difficulties of reinforcement from fifty or sixty miles to the rear were just beginning.

However, all was now elation among the Germans. The disillusionment would come later.

As Rudolf Binding wrote:

> It is impossible to sleep for excitement. Really one would like to be after them day and night, and only longs that there shall be no rest until one can feel the first breath of the Atlantic in Amiens.

The Kaiser himself had come towards the front to bask in the great victory.

Maj-Gen Sir W T Furse KCB, DSO, a former commander of the 9th Division, forwarded a statement to General Smuts to be shown to General Botha, on 31 December 1918. It had been made by Captain G Pierson MC, Brigade-Major 48th Infantry Brigade in the 16th Irish Division, who was taken prisoner in the German advance of March. Furse felt that his statement would be of the greatest interest as it told how gallantly and magnificently the South Africans under Dawson had fought.

> After being captured at La Motte near Corbie I was taken to the German Battalion HQ for examination by an intelligence officer. The officer asked me if I knew the 9th Division. He said that the fight it put up was considered one of the best on the whole front and particularly the last stand of the South African Brigade.
>
> After this conversation I was sent to Le Cateau and on the way many German officers spoke to us, and all mentioned the splendid fight put up by the South Africans.
>
> On reaching Le Cateau I met two officers (British) who said that whilst their party was being marched to this place they were stopped by the Kaiser who asked if anyone present belonged to the 9th Division. The Kaiser then said that had all Divisions fought as well as the 9th Division he would have had no more troops to carry on his attack with...[1]

The SA Brigade had achieved much through their dogged stand. Lt R J Read, 4th SAI, observed: 'As we moved rearwards we found the enemy transport had taken a wide detour round us and were moving along the roads which shows the enemy must have been well past us on either flank.' They had provided the obstacle, the blockage that held back the flood. In doing this the SA Brigade had saved the situation for both the Third and Fifth Armies. General Byng's southern-most troops were at Rocquigny and Barastre, far off from General Gough's left. In fact, the other two Brigades of the latter's 9th Division had operated in Byng's own area. If Dawson had given up in the morning, disaster would have resulted. The link between Gough and Byng would have been severed completely. By holding on after the capture of Combles and Morval, Dawson provided time for a line to be established between Etinehem on the Somme River to Longueval in the north.

Dawson and the other survivors who had been taken prisoner observed with satisfaction that their stand of over seven hours had caused a mammoth traffic jam for miles and miles. The Bouchavesnes-Combles road was choked with an unbroken double line of transport vehicles, artillery and battalions of infantry

1   WW1 Diverse Series, Box 32, SADF Documentation Centre.

stretching from west of Bouchavesnes to Aizecourt le Haut. No advance along the road had been possible until the South Africans had been dealt with. The delay in the German advance had been of inestimable value to the British troops in the rear.

In the *Natal Mercury* of 3 August 1918, Maj-Gen Tudor commanding the 9th Division wrote:

> I think everyone should know how magnificently the South African Brigade fought.....The story of the magnificent stand made by the Brigade after it was surrounded can only be told by those who were with it to the last but this much is certain, that it was a shortage of ammunition alone which made the survivors surrender... They bore the brunt of the fighting on 21 and 22 March of the 9th Division... I am sure they are as proud to be in the Division as the Division is proud to have them. In this last battle they did more than any in the first days of the attack, and no troops could have fought more gloriously.

Medals for gallantry for Marrières are few. Too much was done by too many for recognition. Those who may have witnessed acts of bravery were either dead, wounded or prisoners of war.

Delville Wood has its memorial. There is none at Marrières. In terms of real achievement, there are probably few episodes that can equal the stand made by the SA Brigade at Marrières Wood on the Western Front.

Chapter 27

How young they died: The officer experience

To replace the casualties suffered, new drafts were constantly arriving. For every South African school that had its sons serving on one or other front, each post brought its own crop of letters. Heartbreak, humour and pride were the potential ingredients of each sealed envelope.

The schools kept records of their old boys during the Great War. They make astonishing reading. So many had become officers. Because the obstacles to embark on the great adventure were so great, those who made the effort were the best – men of calibre.

Those who did not were in that position through circumstance rather than choice. Once you were a member of the South African Infantry or South African Heavy Artillery, it was difficult to obtain a commission outside your unit. The South African authorities complicated matters for members of SA units serving in France to seek commissions in the British Army, because if such applications went unchecked, units would be denuded of their members. If, however, you had done your bit in France or had already served in East Africa or Palestine you had a better chance. A large number, of course, proceeded directly to Britain often with the added recommendation of being a veteran of the German South West Africa Campaign. Many were immediately successful in their acceptance on an officers' course. One Johannesburg school, for example, had 307 of its Old Boys serving in Europe, 86 in South African War Service Units; 110 officers in British units while by 1918 another 111 were in the RAF with commissions or as officer cadets. Only six were sewing in British units without commissioned rank.[1]

There were those in the South African forces in Europe who felt they had already put in their time and sacrifice. If there were no commissions in their own units, then they would be forced to look elsewhere. One who felt these sentiments was Pte F Addison, 2nd SAI, who had been wounded at Butte de Warlencourt.

After his discharge from hospital and a period at a convalescent camp at

1   King Edward VII School, Johannesburg.

Epsom, he returned to the SA Brigade Depot.

> I was sent back to Bordon Camp where I found I was a stranger in a strange company. All my former companions were either dead, in hospital, or transferred to other units...
>
> The men who had been to France were more or less excused parades on the barrack square, but we caught the fatigues in the same old way. I picked up used matches and cigarette ends off the roads, and swept the leaves from the paths around the officers mess, and even had to stand to attention with a broom in my hand while my brother Julian came past in a lordly manner without a sign of recognition, except to return my salute. For a week I was on officers mess fatigue which meant we had to do all the kitchen chores... Through a door I could see Julian at the officers mess tables guzzling good grub, and I had to wash his dirty plates.
>
> This was the last straw – so I made application to the proper quarters for a transfer to the field artillery, thinking I would get away from some of the squalor and dangers of the trenches. I later found out I had made a profound mistake. I do not mean that an artillery man has the same hardships as an infantry man, but he certainly slept on no bed of roses. While my papers were going through the red tape machine I continued to pick up match heads, wash plates and scrub out latrines.
>
> At last in March I got orders to report to an artillery school at Exeter in Devon and I left for that glorious county with mixed feelings. All my pals were gone, but I felt a pride that I had served with an infantry regiment as a very humble rifle bearer.[1]

In due course, as Addison puts it, 'Our name appeared in the *London Gazette* as temporary commissioned officers and gentlemen.'

Addison proceeded to take a humorous look at himself in his new found magnificence and enhanced status.

> But who is this artillery officer I refer to above? Can it be the same individual who earlier in the war lived and dressed like a Hottentot in the hot desert sands of South West Africa, and who later as a lousy private, sweated and trembled in the trenches in France? Believe it or not, this answer to a maiden's prayer is the very same human being. He is dressed up like a ham bone, his top riding boots, spurs, buttons and Sam Browne belt are gleaming, but he has not touched a thing himself; he now has a servant

1   Addison F, p2.

commonly known as a batman; he is in charge and responsible for a lot of valuable lives and equipment; he even has a banking account at Cox's Bank, and for all this he is paid ten bob a day, or fifteen quid a month, which is more money than he has ever seen in his life. He is addressed as mister, and the sweetest thing of all the battery sergeant salutes him and even calls him 'sir'.

There were others who were loath to leave their South African unit, so strong were the bonds of camaraderie and regimental pride. Sometimes they were lucky enough to receive a commission in their own unit. Pte G G J Lawrence, 1st SAI, had received his commission in the field. Pte Cyril Choat, 4th SAI, went on an officers' course. Before the opportunity had arisen, he had given the matter much thought.

In a letter to his parents dated 12 July 1917, he wrote:

> What is your opinion on the subject of commissions? Fred van Renen and Neil Johnson are going to register their names in this regiment for commissions and want me to as well, but I am not decided on the point, I think I'm too young in the first place and then one doesn't go to Blighty to an OTC in such a case. If I apply for a commission in some home regiment, and it's not difficult to get one, I go home, if accepted and have six months at an OTC and leave as well... Nevertheless I am quite happy and contented where I am and as long as I get through safely that is the main thing.

Choat was recommended for a commission and accepted to go to the Officers' Training Corps. He still hankered after flying, but he felt that 'it would be nice to come back to SA as an officer in the old regiment'. (4th SAI)

After two weeks leave Choat received a new uniform issue at Woking and then was sent to St John's College, Oxford for the start of his OTC course. What a contrast to normal army conditions:

3 October 1917

> Four of us S Africans have a room together and are very comfortable indeed... We have everything to make things homely... We have been given equipment, badges and white bands for our hats (to signify candidate officer status as is still the case today) and shall be getting the officers' style uniform in a few weeks time I expect. I've bought myself gloves, a stick and pyjamas and slippers to go on with.

We go through a four months course here I believe and each day have some duty to perform. Tomorrow for instance, I am first man to start, I am Orderly Officer and Company Commander in one, and have to act as such. I'll tell you how I get on later. We've been organised in sections and platoons and have been given dozens of books and tomorrow we start work in earnest....There are some beautiful old colleges, fine parks (and) the river Thames where plenty boating can be had. .. There are hundreds of cadets of all regiments and the RFC here. They look very swanky in their Burberrys and uniforms...We get 50 pounds for outfit. I have applied for RFC, only failing our own Regiment, which I think I shall get back to. The class of fellow in this Company and in all the OTC's in Oxford is very good. They're all gentlemanly fellows and of good families. It's really fine to see the fine young manhood in thousands like this.

...The strictest regular army discipline prevails and no details of correct procedure on parade are omitted. Each man is taught to give orders from a distance to a squad and to give clear commands. Then we have lectures on all kinds of things...I purchased a decent Burberry at £5.15s...There are fellows from every imaginable regiment, Australians, Canadians, New Zealanders, Scottish, etc. There are also a lot of American cadets training as Flying Officers I believe. They are a fine big lot, but their uniform is not great and they look rather sloppy.

5 November 1917

...When we get our new uniforms with spats, coloured hose tops, sporran etc., we shall look very swanky.

18 November 1917

...I have been let off all the early parades for next week as being one of the best turned out and best drilled cadets on parade last week. It will be nice to lie in bed and watch the others getting ready for parade...

5 December 1917

...We finish up with distance judging tomorrow...The week has been very interesting anyway and we have had inter-platoon competitions all through...One of the competitions we had was an attack practice by sections. Each section had to advance in rushes for about 200 hundred yards firing at disappearing targets and men were posted to throw tear gas bombs and smoke bombs at us to make us put gas helmets on. I had to fire a Lewis gun on the flank, and after about five minutes I got a stoppage which I repaired after a lot of trouble, lying in the mud with a gas helmet on and smoke flying about...We all got covered in mud but it was great fun all the same, and was done for the benefit of the Colonel...

9 January 1918

...Today we went out to a place near Oxford called North Henksey to do a few more problems in tactics. They give us papers explaining the supposed situation of our own and the enemy's troops and then ask us problems on how we would act under certain circumstances. We've had several similar field days...

27 January 1918

...Today we handed in our tommies' kit, had one or two tips given to us and were interviewed individually by the CO. Tomorrow we are writing the exam all day.

6 February 1918

...Officers will all get a good bonus after the war I expect and that will be enough to start me off again.
Well I passed the exam all right, not brilliantly, but about 20th out of 105...The dinner after the exam was a great success...The concert afterwards wasn't up to much...The results were given out at midnight and we all went to bed then.
Wednesday morning the colonel gave us a final address, and we were then free to go to our various destinations.

...Usually it's about a fortnight before the names appear in the Gazette and then one is given ten days leave to buy kit...

20 February 1918

...I am now a 2nd Lieut. I was gazetted to the S Africans on Saturday but...do not know if I have got back to the Scottish, though it's practically certain I have...I ought to have another ten days leave after I receive this notification to enable me to fix up kit etc.

And so this interlude, almost too good to be true was fast drawing to a close. The hospitality of Mr Urquhart, an Oxford don with South African connections, invitations to tea from Mrs Crewe, a South African, rounds of visits to family during leave, boating, hockey matches, shows in London – Doyly Carte Opera Company's *Mikado* – lunch at the Regent Palace Hotel and the camaraderie of the other members of the OTC at Oxford were all happy memories. Even now there were pleasures still to savour in London.

24 February 1918

...On Friday my instructions arrived. I am to report at Woking with all my kit on Thursday 28th...I left for London on Saturday at 9.5 a.m...I went to Robert Lillico's in Maddox St, off Regent St and there got measured for a tunic, tartan slacks and spats, and also bought a Wolseley Valise (a sort of combined ground sheet, bed and holdall), haversack, a pair of brogues and one or two other things, which I brought up with me. I then proceeded to Holts', the army agents, and got my joining papers and cheque book. Here, strangely enough, I encountered my old Company Commander, Capt Farrell, he who recommended me for a commission. He was very pleased to see me and was very decent altogether. I also met another of our officers, Major Clerk, whom I never knew very well before, but...he advised me to go and add my name to the list at the SA Officers Club...

SA Scottish,
Inkerman Bks,
Woking
5 March 1918

...It's jolly nice to be able to get up in the morning nowadays and find buttons, belt, boots, etc. all ready cleaned for you and to have beds etc. made for you. Quite a change from life in the ranks...
I have at last really commenced life as an officer...all the officers are very decent and soon make one at home...The new tunic and tartan trews have arrived and fit very well. I shall have a photo taken when I next go on leave which will be before very long...

While an officer cadet, Oxford January 1918 (L to R): Crawley (Rugby School); Mr Urquhart of Balliol College and Cyril Choat.
(Photo: Transvaal Scottish Regimental Museum)

11 March 1918

... You mustn't worry about me in France. I don't worry or even think of the possibility of being knocked out and I've every confidence that I shan't be. You mustn't imagine life out there to be what it appears from some accounts. It's not half bad and I can truly say I've been extremely happy in the trenches. You will see fellows, by no means brave ones, laughing and making jokes while shells are pounding on the parapet. The idea of being hit never enters their heads, and these are the people that usually come through. I wouldn't have missed this life for anything and though you may think it strange, I can never think of the time I have already had in France without many fond memories of absolute care-freeness, happiness and true comradeship...I've quite settled down now and everything is going well

17 March 1918

...A new draft arrived the other day and one left for France...

A day or two ago I had a letter from the Defence Dept saying I had fifty eight days leave on full pay due to me...I can take the leave on full pay when I return at the end of the war...

France
29 March 1918

My dearest Mother and Dad,

Here I am once again in this benighted land. We left Blighty on the 26th and arrived here today.

3 April 1918

...I will write when I reach the Regiment...I expect we shall be having a quiet spell for some time...

Choat's 'quiet spell' was the Battle of Messines Ridge. There were others who did not share Choat's optimism of France. It was all a matter of your own personal experiences. This determined your outlook. After coming through March 1918 and having survived the German offensive, Pte 'Bob' Grimsdell, 4th SAI, wrote: 'By this time I was getting nervous, twice wounded and with long service in the line, so when recommended for a commission,

2/Lt Cyril Choat 4th SAI (SA Scottish) studio photograph taken shortly before proceeding to France as an officer. (Photo: Transvaal Scottish Regimental Museum)

I applied to go into the RAF in April 1918.'[1]

To fly in a rudimentary flying machine with a flimsy structure of wire, wood and canvas without the safety measure of a parachute, required a different type of courage. Cpl Arthur Betteridge, 4th SAI, who obtained a commission in the RFC, began his officers' training course with the realisation that 'we were on the threshold of a new life, certainly a new type of training for a new type of warfare, so clean compared with what we had so far experienced on the ground. We were thrilled at the prospect.'[2] He was undaunted by the fact that during his training he collected dozens of snapshots of crashes. It was almost a daily occurrence to see posted up in the Orderly Room lists of pall-bearers for that day's funerals.

At least if you were a pilot, although on your own, you were largely responsible for your own survival. Combat was on a one-to-one basis.

The excitement and thrill of the war in the air acted as a magnet to a number of South Africans. Many joined the Royal Flying Corps or Royal Air Force, as it became in 1918, without previous military experience. Appendix B gives an indication of the very significant achievements of South African pilots.

On the Allied side five victories became the recognised criterion for 'Air Ace' status. The downing of a balloon or aircraft was given equal scoring value. Combat reports were completed by pilots and forwarded to Air Force Headquarters via the relevant Wing and Brigade HQ so that their contents could be checked and claims confirmed. It is interesting to note that the highest score for a British ace was fifty-seven and in second position D M MacLaren of Canada. A W Beauchamp-Proctor, a South African, shares the second highest score for the Great War, within the British Empire, with a total of fifty-four. Individual scores may differ slightly from various sources. Many brave airmen failed to achieve the required minimum number of victories to rank as an 'ace'.

In the air war and in many Imperial units – of the Regular Army, Territorials and Yeomanry – there were South Africans to be found, but in such units they were not easily identifiable. Many would be involved in the battle of Messines Ridge according to the particular role of their unit. However, it would be the fortunes of the SA Brigade at Messines that would steal the newspaper headlines.

1   'Bob' Grimsdell's reminiscences p11. Transvaal Scottish Regimental Museum
2   Betteridge, p112.

Chapter 28

Scraping the bottom of the barrel

At Marrières Wood the SA Brigade had been destroyed. What was left of the Brigade were the remnants of Captains Burgess and Ward's companies; the remainder were base details who had fought the rearguard action to cover the withdrawal of the SA Brigade to the Marrières Wood position. Some of the details had been sent there to reinforce the SA Brigade only to be killed or captured. Lt-Col Young in command of the details, had received a final message from Brigade HQ on 24 March: 'Retain all details with you for present and report numbers available to Division...'[1]

After Young had received a definite report of the capture of the Brigade, these remnants were formed into a Composite Battalion of 450 rifles under his command. Each company represented a Regiment of the SA Brigade.

After a good sleep, a wash and a shave, and a hot meal – the first in five days – the men were greatly refreshed. On 26 March they were ordered back into the line then being held at Dernacourt village on the river. Lt G Lawrence wrote:

> We marched back against the stream (of traffic) on the roads, choked with retiring troops and artillery. We held our heads up and marched proudly with a swinging step as if we were the Guards. I remember the retiring troops looking at us in amazement as if we were going the wrong way. We were singing as we marched, *Mein Gott, Mein Gott, what a bloody fine lot, the Kaiser he will say. Who are we? We are, we are, the SA Infantry.*[2]

The Composite Battalion held their ground in spite of persistent German shelling and machine-gun fire until they were relieved on 28 March. The 9th Division was now withdrawn from the line and sent north to become part of General Plumer's Second Army.

Young's men of the Composite Battalion had detrained in the Dickebusch area on 1 April to await new drafts. The SA Brigade depot at Woking was stripped

1   WW1 Diverse Series Box 32 SADF Documentation Centre.
2   *Militaria* 8/4 1978 p61.

of every man who could be found. Sergeant-Instructors, who thought they had a secure position in England, suddenly found themselves posted for Active Service. By the first week of April drafts of 17 officers and 945 other ranks had arrived.

Continuity was maintained by the appointment of Brig-Gen Tanner, as SA Brigade Commander. He had been commanding 8th Brigade and as a former OC of the 2nd SAI he was no stranger. The 1st SAI was placed under Lt-Col B Young; 2nd SAI under Capt L M Jacobs and 4th SAI under Capt J L Reid. The Brigade strength was now 39 officers and 1 473 other ranks. The 9th Division along with others which had suffered considerable losses during the recent German offensive in the south had been placed here to have a breather to refit and recover or such had been the intention. It was not to be.

Ludendorff had decided that the next move in his spring offensive was to fall on the twenty-four mile front between La Bassée and Ypres-Comines Canal. The British troops here included only one fresh division and five that were battle worn plus two Portuguese divisions. The latter held a front of six miles. When the German massed attack of nine divisions came, it fell on the Portuguese who were the most thinly spread. They were easily swept away. British intelligence had given ample warning of the movement to the north of German infantry and artillery by road and rail, yet General Headquarters were convinced that the attack would continue in the south on the Arras front. Thinking that Ludendorff would be as persistent in achieving his object as he had himself been at Passchendaele, Haig ignored the intelligence reports. In the south when the breakthrough had come in March, it had penetrated to a depth of forty miles. In the north a ten-mile German penetration was far more serious. Here there was only a narrow strip of land between the British lines and the English Channel with no space to manoeuvre. It was not a pleasant thought to be pushed into the sea.

Ludendorff saw this new offensive in Flanders more as a diversion to force the British to send reinforcements from the south. However, his easy initial success through the luck of his first blow falling on the Portuguese, forced him to pursue a strategy that he did not wholeheartedly support. At the time his irresolution was unknown to the British. The rapid German advance caused widespread alarm.

The actual German attack had been prefaced by an intense bombardment on 9 April 1918 before dawn. This had fallen on the eleven mile front between Armentières and the La Bassée Canal. Once again the weather favoured the Germans with a heavy ground mist to screen the advance. All that day the SA Brigade, in reserve, awaited developments.

The next morning, after a hurried breakfast the Brigade began a four hour march which took them through the villages of Voormezeele, Wytschaete, Wulverghem and Neuve Eglise. Brig-Gen Tanner wrote:

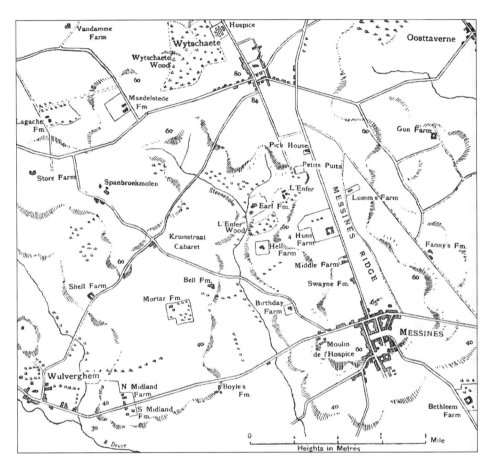

ACTION OF SOUTH AFRICAN BRIGADE ON MESSINES RIDGE.
(Union of South Africa and the Great War 1914-18. Official History, 1924)

The march of the South African Inf.Bde. from La Clytte to Neuve Eglise was one which is never likely to be forgotten...The crash of the enemy offensive which had been delivered that morning had thrown our line back to the line of the Messines-Wytschaete ridge... As a result a large belt of country previously unmolested became subjected to a terrifying storm of long range projectiles and the inhabitants, who up till then had continued to peacefully conduct their farming operations, were compelled to fly to areas beyond the range of the enemy guns.

As we approached Neuve Eglise, the road from Scherpenberg onwards presented a constant stream of fugitives, of old men, women, and children laden with what household goods they were able to remove in carts, wheelbarrows, and perambulators. The most pitiable sights were those of infirm old men, and women, being removed in wheel barrows, which were being pushed and pulled by women and children. The distress of these unfortunate people, flying for their lives, and with the knowledge that all their worldly possessions were being battered to pieces by the guns of the enemy, was clearly marked in every face.[1],

On arrival at Neuve Eglise, he received a message to report to 19th Division Headquarters under whose orders the SA Brigade would fall. The 19th Division, along with the 25th and 9th Division, were holding the Messines Ridge in a line just north of the River Lys. The South African battalions were ordered to have lunch at once and to move to an assembly point in the rear of North Midland Farm by 2 p.m.

Tanner returned from 19th Division HQ with a written order, all available information about the terrain from the OC 57th Infantry Brigade and details of artillery support. He was now ready to address his battalion commanders. They assembled in a Nissen hut for their briefing. Lt Geoffrey Lawrence, 1st SAI, was there and recorded:

> Brig-Gen Tanner told us that as a result of the attack that morning the position was very serious. The line had been broken and there was a mile gap between two British divisions. Our orders were to counterattack and re-take the ground lost and to hold it at all costs. Unfortunately there were no maps to be had. There would be one battery of New Zealander field guns to support us. Our objective was the Messines-Wytschaete road on the crest of the Messines Ridge. He finally asked if there were any questions. I jumped up and said as commander of the platoon on the extreme right,

1   WW1 Diverse Series Box 32 SADF Documentation Centre.

were there any landmarks that would serve as a guide. He gave me what he said were only very rough directions. We all piled out of the hut looking pretty glum at the idea of tackling a forlorn hope and got busy.

Our chances of surviving this attack were very slim...Talking to some of our officers, I said, 'I hope this time I shall get either a really good smack or not survive.' How can one explain the psychological state of a young man who has had two years of constant strain and been face to face with death so often? Probably the hardest strain is in being a young officer as fearful as any, who has not only to pretend to be unafraid, but has to be cool and calm in the heaviest shell fire and set an example that will steady his men.[1]

Because Lawrence was second in command of 'A' Company, he was called to their temporary orderly room by Captain Ward to help him deal with a very distressing case. A sergeant, who in pre-war days had been billed a 'strong man' in entertainments up and down South Africa and was the favourite of the crowds had, until recently, been a PT and bayonet instructor at Woking. Here he had led the good life in uniform, consistently evading the many replacement drafts called to France. Now with the urgent call for men, especially NCOs, to replace the Marrières Wood losses, no excuses were taken from anyone. His expertise as an instructor and tutor of recruits had been overruled by the greater need. He was sent out with this last draft. Now he was pleading with Capt Ward to be left out of the attack.

> To see a man, [wrote Lawrence], completely broken down, begging for his life was most upsetting. We, who were not too happy ourselves, had to refuse and tell him that we were all in the same boat...Finally, he was sternly told, 'You are a sergeant – pull yourself together and fall in with your platoon.'[2]

The sergeant went into the attack. Lt J Carstens, 1st SAI, kept his eye on him 'but it was not long before the fatal bullet struck and he fell almost within an arm's length of me. The bullet had caught him right in the middle of the forehead and he never moved again.'[3]

During June of the previous year the victory at Messines had established the British line two miles east of the Messines Ridge. By that morning of 10 April

1   *Militaria* 8/4, p64-65.
2   *Militaria* Ibid p64-65.
3   Carstens, p29.

1918, the German attack had forced back the line to the western slopes of the ridge. The SA Brigade was to attack the deeper gap that had been forced in the British line between Messines village in the south and Pick House in the north. The distance between these points was just over a mile. It was considered possible that isolated groups of British troops still could be holding parts of this line.

At 5.15 p.m. the battalions of the SA Brigade moved to the assembly line along the Steenbeck stream. Zero hour was 5.45 p.m. The 1st SAI was on the right attacking Messines village, with the 2nd SAI attacking the front between Messines and Pick House. The 4th SAI was in support of both battalions. One of their companies was detached to assist the 1st SAI. The spring day had clouded over and a slight drizzle with mist, partly screened their advance. Lawrence wrote:

> Before extending into attacking order the boys were singing, though well aware of being sacrifice troops with a grim future before them. The song they sang was, *'Goodbyee, don't sighee, wipe the tear, baby dear, from your eyee, – Goodbyeee.'* We passed over other front line troops dug into little slit trenches; they looked up and seemed astonished to see us moving over them into the open. When about 800 to 1 000 yards from the crest of the ridge and our objective, Captain Ward blew his whistle and gave the signal for us in conformity with the adjoining companies to extend. We formed into three lines, or waves, of attack. Captain Ward now came up to me and said, 'You know, Lawrence, this is not fair, you and I have been through it time and again – we can't go on like this and get away with it.' I said, 'I know, skipper, it's bad luck', and to break the tension suggested I should take the front wave and guide our right flank. He agreed and took charge of the second wave with 2/Lt L R Hopgood...We shook hands and all moved forward at his signal. Going forward at a sharp pace, something prompted me to do a thing I had never thought of doing before. I quickly stooped down and picked up an abandoned rifle and bayonet, slung it over my shoulder and carried on. This very likely saved my life for officers were always picked off first. Wearing, as we did then, a worsted star on a private's tunic I was not conspicuous when carrying a rifle.
> Machine-guns and rifle fire opened up on us. They had been holding their fire until now. The chattering machine-guns were sweeping first one way and then back. Men were dropping here and there. As the sweep of the machine-guns came on to me the bullets gave a clap like a whiplash in my face and then moved by, coming back and forth each time with that sharp crack. I moved as fast as I could as more and more men were dropping. I

went on until looking around I saw there were only three of us left in the front wave. I put my hand high up in signal for halt and dived for a shell hole. The two men on my right and a few yards behind unfortunately tried to come up in line with me. As I looked from the shelter of my shell hole one fell dead, the other ran up and stooped over the first to help, when he too fell dead on top of his pal.

I remember I had a small Scotch thistle growing on the edge of my shell hole and I tried to hide as much as I could behind it. I opened fire at once with my rifle at the Germans now only seventy-five yards distant, some of them standing up and firing. I accounted for five certainties very quickly and continued picking off more in the trench as I was looking down its full length. I then threw clods at the sergeant and two men in their shell hole on my right and told them to open fire. This they did with good effect. At this stage 2/Lt Clarke and a man from the third wave came up and jumped into cover near me. He told me Captain Ward and 2/Lt Hopgood had been killed and he thought all the other officers in our regiment were either killed or wounded. This left me in charge. We had now quietened down

Survivors of the 1st SA Infantry Brigade – members of Lt-Col Young's Composite Battalion resting by the roadside while on the march out of action at Dernacourt, before proceeding to Candas to rest, 31 March 1918.
(Photo: SA National Museum of Military History)

Another group of survivors of the SA Infantry Brigade near Albert, 31 March 1918, with 'Jackie' in his element. (Photo: SA National Museum of Military History)

the fire from the trench in front of us. I decided that as we had not reached our objective on top of the rise I had to get to the centre and organise a further attack.

I told Clarke and the others to open up with rapid fire to cover me. Leaving my rifle I ran across the enemy front to our centre. I jumped from shell hole to shell hole and reached a collection of broken-down walls where I found a young 4th Regiment officer with about twenty men. I suggested we make a dash forward to gain our objective. I was about to look over the wall we were behind when someone stopped me and said a man had just been shot through the head looking over. After talking things over a short while, I said, 'I will lead if your men will follow me'. They agreed. I blew my whistle, drew my pistol and set off into the open skirting a large shell hole on my right. I had not got more than forty yards when something hit me like a sledge hammer in my left thigh. It seemed red hot and spun me round completely before I fell I lay perfectly still, as I thought, for the second bullet. There was another big shell hole right alongside me so I gave a quick lurch and rolled down out of sight and into the green water

Albert Cathedral with its famous falling angel which the Germans finally demolished by shell-fire in March 1918. The year the angel fell, the men had it, the war would end. (Photo: SA National Museum of Military History)

at the bottom. I pulled myself out and on to the slope at the side above the water.[1]

The bullet, fired at short range, had turned on the thigh bone and gone through sideways making a fist-sized hole where it came out. Help came just before dawn, some ten hours after Lawrence had been wounded. After graduating from being dragged over the uneven ground of No Man's Land on his raincoat to a wheeled stretcher, Lawrence was abandoned whenever a known 'hot spot' was reached. The two stretcher-bearers dived for cover as shells rained down, then they resumed the journey at full speed. Before finally reaching the casualty clearing station and a welcome bed, several doctors had ominously sniffed the wound at dressing stations along the way to check for gangrene.

Soon, [Lawrence continued] I was taken into the operating theatre sited in a makeshift little room in which the doctors waded in blood in thigh gum

1   *Militaria* Ibid p64-65.

boots. I looked apprehensively at a great pile of legs and arms in the corner. When the very sweet sister came to give me chloroform I begged her not to let them take my leg off as seemed very likely in their haste to deal with gangrene cases.

With the front line nearby in danger of pulling back at any moment, casualties had to be summarily treated. She was very soothing and hoped they would just clear the gangrenous tissues in the path of the bullet. This was done and I next awoke in a hospital train that landed me in a Rouen hospital.[1]

Obviously Lt Lawrence could only give a view of the fighting in the 1st SAI area until he was wounded. The weak supporting fire from the New Zealand Artillery Brigade did nothing to discourage the many German machine-gunners and snipers established in the old strong points and shell holes. The South African advance was literally from shell hole to shell hole as this was the only cover towards that exposed ridge. Heavy fire came from the German positions at Bethlehem Farm on the outskirts of Messines village, which Lt Lawrence had encountered, as well as from Middle Farm, Four Huns Farm and Pick House. By 6.30 p.m. on 10 April, the 2nd SAI had nevertheless taken its first objective – the Messines-Wytschaete Road just below the ridge.

Shortly afterwards a company of 2nd SAI had taken Four Huns Farm, Middle Farm and Swayne's Farm with four machine-guns and fifty prisoners. Then 'D' Company 2nd SAI and a company of 4th SAI had pushed on ever further to take Lumm's Farm in the centre with two machine-guns as the prize. These positions had been taken in spite of the heavy machine-gun and rifle fire that swept the whole ridge as the South Africans advanced through the mist. Casualties were particularly heavy when the top of the ridge was crossed. Further advance was held up on the flanks by very heavy enfilade machine-gun fire from pill-boxes north of Messines village on the right and Pick House on the left. The latter proved too strongly held and was not taken.

Pte Y E Slaney, 4th SAI, a veteran of other battles since 1916, who had just rejoined the SA Brigade recalled going into action that day.

I, at that time, was an experienced soldier; we attacked in artillery formation, with no artillery support. We had in our force many rookies – their first action. I laughed at some of their antics, particularly on one occasion when they saw one of our men was killed and fell on the barbed wire, Jerry used his body as a target.

They shouted that he should be rescued. I shouted at them to stop being

1   *Militaria* Ibid p64-65.

fools. We then got the 'extend order'. I moved over. That is the last I remember of the action,...[until] a voice said: 'You poor bastard' and to someone else said 'Help me the bastard's bleeding to death'.

After pouring iodine over my wound they left me...Orders were (that) any wounded had to look after themselves...What happened during that period is very faint. I know I bled a lot, as I can remember emptying my tin hat which I had used in reverse as a pillow, of some of the blood which must have poured from me. Some hours after – it must have been hours – I saw about four men searching around very carefully. I lifted my kilt to use as a flag and fortunately they saw me...I was transported to the nearest Casualty Clearing Station where I was disrobed and medically examined. Not one louse was found on my body. NO BLOOD LEFT.

My parents received a telegram referring to me 'MISSING BELIEVED KILLED'.

The casualties of 'D' Company, 2nd SAI and the 4th SAI company had been light compared to those of the 1st SAI: all their officers were casualties. Capt A E Ward; Lieut C J C Griffiths and 2/Lt L R Hopgood had been killed while among the wounded were: Capts E J Burgess, W A Larmuth and G W Tobias; Lieuts G G J Lawrence and R E Neville; 2/Lts J Carstens, C F Christenssen and W W Clarke MM. The 2nd had been involved in particularly heavy fighting. They had

Messines Ridge – recaptured by the Germans, April 1918 – already devastated by the fighting of 1917. (Photo: Cloete-Smith Collection)

charged the Germans with fixed bayonets and driven them over the ridge, but on the east side of the village, as we have seen, it was another story. The 1st SAI had abandoned their position and concentrated on a line about one hundred yards west of the village because of the shortage of men.

In the centre of the South African line the right companies of 2nd SAI had not given any ground but nevertheless their effective strength had suffered fifty per cent casualties including 2/Lieut B Pope-Hennessy MC killed and Lieut D Jenner wounded.

During the night of Wednesday 10 April, the South Africans were holding a crescent-shaped position that straddled the Messines-Wytschaete road with its right resting on the western edges of Messines Village, through the Moulin de l'Hospice, Middle Farm, Lumm's Farm to the north and then back to Petits Puits with a forward post at Romman's Farm. The 4th SAI had reinforced the depleted 1st SAI, soon making their presence felt.

Some of their men were responsible for bringing down a German aeroplane which had been machine-gunning the South African line, presuming immunity. The Lewis gun, directed by this group of kilted Transvaalers, set the 'plane's petrol tank on fire and it landed in flames just across the German line. Two very scared and singed German aviators tumbled out of their burning wreck amid brisk rifle fire from the South Africans.

On the afternoon of 11 April, German General Sixt von Armin launched fresh attacks in great strength on the British front at Messines. The SA Brigade holding the position between Middle Farm and Petits Puits came under heavy attack and the 2nd SAI was pushed back to a line 600 yards west of and parallel to the Messines-Wytschaete road. With the wounding of Capt L M Jacobs that morning, Capt L Greene was now in command of the 2nd SAI. He launched a counterattack along with men of the 4th SAI under Lt S G Thompson. The lost ground was regained. The success was not without casualties.

One of those to fall with a machine-gun bullet through his hips, penetrating the bladder, was 2/Lt Cyril Choat, 4th SAI. He was taken into a captured pill-box, cheerful all the time. He had his wounds dressed and was carried out on a stretcher. His debut as an officer leading his men into action had been ended in its first moments. On 27 March he had telegraphed his parents in East London from Cambridge, England: 'Leaving Choat'. When they received his telegram on 12 April he was already a casualty, having been admitted that day to the New Zealand Stationary Hospital. On 16 April he wrote his last letter to his parents telling them that

they are looking after me splendidly in this place, and I am quite happy to

Wounded from the battle coming down the line.
(Photo: SA National Museum of Military History)

> be here – you must not worry about me – I'll be all right. I have written a
> note to Aunt in England to let her know I will write a longer note as soon
> as I am more fit.
>
> Your loving Son
Cyril

The matron had hoped that he would recover but he died at 12.30 a.m on 24
April. She expressed surprise 'that he lasted so long – it was just his spirit that kept
him up.' And then the letter from the hospital chaplain. How many millions of
similar letters were written during those four years of waste and needless suffering?

> ... The wound became septic and as you know in such a case there is
> then very little hope. He put up a good fight but grew gradually weaker.
> Needless to say, we did everything possible for him – both surgically and
> for comfort's sake. He suffered a good deal of pain, but was very patient
> in it all and didn't complain. I saw a good bit of him but he was not very
> communicative, doubtless on account of his pain. The night before he died,

he asked me to say a prayer with him which I did. He knew he was very ill but did not expect to die although he was quite ready.

He passed away quietly and without pain.

His body is buried in Longuenesse Military Cemetery, St Omer Plot V Row A Grave 69 and a cross has been erected.

I am yours sincerely
S Parr
Chaplain.

Besides the letters there was finally the heartbreak of the arrival of a small strongly-made cardboard box with the label: 'OHMS The High Commissioner for the Union of South Africa, 32 Victoria Street, Westminster SW1, 3906 2nd Lieut J C Choat, 4th Battn S. African Inf. per Small Effects.'

Capt J H Begg, 4th SAI, also wounded in the same attack as Choat, recalled how the Germans had twice turned and run in the face of a bayonet charge. This success was short lived. Messines Ridge was now lost once again, but the line still held.

Because the Germans had now taken Hill 63, south-west of Messines Ridge, it was necessary for the 57th, 108th and SA Brigades to withdraw to a line running along the ridge west of Steenbeck Stream. The withdrawal was completed with very few casualties by 5 a.m. on the 12 April.

Throughout that day the Germans rested. Having regained the Messines Ridge they made no attempt to carry forward the attack. From their vantage point they contented themselves with inflicting casualties from a distance. On the night of 13 April, the SA Brigade was relieved in the line.

Out of the 39 officers and 1 473 other ranks of the SA Brigade, losses for the four days under review were as follows:

	Officers	Other Ranks
Killed	4	82
Died of Wounds	1	8
Wounded	16	251
Wounded and Missing	3	
Missing	2	278
TOTALS	23	616

GV RI

Dieu et mon droit

HE whom this scroll commemorates was numbered among those who, at the call of King and Country, left all that was dear to them, endured hardness, faced danger, and finally passed out of the sight of men by the path of duty and self-sacrifice, giving up their own lives that others might live in freedom. Let those who come after see to it that his name be not forgotten.

2/Lieut. Joseph Cyril Choat
4 Bn., S. African Inf.

Memorial Scroll, 2/Lt J C Choat. (Transvaal Scottish Regimental Museum)

The majority of those listed as missing were later found to have been killed. John Buchan recorded that in spite of these losses, 'as the men marched back from the line, their spirits seemed to be as high as when they entered it'.[1] They were no beaten army but had every reason to be proud. The SA Brigade had succeeded in filling the mile gap lost to the Germans between two divisions. The gap was held for thirty hours against heavy attacks until relief had come.

Recognition of this achievement was expressed in messages from official quarters such as IX Corps and 19th Division Headquarters. Perhaps the most surprising yet telling tribute comes from Winston Churchill in his book *The World Crisis:*

> The whole front to the southward having been beaten in, its right flank was turned back and the resurrected South African Brigade on the afternoon of the 10th drove the Germans from the Messines crest. All efforts to oust this division from the position into which it had clawed itself, failed. Thus the buttress stood immovable although the wall between them was completely battered in. Upon this fact the safety of the whole front and the final result of the battle unquestionably depended.

And then there is a postscript to the whole episode from Captain Frank Theron, (the Major-General of World War II), a son of the veld, of Boer descent. His elation is revealing as it shows how the South African Brigade had been responsible for welding a national, a South African pride in its soldiers. This spirit would carry South Africa into a Second World War where there was no thought of Englishman or Afrikaner but of South Africans: Springboks one and all. Theron, a staff captain, wrote from France to a fellow officer:

> ...By Jove, they were grand. I count it one of the greatest privileges in my life to have been associated with this Brigade and its traditions...and we can never be too proud of them. They drove the Bosch [*sic*] before them...They were frequently attacked and heavily shelled, but never gave ground; and of all the brave spirits, Greene – old Colonel Greene's son, of Natal – with the remnants of the Second was the outstanding personality. He hung on to Hell Farm through thick and thin, and the Bosch could not shift him. He came out last night with 130 men, and was prepared and cheerful to carry on in the new position. He ought to get the DSO at least![2]
> Jenkins and I ran the advance Brigade Headquarters – getting in the

1   Buchan, p205.
2   Greene was awarded the Military Cross.

messages, sending up ammunition, SOS rations, and that sort of thing; switching barrages.

Tanner has been magnificent. He was so proud of the Brigade and pleased with the recruits, and it must have been a severe shock to him when he was ordered to counterattack and restore the position at Messines...He never flinched, never lost courage, and maintained his good spirits...His message to me through the Brigade Major was when retirement was general that the Brigade was to maintain its ground, and I sent out a message to the units 'General Tanner has ordered that the South Africans must hold their positions at all costs', and thank God they did until they were ordered to retire to conform to the movement on the right. General Plumer wired tonight that he was very pleased with the way his Army had stood the shock of the Bosch onrush, and specially singled out the South Africans for praise of the splendid work they have done. So tell the people in South Africa to be proud of their Brigade, and do all in their power to keep it going, – *sê ons trap vas en is vol moed.*

I don't know what will happen to us, as we are only about 600 strong now, all told...

Capt Theron and indeed many others had every reason to ask that question. Once again the SA Brigade had been reduced to battalion strength in a space of three weeks. The old Brigade of Egypt and Delville Wood days had disappeared from the scene at Marrières Wood. Around the base details and lost men who had become detached during the March offensive and then rejoined had been added every man from the depot at Woking. The resurrected Brigade had suffered casualties that could not be replaced. There were no reserves to draw on.

Chapter 29

From brigade to battalion

From La Clytte the remnants of the SA Brigade were given marching orders. In this period of alarms and activity there could be little hope of rest. What Ludendorff had begun as a diversion now developed into a full-scale offensive. The pressure on the British front did not let up.

On the way to the area of Reninghelst, some two miles north-east of La Clytte, the Brigade was heavily shelled. One of the casualties was Jackie, the Brigade baboon-mascot. His earlier history has been told in previous chapters. Jackie was seen frantically trying to build a wall of stones about himself, as shelter from flying shrapnel, while shells were bursting all around. The wall was never completed. A jagged piece of shrapnel wounded him in the arm and another in the leg. At first Jackie refused to be evacuated by the stretcher-bearers; he tried vainly to continue with his wall, hobbling around in excruciating pain, on what had been a leg.

The remarkable story is best told in the words of Lt-Col R N Woodsend of the Royal Army Medical Corps.

> It was a pathetic sight: the little fellow, carried by his keeper, lay moaning in pain, the man crying his eyes out in sympathy, 'You must do something for him, he saved my life in Egypt. He nursed me through dysentery.' The baboon was badly wounded, the left leg hanging with shreds of muscle, another jagged wound in the right arm.
>
> We decided to give the patient chloroform and dress his wounds. If he died under the anaesthetic perhaps it would be the best thing; as I had never given an anaesthetic to such a patient before, I thought it would be the most likely result. However, he lapped up the chloroform as if it had been whisky, and was well under in a remarkably short time. It was a simple matter to amputate the leg with scissors and I cleaned the wounds and dressed them as well as I could. He came round as quickly as he went under. The problem then was what to do with him. This was soon settled by his keeper: 'He is on army strength'. So, duly labelled, number, name, ATS injection, nature of injuries, etc. he was taken to the road and sent by

'Jackie' after the amputation of his leg, with Lt-Col R N Woodsend, Royal Army Medical Corps. (Photo: Author's Collection)

a passing ambulance to the Casualty Clearing Station. It was several days before I could visit the CCS. 'Oh yes', said the commanding officer, 'he was pretty bad when he arrived, but we put him to bed and that night when I was doing the rounds he sat up in bed to salute me. He went down to the base hospital the next day.'

This hospital was on the French coast and it was a common sight to see Jackie frolicking on the beach with the other patients.

It was the end of active service for Pte Albert Marr, Jackie's keeper, and Jackie, with the war drawing to a close. They received much publicity in newspapers such as *The Times*. On September 28 the two friends were at Inkerman Barracks, on the occasion of the 2nd SAI Reserve Battalion's sports day. During the course of the afternoon, Maj-Gen Sir H T Lukin KCB, DSO, who had commanded the SA Brigade in France, introduced Jackie as the mascot of the 3rd SAI. Private Marr went round the ring of curious onlookers and collected funds for the Red Cross.

The wounding of Jackie and Pte Albert Marr, his keeper, being thrown into the air by the explosion of the same shell, was one of thousands of similar incidents in those eventful days of April, 1918.

'Jackie' and Pte Albert Marr 3rd SAI. The famous postcard that raised hundreds of pounds for Red Cross funds. (Author's Collection)

Jackie's official army identity disc. (Author's Collection)

At Reninghelst on the evening of 15 April, the SA Brigade received orders from 9th Division Staff to move at an hour's notice to take up a position on the Wytschaete Ridge in the Vierstraat line between La Polka just east of Kemmel village and Desinet Farm. The panic was on. Wytschaete village had been lost to the Germans. By 12.30 p.m. on 16 April, the depleted SA Brigade – the all ranks strength of each regiment was as follows: 1st: 250; 2nd: 280; 4th: 250 – had occupied the front line. For the next two days elements were detached to strengthen other brigades and divisions, when needed.

By the 18 April, although not realised at the time, the German storm had subsided. It was only on 29 April that the German offensive was abandoned.

The whole SA Brigade was reunited at Hopoutre on 23 April. Since 21 March, from a position where the SA Brigade had been over strength, its numbers had been consistently whittled away. Because of the lack of sufficient reinforcements it was decided to form one composite battalion which included a Light Trench Mortar Battery. Command of the new SA Composite Battalion, the old Brigade in miniature with a 1st, 2nd, 3rd and 4th Company, constituted of men of the lst, 2nd, 3rd and 4th SAI respectively, was given to Lt-Col H W M Bamford MC, 2nd SAI. Major H H Jenkins, 1st SAI, was second-in-command and Lieut T G McFie MC, 4th SAI, the Adjutant. The work to re-form and re-fit began. The disbanded 3rd SAI enjoyed a brief reincarnation in the 3rd Company. Pipers N McNeil and M Strang were given sets of pipes of two pipers who had been elsewhere when all the 4th SAI pipe band instruments were destroyed. While the rest of the band languished at Rouen, McNeil and Strang kept the 4th Company of the Composite Battalion marching to the rousing notes of the bagpipes. Drafts from England brought the strength of the Composite Battalion to 59 officers and 1 527 other ranks – more than the SA Brigade had totalled when it went into action at Messines Ridge.

Although still known as the SA Brigade, the other two units which constituted the 'SA Brigade' were 9th Bn Cameronians and 2nd Bn Royal Scots Fusiliers. In spite of the old name, for the moment, the history of the doings of the SA Brigade was actually that of the Composite Battalion. Brig-Gen Tanner remained the Brigade Commander. That the name 'South African Brigade' was to remain was the greatest possible tribute to the Brigade's reputation.

In a last vain hope to broaden his salient and show some return for the very heavy loss of German lives in the Lys offensive – one German war cemetery at Sailly sur Lys contained 5 000 German graves alone – Ludendorff now attempted to seize Kemmel Hill that overlooked the junction of the French and British lines.

This, supposedly, was the weakest point in the British line. At first Ludendorff seemed to be making progress. Launching his attack in the early hours of 25

April, by 10 a.m. he had taken Kemmel village and Kemmel Hill itself, although some pockets of French troops held out. The 9th Division was later forced back to Vierstraat and pressure on the 21st Division had caused a general withdrawal of the British line to La Clytte in the south, through Ridge Wood, Voomezeele, to Hill 60 in the north.

The Composite Battalion strength here was 23 officers and 718 other ranks. Two days of heavy shelling had resulted in sixty casualties. During this period in support the battle raged on. The Germans were repulsed in their attack of 29 April.

The Composite Battalion relieved the 2nd Royal Scots Fusiliers on the 30 April. The South Africans held one slope while the Germans held another. The crown of Kemmel Hill was unoccupied. The vigorous British shelling kept the Germans from it. Snipers and machine-gunners on either side showed no mercy to the ordinary combatants, but the wounded, including several Springbok officers, owed their lives to the fact that snipers of both sides refrained from firing on wounded men who were moving towards the rear. Misty weather and poor visibility saved the casualty figure from rising beyond the 200 mark because the Germans on Kemmel Hill had a perfect view of the South African trenches. Two officer casualties during this time were Lieut B W Goodwin and 2/Lt E C Addison who were killed by shells.

Activity now moved to the south with Ludendorffs big push on the Aisne and then on the Marne, but the 9th Division remained in the north as part of General Plumer's Second Army. After nine weeks of action the divisions stationed in the northern area needed a rest. Nevertheless throughout this period there was uncertainty as to where the next German blow would fall.

The Composite Battalion was withdrawn on 5 May to rejoin the 9th Division with its two new sister battalions. The 9th Division front stretched from Locre north of Bailleul down a line west of Méteren village to halfway between Strazeele and Merris. The 'SA' Brigade was holding the area opposite Méteren between the Méteren-Cassel road to the Méteren Becque stream that ran south-east of Flêtre. Méteren, was held in strength by the Germans.

On 24 June, during the Composite Battalion's second stint in the front line, they provided two companies to co-operate with the 1st Australian Brigade in a minor operation to adjust the configuration of 2 000 yards of front line to a depth of 500 yards. The objective was speedily taken with the minimal loss of five other ranks killed and 23 wounded including 2/Lts J N Harvey and D C Uys.

Encouraged by this and three successful raids on the night of 11/12 July on the 9th Division front, Brig-Gen Tanner received the necessary authorisation to attack and take Méteren so that the British front line would be advanced east of

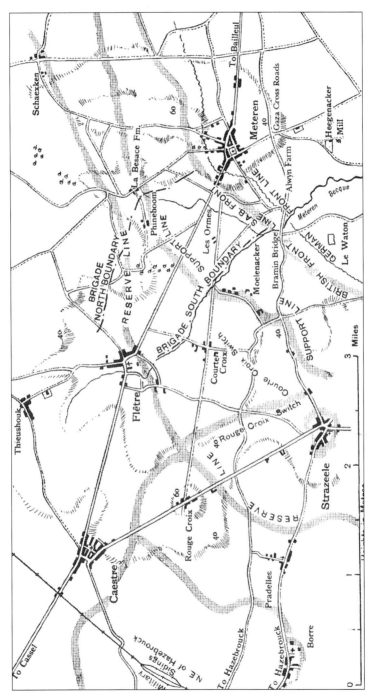

THE FIGHTING ABOUT MÉTEREN.
(South Africa and the Great War 1914-18. Official History, 1924)

the village. The German occupation of the village had long been a thorn in the side of the 9th Division – not only because of its proximity to the British front line, but because of the commanding view it gave. Indeed after Méteren had fallen, there was much astonishment that the Germans had not shelled the British front more frequently.

Experience at Longueval in 1916 recommended the necessity of completely flattening Méteren. So, for two weeks prior to the attack, projectiles poured into the doomed village. By the 19 July, the date of the scheduled attack, Méteren had been levelled completely. The assaulting battalions were the Composite Battalion on the right and the 2nd Royal Scots Fusiliers on the left. The attack had been well practised at a nearby RAF aerodrome in conditions similar to those they would encounter plus the usual model of the ground.

As a result of this thorough training, success was complete. The two battalions emerged from their trenches at 7.55 a.m. in artillery formation. Under cover of an accurately timed and placed smoke and high explosive barrage, the German front line posts were rapidly over-come. After that, by close hugging of the artillery barrage, the numerous German machine-gunners were given little chance of using their guns. The total bag was eleven heavy machine-guns and thirty-six light machine-guns. A number of these made their way back to South Africa as trophies of war and are still to be seen in Museums in Cape Town, Johannesburg and Durban with the legend painted in white 'Captured by the South African Composite Battalion at Méteren 19 July 1918'.

So accustomed had the Germans become to the daily plastering of Méteren with high explosive, smoke and gas shells that the bombardment of 19 July had seemed part of the daily routine. Some of the prisoners taken were still wearing gas masks. The surprise attack in broad daylight after 'stand to' and breakfast was quite unexpected. As a newspaper reporter of *The Star* wryly expressed it, 'This indecent departure from routine threw the enemy's entire local machinery out of gear and before the enemy was aware of it No Man's Land was crossed'.[1]

Scotsmen and South Africans swarmed among the German's places of refuge and looked down at them grimly from the lips of craters with bayonets poised. Further support came from the SA Stokes Mortar Battery and one and a half Batteries loaned from the 1st Australian Brigade which directed their fire at various specified targets. The break with routine that the Germans had complained of had not been without danger. Although safe in their forward positions, well before dawn, the attacking battalions were subject to observation during the hours of daylight until zero hour arrived. To avoid detection, the trenches had been covered with coconut fibre matting, along which a wide black strip had been painted, to

1   *The Star*, 25 July 1918

simulate the appearance of an empty trench from the air.

All objectives on the right were secured on time. Instead of the advantage the Germans had expected from the heavily wired and defended hedges that ran north and south on the west side of Méteren, it resulted in their suffering heavy casualties as they were attacked sideways instead of frontally. A pocket of opposition in a shallow trench on the left behind a wired hedge, offered stout resistance until overcome. When the barrage lifted, a company of the Composite Battalion, which occupied the far right, south of the point on which the operation hinged, was tasked to exploit any likely opportunity that arose to harass the Germans. This company was also to extend patrols along their front and hopefully capture the German trench between the Méteren Becque stream and the Brahmin Bridge – Alwyn Farm road. This was speedily accomplished. Seven machine-guns and prisoners were taken.

Consolidation and wiring of the captured Méteren village and ridge was rapidly undertaken and completed. Strong machine-gun nests were a feature of the German defensive system. As many as ten machine-guns were discovered in short, single strips of trench.

On the morning of 20 July the 2nd Royal Scots Fusiliers brought in a German field gun they had found fifty yards south of and parallel to Brahmin Bridge-Gaza crossroads. Shortly after 6 a.m. the Composite Battalion sent out fighting patrols to test for German resistance in the same direction, forcing the Germans to withdraw to a line 400 yards further south. Capt J C Scheepers, 1st SAI, who had rejoined the Composite Battalion two days before, was killed while this was achieved.

In this perfectly planned and executed minor action at Méteren, 70 Germans are known to have been killed and 225 prisoners were taken by the 'SA' Brigade. There is no record of the wounded suffered by the Germans. Besides the trophies already mentioned six heavy and six light trench mortars had been taken and one stick-bomb thrower. Total casualties suffered by the Composite Battalion between 19 and 21 July were five officers and 21 other ranks killed with one officer, 2/Lt L G MacKay, and 93 other ranks wounded, seven missing and one died of wounds. Success – had been at great cost as casualties among the junior officers had been particularly high: 2/Lts C A Anderson (ex 3rd SAI); F Douglas 4th SAI; D C MacKie MC 1st SAI and E C Male 4th SAI, had all been killed in action, while 2/Lt E J Keeley 4th SAI was to be killed on 23 July.

On 28 August, after a period of routine activities, the SA Composite Battalion marched to Lumbres to prepare for disbandment. The period of a titular 'SA' Brigade had ended. A new, wholly South African Brigade would arise like a Phoenix after a four-month period that at first seemed an embarrassment, but had not been without its moments of glory and achievement.

All that was left of Méteren after its capture. (Photo: Cloete-Smith Collection)

Chapter 30

A new Brigade is born

A birth is painful. This one meant farewell to the 9th Division. On 11 September the SA Composite Battalion was withdrawn from the 9th Division to be reconstituted as a brigade. Great was the dismay when it was heard that the withdrawal was to be permanent.

The SA Brigade was now attached to the 66th Division. As John Buchan stated:

> It was not easy for the South Africans to leave the 9th Division, or for the 9th Division to part with them. Together they had fought in the bitterest actions of the campaign (on the Western Front), and their glory was eternally intertwined.[1]

Maj-Gen Tudor, Commander of the 9th Division, wrote to Brig-Gen Tanner, who had been appointed to command the re-constituted SA Brigade:

> ...The cheery keenness and comradeship with which the South African Brigade has always worked and fought will be very much missed by me personally, and by all the 9th Division. We wish you and your Brigade the best fortune, and know that you will always fully maintain the splendid name you have earned.[2]

The 66th Division, reduced to a shadow of its former self during the German March offensive, had been re-formed late in the summer of 1918 under the command of Maj-Gen H K Bethell. It included the 198th Brigade (6th Lancashire Fusiliers; 5th Royal Inniskilling Fusiliers and 6th Royal Dublin Fusiliers) and the 199th Brigade (18th King's Liverpool Regiment; 9th Manchester Regiment and 5th Connaught Rangers). The pioneer battalion was the 9th Gloucestershire Regiment.

---

1 Buchan, p225.
2 Ibid p232.

The SA Brigade was organised as follows:

1st SAI: OC Major H H Jenkins; 2nd SAI: OC Lt-Col H W M Bamford; 4th SAI: OC Lt-Col D M Macleod DSO DCM. Of the original battalion commanders, appointed in August 1915 at Potchefstroom, only Macleod remained, having just returned from hospital. Macleod wrote a letter shortly afterwards, in which he exuded the same spirit that had always inspired his men.

> It is just glorious to get back and find the Brigade in shape once more. My right hand is quite out of action, but it is not so bad as it sounds, as I still have a good left...The last men sent across are as fine a looking set of chaps as I have ever seen and as keen as mustard. I am getting a band together again and we now have seven sets of pipes and six sets more are on the way so that we shall soon be quite all right again.[1]

Among the sets of bagpipes now purchased was a special one with hall-marked silver and real ivory mounts for Pipe-Major 'Sandy' Grieve of the 4th SA (SA Scottish) and an embroidered pipe banner. The banner was later to be awarded as a pipe band floating trophy at the annual Royal Scottish Gathering in Johannesburg.[2] Now pipes and banner are displayed in the Transvaal Scottish Regimental Museum. Grieve was permitted to retain the pipes on demobilisation and proudly played them with the Cape Town Highlanders and thereafter, until his death in Bloemfontein during the late 1940s. The new horsehair sporrans for the pipe band carried a new badge – a springbok enclosed in a fern half-wreath with the Gaelic motto 'Buadh nam bhas'. Loosely translated this means: 'We're the best', which is indicative of the arrogance and pride of a pipe band.

While the SA Brigade prepared, Ludendorff had launched a third offensive on the Aisne on 27 May, pushing forward until the Germans reached the Marne by the end of the month. In spite of this success he had manoeuvred himself into a dangerous salient, where he was threatened on both flanks. In order not to destroy the morale of his armies he decided to make two further attacks against the Soissons and the Noyon – Montdidier sectors in order to threaten Paris. The French succeeded in frustrating this plan and once again the Germans suffered heavy casualties.

The Allied Commander-in-Chief, Marshal Foch, had been building up reserves while attacking at different points without heavily engaging the Germans. In this way they would be worn down gradually through the constant movement of

1   Cloete-Smith newspaper-cutting collection.
2   Called the Mackintosh-Dalrymple Banner. The author saw to it that a new trophy was procured so that the pipes and banner could be reunited. They had been separated since 1919.

men and supplies to wherever their line was threatened. The advent of American Divisions to the Western Front had also bolstered the Allied forces. Throughout August and September, British and French armies were active all along the front and the Germans were pushed back.

These moves culminated in Haig's bold decision, in the face of scepticism even from Foch, to attack the main German defensive position between Cambrai and St Quentin – the Hindenburg Line, prepared, strengthened and then reinforced over nearly four years. Germany regarded the position as impregnable – a bastion behind which the German forces could stand for the duration of a long winter. They reasoned that with the Allies exhausted, a negotiated settlement with them in the Spring of 1919 could become a distinct possibility.

Nevertheless Haig was not dissuaded and between 27 September and 7 October, the Canal du Nord and Scheldt Canal were crossed in quick succession, the Hindenburg fortifed zone penetrated, St Quentin taken and Cambrai outflanked. All but the final zone of the Hindenburg Line had not been pierced.

The 66th Division was transferred to General Rawlinson's Fourth Army on 28 September 1918 as part of XIII Corps. The other divisions of the XIII Corps were the 18th, 25th and 50th Divisions. On 5 October the SA Brigade began their move across the old Somme battlefields. This afforded the opportunity for a detour, once again, to the Delville Wood battlefield. Here the 4th SAI found that their cairn with the cross was still standing but had been hit in a few places by shrapnel. The cross now reposes in St George's Presbyterian Church, Johannesburg. It had been erected at Delville Wood at the memorial service of February 1918. On 25 May 1924 it was rededicated and unveiled by Lt-Col D M Macleod in its new location. A number of the temporary wooden memorials were removed from Delville Wood and transported to South Africa when work on the Delville Wood Memorial was begun. They were positioned in similar places of honour in various centres.

Soon the Rossoy area was reached. Here the 66th Division was to take part in a major operation involving both the Fourth Army and General Byng's Third Army. The remnants of the Beaurevoir Line were to be the objective. With its destruction, the Hindenburg Line would be no more. John Buchan described the nature of the countryside as follows:

> The country was the last slopes of the Picardy uplands, where they break down to the flats of the Scheldt – wide undulations enclosing broad, shallow valleys. There was little cover save the orchards and plantations around the farms and hamlets, but there were many sunken roads, and these, combined with the perfect field (of fire) afforded everywhere for

machine-guns, made it a good land for rearguard fighting.[1]

The morning of Byng's and Rawlinson's advance of 8 October on a seventeen mile front, from Cambrai to Sequehart, dawned wet and unpleasant. The 66th Division formed the centre of XIII Corps and had been set the task of capturing Serain, attacking on a two-Brigade front. In the case of the SA Brigade, the 2nd SAI was on the right, the 4th SAA on the left with 1st SAI in support. The Brigade front was the section of the line from the cemetery, south-east of Beaurevoir, to a point in the northern outskirts of Beaurevoir.

Unfortunately, at 1 a.m. while the SA Brigade was moving to the assembly position, a heavy German barrage came down on Beaurevoir and caused numerous casualties, including Lt-Col Bamford, OC of 2nd SAI, who was wounded. Major L F Sprenger took his place. The barrage had been quite unexpected and was in response to the barrage laid down by the 50th Division preparatory to their attack on the left of the 66th Division. No 4 Platoon 4th SAI was reduced to one corporal, four men and a Lewis gun team.

Major L W Tomlinson DSO, 4th SAI, prepared a special summary of the operations of 8/9 October for Brig-Gen Tanner. The document provides a very good idea of the nature of the fighting and the vast quantities of equipment that were being captured by the SA Brigade.

Major Tomlinson was in command of 'A' Company on the left and Capt A M Cameron in command of 'B' Company on the right. To ensure that touch was kept with the 198th Brigade on his left, Tomlinson visited their extreme right flank company commander, but encountered an unsympathetic response to this logical suggestion of co-operation. Once again the SA Brigade was to suffer the problem of a flank 'in the air' which had been the annoying reality in most of the actions of 1918. Zero hour for the Fourth Army was 5.10 a.m. on 8 October.

The first objective, La Sablonnière, was captured at 7 a.m. A total of sixteen heavy and ten light machine-guns with four prisoners were taken by Tomlinson's company. Hamage Farm on the left proved to be a harder nut to crack. Its capture was essential to any further advance.

> [Tomlinson wrote] we were being shelled by 77s over open sights, and experienced heavy machine-gun fire, which we found most difficult to locate. Our first attack on Hamage Farm failed, I quickly re-formed and re-attacked, detailing Lt R H Hill, to work round on the west of the farm, taking advantage of the ground there, and I led the attack on the eastern side, gaining the railway cutting. I observed that a battery of 77s (four field

1   Ibid p232.

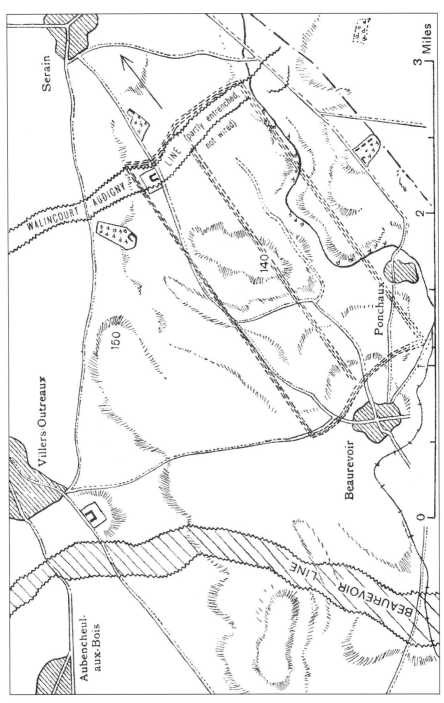

SOUTH AFRICANS' ATTACK BEYOND BEAUREVOIR, 8TH OCTOBER 1918.
(Union of South Africa and the Great War 1914-18. Official History, 1924)

370

guns) supported by machine-guns was in action in the cutting on the high ground immediately north of Hamage Farm.

The field guns were soon captured and Hamage Farm taken. Tomlinson could now add four 77mm (whizzbang) field guns; six heavy and three light machine-guns, six anti-tank rifles, ammunition and stores to his captures. The 198th Brigade on the 4th SAI left had not advanced, but was far in the rear, being heavily counterattacked. Tomlinson directed long range enfilading fire on the Germans, which seemed to cause their retirement, so the 198th Brigade's right flank could advance. Capt Style, a staff captain, questioned Tomlinson as to the number of guns he had captured, so he went back to check totals, only to find the record of his capture had been crossed out. The new legend read: 'Captured by the Dublin Fusiliers.' Later while in Serain, much to Tomlinson's irritation, he found Style still had not received the list of captured guns.

> ...I again visited these guns with my orderly, armed with a tin of white paint, and on arrival noticed that my record was again obliterated and the legend read: 'Captured by No 2 Balbon Section'.[1]

On the right of the SA Brigade, the 2nd SAI's casualties were far higher. Major Sprenger, OC 2nd SAI, described the action on his front line from the time the creeping barrage ceased.

> Heavy machine-gun fire was experienced on the first crest reached and after a bit of a fight a round number of machine-guns were captured, many of the enemy being killed and captured in the sunken roads and trenches. In the Usigny Ravine considerable opposition was experienced, the enemy bringing a great number of machine-guns and much sniping to bear. The timely arrival of a tank helped to finish up this particular portion of the front.
> Although resistance was stubborn the advance forward was brisk, the troops of the 25th Division being unable to maintain the pace resulting in somewhat thick machine-gun fire coming from Ponchaux to the right rear, (causing)...the right company ('A' Company) to suffer severe casualties, not an officer being with this Company at this stage.
> The line was now reinforced by the two support companies, 'C' and 'D', and the advance was continued by short rushes covered by fire from Lewis guns and riflemen. Four enemy field pieces firing over open sights at point

1   Box 148 GSWA Series SADF Documentation Centre.

blank range were the cause of a number of casualties, but Lieut E J Brook with Sgt S J Hinwood and a few men, with a determined rush, pushed forward and captured the guns on Red Line, the crews surrendering.[1]

Hinwood was awarded the Military Medal. The four captured field guns were now turned around and about forty rounds were fired at the fleeing Germans. Besides the field guns, the 2nd SAI had been responsible for capturing two anti-tank guns, twelve heavy and seven light machine-guns as well as 450 to 500 prisoners excluding a further group who were utilised as stretcher bearers.

'A' Company had suffered the most severely in officer losses with 2/Lt R G A McCarter killed and Capt T H Symons MC with 2/Lts O S Giddy, E D Birrell wounded; 'B' Company 2/Lt G S Fernie wounded; 'C' Company 2/Lts C W Roberts and H L Francis wounded; 'D' Company Lieut C M Egan and 2/Lt H C H Gunn wounded.

The SA Brigade stopped on the Red Line, having taken their objective, while the 199th Brigade leapfrogged through them to continue the advance of the 66th Division to Green Line, which included the town of Serain. The 198th and 199th Brigades were to attack Maretz the next day (9 October). It was then the turn of the SA Brigade to leapfrog through the 199th Brigade. At about 10 a.m. they moved off on a three mile trek to the villages of Maurois and Honnechy to take up a line beyond them. The order of attack for the SA Brigade was the same as the previous day. Once again German machine-gunners and snipers were the main problem to overcome – particularly from Gattigny Wood on the left of the 2nd SAI. With the aid of two armoured cars the objective was reached after half an hour's hold up along the railway embankment west of the wood where strong opposition was experienced. The losses suffered by the SA Brigade were wholly disproportionate to the strength of the positions captured. Machine-guns and many prisoners were taken.

Now with the way clear, the two villages in the path of the SA Brigade seemed quiet. Many of the houses were flying white flags. The advance was continued with little opposition and the new objective reached by 1 p.m. Two and a half hours later the Division on the right came into sight and the extended 2nd SAI line shortened. Second Lieutenant J Peters, 4th SAI, took the village of Maurois with two men and a couple of Mills grenades. The civilians of the villages were at last free. Major C M Browne MC, 4th SAI, wrote:

> Their pleasure at seeing us was too pathetic for words. They gave the boys coffee and anything they had in the way of food. It almost brought tears to

1   Box 8 WO1 DA Series SADF Documentation Centre.

one's eyes to see the relief of those poor French civilians being released from the clutches of the Hun.[1]

Only an hour after the arrival of the right flank division did the 4th SAI finally close the line. The 4th SAI had been involved in a tough fight. Lt-Col Macleod and his unit had eliminated determined resistance from the northern edge of Gattigny Wood by a flanking movement, only to discover that the brigade on his left had not reached its objective – the village of Bertry. This dominated the whole of the SA Brigade's objective. Although not within the Operation Order, circumstances justified the capture of Bertry by Major Tomlinson and 'A' Company.

Here Tomlinson made an interesting capture. This time it was a German staff car which Lt J J Young MM had stopped. The wounded German officer in the car stated that his mission was to fire mines and charges, placed at various points to retard the British advance. Next day a party was sent to recover the car, but it was nowhere to be found. Once again Tomlinson had found to his cost that to take a prize was one thing but to retain possession another.

While waiting for the 4th SAI and the right flank division to come up to his line, Major Sprenger had reconnoitred Reumont which seemed unoccupied. Snipers began firing at him and the horse he had borrowed from the nearby Cavalry Division was killed. On the high ground beyond Reumont the German guns were firing rapidly over open sights to cover their infantry, cavalry, as well as motor cars and vehicles of every kind that were rapidly retiring. This was about 2 p.m. An aeroplane dropping a message saying: 'All clear ahead' confirmed their retreat. The 2nd SAI machine-gunners had fallen behind so they lost the opportunity of scything down the retreating Germans.

Only after Bertry had been captured did Macleod proceed to link up with Sprenger's line. Major Sprenger's irritation was no doubt some-what mollified when he realised that the activities of the 4th SAI were the reason for his rapid progress.

In the light of the day's achievements, losses had been small. 4th SAI: Lieut R Hill and 23 other ranks killed with four officers including 2/Lts E N Cummings, N J Johnson, G C Strickland and 71 other ranks wounded; 2nd SAI: 2/Lt H Perry wounded.

The German retreat had reached a stage where it was essential for them to make a stand in order to delay the Allied advance east of Le Cateau and the River Selle. If this were not done the chances of failing to extricate their forces to establish new lines of resistance would be much increased. The 66th Division, had reached the western extremities of Le Cateau. Here they began to feel a stiffening

---

1   Cloete-Smith newspaper-cutting collection.

of German resistance, that the SA Brigade would be called upon to pierce in the wake of other brigades who had failed to do the job.

All along the British front, there were units, brigades, divisions and army corps pushing forward. Each had their own tale to tell. In this great movement the efforts of the SA Brigade went unnoticed. This was only to be expected in a major offensive on many miles of front. The activities of a single brigade were lost in the sheer magnitude of the offensive.

The old sporran badge of the pipe band of the SA Scottish (left) and the new (above). (Photo: Transvaal Scottish Regimental Museum)

Chapter 31

General Bethell's impossible task on the Selle

In spite of the SA Brigade losing its identity in so large an offensive, there was to be a last demonstration of the calibre of the South Africans on the River Selle before the war ended. Careful scrutiny of the map of the area will highlight what was achieved.

In its advance from Beaurevoir on 8 October, the 66th Division had been moving forward in a north-easterly direction with no deviation from a definite path that had been laid down in operational orders. To its right and left similar routes for divisions all along the whole seventeen mile front of the Third and Fourth Armies had been mapped out. There was to be no skirting of obstacles. Directly blocking the advance of the 66th Division from Reumont was the town of Le Cateau and a particularly well-fortified stretch of the River Selle.

It was to be the task of the SA Brigade to draw the tooth that had proved to be too difficult for the 198th and 199th Brigades of the 66th Division. On the left of the SA Brigade the 18th King's Liverpool Regiment of the 199th Brigade had reached Montay, but could not cross the Selle because the river banks were too heavily wired. On the right, the 5th Connaught Rangers of the 198th Brigade had reached the railway east of Le Cateau. However, they had been withdrawn to the west side of Le Cateau to hold the course of the Selle where it passed through the town.

Le Cateau, normally with a population of 10 000, for the most part lay on the eastern slopes of the river, consisting of solidly built houses and factories. In this eastern sector of the town, roughly from north to south, ran the railway to Solesmes. Its embankments and cuttings had been the main focus of German attentions and had been turned into an impregnable fortress of machine-gun emplacements, reinforced with most comprehensive barbed wire works which were considered impenetrable. As well as this to contend with, there was the railway yard and station: now a strong point bounded on its east side by a bank thirty feet high and a concealed mound which provided excellent observation

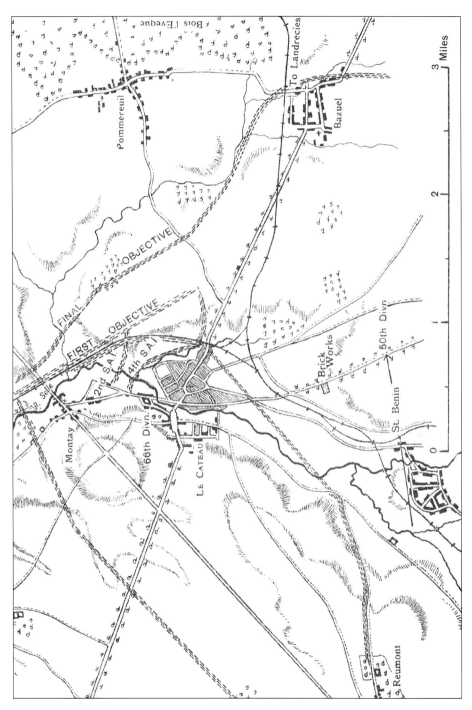

THE FIGHT FOR THE CROSSING OF THE SELLE.
(Union of South Africa and the Great War 1914-18. Official History, 1924)

to the south. Buildings and cellars had been adapted for a long defence and the area along the Selle had been christened the 'Hermann Line', so important was it considered in the stand that was to be made. Four German divisions – two of them fresh from the reserve – held the line here. It was not surprising therefore that the advance had been held up – not only the 66th Division but further right the 25th Division and 2nd American Corps had ground to a standstill.

It was the most strongly held area just south of Montay and north-east of Le Cateau that blocked the path laid down for the advance of the SA Brigade. The 1st SAI had tried from 12 to 15 October to push forward the line north of Le Cateau to the bank of the Selle. The Selle ran roughly south to north, but just as it passed through the northern part of the town the river bent round in a large arc with the bulge towards the east. The 1st SAI had moved towards the river bank in this bulge, finding forward progress almost impossible. Strong German patrols were proving very troublesome among the numerous houses along the western banks as well as further north as far as Montay. The valley was dominated by the fortified German position along the whole eastern bank, already described. The 1st SAI had lost some 20 all ranks killed and wounded with a further 8 other ranks missing.

Because of the impending attack, the capture of two bridges, in the western outskirts of Le Cateau was considered vital if bridgeheads were to be established on the narrow strip of land on the east bank to the front of the fortified positions and railway embankment. On 15 October the capture of one of these bridges was assigned to 2/Lt R D Hewat, 2nd SAI, with a Lewis gun section and a rifle section. Major Sprenger recorded Hewat's exploits in his report.[1] Hewat did all and more than was required of him.

Late on the afternoon of 17 October, with only seven men left, he was relieved by the battalion mopping up Le Cateau. Hewat had held out for over thirty-six hours. He returned to report back to Battalion Headquarters.

On the morning of the 17 October the rest of the 2nd SAI and 4th SAI had been ordered to attack. The assembly area was on the east bank. The 1st SAI was now in support with the 2nd on the left and 4th on the right. The attack had been planned so that Le Cateau itself would not be taken by direct attack but enveloped by means of the SA Brigade attacking from the north and the 50th Division from the south. A battalion of 198th Brigade would afterwards mop up the town – Lieut Hewat had encountered them doing this.

After a move across light foot bridges constructed by the Royal Engineers during the night, the assembly was completed by 4.45 a.m. Two companies of each regiment remained in support on the west bank. The 1st SAI guides, who

---

1   Box 8 WOIDA Series SADF Documentation Centre.

covered the engineers, cut openings through a strong barbed wire entanglement that had been erected along the east bank. In this way the assembly area could be reached.

Under normal circumstances the narrow assembly area on the east bank would have been a death trap because it lay at the foot of the German fortified line, but for once the weather was on the side of the British. Just before dawn, nature provided an excellent shield in the form of a heavy mist which prevented the Germans from obtaining observation of the concentration of the SA Brigade. Because of this, the German barrage fell just over the British line. Had the weather not intervened the story would have been very different. In the short space of time available only scanty trenches could be dug. During the wait between dawn and 8.05 a.m., the South Africans would have been sitting ducks. Besides the closeness of the German positions, a line of their machine-gun posts was sited along the road immediately south east of the lower bulge of the Selle. In places these posts were within fifty yards of the South African assembly position. Slaughter would have been complete. As it was, casualties were still very high as assembly had taken place at point blank range of the German machine-gunners. Lieut E J Brook, 2nd SAI, was one of those killed, his riddled body being found about five yards from the muzzle of a German machine-gun.

The SA Brigade advanced at 8.05 a.m. under the cover of an artillery and machine-gun barrage. They were hidden by the thick mist made even more dense by smoke shells. From the outset, thick belts of single and double-apron wire were encountered. Because these belts were too close to the assembly area, the wire had to be cut by hand. All the time heavy machine-gun fire was directed blindly through the mist at the SA Brigade's front, right rear and left flank.

At about 150 yards from the assembly area the first substantial obstacle was reached. This was a sunken road running parallel with the line of the Selle, defended by a brushwood palisade reinforced in places with wire entanglements and was only penetrated after suffering many casualties. An extract from the Military Cross citation of Capt R B Marshall, 4th SAI, gives a vivid impression of the fighting at this point on the 4th SAI's left.

> In the face of close range machine-gun fire he took and consolidated a trench system fortified with three uncut belts of wire. On reaching his objective he found himself enfiladed and taken in reverse by enemy machine-guns. These he dealt with, and with rifle fire broke up several enemy attempts to encircle his flanks. At the outset he was left the only officer in his company, and his handling of a most difficult situation was admirable.

The next obstacle, even more formidable and stretching along the whole Brigade front, was the railway cutting. This was defended by machine-guns and protected by a belt of inter-wired barbed wire entanglements sixty yards deep. One company of 1st SAI under Capt A M Thomson, detailed to attack an area north of the 2nd SAI left, to form a strong defensive flank, came under very heavy fire. This, with the wire obstacles, forced them to fall back to the northern extremity of the 2nd SA positions. During that day every officer of this 1st SAI Company was wounded.

The railway along the 2nd and 4th SAI front was contained in a deep cutting. All along the sides of the cutting the Germans had established machine-gun posts and rifle pits. It now appeared that any further advance would be impossible but the 4th SAI came to the rescue.[1] A gap in the wire, cut by Lewis gun bullets, was discovered. This in turn led to a shallow communication trench running under the wire to the railway cutting. In single file they followed this twisting path used by German patrols. Major E G Clerk, 4th SAI, shot the two sentries on duty. He was then wounded in the hand while moving forward. The 4th SAI came under heavy fire. Undaunted, they were soon fighting in the cutting. Machine-gun posts were individually bombed or their crews driven out by Lewis gunners until the cutting was clear, but heavy enfilade fire came from the station on the right and the signal box on the left. The Germans kept up heavy sniper, machine-gun and trench mortar fire, but did not attempt to counterattack. The 2nd SAI experienced similar opposition. The success achieved so far had been due to following the German March offensive tactic of infiltration in miniature. By 9.25 a.m. the cutting was captured.

In spite of having progressed so far, the Brigade's first objective of the day still lay beyond the railway to the east, on a line running north to south. The open ground between the railway and this line was so swept by shot and shell from a sunken road parallel to the front and from the flanks that the SA Brigade had to fall back and dig in along the railway cutting. Major Sprenger recorded an unusual occurrence that took place at this stage.

> When the line was withdrawn to the railway line, several wounded, who could not be brought back at the time but were recovered during the night of 17th and 18th, were left lying on the objective. The enemy, who returned to the position, found one of our NCOs and examined his identification. Hearing that he was a South African they immediately rubbed his hands for him and gave him a drink of rum before passing on.[2]

1   SADF Documentation Centre.
2   SADF Documentation Centre. 2nd Regt Operations 8-18 October 1918.

The 1st SAI was now called upon to reinforce the 2nd and 4th SAI because of the heavy casualties suffered.

The night of the 17 October allowed no rest. The German bombing and machine-gun patrols never let up. Accurate and intense fire was kept up by machine-guns and trench mortars, while there was almost continuous artillery fire with light, heavy and gas shells. The Germans were desperately trying to dislodge the South Africans.

The next day the position along the railway cutting was consolidated. Relief had been expected, but the order was cancelled late that afternoon. 'B' Company, 1st SAI, did not receive the cancellation and after withdrawing had to return to their original position, losing thirteen killed.

The 4th SAI succeeded in both securing and consolidating the second objective by 3.12 a.m. on 19 October without any casualties, through the large scale withdrawal of the Germans, because of pressure elsewhere from another division.

Casualties for the SA Brigade had been high:

	Officers	Other Ranks
Killed	6	155
Wounded	40	988
Died of wounds	1	29
Missing	1	46
Gassed	-	17
Total	47	1 227

But there was something substantial to show for these losses in the list of the following captures: Prisoners – four officers and 1 238 other ranks; 5 000 rifles; 367 machine-guns; 19 light trench mortars; 22 field guns; four anti-tank guns; 15 bicycles; one lorry; three motor cars.[1]

Brig-Gen Ian Stewart, XIII Corps HQ Staff wrote to Tanner: 'I shall always look on the capture of the railway embankment north of Le Cateau as one of the most astounding feats of the War.'

In 1919, with the War over, and the SA Brigade on the point of departure from the 66th Division, Maj-Gen Bethell, the Divisional Commander, wrote in his special order of the day:

1   Box 32 WW1 Diverse Series SADF Documentation Centre.

In after life if any of you are up against what you imagine to be an impossible task of any description, call to mind the Boche position on the east bank of the Selle River north of Le Cateau, or ask some one who was there to depict it to you. Then remember that the South African Brigade crossed that stream and took that position, which the enemy thought impregnable to attack from that direction, and that, on looking back at it from the enemy's side, it was hard to understand how the apparently impossible had been done by you.

Notice-board used in France 1916-19 by the SA Scottish and thereafter by the Transvaal Scottish on camp and active service until the 1970s. Certain painted alterations were removed to reveal all the original detail. (Transvaal Scottish Regimental Museum)

Chapter 32

Curtain call

That the war was at last drawing to a close was apparent. If any members of the SA Brigade had been unconvinced, then the forward progress, culminating in the crossing of the River Selle at Le Cateau would have confirmed their suspicions. The great adventure was about to end. Where was there still action that was likely, for a time at least, to remain unaffected by the progress of events on the Western Front? The answer was Russia.

The background to the call for officers and men to serve in Russia dated back to events in 1917. In December that year the Don Cossacks had risen in revolt against the newly-established Communist Government. At first the Cossack army clashed indecisively with Red Army militia. The fighting between the two opposing forces embraced a broad sweep of territory from Odessa through Kiev, Oren Voronezh, Isartzin to Astrakhan and the estuary of the Volga.

As early as August 1918, a small British-American-French expeditionary force under the command of Maj-Gen Sir Edmund Ironside, a British general, had settled themselves in Archangel. Ostensibly their task was to retrieve Allied war equipment loaned to the old Tsarist regime. The actual purpose was to move south and east to link up with the 42 000 strong Czech Legion and assist them in their efforts to return home. It was optimistically hoped that the presence of this Allied force would contribute to a White Russian counter-revolution to oust the communists, so Germany could be threatened on two fronts once again. For over a year South African officers participated in this hard-fought yet unknown war in which White Russians and Reds were fighting for mastery.

One of the first South Africans to become involved was Maj-Gen Kenneth R van der Spuy, then a lieutenant-colonel in the Royal Flying Corps. He had already served on the Western Front with the British Expeditionary Force in 1914 and thereafter with the SA Aviation Corps in the German South West and East African Campaigns. He was posted back to Europe where he was officer commanding of a Training Wing and then a Group of the RAF. In early 1918 he was invited to establish and command the Slavo-British Aviation Corps which was to operate with the British, French and White Russian forces, with Archangel as headquarters.

The unit Van der Spuy was to command was given the title of the Elope Expedition. Its organisation was shrouded in secrecy so the Bolsheviks would not become aware of the aid that was being given to the White Russians. He was given a free hand in choosing his officers and he selected three South Africans, three Australians and two Canadians.

Van der Spuy was on board the same ship that was transporting Maj-Gen Ironside to take over the command of the North Russian Expeditionary Force. Van der Spuy wrote:

> He stood about six feet seven, was as broad and as strong as an ox and equally strong-minded in his dealings with those who did not carry out his orders...He was a great linguist, a sworn interpreter in twelve or more languages and spoke seventeen. I recollect my surprise when on one occasion on the voyage he addressed me in Afrikaans!

Maj-Gen Sir Edmund Ironside. (Photo: Cloete-Smith Collection)

Van der Spuy had the bad luck of crashing his plane after engine failure. As he was over hostile territory it was only a matter of time before he was captured. In his autobiography *Chasing the Wind* he graphically describes his incarceration in a series of Moscow prisons where his diet consisted of black bread and cabbage-leaf soup, with a period of solitary confinement in insanitary conditions of unspeakable squalor. This resulted in his becoming ill and being removed to the prison hospital. After a transfer to the notorious Burturkri Jail he encountered many of the elite of old Russia – nobles, aristocrats, landlords, chiefs of the navy, army and airforce and those who had held ministerial and high-ranking posts. Van der Spuy was finally released and arrived at Southampton in the same clothes he had worn when captured nineteen months before.

For the majority, the move to Russia had come after the cessation of hostilities in Europe. The signing of the Armistice had sounded the release of millions of men from the horrors of war. There were those, however, who looked into the future with dismay. Captain Hugh Boustead MC, 4th SAI, voiced the feelings of quite a number of others when he wrote:

> I had found the ardours and endurances and dangers of the past years, shared in company with men whom I admired, greatly stimulating in spite of the horrors of the Western Front.
>
> As the months passed and release from anxiety and strain brought new vitality into the minds of the young men who formed the Brigade, our thoughts were turning to what we would do in the future. Places were being offered at Oxford and other universities for forestry, agriculture, medicine. I was unsure that peacetime soldiering would be in my line, if indeed I were to be selected for it. Suddenly out of the blue an officer called Pougnet, who was serving with the Brigade, told me that the Brigade had requests for officers to go out to a mission in Russia. He had the forms with him.
>
> I told Pougnet that he could send in my application straight away...The idea of riding across the steppes of the Don or Ukraine with a Cossack brigade fired my imagination; all thoughts of Oxford or the forest service vanished into the background. By March we were in England in Shoreham camp preparing to disband for home. The War Office sent for me (for Russia). I said goodbye to the Colonel and to all my friends, and embarked at Southampton in late March.[1]

Col Sir Hugh Boustead KBE, CMG, DSO, MC in 1975.
(Photo: Pretoria News)

T/Major R Beverley DSO MC, former Brigade Major to Brig-Gen F S Dawson, expressed in a letter to his former chief an ulterior motive

1   Boustead, p47.

for volunteering to serve in Russia. Anticipating the likelihood of reverting to his substantive rank after demobilisation, Beverley regarded service in North Russia as a means of forestalling this.

Lt D'Eyncourt Chamberlain serving in the 2nd Hampshire Regiment wrote to his old school, Bishops, in Cape Town describing his voyage to Archangel in North Russia.

On Tuesday, 13th May 1919, we left England to go to the relief of the troops in North Russia. I was with several fellows with whom I had been at Sandhurst, but I felt a bit of a hero as I was off to represent 'Bishops' in Russia...We had an exceedingly good voyage, calm and fairly warm, there was plenty of boat drill as well on account of the unswept minefields, we had to go through.

The next bit of excitement was going through the icefields after leaving Murmansk. There was a bitterly cold wind blowing but that made the excitement more keen! An icebreaker pushed on in front and loosened the ice for us, then we came on crashing through large blocks of snow-covered slabs of ice, pushing some underneath us, cutting our way neatly through some but forever forging slowly ahead. At times the slabs were so large that one could feel the ship do a kind of side-slip out of its course. It took us thirteen hours to go through the first...We had a great reception at Archangel.

Eventually we went up the Dvina River on our mission of relieving the Royal Scots in the line, a phrase borrowed, I take it, from France, because I can't see any semblance in a block house system to a trench system. After a show, we were sent down the river to raise the Russian morale on another front. We have just arrived after six nights' march (we turned day into night on account of the colossal heat during the day), through forests and across rivers, and now are anxiously wondering whether we shall leave before the winter or do a winter campaign out here.

Another Bishop's boy, Capt Dennis Kilpin, was also in Siberia and wrote from Taigain on 14 May 1919.

In the evening of the 7th May, we reached Taishe [on the way from Vladivostock to Ekaterinberg], and found the station packed full of trains, and the line had been destroyed a little further up. About an hour after we got there we heard that the line had been taken up behind us as well. However, it is one of the practices of the Bolsheviks, so we didn't think much of it; but I'm blest if they didn't attack us at dawn next morning.

Fortunately there was a garrison of Czechs, some 500 strong, or I shouldn't be here to tell the tale.

It was just beginning to get light when I woke up, and very cold. I could hear firing on both sides of our truck, above and below, and nobody seemed to have the slightest idea where the attack was coming from. I got on a few clothes, loaded my rifle and jumped out, but all one could see in the faint light were the Czechs kneeling and taking cover behind the wheels. A fellow named S. .. and I climbed through about six trains and saw about fifty feet from the line a wooden fence, behind which the Czechs had taken up a position...Just to our left we heard a lot of machine-gun fire, but it turned out that the Bolshies had captured the railway station. A shot from a field gun on an armoured train set the station on fire, and out came our friends, bolting like rabbits, unfortunately for them into a road covered with machine-guns, so none of them got away. About 1 000 are supposed to have attacked, and they lost over 100. The casualties on our side were ten Czechs wounded, five killed and a few Russians killed. The armoured train went out and repaired the line, and the next day we moved on.

Also serving in the RAF like Van der Spuy was Flying Officer S M Kinkead. Hailing from Johannesburg, he had served in the Royal Naval Air Service gaining a DSC and Bar and DFC and Bar. By the end of the war he had chalked up a total of thirty kills. He was stationed in South Russia with 47 Squadron. The RAF was the only British unit supporting the White Russian General Denikin. Otherwise, British officers attached to the Military Mission served in White Russian units as advisers. The three flights of No 47 Squadron were equipped with DH9 and DH9A bombers and Sopwith Camels respectively.

The period of Kinkead's involvement saw intense fighting and was the first recorded clash between the RAF and the Soviet Air Force. The latter, although becoming more aggressive, had many of their planes destroyed by the experienced pilots of 47 Squadron. However, Kinkead, because of a shot-up engine, was forced to land his Camel on the banks of the Volga River. Kinkead's pursuer was shot down by a fellow officer who proceeded to land. He rescued Kinkead, who squeezed himself into the confined area between the upper wing and the machine-guns mounted in front of the cockpit. He was nearly blown away by the slipstream during the uncomfortable flight back to Beketovka. Kinkead, besides being awarded the White Russian Orders of St Anne (2nd Class), St Stanislas (2nd Class Military), St George (4th Class Military) and St Vladimir (4th Class Military) was awarded the Distinguished Service Order. His citation in the London Gazette dated 1 April 1920 reads as follows:

On 12 October 1919, near Kotluban, this officer led a formation of Camel machines and attacked the Cavalry Division of Dumenko. By skilful tactics in low flying he dispersed the force, which had turned the left flank of the Caucasian Army, and threatened to jeopardize the defence of Tsaritzin, Flying Officer Kinkead has carried out similar attacks on enemy troops, batteries, camps and transport with great success and at considerable personal risk.

Perhaps one of the most spectacular successes enjoyed by the White Russians was achieved by the North Russian Relief Force on the Dvina River on 9/10 August 1919. These operations were under the command of Brig-Gen L W de V Sadlier-Jackson CB, CMG, DSO. The Sadlier-Jackson Brigade, as it was called, consisted of a RFA Battery, a field as well as a signal company of the Royal Engineers, a battalion of the Machine-Gun Corps, a field ambulance detachment, the 1/3rd North Russian Rifles as well as two infantry service battalions – the 45th and 46th Battalions of the Royal Fusiliers. The latter was commanded by Lt-Col H H Jenkins DSO, formerly of 1st SAI. Two other South Africans, Lt Alex Smith DCM and Sgt (formerly Lt) J Whammond MC were also serving with him. 'Jock' Whammond is better known as the renowned Garrison Sergeant Major of Roberts Heights during the 1930s. The Mess at the Military College, Pretoria, is named

after him. Another South African, Sgt Malcolm McCorkindale, was serving in the 201st Machine-Gun Battalion. Although a survivor of Delville Wood and having been gassed three times and wounded on five occasions, he had grabbed the chance of serving in Russia. As he put it, this was an 'offer of more adventure and another fight', after seeing a poster in Southampton Docks with the headline 'Russia needs men like you!'

The North Russian Relief Force was on the Dvina

Brig-Gen LW de Vere Sadlier-Jackson CMG, DSO.
(Photo: Cloete-Smith Collection)

River. Lt-Col Jenkins was in charge of operations on the right bank with three columns under his command. The Communist forces were completely surprised and soundly defeated. A total of about 750 prisoners were taken including one regimental and two battalion commanders. At least forty, but probably a great many others who disappeared into the forests, were killed. Captured equipment was also extensive: 9 artillery pieces, 16 machine-guns and 900 rifles were included in the tally. All this was achieved at a cost of only three killed and nine wounded. This battle was the culmination of the campaign in the area and left the Bolshevik forces completely crushed. During the campaign the Reds had lost 3 700 killed, wounded and missing out of a total of 6 000 effectives.[1] Jenkins was awarded the CMG for his efforts.

The 4th SAI was not without representation. First and foremost there was the OC, Lt-Col D M Macleod DSO, MC, DCM, who from start to finish between wounds, had remained with the SA Scottish as commanding officer. After his return to England from France for demobilisation in 1919, the War Office had sent him to Perham Downs on Salisbury plain to solve the problem of a 'strike' of troops that was causing the authorities a headache. The camp theatre was opened and one curious soldier asked the duty sergeant 'What's the lecture today?' 'Oh, the War Office have sent down a little chap, Macleod, to see what he can do with the strike'. No one who was present can forget the diminutive figure all alone on the stage and the electrifying effect of his fluent rhetoric as he dealt with the problem.....'You – you who want to get back to Africa, before men, men who have shown the world that Africa could breed men. Get out of my sight....' Within half an hour the strike had ended. Obviously this taste of what peace had brought was not to his liking. On 5 April 1919, Macleod left hurriedly for North Russia, the call of action being too strong to resist.

Now it was to join Maj-Gen Sir Edmund Ironside's staff. During the Archangel relief operation he was in charge of the British Military Mission to Oost Pinega and was given command of a Russian regiment which had mutinied. Macleod, with five other officers, took over and made an efficient unit out of the dispirited men. When this force was withdrawn, Macleod was given the command of the 2nd Hampshire Regiment. That he should have been given command of a British Regular Army unit in Russia indicates the esteem in which he was held. It is interesting to note that he took over command from another South African, Lt-Col J Sherwood-Kelly VC, CMG, DSO, who had previously commanded battalions of the Norfolk Regiment and Royal Inniskilling Fusiliers.

---

1   Singleton-Gates, G R, *Bolos and Barishynas* – For Private Circulation, Gale and Polden 1920 p120. For a full account of the exploits of the Sadlier-Jackson Brigade this book should be consulted.

A letter from Maj-Gen Ironside from Archangel dated 11 June 1919 indicates the close cordiality that existed between the two men.

> Archangel
> June 11th
> Dear Macleod,
>
> Your lads appear to have done very well at Pinega and that is what was required. I am going to give MacFie a DSO. What about Boatswaine?
> Keep going with the training while you are in command. I have spoken to the Russian authorities and they are issuing orders that the training is to be continued under British instruction.
> The last lot of Sadlier-Jackson's Bde came in here today and we had the official reception this afternoon. I shall be glad to get rid of some of these functions.

Lt-Col J Sherwood-Kelly VC, CMG, DSO. (Photo: SADF Documentation Centre)

> I shall be doing a small stunt on the Dvina about the 17th and things depend upon how that goes. It ought to go well enough and then we shall be in possession of the mine area and so open the way to our advance on Kotlas.
> All the points mentioned in your letter are in hand. I have a lot of Kurdish Russian officers coming out thank goodness, and that will improve things greatly.
> Keep your men employed training and playing games if possible, but don't do any offensives, except raids until I can send a Bn up to you and then we will finish things off properly.
>
> Best regards
> Yours sincerely
> Edmund Ironside.

MacFie, whom Ironside refers to, was Macleod's adjutant when the SA Scottish was at Shoreham-on-Sea.

Capt T G MacFie's citation for the DSO published in the *London Gazette* of 3 October 1919 reads:

> On 2 June 1919 he was near the 18-pounder position on his way to the observation post. He collected and organised some infantry at this point. He then went back to Priluk, rallying and encouraging Russian infantry who were disorganised and himself led a counterattack against Priluk, which was recaptured together with all the guns. The success was due to his marked gallantry and ability to command.

Another officer of the SA Scottish who had left before Macleod or MacFie, was of course, Captain Hugh Boustead. He had joined the British Military Mission in South Russia under General Holman where the role of British officers was primarily a training and an advisory one. They were not supposed to participate actively in the campaign. General Holman's mission was attached to the army of White Russian General Denikin with headquarters at Ekaterïnodar. Denikin's 200 000 strong Army was in particular need of training in the use of Vickers and Lewis guns that they had received from Britain as part of a consignment of over a million pounds of surplus war stores. The instruction of Lewis gunners was Boustead's particular forte. Boustead wrote:

> Before we set off, we were inspected by the Commander-in-Chief, General Sidorian. On one of the hottest July afternoons the battalions marched past singing as only Russians can. The leading sections of four start the first line and the columns take up the chorus in strong, clear, ringing voices. The effect is wonderful, and no band or pipe music can approach the inspiring effect of these songs on long marches.
>
> After the march past, the men were inspected. No British officer could see the condition of their clothing and their lack of equipment without pity. From General down to Plastuni, the dress order of the day was sacking, small caps which gave no protection from the sun and, for at least half the men, no boots. Even the sacking tunics did not meet across their chests, and they wore no underclothing. They had fought through a Russian winter in this state, and more awful hardships lay ahead of them.[1]

Boustead wrote of the first occasion in which his newly-trained Lewis gunners

1   Boustead, p52.

were in action and their surprise at the effectiveness of the weapons during a move to occupy the village of Schakin.

> Before the company had time to deploy, three squadrons of Red cavalry burst from the fringe of the forest, with sabres already drawn, and it looked as though we were trapped.
>
> It was a very bad moment, but Sergeant Sultricov, a very intelligent Roumanian Lewis gunner, saved the situation. Rushing his two gun teams to the left of the column, which had had no time to extend, he fired the guns from the men's shoulders, one man supporting each gun on his shoulder. Owing to the high grass, this was the only effective way of working the Lewis gun.
>
> This was the first cavalry charge that I had seen, and it was the first action for most of these young Plastunis. It looked at one moment as if nothing could stop the dense mass of horsemen, and the effect of their determined rush with flashing sabres and cheering shouts was enough to cause an intense state of 'wind up', even amongst old soldiers. The line of cavalry looked as if they were almost on top of us. But the effect of the Lewis gun fire was devastating. Sabres flew, and horses reared and fell on their riders; through a cloud of dust the screaming of the horses and the shouts of their riders were loud in our ears.
>
> The enemy line melted under the fire at this range. As those in the rear turned and fled, they were followed by bursts from the other two machine-guns that had by now opened up.
>
> The Plastunis could hardly believe their eyes. Hardly a man had fired a shot from his rifle. It was all over in two minutes.[1]

This was the first of similar successes which served as some consolation during the autumn retreat of the Don Cossack Army. Boustead also took part in a nightmare cross country journey to fetch spares for the machine- guns from the Mission HQ at Taganrog, where Boustead's immediate superior greeted him with 'Good God, I thought I'd seen a ghost – you were reported captured and killed weeks ago'. Here he also heard that the officer commanding the Don Plastuni Brigade and Division Commander had written to say that at Kardail the situation had been saved by the right flank action and the effectiveness of the Lewis guns. General Holman recommended Boustead for the award of a bar to his Military Cross and on Colonel Efanov's recommendation he received the Order of St Vladimir with Bow and Crossed Swords, the equivalent in Russian terms of a DSO. After three

1   Boustead, p58.

days Boustead, with a young British Ordnance sergeant made the journey back with a lorry full of spares for the Lewis and Vickers guns. While crossing a bridge across a tributary of the Don River the lorry fell through the bridge and was extricated by a team of farmers with oxen. After arriving safely with the lorry of vital spares, Boustead found orders from General Holman to return. After three days of feverish activity in refitting the guns, Boustead said goodbye and was given a tumultuous send off by the brigade.

Boustead received a fortnight's leave and on New Year's Day 1920 he arrived at his parents home in England. During this time the War Office informed Boustead that he was not to return to Russia as the Mission was about to be recalled. Throughout the campaign Boustead wore his SA Scottish uniform with his kilt so he must have been one of the last, if not the last member of the SA Brigade still wearing the uniform of a unit of the Brigade.

Boustead continued to serve in the British army and in 1975, on the 60th Anniversary of the lst South African Infantry Brigade he was appropriately invited to South Africa as Guest of Honour, now as Colonel Sir Hugh Boustead KBE CMG DSO MC. In South Africa the author had the opportunity of renewing his friendship with Sir Hugh that had begun in London in 1973, when he had dined with him at the United Services and Royal Aero Club, Pall Mall. Now he could reciprocate and he had the great man to stay with him for a weekend.

A list (See Appendix C) of those South Africans, although there may well have been others, who were engaged in the Russian adventure, shows the remarkable calibre of those involved. Two were already holders of the Victoria Cross while many had been decorated during the War.[1] Most received further honours and awards for their service in Russia. All had been prepared to put their lives at risk as volunteers while others were streaming home in their thousands after the most horrific war in the history of mankind.

These numbers are very small and insignificant and are perhaps not even worthy of mention in the context of the whole First World War. Many had been members of the SA Brigade. However, the achievements of these men, the valuable contribution they made to the cause of the Allies and White Russians must not be forgotten. For them the war did not end on 11 November 1918. Instead they ensured for themselves a curtain call far beyond the final act.

---

1   With acknowledgements to Commander W M Bissett, *Militaria* 15/4 1985 p48.

Chapter 33

The final act

At last came a well-deserved rest. Withdrawn from the line at 1.30 a.m. on 20 October, the SA Brigade marched via Reumont to Serain, where it remained until 1 November 1918. Then began a succession of daily marches through Reumont, Le Cateau, Pommereuil, Landrecies, Basse Noyelles, Taisnières, to Dompière, arriving there on 8 November. The Brigade was billeted in and around the village.

As the Brigade set out the next day from Dompière via Beugnies to Solre le Chateau, verbal orders were received from Maj-Gen Bethell, that

> ...in order to deal with the situation created by the rapid retirement of the enemy in the Fourth Army front, it has been decided to create a Mobile Column under the command of the South African Infantry Brigade Commander. This force will concentrate at Solre le Chateau immediately (after arriving there from Dompière via Beugnies) and push on with the utmost rapidity. Definite orders will be issued later in the day.[1]

The newly created Column consisted of: 1st and 2nd SAI (the 4th SAI was in Divisional Reserve); 331st Brigade Royal Field Artillery – 'B' and 'D' Batteries; 430th Field Company Royal Engineers; 'C' Company 100th Machine-Gun Corps Battalion; two armoured cars and two platoons of XII Corps Cyclists. The Signal Section and the SA Field Ambulance naturally formed part of the force as well. No doubt the South Africans were selected for this assignment because of their reputation in earlier campaigns for this type of warfare.

The last lap of the forward advance to Solre le Chateau was slow and difficult because the Germans had destroyed bridges and roads in the wake of their withdrawal. At times field tracks were resorted to and long detours made.

Even so the advance had been very rapid. However, the march of events had been even faster. On 23 October Field Marshal Haig had begun an offensive on a fifteen mile front to attempt to penetrate a ten mile gap in the German positions between Mormal Forest and the Scheldt Canal. By 31 October he was through

---

1   Appendix 47 Box 137 GSWA Series SADF Documentation Centre.

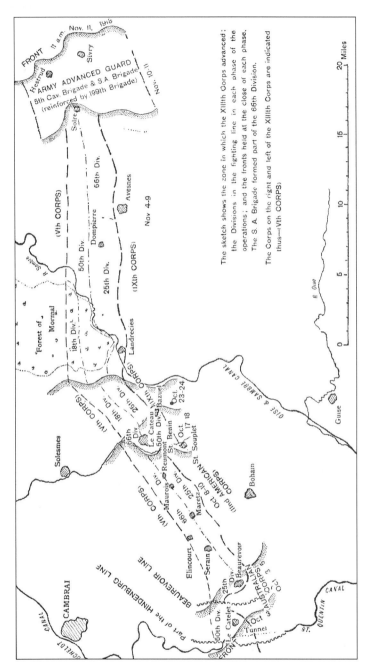

A map showing Hestrud, where the 1st South African Infantry Brigade was in action on the last day of the Great War – the furthest point of the advance reached by any of the British Forces. L/Cpl C D Thompson (please see the back of the dustjacket for a photograph of his grave in the Hestrud Village Cemetery, where seven South Africans lie) was killed in action some 30 minutes before the war ended. He was on the point of leaving to go to England for a commission.

(Union of South Africa and the Great War 1914-18. Official History, 1924)

the gap. The Allies had attacked all along the line held by the Germans. It was time to make a final move towards the German border. Events in Germany were to forestall this. The new government that had come into power in Berlin early in October began negotiations with the Allies. The terms presented by President Wilson of the United States of America were accepted on 29 October and the day before, General von Ludendorff resigned. All through this period the Germans were waging a most determined rearguard action all along the line as they withdrew. By the first few days of November the tempo of the German retreat had increased, so great was the pressure upon them. There was a danger that they would be cut off. Only an armistice could save the German army from actual defeat in the field. On 9 November, Kaiser Wilhelm II was forced to abdicate and a republic was proclaimed. Meanwhile the last phase of the Allied offensive was in progress.

It was in this final act that the SA Brigade had been chosen to play a part. The mobile column, formed by the SA Brigade, along with the 5th Cavalry Brigade, was to be an advance guard to cover the front of the Fourth Army. The Column moved out of Solre le Chateau at 7.00 a.m. on 10 November, along the road to Beaumont. Ahead of them trotted the 12th Lancers while the rest of the 5th Cavalry Brigade moved off on the southern flank of the column. The 1st SAI,

Ready to leave: The last draft for France, Potchefstroom, 13 August 1918.
(Photo: Transvaal Scottish Regimental Museum)

under Lt-Col H H Jenkins, with various attached troops, formed the advance guard behind the Lancers. The road ahead had been blown up where it crossed a culvert so only at 9.30 a.m. did the 1st SAI reach Hestrud which already had been occupied by 12th Lancers. The OC of the Lancers reported the Germans in considerable force on high ground north and south of Grandieu – in fact along the whole front of about one and a half miles. Under cover of the Bois de Madame, the column halted. The area before them was briefly reconnoitred and the 1st SAI began to deploy for the attack, on a three company front, to clear the way for the column to move forward. The assaulting troops first had to wade through the River Thure as the road bridge at Hestrud had been blown up. No doubt miscalculating the rapidity of the South African attack, shortly after the 1st SAI had crossed the river, the Germans rendered the Thure unfordable by opening the sluice gates of a reservoir further upstream. No other troops could cross until 2 p.m.

The progress of 1st SAI was extremely slow because almost at once they had been subjected to heavy machine-gun fire from strong positions. This was no retreat that the South Africans were facing, but a well organised, strongly held rearguard position with artillery support.

The Germans heavily shelled Hestrud with high explosive and gas. Machine-guns systematically raked the area. Then the main body of the mobile column was spotted and also heavily shelled. The Column's RFA batteries were completely outgunned. Without proper artillery support the advance could not succeed. Casualties began to rise and the shelling of the mornings targets was continued into the afternoon by the superior German artillery. In spite of some help from the Column's machine-gun company, there was a further problem. Both flanks, once again, were exposed. The 5th Cavalry Brigade had not arrived as scheduled. Tanner's instructions were not to press home the attack if heavy opposition was encountered from a well defended position.

This could have been partly because there was an awareness of the weakness of the SA Brigade. From 8 October to 11 November no reinforcements from the SA Brigade Depot at Inkerman Barracks, Woking, England, had reached the Brigade. From 9 October onwards, the tasks allotted to the Brigade were undertaken by three battalions very depleted in numbers – each some 300 strong. Ironically the first draft to make good the great deficiency, arrived at Hestrud on the evening of 11 November, approximately 500 all ranks. They were too late. Their superhuman effort to arrive in time to participate was to no avail. They had marched twenty-three miles that day from the railhead. Tanner's congratulations on this feat could not wipe out their disappointment. The new arrivals were only one-third of the Brigade's requirements, yet at the time there were 4 000 men of all categories at Woking! Until the last, there had been a desire to get to the fighting to be part

Civilians in a newly captured village, delighted at the arrival of advancing British troops, November 1918. (Photo: SA National Museum of Military History)

of the experience that was the Great War, even if the paths of glory led to the grave! It had been the influenza epidemic that was rife at the time that had been responsible for the War Office stopping drafts leaving Woking.

So, instead of resuming the offensive, on the afternoon of 10 November, the 1st SAI had been ordered to dig in on their present line. This was 200 yards east of the Franco-Belgian border. Low flying German aeroplanes were very active at the time. In spite of the Germans' shelling of Hestrud during the night, the engineers completed the repair of the Hestrud Bridge in record time.

The next morning the situation was unchanged. Orders were received to try and force an advance. This was tried. 2/Lt R C Cawood pushed his patrol some distance forward.

Pte A F Germishuys, 1st SAI, described the last hours of fighting on 10 and 11 November 1918.

> We went over the top in the morning, the two other (companies) remaining in the village in reserve... The enemy had a fairly strong line, which they defended by rifle fire and machine-guns, especially from a white house in front and a wood on our left flank. Though our cavalry (12th Lancers) had gone on ahead and somewhat to the right in pursuit of the main body of the retreating enemy, it was difficult for us to get forward. But we took the

ridges around the villages and pressed the attack right up to the last.

(The next day – 11th) we were given a hint to do our best before eleven o'clock and we did it. In this connection 2/Lt Cawood earned his Military Cross, Colonel Jenkins being very proud of the distance covered. The machine-guns were our worst trouble and caused many casualties. We found afterwards that there had been seven machine-guns in the white house. But the enemy were firing on us from a dozen different points and especially from the wood. Our platoon, which went into the fight 24 strong, lost 10 killed and wounded.

Among the killed were: L/Cpl C D Thompson, a Rhodesian, and Private R G Haw and T J A Taylor, while Pte N W Johnson died of the wound he had received that day. Thompson had been on the point of leaving to go to England for a commission.

At 10 a.m. at Column HQ, Tanner received telephonic advice that an Armistice had been signed. Hostilities would cease at 11 a.m. The actual Divisional order read:

> Hostilities will cease at 11.00 today, November 11th. Troops will stand fast on line reached at that time which will be reported immediately by wire to HQ. Fourth Army Advance Guard Defensive precautions will be maintained. There will be no intercourse of any description with the enemy until receipt of instructions.

The news must have reached the Germans before it reached the Column HQ as the Germans celebrated the occasion with a considerable increase in their bombardment, which at times became very severe. It was as though there was a determination not to have any ammunition left when the fateful hour arrived. At 11 a.m. exactly, the firing on both sides suddenly ceased. The silence that followed was most dramatic.

John Buchan wrote of the moment after the silence.

> There was then a sound as of a light wind blowing down the lines – the echo of men cheering on the long battle front. The meaning of victory could not in that hour be realised by the weary troops; they only knew that fighting had stopped, and that they could leave their trenches without disaster. The final 'gesture' fell to the arm which from the beginning of the campaign had been the most efficient in the enemy service. At two minutes to eleven a machine-gun opened about two hundred yards from our leading troops at Grandrieu, and fired off a whole belt without a pause.

A German machine-gunner was then seen to stand up beside his weapon, take off his helmet, bow, and, turning about, walk slowly to the rear.

At the hour of armistice the line reached by the advanced guard ran from Montbliart in the south, west of Sautain, through the Bois de Martinsart, round the edge of Grandrieu to the western skirts of Cousolre. It represented the easternmost point gained by any troops of the British Armies in France. The South Africans had the honour of finishing the War as the spear-point of the advance to victory.[1]

In the last two days of fighting before the armistice the SA Brigade had suffered the following casualties:

1st SAI – five other ranks killed and one officer and 28 other ranks wounded; 2nd SAI – one other rank killed and six other ranks wounded; 4th SAI – two other ranks killed; The SA Field Ambulance suffered five other ranks killed and one officer and nine other ranks wounded.

As soon as the eleventh hour of the eleventh day of the eleventh month of 1918 had struck, the combatants on both sides came out of their trenches and protected positions. They walked about in full view of each other. There was initial caution in case something led to a new outbreak of fighting, so novel was the idea of peace.

At noon two officers of the 443rd Regiment Prussian Guards came over to discuss the line they should hold. They were blindfolded and taken to Brig-Gen Tanner, who gave them short shrift. He told them that to prevent fraternisation they should remove their men to a safe distance. They agreed and the next morning the last of them were seen disappearing over the high ground toward Beaumont.

Pte A F Germishuys, 1st SAI, continued his narrative by describing how the end came:

> At eleven o'clock on the morning of the 11th we had the surprise of our lives. From the wood on the left there came 900 Germans – rather fine looking Prussians, who had been told off to hold us up. Our Lewis gunners were on the point of opening fire on them, when we suddenly realised what must have happened. Jerry slung down his rifle and came forward, throwing up his hat and offering us cigarettes. They wanted to talk to us and told us that if the armistice had not been signed they had arranged to counterattack at twelve o'clock. However, they were jolly glad that the fighting was over; in fact, they went mad with joy and cut capers all over the veld. We were told not to associate with the Germans, but none of us

1   Buchan, p255.

felt inclined to. They went right past us along the road into the village, and managed to get some coffee and other things from the French people, who, of course were delighted that the fighting was over, for their village had been briskly shelled by the German artillery. As soon as eleven o'clock struck the enemy abandoned their arms and nearly everything else, and the same evening they were in full retreat towards home.[1]

The Allies advanced in the path of the retreating Germans up the Meuse valley into Belgium. British Cavalry had gone on ahead, but over most of the route the South Africans were the first British infantry to be seen. They received a warm welcome from French and Belgians alike.

From Hermeton, in the valley of the Meuse River, Major Claude M Browne MC, 4th SAI, wrote to his Honorary Colonel in South Africa, Colonel William Dalrymple[2]:

Our gallant Colonel (Lt-Col D M Macleod) stood by his men until the last shot was fired. Suffering still from his wound received in the retreat earlier in the year, he at last consented to go home and undergo a further operation which accounts for my being in command.

We have had rather bad luck this week. Poor old Springbok, 'Nancy', the regimental mascot, who served with us ever since the first, died, but she saw us through until the armistice. She was suffering from the cold, and some infection of the neck, which she had last winter. We buried her in the village and we put up a cross with a French inscription so that the grave will always be left undisturbed. Before we buried her, we skinned her, and I have had the skin sent home to a very good taxidermist in Bond Street, and I am having it stuffed and mounted.

At the present moment we lie at Hermeton...I believe that we shall probably stay here about another ten days...The regiment had the usual dinner on St Andrew's Nicht. Major Power and Captain Lawrence came from the SAMC and the General (Tanner) came with Style, who is acting Brigade-Major. Colonel Jenkins and Forbes from the 1st ..We drank to the Colonel's health with Highland honours. It was very difficult to get liquor, and one of the most difficult was liqueurs. Some one, however, had a brain wave and made a concoction of rum and sugar. It may seem rather peculiar, but nobody knew what it was and everybody liked it, and I am

1   Cloete-Smith newspaper-cutting collection.
2   Col Dalrymple was OC of the Scottish Horse, Transvaal Volunteers 1902-08. Thereafter he became Hon-Col of the Transvaal Scottish and 4th SAI (South African Scottish).

Nancy's grave, Hermeton, Belgium. (Photo: Transvaal Scottish Regimental Museum)

sure it added to the hilarity of the evening.[1]

That day Captain H R Lawrence had received the news of the award of a Military Cross for his bravery at Le Cateau. 'He was delighted and celebrated tremendously,' recorded Captain Hugh Boustead.[2] In the pre-vailing atmosphere of unrestricted

1   Cloete-Smith newspaper-cutting collection.
2   Boustead, p46-47.

celebration, after months of tension Lawrence became a casualty of the Great War, as surely as if he had received a German bullet in his heart.

> He was billeted in a farmhouse outside Huy and his friends, who were in no fit state to take care of him, insisted on seeing him safely to bed. But they took him to the 'wrong' house and put him into a large double bed where an old farmer's wife was lying huddled in a corner of the bed in the dark, too terrified to speak or move.

The farmer was also out celebrating. When he returned home he discovered the doctor in bed with his wife. He unceremoniously dumped the unconscious Lawrence on the doorstep for the night in the bitter cold. On 14 December 1918 the beloved doctor of the 4th SAI died of pneumonia as a result of man's stupidity and inhumanity.

Major Browne's efforts had a sequel. The stuffed and mounted 'Nancy' was dispatched back to South African to Colonel Sir William Dalrymple, as he now was. For a number of years 'Nancy' stood in his Westcliff home, 'Glenshiel', before Sir William presented her to the Transvaal Scottish Officers' Mess at the Drill Hall, Johannesburg, from where in the early 1950s she was moved to the SA National War Museum, as it was then called, by the Transvaal Scottish Regimental Council, on loan. Nancy is not forgotten.

Nancy's counterpart, Jackie the baboon, mascot of the 3rd SAI, enjoyed yet other momentous occasions after he recovered from his wounds and the amputation of his leg. His earlier history is recorded in previous chapters.[1] Surely his proudest hour came with his participation in the Lord Mayor's Day procession of the Right Honourable Sir Horace Brooks-Marshal. In the printed programme of the Order of Procession, of Saturday 9 November 1918, appears the following note: '77mm German Gun captured by SA troops, with Jackie the baboon (twice wounded in action)'. So from that vantage point, Jackie rode through the streets of London like royalty.

From early September to 14 February 1919, Jackie and Private Marr were lent to the Red Cross by the War Office and the South African Government for the purpose of collecting money for sick and wounded soldiers. Between them they raised over £1000. At one Red Cross fête in Leicester, for example, Jackie appeared – 2/6d for a handshake and 5/- for a kiss. Much of the money the pair made was from the sale of postcards depicting Jackie and Private Marr.

On 5 May 1919, Jackie and Albert were on the last leg of their long journey home to Pretoria and Cheshire Farm. That day, a Sunday, Jackie dined at

---

1   See Chapters 2, 3 and 31.

Johannesburg's Park Station Restaurant. Sitting on a chair next to Albert, he demolished the excellent fare provided for him by the buffet. As a reporter on the spot wrote: 'Jackie is endowed with a lot of intelligence. He has an affectionate countenance and seems to understand all Marr said – "Now shake hands with the gentleman" and there was no hesitation about doing it.'

Jackie had been officially discharged at Maitland Dispersal Camp, Cape Town, on 26 April. On his arm Jackie wore one gold wound stripe and the three blue service chevrons, indicating three years' frontline service. At Maitland he received the usual parchment discharge papers, a military pension, plus a 'Civil Employment Form for Discharged Soldiers', which had been filled in, signed and witnessed like any other such document. Some of the entries on this document make amusing reading.

Another relic that has survived the ravages of time is Jackie's identity disc that

Nancy, stuffed and mounted, back in South Africa at 'Glenshiel', the mansion of Col Sir William Dalrymple (extreme right), Honorary Colonel of the Transvaal Scottish. (Photo: Transvaal Scottish Regimental Museum)

Jackie on the last leg of the long journey home, at Park Station Restaurant, Johannesburg 1919. (Photo: Author's Collection)

was worn round the neck of this small baboon throughout the War

After their arrival home, Jackie was again fêted and became the centre of attention on occasions such as the parade to welcome back officially the 1st SAI Brigade and at the Peace Parade on Church Square, Pretoria, on 31 July 1920, where he received the Pretoria Citizen's Service Medal.

Jackie was able to live out his days in peaceful retirement. To have gone to war was one thing, but to actually return home was quite another. Life on the farm continued until his death on 22 May 1921 the day after a fire destroyed the Marr home. The shock and perhaps unconscious reminder of the war was too much for Jackie. He was buried in an unmarked grave on Cheshire Fann, Villieria.

Thus died the lovable Jackie, an unsung hero, yet he had made a unique contribution to the tapestry of South African military history.

Albert Marr died in Pretoria, aged 84, in August 1973.

Capt Hugh Boustead MC, 4th SAI (SA Scottish), described this new phase in the advance of the SA Brigade in the days after the signing of the Armistice in his memoirs.

> It was now a peace time march in column of route with pipes and drums going full blast and all the panoply that we could muster.
> The country around us was beautiful upland with wide green pastures

stocked with Belgian cattle. At Marche, on the edge of the Ardennes forests, we spent the next few months mainly engaged in one form of sport or another...We boxed against the Army on the Rhine in Bonn, we steeplechased and hunted wild boar in the Ardennes. Leave parties went home through Brussels...The hotels were filled with young officers from all the allied armies out for a splendid time...[1]

In March 1919 the SA Brigade left the 66th Division for England and demobilisation at Shoreham-on-Sea in Sussex, prior to their sailing for South Africa. The 1st, 2nd and 4th SAI had been sent King's Colours which they received while in Belgium.[2] They had not been consecrated. Because of the pending demobilisation, such ceremonies were to be undertaken only when the regiments arrived in South Africa. It was considered likely that the units would have a place in the post war Union Defence Force.

Before their departure from Belgium, Farewell Orders were received from Maj-Gen H K Bethell CMG DSO, Commanding 66th Division and from Field Marshal Sir Douglas Haig.

The disbandment of the Brigade was tinged with sadness. Lieut W A 'Alf' Beattie penned a poem that refers to the 4th SAI, but his sentiments speak for the other units as well.

The Passing of the 'Scottish'

Scottish! your task is done – your martial fame
Emblazoned on a flag. Your dead are dust.
Your Highland garb that borrowed Atholl's name
Lies limp, dejected – food for moth and rust.

Twelve hundred strong from Table Bay you sailed,
Your mettle still untried, your name unsung.
In Egypt's desert wastes your strength prevailed,
Then into Flanders furnace you were flung.

A fierce and fiery test that might have tried
The courage of a veteran hero host,
Yet there in Delville Wood your hundreds died
Unvanquished, undismayed – that we may boast.

1   Boustead, p46.
2   4th SAI File of Dress Regulations – Transvaal Scottish Regimental Museum.

Bludgeoned and crushed by mighty shells that tore
And blasted smiling lands with poison breath,
Stubborn you stood, and ever proudly bore
Your ducal motto, 'My Reward is Death'.

Your valiant leaders – Lukin, Jones, Macleod –
Each of the stuff that Greater Britain breeds,
Gallant, defiant, debonair and proud,
And modest, too, for all their doughty deeds.

Forward they led, or held the foe at bay,
Manning the trench whence even hope had fled.
Time and again they dashed into the fray,
With all Hell's fury lashing overhead.

And so from day to day you lived or died,
Firm in the faith that Right must conquer Might;
Comrades in arms, blood brothers side by side,
Each fought for all as all for each would fight.

Pass, Friends! All's well – and may your simple story
Ring through the years to come, that sons of men
May gather strength to emulate the glory
That such as you bestow on us. Amen.

Another farewell communication, dated 17 February 1919, was received at about the same time by the commanding officer of a South African unit that had led such a cloak and dagger existence that many were unaware that it had even existed.

The unit in question was Bailey's Sharpshooters, otherwise known as the South African Sharpshooters. The initials of their title SAS highlight for the present generation the actual nature of this force. Its strength was sixteen men. The commanding officer and only officer in the unit was 2/Lt (later Lt) Neville William Methven. The letter was from Maj-Gen E P Strickland, Commanding 1st Division, thanking Methven for his and his men's 'splendid services' to the whole division in all its actions. Strickland particularly made mention of the high toll Methven's men had taken of the Germans at Passchendaele in 1917 and during the German spring offensive of 1918. He also recorded that 'I am indebted to you personally for some very fine reconnaissance and observation work in action as well as in training a large number of men in marksmanship of a very high order.'

Group photograph of the South African Sharpshooters, Lt N W Methven MC seated front row centre. (Photo: Mrs P Methven)

In 1916 the War Office in London had approached the Union Defence Force informing them of the urgent need for a unit of expert marksmen to operate in the front line in France. Sir Abe Bailey recruited and carefully selected the men for the unit from Northern and Southern Rhodesia and the Union of South Africa. Bailey financed the equipping of this elite group throughout the war and paid the men's salaries.

When Bailey's South African Sharpshooters arrived in France in 1916 they were attached to the 1st Division and remained under the control of Maj-Gen Strickland, Officer Commanding the 1st Division. Methven and his men saw service with the 1st Northamptonshire Regiment, 1st Loyal North Lancashire Regiment, 2nd Royal Sussex Regiment and 2nd Kings Royal Rifle Corps. Lt Methven, who was awarded the Military Cross on 3 June 1917, accounted for well over one hundred Germans himself while his unit is reckoned to have killed more than 3 000 Germans during their two and a half years in France. They led a life of extreme hardship operating for the most part in No Man's Land, summer and winter, in the muddy wasteland of shell holes, abandoned trenches and shattered heaps of brick. In the pursuit of such extremely dangerous work, the casualties were high.

BUCKINGHAM PALACE

1918.

The Queen joins me in welcoming you on your release from the miseries & hardships, which you have endured with so much patience & courage.

During these many months of trial, the early rescue of our gallant Officers & Men from the cruelties of their captivity has been uppermost in our thoughts.

We are thankful that this longed for day has arrived, & that back in the old Country you will be able once more to enjoy the happiness of a home & to see good days among those who anxiously look for your return.

George R.I.

A rare scroll issued to released Prisoners of War.
(Transvaal Scottish Regimental Museum)

Six of the unit survived the War. These were:
Lieut N W Methven MC of Umtali; Cpl S Evans of Umtali; L/Cpl Horne of Salisbury; L/Cpl G E Lugg of Durban; L/Cpl L C W Schuurman of Benoni; L/Cpl F H Spence of Lusaka.

All the men in the unit owed their selection to their being expert shottists. Methven, himself, already held sixteen shooting medals and numerous other trophies when he joined up at the age of thirty-two in 1916. It is appropriate that a group photograph enlarged to half life-size adorns the wall of the officers' mess of 5 Reconnaissance Regiment in Phalaborwa, particularly because of links this unit has with the Selous Scouts and Rhodesia. Someone with a fine knowledge of military tradition and history must have known of Methven's background.

It was a time of farewells and the parting of friends who had shared life and death. There was the long wait until their turn came round. Dispersal camps for demobilisation were set up at Cape Town, Durban, Roberts Heights in Pretoria and at Potchefstroom. To prevent overcrowding and delays in the release of troops, the Imperial Authorities were requested to return them in batches not exceeding 2 000 and at two week intervals. Union-Imperial service contingents arriving from Europe came via the West Coast route and were demobilised at the Maitland Dispersal Camp in Cape Town, close to the railway station. Troops from Europe

Members of the South African Scottish, after demobilisation, marching to the Maitland Dispersal Camp, Cape Town, back to civilian life. All men are carrying full equipment – some with birdcages – 1919.
(Photo: Transvaal Scottish Regimental Museum)

THE GREAT WAR

1914 — 1919

UNION IS STRENGTH. EENDRACHT MAAKT MACHT.

PEACE.

To

L. Dickason

The Residents of Sea View and South Coast Junction, while extending a Public Welcome to those who have returned after serving their King and Empire during the Great War which has just been brought to a close, gratefully acknowledge the splendid services, the gallant deeds and noble sacrifices displayed by the men who left the Union of South Africa to share in the struggle against a cruel and powerful foe.

They are proud to know that those who went from this District were no whit behind others in their determination to uphold the cause of Humanity on the Field of Battle, on the Sea, in the Air, or among those who served so nobly in the Hospitals.

It is their wish that you should accept this as a token of their appreciation of the part you personally have taken in those operations which conduced to Victory, the honour of the Throne and Empire, and the maintenance of the best traditions of our historic province. In offering you their heartiest congratulations on your safe return, they trust you may long be spared to a life of happiness and continued usefulness.

J. M. Ross.

Chairman of Committee

South Coast Junction,
27th September, 1919.

Small recompense for it all. (Author's Collection)

began to arrive early in 1919. Arrivals reached their height in April 1919. The majority had arrived by August. Regulations were drawn up by the Demobilisation Board to assist the soldier in bridging the gap between military and civilian life. Fifty-four Returned Soldier Employment Committees were established in larger towns while in smaller centres, magistrates fulfilled this function. Each soldier received twenty-eight days' leave on full pay after demobilisation; free rail and meal tickets to get him home; a thorough medical inspection and, if necessary, hospital treatment. In addition, the soldier was given £4 to buy civilian clothes and was allowed to retain his uniform, greatcoat and two blankets.

The arrival of the South African Scottish and their march up Adderley Street, Cape Town, on their way to the Maitland Dispersal Camp was somewhat reminiscent of that never-to-be-forgotten march through Marseilles in 1916. The crowds were almost as numerous but the feelings of the men were quite different. Afer what they had seen and experienced would anyone at home understand?

One of the first to arrive home was Father Eustace Hill. The restrictions and hardships of prison-camp life had caused him more suffering than his wound. He was ill and weak when he returned to England. He arrived in South Africa early in 1919,

> as a national hero, known and loved by hundreds of South African soldiers and their families. Bishop Furse was at Park Station [Johannesburg] to meet him and invited him to come along later to the session of the Diocesan Synod in St Mary's Hall. The occasion was memorable. As Eustace Hill entered the building, the whole Synod, clergy and laity alike, spontaneously rose to their feet and remained standing, as a tribute to their admiration and affection. Hill appeared quite unconscious of this gesture, went up to the dais, warmly greeted the Bishop, and sat down beside him.
>
> Bishop Furse, speaking with obvious emotion, welcomed him back on behalf of the Synod. 'I know,' he said, 'that you are the last person to realise how much you have meant to all those you have served in all sorts of conditions during the past five years. Of all the thousands of gallant men who went to represent South Africa in the Great War on many different fronts, there can be none whose name is held in higher honour and who was loved with such personal affection as you...We thank God that you are safely back.'
>
> Hill's reply was characteristic: 'I'm a little bit deaf nowadays, but the amount I have heard is enough to knock me over. It was an enormous privilege to be Chaplain to our men, and I thank the Bishop for letting me go. I can't live up to the character I have been given – but all I can do is to try to be

better than I am.'[1]

Hill was appointed Headmaster of St John's College in 1922 and retired in 1930.

What shines through all Hill wrote in his letters back to St John's was his admiration and devotion for the men of the 1st SA Infantry Brigade that he had served.

Compared to the contingents from India, Australia, New Zealand and Canada the 1st SAI Brigade was very small – one of several hundred such brigades of the British Army in France. The German South West and East Africa Campaigns were more in the nature of a response to the defence of the borders of South Africa and African interests, but the war in France was different. The serving together of the members of the two sections of the white population thousands of miles from home reflected the true spirit of the Union of South Africa that had taken place in 1910.

On all fronts nearly ten per cent of the white population of the Union of South Africa had seen service during the war. The percentage on the Western Front was even smaller.

It is appropriate to allow John Buchan to have the last word about the Brigade itself, as he was the Brigade's official historian.

1   Lawson, KC, p131.

Veterans gather: after the laying up of the Colours of the 4th SAI, Pretoria, 2 October 1927. Front Row: (1) Lt W A Beattie, (2) Capt J L Reid, (3) Unknown, (4) Lt-Col D McL Macleod DSO, MC, DCM former OC 4th SAI, (5) Col Sir William Dalrymple KBE, VD former Hon. Col. 4th SAI, (6) Lt-Col C S Rendall (OC Transvaal Scottish) (7) Major D R Hunt (8) Lt W D Charlton MC (9) Major D F Smitheman (2IC Transvaal Scottish). (10) unknown (12) Capt V N Pougnet MC.
(Photo: Transvaal Scottish Regimental Museum)

In the long road to victory the Brigade had left many of their best by the wayside. The casualties in France were close on 15 000, nearly 300 per cent of the original strength. Of these some 5 000 were dead. As evidence of the fury of the Western campaign, it may be noted that the South African contingent in East Africa was nearly twice the size of the forces in France from beginning to end, but its losses were not more than a quarter of theirs. How many, especially of the younger officers, whose names are recorded in the earlier actions, survived to advance on Le Cateau? Yet the amazing thing is that in a Brigade which was so often severely engaged, and in which the uttermost risks were cheerfully and habitually taken, many came through the three years' struggle. There are men who fought from Agagia to Le Cateau and have now returned to the mine and the farm to be living witnesses to their miraculous Odyssey. There is one quality of the South Africans which deserves special mention – I mean their curious modesty. To talk to them after a hard-fought action was to hear a tale of quite ordinary and prosaic deeds. They had that gentle and inflexible pride which is too proud to make claims, and leaves the bare fact to be its trumpeter.

It is not glorious deeds but ordinary men – friends – that members of the Brigade remember. F Addison ended his brief personal memoir of his Western Front experiences with the SA Brigade by listing twenty-five names prefaced only with nicknames or initials. Ranks are omitted. Addison's simple statement draws together the total experience of all those thousands who served South Africa in that experience that was the Great War.

> These are just names to you, but to me as I write them down I can vividly recall their faces, their voices and the laughter in their eyes, and they did take part, and see the events recorded in these pages, but I am unable to recall them home because they cannot come. I marched, lived and laughed with these companions, who make up the number of those killed in the 2nd Regiment to well over a thousand men and forty officers. So let their names be written down in these sketchy memoirs for they lived in these pages as much as I did.[1]

1   Addison, *Foot* p31.

Postscript

Ignored and unsung still

Delville Wood to a South African, who knows something of his past, will conjure up the same pride as Gallipoli does for the Australian or Vimy for the Canadian. In Australia and Canada and indeed throughout the whole British Empire that was, the battle honours won in France and Flanders fly proudly on the regimental colours of their units. In South Africa this is not the case. Even the epic battle honour of Delville Wood is not to be found on any colour of the entire South African Defence Force.

No proud Australian would accept the omission of Gallipoli, yet this situation has been perpetuated in South Africa since the end of World War I. The battle honours gained by South African units beyond the borders of South Africa in the Great War are still unrecognised. How this state of affairs came about is detailed in Appendix E.

Appendix
A

1st South African Infantry Brigade

NOMINAL ROLL OF THE ORIGINAL OFFICERS, POTCHEFSTROOM 1915

1st Regiment South African Infantry

Honorary Colonel: Brig-Gen the Hon Charles Crewe CB, who was Director of Recruiting for South Africa.
OC: Lt-Col F S Dawson
Adjutant: Captain E T Burges
Major: F H Heal
Captains: H H Jenkins, P J Jowett, J J Harris, J R Leisk, T G McEwen, G J Miller, T Ormiston
Lieutenants: J T Bain, C I Bate, E J Burgess, E A Davies, W D Henry, K Keith, W A Larmouth, A W Liefeldt, C B Parsons, T O Priday, S W E Style
2nd Lieutenants: W N Brown, A W Craig, W S Dent, H C Harrison, L I Isaacs, C F S Nicholson, C W Reid.
Quartermaster: Captain A C Wearner
Medical Officer: Major R A St Leger
Chaplain: Church of England: Captain the Revd Father E StC Hill CR

2nd Regiment South African Infantry

Honorary Colonel: General Louis Botha, the Prime Minister
OC: Lt-Col W E C Tanner
Adjutant: Captain H M Bamford
Majors: E Christian, H H A Gee
Captains: E Barlow, H E Clifford, W J Gray, C R Heenan, W F Hoptroff, A A Sullivan, J D Walsh
Lieutenants: H E F Creed, F M Davis, L Greene, R N Jenkins, C L H Mulcahy, W G Stranack, T H Symons, H E Turnley
2nd Lieutenants: R Beverley, J M Forrester, A R Knibbs, C T K Letchford, B N

Macfarlane, R G Miller, T F Pearse, W J Perkins
Quartermaster: Captain E A Legge
Medical Officer: Major H C Baker
Chaplains: Church of England: Captain the Revd Father H Harris Roman
Catholic: Captain the Revd Father P J Walshe

3rd Regiment South African Infantry

Honorary Colonel: Lt-Gen J C Smuts, the Minister of Defence
OC: Lt-Col E F Thackeray
Adjutant: Captain J W Webber
Majors: H S J L Hemming, B Young
Captains: J W Jackson, D R Maclachlan, R F C Medlicott, H P Mills, L F Sprenger, E V Vivian
Lieutenants: J G Baker, H M Burrough, B H L Dougherty, H C Elliot, H M Hirtzel, A L Paxton, D A Pirie, S E Rogers, O H de B Thomas, A M Thomson
2nd Lieutenants: D M Abel, A H J Bliss, F W S Burton, A P Gairdner, A E Sharpe, W E Tucker, C Wilson
Quartermaster: Lt A W H McDonald
Medical Officer: Captain S Liebson

4th Regiment South African Infantry (SA Scottish)

Colonel-in-Chief: His Grace the Duke of Atholl
Honorary Colonel: Colonel W Dalrymple
OC: Lt-Col F A Jones DSO
Adjutant: Captain C M Browne
Majors: D M Macleod DCM, D R Hunt (OC 'C' Company)
Captains: R Anderson, E G Clerk (OC 'D' Company), E E D Grady, G E W Marshall, F Mc E Mitchell, R L Morton (OC 'A' Company), T H Ross (OC 'B' Company)
Lieutenants: C S Bell, A H Brown, A M Cameron (Maxim Officer),W D Charlton, J C French, C M Guest, H M Newson, M L Norton, J L Shenton, G Smith, R B Thorburn, J E Watkins.
2nd Lieutenants: J S M McCubbin, W McLean, H G Oughterson, A Young VC
Quartermaster: Captain H McVeigh
Medical Officer: Major M Power
Chaplain: Presbyterian: Captain the Revd S Thomson

Appendix B

Achievements of South African airmen who served in the Royal Flying Corps, Royal Naval Air Service and Royal Air Force 1914-19

SOUTH AFRICAN AIRMEN WHO SCORED FIVE OR MORE VICTORIES

NAME	RANK	DECORATIONS	SQUADRON	SCORE
BEAUCHAMP-PROCTOR Andrew Weatherby 'Proccy'	Capt	VC, DSO & Bar, MC & Bar, DFC	84	54 Includes 16 Balloons
KINKEAD Samuel Marcus 'Kink'	Capt	DSC & Bar, DFC & Bar DSO, Several Russian Orders	201 (Originally 1 RNAS) 47	30 10
VENTER Christoffel Johannes 'Boetie'	Capt	DFC & Bar POW 18 August 1918	29	22 or 16
HARRISON Thomas Sinclair	Capt	DFC & Bar, Croix de Guerre (Belgium)	29	22
BELL Douglas John 'Ginger'	Capt	MC & Bar KIA 27 May 1918	27,78,3	21
BARTON Horace Dale	Capt	DFC & Bar	24	20
ROSS Charles Gordon	Capt	DFC & Bar, Croix de Guerre (Belgium)	29	20

NAME	RANK	DECORATIONS	SQUADRON	SCORE
SOUTHEY Walter Alfred	Capt	DFC & Bar	48,84	20 (Includes 5 balloons)
REED Arthur Eden	Lt	DFC & Bar	29	19
SAUNDERS Hugh William Lumsden 'Dingbat'	Capt	MC, DFC, MM (Later knighted)	84	19
HAYNE Edwin Tufnell	Capt	DSC, DFC Killed flying accident 28 April 1919	203 (Originally 3 RNAS)	15
KIDDIE Andrew Cameron 'The Old Man'	Capt	DFC & Bar, Croix de Guerre	74	15
TUDHOPE John Henry	Capt	MC & Bar	40	15
GRAHAM Gavin Lynedoch	Lt	DFC, Legion of Honour Chevalier, Croix de Guerre with Palms	Observer 70 Pilot 73	13
CHAPPELL Roy Williamson	Capt	MC	27,41	12
QUINTIN-BRAND Christopher Joseph	Major	DSO, MC, DFC (Later Knighted) Pioneer Night Fighter 1,112,151	1,112,151	12
Shot down Gotha GV 979 off Staffel 15 during German bombing raid on England 19.5.18				
AMM Edgar Oxenham	Lt	DFC & Bar, Croix de Guerre (French)	29	10
PITHEY Croye Rothes	Lt	DFC & Bar Lost over Irish Sea Believed drowned 21 February 1920.	12	10 Shared with his observer
REDLER Herbert Bolton	Lt	MC Killed flying accident 21 June 1918	40,24	10
DANIEL Hector Cyril (Youngest Brother)	Capt	MC	43	10

NAME	RANK	DECORATIONS	SQUADRON	SCORE
SLATTER Leonard Horatio	Capt	DSC & Bar, DFC (Later Air Marshal)	Seaplane Defence Flight 13 RNAS, 213 4 ASD 47 (Russia)	10 or 7
WILLIAMS Thomas Mellings	Capt	MC, DFC (Later knighted)	65	10
MOODY Basil Henry	Lt		1	9
ANDERSON Gerald Frank	Lt	DFC He and his observer wounded 30 October 1918	88	8
HEMMING Alfred Stewart	Capt	DFC	41	8
LLOYD George Lawrence 'Zulu'	Major	MC, AFC	60,40	8
MEINTJES Henry 'Duke'	Capt	MC, AFC	60,56	8
NEL William Joseph Baynes	Lt		84	7
MACDONALD Hector Omdurman	Lt		84	7
FINDLAY John Pierce	Lt		88	6
LAWSON George Edgar Bruce	Lt	DFC When entrapped alone in a dogfight by some 15 opposing Fighters (27.9.18) he charged straight at the nearest fighter. Lawson's undercarriage struck the top of the enemy's machine. Lawson managed to land safely in his own lines. Lieutenant Fritz Rumey (German) (45 victories) crashed to his death out of control.	32	6

NAME	RANK	DECORATIONS	SQUADRON	SCORE
THOMSON Cecil Robert 'Ruggles'	Lt	DFC	84	6
TUDHOPE Philip Murray	Lt	DFC	46	6
WESTWOOD William Graham	Capt		88	6
ARMSTRONG D'Urban Victor	Capt	DFC Killed while stunting 13 November 1918 Camel specialist flyer	60,78,39,151	5
BLAKE Arthur Winston	Lt		19	5
HALL Robert Norwood	Capt	MC Earned while with RFA	40,44	5 Includes 3 balloons
SMUTS Neil Reitz	Capt	DFC	3	5
STEAD Ian Oliver	Lt		22	5
VOSS Vivian	Lt		48,88	5
VAN RYNEVELD (Andrias)	Lt-Col	DSO, MC, French Croix de Chevalier, Legion d' Honneur, Belgian Croix D'Officer de L'Orde de Leopold with Croix de Guerre. Later knighted.	17, 78HD[1] 45, OC 11th Wing	
LINDUP Ernest	Lt	MC	20	5 Shared with his various observers.
OLIVIER Eric	Capt		19	8

1   Home Defence

Indeterminate scores

A few of the South African airmen known to have achieved successes but whose total scores (possibly below 5) are unknown.

NAME	RANK	DECORATIONS	SQUADRON	REMARKS
BARBOUR Robert Lyle McK	Lt	DFC	205 Ex Naval No. 5	Several, shared with various observers
BETTERIDGE Arthur Henry	Lt		3	Includes one balloon
BRANDON Arthur Frank	Flt/Lt	DSC Killed in flying accident 26.10.1917	RNAS War School Manston	Brought down a Gotha at Vincent Farm, Manston, 22.8.1917.
BURGER Malcolm Graham Stewart	Lt	DFC	54	At least three.
CLOETE Dirk	Major	MC, AFC	23	
CURLEWIS Ivan	Lt	MC Wounded POW 9 November 1916	29	Includes one balloon.
DANIEL Arthur Hector Ross 'Artie' (Eldest of the three brothers)	Lt	Killed 29.8.1918 at Bertangles in puzzling aircraft crash. After taking off and climbing machine suddenly nosedived. Pilot was seen to be hanging over the side as if ill. Sudden onset of 1918 flu?	85	
DANIEL John (Middle Brother)	Lt		92	

NAME	RANK	DECORATIONS	SQUADRON	REMARKS
FLEMING Ian G	Lt		88	Shared with his observer
FORBES Haldane	Lt		43	
FORD Hedley	Lt	DFC	49	Shared with his observer
GILES G A[1] Gowan Arbuthnot	Capt		60, 209 Special School of Flying, Gosport.	Shared with two other Pilots
GILCHRIST Euan James Leslie W	Major	MC, DFC	60,56 OC 56	Includes one balloon.
GRAHAM Robert Lynedoch (Brother of Gavin Lynedoch)	Lt	MID KIA 16.9.1917 Passchendaele	19	
GREEN Jack Courtenay	Lt	DFC	54	Several. One shared
JOHNSTON Ernest Henry	Major	OBE, DFC. OC, 20 Squadron October 1917-Jan 1919	5, 20	Shared with his observer
JOOSTE G D	Capt		20	Shared with his observers.
LINDBERG Charles L	Lt		79	
LOVEMORE Robert Bailie	Lt	DSO	29	Includes one balloon.
LOWEN FrederickWilliam	Capt	Croix de Guerre with palms	49	Shared with his observer

1   SPECIAL NOTE Ironically Capt Giles was KIA (Abyssinia) during WW II 3.6.1941, while flying as pilot with 41 Squadron (SAAF) – Hawker Hartbees. The bodies of Giles and his Observer/Air Gunner F/Sgt M McWilliam, were recovered and buried five miles east of Oma Village. Giles was in his forty-third year and seems to have been SAAF's then oldest combat pilot.

NAME	RANK	DECORATIONS	SQUADRON	REMARKS
McCUBBIN[1] George Reynolds	Capt	DSO	25	He and his observer J H Waller credited with downing German 'Air Ace' Max Immelman 18.6.1916.
MILLER Allister Mackintosh	Major	OBE, DSO OC 45 Squadron 1918	3, 45	Shot down one enemy aircraft.
OLIVER Cyril Kingsley	Lt	RAF Communiques 1918 refer to him as 'Lt LCK Oliver'	87	
ORPEN Harold Claude Millard	Lt		60	
PALMER John	Lt		24	
PILDITCH Gerald	Lt	MC	73	2 destroyed 3 out of control
PYOTT Ian Vernon Jeffrey	Capt	DSO	36HD	Shot down Zeppelin L34 in flames off mouth of River Tees (Durham) on 27.11.16.
SHACKELL Cecil John	Lt	KIA 18.6.1918	210	Includes one balloon.

1 Germans claim Immelman's fatal crash caused by: i) Structural failure ii) Immelmann once again 'shot up' his own propeller through interrupter gear malfunction.

NAME	RANK	DECORATIONS	SQUADRON	REMARKS
SOUTHEY J H	Lt		24	At least one balloon. One known shared East African victory.
STOKES Rachfort Clive	Lt	According to 1934 *Who's Who in SA* he was awarded the DFC but not confrmed elsewhere.	49	Shared with his observer.
VAN RYNEVELD Theodore Victor	Lt	MC, Earned in 3SAI wounded at Arras 9.4.17.	29	Includes one balloon.
VORSTER William Lennox		KIA, 23.7.18 Italy	139	
WALTERS Stanley	Lt		20	Probably one shared with observer.
WILSON Felix Beamish	Capt	DFC		
WILTON Frederick Charles	Lt	DFC	98	Shared with his observer.

Appendix C

List of South Africans who Served in the Civil War in Russia 1918-1920

SURNAME	RANK AND INITIALS	HONOURS AND PREVIOUS UNIT OR UNIT IN RUSSIA	HONOURS FOR SERVICE IN RUSSIA
ALBU	CaptWG	RAF	Croix de Guerre with Palm, Order of Stanislas 2nd Cl. North Russia
BEVERLEY	Capt R	DSO, MC, late SAI	Siberia
BOUSTEAD	Capt H	late SA Scottish and Gen Denikin's Army	Bar to MC, Order of St Vladimir. South Russia
BROWNE	T/Maj C M	MC, Gen List, SA Forces British Military Mission South Russia Romanian Order of the Crown	OBE, despatches, South Russia. Order of St Anne, 2nd & 3rd Class. Order of St Vladimir
CHAMBERLIN	L D'E	2nd Hampshire Regt.	North Russia
CLARKE	Lt-Col W J	OBE, late 2nd SAMR	Despatches. North Russia
DODGSON	Capt	Intelligence Officer, RAF	North Russia
EPSTEIN	Lt M G	RAF	North Russia
FEATHERSTONE	T/Capt C	Gen List attd 241 Trench Mortar Bty	MC. North Russia
FRASER	Maj	late Border Mounted Rifles	North Russia
FRASER	Capt R D	Hampshire Regiment	

SURNAME	RANK AND INITIALS	HONOURS AND PREVIOUS UNIT OR UNIT IN RUSSIA	HONOURS FOR SERVICE IN RUSSIA
GREEN	Lt L L	MC, Rifle Brigade attd 46 Bn Royal Fusiliers	DSO, Archangel. North Russia
GWATKIN	T/Capt R D S	RFA (Lt SA Forces)	MBE, despatches Dunsterforce
HASELDEN	Lt-Col F	DSO, MC, late SAI (wounded)	North Russia
HERSCHELL	Maj A	MC, 2TS and RE	OBE South Russia
HEYDENRYCH	Lt L R	RNVR (SAD) Seconded RN Naval Secretary, British Military Mission, Taganrog.	Orders of St Anne and St Stanislas, 4th Class. South Russia
JENKINS	Lt-Col H H	DSO, late SAI, OC 46th Royal Fusiliers	CMG, despatches, Order of St Anne, 2nd Cl. North Russia
KILPIN	Capt D	Staff	
KINKEAD	Flt-Lt S M	DSO and Bar, DFC, RAF	DSO, Orders of St Anne, St Stanislas, St George and St Vladimir. South Russia
KNOWLES	Lt-Col		North Russia
LUNN	Capt W S	MC, late SAHA, RE	Caucasus. South Russia
MACFARLANE	2/Lt B N	MC, late SAI	
MACFIE	Capt T G	MC, late 4th SAI	DSO, despatches. Archangel. North Russia
McCORKINDALE	Sgt M	Cossacks and Machine Gun Corps	Despatches and Order of St George. North Russia
MCKENZIE	Lt D M R	6th Dragoon Guards	'Elope' North Russian Expeditionary Force. Archangel.

SURNAME	RANK AND INITIALS	HONOURS AND PREVIOUS UNIT OR UNIT IN RUSSIA	HONOURS FOR SERVICE IN RUSSIA
MACLEOD	Lt-Col D M	DSO, MC, DCM, late OC 4th SAI, OC 2nd Hampshire Regt. Croix de Guerre	Order of St Anne, 2nd Cl.
NORCUTT	Capt H J	MC, Royal Garrison Artillery	Order of St Anne, 2nd Cl. North Russia
REID	Capt O A	VC	Russia
SHERWOOD-KELLY	Lt-Col J	VC, CMG, DSO, OC 2nd Hampshire Regt.	Archangel. North Russia
SMITH	Lt A	DCM 46th Royal Fusiliers	North Russia
STEWART	2nd Lt	Ex Natal Police	Commissioned for gallantry. North Russia
SUMNER	Lt H L	Ex 4th SAI, MC MM	
VAN DER SPUY	Lt-Col K R	MC, RAF, OC Elope Force	Orders of St George and St Vladimir. North Russia
WHAMMOND	Sgt J (ex Lt)	MC, DCM, MM, 46th Royal Fusiliers	North Russia

Appendix
D

Battle Honours of the 1st South African Infantry Brigade

The Battle Honours in bold print are those actually emblazoned on the regimental colours of the four regiments.

1st SA Infantry (Cape of Good Hope Regt.)	**Agagiya, Egypt** 1916, **Somme** 1916, **Delville Wood**, Le Transloy, **Arras** 1917, Scarpe 1917, **Ypres** 1917, **Menin Road**, Lys, **Messines** 1918, **Kemmel**, Hindenburg Line, **Cambrai** 1918, **Selle**, France and Flanders, 1916-18
2nd SAI (Natal and OFS Regt.)	**Egypt** 1916, **Somme** 1916, **Delville Wood**, Le Transloy, **Arras** 1917, Scarpe 1917, **Ypres** 1917, **Menin Road**, **Lys, Messines** 1918, **Kemmel**, Hindenburg Line, **Cambrai** 1918, **Selle**, France and Flanders, 1916-l8
3rd SAI (Transvaal and Rhodesian Regt.)	**Agagiya, Egypt** 1916, **Somme** 1916, **Delville Wood**, Le Transloy, **Arras** 1917, **Scarpe** 1917, **Ypres** 1917, **Menin Road, Passchendaele, France and Flanders** 1916-18.

4th SAI (SA Scottish)

Egypt 1916, **Somme** 1916,
Delville Wood, Le Transloy,
Arras 1917, Scarpe 1917,
Ypres 1917, **Menin Road**,
Lys, **Messines**, 1918, Kemmel,
Hindenburg Line, Cambrai 1918,
**Pursuit to Mons, France and
Flanders** 1916-18.

The 1st SA Field Ambulance that accompanied the SA Brigade was
also awarded battle honours:

1st SA Field Ambulance

Egypt 1916, **Somme** 1916,
Delville Wood, Arras 1917
Scarpe 1917, **Ypres** 1917,
Menin Road, Passchendaele,
Hindenburg Line, Beaurevoir,
**Selle, Sambre, France and
Flanders** 1916-18,

Appendix
E

Why South African Regiments have been deprived of their First World War Battle Honours 1916-1918

On 10 October 1926, the South African Memorial at Delville Wood was unveiled. The Chairman of the South African National Memorial Committee, Sir Percy Fitzpatrick, who had purchased Delville Wood and presented it to the Union of South Africa, made the opening address and stated that:

> The choice of Delville Wood as the site of this Memorial has been interpreted to mean the Memorial is to those only who fell on this field. This is not so. It is inscribed:
>
> *To the immortal dead from South Africa who, at the call of Duty, made the Great Sacrifice on the battlefields of Africa, Asia and Europe, and on the Sea, this Memorial is dedicated in proud and grateful recognition by their countrymen.*[1]

Some sixty years later 400 South Africans came to Delville Wood on 11 November 1986. The purpose of this gathering was to pay tribute to all South Africans who had given their lives for South Africa during the long course of its history.

> Let this commemorative museum honour the sacrifices of the past, and for future generations, be a symbol of the steadfastness of purpose of the soldiers of South Africa...The South African National War Memorial here at Delville Wood is thus a symbol of national unity and reconciliation for all South Africans of all times on all battlefields...

So spoke the State President, The Hon P W Botha, at the opening of the Museum at Delville Wood.

---

1 Delville Wood Memorial Book extracts from Sir Percy Fitzpatrick's speech p6-11.

Such memorials are very necessary yet these men have been denied the living memorial that is their due. The living memorial takes the form of the battle honours emblazoned on colours carried by regiments. These battle honours record the distinctions and names of places associated with honourable service on the field of battle. Those battle honours go marching into the future carried by the successors of the men who won them. The sight of these honours on a colour creates a feeling of pride in soldiers and ex-soldiers alike and are the outward and visible signs of sacrifice of the people of a country. They are a record of gallant deeds and an inspiration for the future. They embody the memory of the illustrious achievements of thousands of soldiers: their comradeship in battle and countless examples of courage and selfless devotion to duty. These qualities found expression in the Great War perhaps more than in any war before or since. South African units were awarded a host of battle honours as were their Australian, Indian and Canadian counterparts.

Australia, in the same way as South Africa, had a Defence Act in terms of which it was not contemplated that the citizens' forces brought into existence by the Australian Commonwealth Defence Act of 1909 would serve outside the Commonwealth of Australia. Because of this, the Australian Government raised a new volunteer army for service overseas under the title of the Australian Imperial Force. The Great War battle honours awarded to the battalions and regiments of the AIF were inherited, in 1927, by perpetuating units of the Citizen Military Forces of Australia. There are instances where the perpetuating unit had no connection with the war service unit. An Australian Military Order actually had the designations of the Citizen Military Forces altered to conform to the numbers borne by the AIF that had served abroad 'in order to maintain the traditions and perpetuate the records of the 1914-18 War.' (Military Order 364 of the 3 August 1918.)

At the start of World War I, in Canada, like Australia, a new force known as The Canadian Expeditionary Force was brought into existence. After the War, CEF units were also perpetuated. Their battle honours also survived the War.

Like Australia, and other parts of the Empire, South Africa had a Defence Act that precluded the dispatch of its existing units beyond its borders or abutting territories. Botha and Smuts were bound by the terms of the Defence Act, so it was necessary, like Australia and Canada, to create a new force – The South African Overseas Expeditionary Force – but if this force were to be paid and financed by the South African Government, Botha and Smuts would have been voted out of office. They found a way round the problem. The way out is contained in General Order 672 of 1915: 'The South African Overseas Expeditionary Force will be Imperial and have the status of British Regular Troops.'

The word 'status' says it all. This is merely a reference to administrative standing or 'position – rank' of the force.[1] It meant that as Britain was footing the bill for the sake of political expediency on the South African home front, South African troops would receive 'Pay, separation allowance and pension at Imperial rates'. Thus their status would be the same as the British Regular Army because Britain was paying. In no way did this make the South African Overseas Expeditionary Force British. Like the Australians and Canadians these War Service Units received designations for service overseas. They continued to wear South African cap and collar badges and shoulder tides. Their recruitment thus differed little from the methods employed in other parts of the Empire. Veterans of those War Service Units never regarded themselves as anything other than South Africans. If Britain had regarded them as such, the units would have been given a British identity.

There was also ignorance in South Africa in Defence Force circles as to what was in fact being done elsewhere in the British Empire. Unfortunately this parochial view has been pursued blindly by subsequent researchers without making a fresh evaluation of the facts. On 8 June 1916 an unknown lieutenant-colonel who was based at Defence Headquarters in the Adjutant-General's office wrote:

> The Force now sent to German East...is raised locally for the purpose of assisting the Imperial Authorities in carrying out a special undertaking. It really only amounts to this that the Union Government has allowed the Imperial Authorities (and has assisted) to recruit men in South Africa for this Force. It is certainly not raised under the Defence Act (of the Union of South Africa), and this being so, the Union Government can grant no commissions. Besides this Force is paid by the Imperial Government and subject to the Army Act. The only competent authority to grant commissions is the Imperial Army Council. Such commissions will be of a temporary nature and lapse at the conclusion of hostilities.

No one in South Africa, at the time or subsequently, has researched the position of Imperial Service Forces raised for war service in other parts of the British Empire. If they had, they would have discovered that what had taken place in South Africa, except regarding pay, was identical to the position throughout the British Empire. With Britain's aid, whether through the provision of instructors, equipment or funding, locally raised forces were brought into existence to assist the Imperial Authorities in the war effort. All officers held Imperial Service Commissions whether Australian, Canadian, Indian or South African, while their services were needed. The blueprint for the scheme had originated in India.

1 Concise Oxford Dictionary

To mark the Jubilee of the Queen-Empress (Victoria), the larger (Indian) States decided to earmark certain units of their armies for the defence of the Indian Empire. Financed by the Princely rulers, their training supervised by officers loaned by the Indian Army, these Indian States' units – which became known as Imperial Service Troops – began to play a part in Indian defence. By 1914, the Imperial Service Troops had a combined strength of over 20 000 officers and soldiers, most of whom served with distinction for up to four years in the overseas theatres of war...by the end of the Great War, India had sent overseas a total of 290 battalions or more than 1 300 000 volunteer soldiers.[1]

The identity and battle honours won by the Imperial Service Units of the British Empire during the Great War, as well as the identity of these units, were perpetuated with pride. In South Africa, when the end of the Great War came, the need to perpetuate the identity and achievements of South African War Service Units was overlooked.

General Smuts, as Minister of Defence and later as Prime Minister, was too involved on the world stage to concern himself with such parochial matters. This contributed to his own fall at home. In 1924 he found himself defeated at the polls by a Nationalist-Labour Coalition with General Hertzog as Prime Minister. It had been Hertzog who had bitterly opposed South Africa's involvement in the War, particularly in France. Nothing was done about the matter of battle honours for the Imperial Service Units.

By 1935 attitudes in government circles had mellowed. An extract from a letter from Col F H Theron, OC Roberts Heights, to the Adjutant General dated 15 October 1935 reads as follows:

In a recent informal discussion at which Mr. Pirow, Brigadier-General van Ryneveld, Colonel Theron and Lieut-Col. Smitheman were present, the Minister expressed himself as being in sympathy with the suggestion that the existing ACF units which could be regarded as having been the components of those South African units which served overseas during the Great War, should be granted the Battle Honours of the latter.

In 1936, acting on this suggestion, it was decided that

before the matter can be considered it will be necessary to ascertain the number of officers and other ranks who, whilst serving members of units of the Active Citizen Force, enlisted for service overseas with the South African Infantry Brigade.

---

1   Cox R H W, *Military Badges of the British Empire* 1914-18 p253.

The units could not supply such information as all records were held at Defence Headquarters in Pretoria. The units appealed for assistance and voiced their inability to supply the information from their own regimental records.

At Army Headquarters, without an archival service or documentation centre, there were no facilities to conduct such research. A military pensioner was assigned the task of supplying information to units. Such untrained personnel failed to locate the required information.[1] Subsequent requests to supply this information were blocked with the excuse that the attestation forms required for such an investigation did not exist or would be too difficult to extract from the personal files of soldiers. The fact that these documents, along with record cards and embarkation rolls with previous service in the German South West Africa Campaign do exist in 1992 in the SA Defence Force Archives is further evidence of the incompetence of the Defence Force administrative capacity in the 1930s. Obviously no unit could claim or accept battle honours unless proper research was undertaken. The Adjutant-General of the time also ruled that further investigation would be impracticable – a convenient way to conceal the ineptitude of his section.

The whole question had been approached incorrectly. Unit commanders of the day, who may have been very junior officers or too young to serve in the Great War, had been written to. The men who had the answers were ignored. The commanding officers or senior officers of the old Imperial Service Units were still alive and available to be consulted in 1936! They would have been best equipped for the task of evolving a method for the perpetuation of the battle honours of the War Service Units as had been the case in Canada, Australia and elsewhere in the British Empire.

Then came the Second World War and interest in a new crop of battle honours. Once again the matter was conveniently overlooked.

When the Smuts Government was defeated in the 1948 General Election a cloud fell on the Defence Force. The new Minister of Defence, the Hon F C Erasmus, tried exceedingly hard to eliminate every vestige of British tradition from the Union Defence Force. It is ironic that during the period that Erasmus was in office, units of the same World War I designation were coincidentally established: 1 SAI in 1951; 2 SAI, 3 SAI, 4 SAI, 5 SAI and 6 SAI in 1962 as well as a 7 SAI and 8 SAI in 1973. Even though Minister Erasmus passed off the stage, his influence has lingered on. He had inculcated an ignorance of and particular attitude to all tradition and history of the South African Defence Force that has a British connection. No one looked to the World War I Service Units. Very likely

---

1   Evidence of their bungling efforts at research are available for scrutiny in the Transvaal Scottish Regimental Archives.

their PF Unit Commanders were unaware that these units had even existed!

In 1984 the OC 4 SAI, when asked to design a cap badge, actually based the design of his new cap badge on one of the Israeli Army! Certainly under such circumstances the long defunct Regimental Associations of the SA Brigades would not have wished their cherished honours to fall prey to a unit 'tradition' that was so far removed from their own.

In 1965 the Chief of the Army and Commandant-General did pass a ruling that the present day 4 and 5 SAI Battalions had no connection with those of the same designation in World War I. Nor could they claim any World War I battle honours. However, in direct contradiction to this ruling, the World War I battle honours of the Cape Corps, (which was an Imperial Service Unit that had been established on the same basis as 1st SAI to 12th SAI and the SAHA Batteries), were given to the present day Cape Corps of the SA Defence Force. The occasion was the unit's tenth birthday. The reason for this departure was once again politically motivated: 'This decision (in 1973) was taken in the spirit of the prevailing political climate and coincided with the commissioning of the Unit's Colours on the occasion of its tenth birthday.'[1]

Only in 1985, shortly before the opening of the Delville Wood Museum was the matter of battle honours re-opened. South Africa would be in the spotlight in Europe – not a single battle honour won in the Great War would be in evidence if regimental colour parties were sent to France as part of the contingent. Once again unit commanders were consulted regarding the possible award of battle honours to existing ACF units, but they were not supplied with the real background and motivation behind the letter they received. The true meaning of Imperial Service Units – that they were universally applicable throughout the British Empire during the Great War – was not explained. Nothing was said regarding the position of battle honours awarded to the successors to or the perpetuating units of the War Service Units in Canada or Australia. The unit commanders of 1986 were even less qualified to respond to such a suggestion as those of 1936. Regimental histories were vague on the matter.

As was to be expected, responses were negative, uninformed and even sometimes on the verge of the ridiculous as the following outburst illustrates:

> Such an award (of battle honours) would constitute an immoral prostitution of the battle honours concerned which would taint not only the recipients but also the South African Army with the shabbiness of fraud and deceit.[2]

However, this is exactly what was done in Canada and Australia and the fact of the

---

1   AMI/MIB (Arg) C/521/3/7/1/2
2   From a letter written by young officer in 1985.

matter is that certain South African ACF Units did get absorbed virtually *en masse* by Imperial Service Units and I know of at least one Imperial Service Unit's senior NCO and officer element that returned to its ACF unit in 1921 virtually *en bloc*.

What must not be lost sight of is that just as Canadians and Australians fought in World War I and the battle honours of those units were perpetuated in new units filled with a new generation, so are there still units in the South African Defence Force filled with the grandsons or great-grandsons of the men who fought in the Great War. In addition, the majority of the ACF Units that supplied the men for the War Service Units still exist.

No error or oversight is too late to correct, especially in the climate of the South Africa of today.

In a letter of 5 November 1985, the then Chief of the SA Defence Force, General J J Geldenhuys SSA SOE SD SM, addressed the problem with great perception. As yet no one has responded to some very valid points he made regarding requirements for the award of battle honours to units that participated in World War I. These were:

– Motivation for and the changing of the existing rules and regulations for the award of battle honours.
– The discovery and formulation of an acceptable formula by which battle honour; may be awarded to units that took part in World War I.

(Translated from the Afrikaans.)

Here at last is recognition that a new formula has to be found for the perpetuation of Imperial War Service battle honours.

What has been achieved through doing this in countries such as Canada and Australia through perpetuating units so these units become the custodians of the battle honours of the Great War, cannot be ignored. In South Africa there must be a proud and equitable solution to such a problem, but only the concern and commitment of interested parties will bring it to fruition. Even now it can be done.

1st SA Infantry Brigade Christmas Card 1918-19 sent by Captain H R Lawrence MC, Medical Officer 4th SAI, to the Adjutant Captain F McE Mitchell MC and his wife. This must have been the last document Lawrence signed before he succumbed to pneumonia on 14 December 1918. (Transvaal Scottish Regimental Museum)

Appendix
F

Battle Honours of the South African Heavy Artillery

NOTE: Only on three occasions during the entire duration of their Western Front service were the SA Heavy Artillery in action in support of the 1st SA Infantry Brigade. When this occurred it was only one of the six batteries that was involved: the 75th Siege Battery at Butte de Warlencourt, the 71st Siege Battery at Third Ypres and the 74th Siege Battery at Arras. This was purely co-incidental. The units of the SAHA acted independently, being allotted to British Army Corps and Heavy Artillery Groups across the length and breadth of the Western Front from summer 1916 to November 1918. Even on the formation of the 44th and 50th South African Artillery Brigades in 1918, the SAHA batteries never had the same corporate identity as the 1st SA Infantry Brigade. The six batteries of SAHA were each issued with four 6 inch 26cwt Breech Loading Howitzers with an elevation of 45 degrees and a range of 9 500 yards for a 100 lb shell.

The record rate of fire was achieved by 73rd Siege Battery, doing 32 rounds in 8 minutes with each gun. This record was never broken in France. There were 1 246 of the 26cwt Howitzers used by British artillery in the line from late 1915 to November 1918 and over this period the ammunition expenditure in France and Flanders for these guns was 22 400 000 rounds. The 74th Siege Battery recorded firing 1 733 rounds on 1 July 1916 while the 75th Siege Battery fired 1 312 rounds before noon on the same day. The tons of metal thrown at each side becomes mind-boggling when it is realised that these records reflect one calibre of gun and only those used by the British.

The following list of battle honours awarded to the South African Heavy Artillery during the Great War, spell out their achievement which took them to every corner of the Western Front. The Battle Honours in bold type were those selected from each list of battery honours, to be regarded as the Battle Honours to be carried by that battery. The battery could select a minimum number from the approved list:

439

THE GREAT WAR – FRANCE AND FLANDERS, 1916-18

As granted to the South African Heavy Artillery by GO 5997 of 21 April 1926.

UNIT PARTICIPATING	HONOURS
71st (Transvaal) Siege Bty RGA	**Somme** 1916, Bazentin, **Pozieres, Flers-Courcelette, Thiepval**, Ancre Heights, Bapaume 1917, **Bullecourt, Ypres** 1917, Menin Road, Polygon Wood, Broodseinde, **Passchendaele, Cambrai** 1917, **Lys**, Estaires, Bethune, **Pursuit to Mons**, France and Flanders, 1916-18.
72nd (Griqualand West) Siege Bty RGA	**Somme** 1916-18, Albert 1916, Bazentin, **Pozieres**, Flers-Courcelette, **Thipval**, Ancre Heights, **Ancre** 1916, **Arras** 1917-18, Vimy 1917, Arleux, Oppy, Hill 70, **Ypres** 1917, **Passchendaele, Scarpe** 1918, **Droucourt-Queánt**, Hindenburg Line, Canal du Nord, Cambrai 1918, **Pursuit to Mons**, France and Flanders, 1916-18.
73rd (Cape) Siege Bty RGA	**Somme** 1916, Bazentin, **Pozieres**, Flers-Courcelette, **Thiepval**, Ancre Heights, **Ancre** 1916, **Arras** 1917, Vimy 1917, Arleux Oppy, **Ypres** 1917, **Menin Road**, Polygon Wood, Broodseinde,

Passchendaele, **Lys**,
Estaires, **Bethune**,
Pursuit to Mons,
France and
Flanders, 1916-18.

74th (Eastern Province) Siege Bty RGA	**Somme** 1916-18, Albert 1916, **Pozieres**, Flers-Courcelette, Thiepval, Ancre Heights, **Ancre** 1916, **Arras** 1917-18, Vimy 1917, Scarpe 1917, **Oppy, Messines** 1917, **Ypres** 1917, **Menin Road**, Polygon Wood, Broodseinde, **Passchendaele**, Scarpe 1918, Drocourt-Queánt, Hindenburg Line, Canal du Nord, Cambrai 1918, **Pursuit to Mons**, France and Flanders, 1916-18.
75th (Natal) Siege Bty RGA	**Somme** 1916-18, Albert 1916, **Bazentein, Pozieres, Flers-Courcelette**, Ancre Heights, Ancre 1916, Bapaume 1917, **Ypres** 1917, Pilckem, Langemarck 1917, **Poelca-Pelle**, Passchendaele, Arras 1918, **Scarpe** 1918. **Droucourt-Queánt**, Hindenburg Line, Canal du Nord, Cambrai 1918, **Pursuit to Mons**, France and Flanders, 1916-18.

125th (Transvaal) Siege
Bty RGA

Somme 1916, **Flers-
Courcelette**, Morval,
Thiepval, LeTransloy,
Ancre Heights,
Ancre 1916,
Arras 1917, **Scarpe** 1917,
Oppy, Hill 70, **Ypres** 1917,
Cambrai 1917, **Lys**, Estaires,
Bethune, Pursuit to Mons,
France and Flanders, 1916-18

Eleven honours are shown in block capitals which is contrary to Army Order 470/22.

Appendix G

Battle Honours of the South African Field Artillery

The SAFA was recruited for service in France in September 1915, but when it was announced that the SAFA was destined for German East Africa, some 280 men of all ranks transferred to the SAHA. After completing their stint in East Africa, the five batteries of SAFA returned to South Africa in April 1917. Thereafter their new destination was Palestine, not France. Only later did the 3rd and 5th Batteries follow the other three to Palestine, after a second period of service in East Africa.

The following Battle Honours were awarded to the SAFA:

UNIT PARTICIPATING	HONOURS
1st Bty SAFA	**Kilimanjaro, E Africa** 1916, **Gaza, El Mughar, Nebi Samwil, 'Tel'Asur', Megiddo, Sharon, Palestine** 1917-18.
2nd Bty SAFA	**Kilimanjaro, E Africa** 1916, **Gaza, El Mughar, Nebi Samwil, 'Tel'Asur', Megiddo, Sharon, Palestine** 1917-18.
3rd Bty SAFA	**Kilimanjaro, E Africa** 1916, **'Tel'Asur', Megiddo, Sharon, Palestine** 1918.

4th Bty SAFA

Kilimanjaro, E Africa 1916,
**Gaza, El Mughar, Nebi
Samwil 'Tel'Asur',
Megiddo, Sharon,
Palestine** 1917-18.

5th Bty SAFA

Kilimanjaro, E Africa 1916-17,
**'Tel'Asur', Megiddo,
Sharon, Palestine** 1918.

Bibliography

1. *A History of the Seventy First Siege Battery South African Heavy Artillery* – no date.
2. Addison, F – *Horse, Foot and Guns 1914-1918* – unpublished manuscript.
3. Adler, Lorch and Curson – *The SA Field Artillery in German East Africa and Palestine 1915-1919* – Van Schaik 1958.
4. Adler, Major F B – *The History of the Transvaal Horse Artillery* – Speciality Press 1927.
5. Barnes, Major R Money – *The Uniforms and History of the Scottish Regiments* – Seeley Service: no date.
6. Betteridge, Arthur H – *Combat In and Over Delville Wood Vol 1-3* – Edited and privately published by Ernest Slatter, Pretoria.
7. Bissett, Cmdr W M – *A Short History of Kyk in de Pot Battery and Fort Wynyard* – no date.
8. Bouch, R J – *Infantry in South Africa 1652-1976* – Government Printer, Pretoria 1977.
9. Boustead, Col Sir Hugh – *The Wind of Morning* – Chatto and Windus 1972.
10. Brice, B – *The Battle Book of Ypres* – John Murray 1927.
11. Buchan, J – *The South African Forces in France* – Nelson 1920.
12. Bowyer, C – *Sopwith Camel: King of Combat* – Glasney Press.
13. Butcher, P E – *Skill and Devotion (No 2 Squadron RFC)* – Radio Modeller Book Division 1971.
14. Buxton, Lord – *General Botha* – John Murray 1924.
15. Captain – *With the Springboks in Egypt* 1916.
16. Carstens, J – *A Fortune Through My Fingers* – Howard Timmins 1962.
17. Choat, 2/Lt C – Collection of Letters 1916-1918 (unpublished).
18. *Chronicles of a Family* – privately published.
19. Cloete-Smith, Cpl A W – Collection of Letters 1915-1918 (unpublished).
20. Clothier, N – *Black Valour* – University of Natal Press, 1987.
21. Cole, C (and others) – *Royal Flying Corps 1915-1916 and Royal Air Force*

Communiques 1918.

22. Cox, R H W – *Military Badges of the British Empire 1914-18* – E Benn Ltd 1982.

23. Creagh and Humphris – *The VC and the DSO* (3 Vols) – Standard Art Book Co.

24. Croft, Lt-Col W D – *Three Years With the 9th Scottish Division* – John Murray 1919.

25. *Cross and Cockade International Journals.*

26. Curson, H H – *Colours and Honours in South Africa 1783-1948* – Wallachs 1948.

27. Curson, H H – *The History of the Kimberley Regiment 1876-1962* – Northern Cape Printers 1963.

28. *Delville Wood Memorial Book* – 1926.

29. Digby, Capt P K A – *The Affiliation Cap Badges of the South African Defence Force 1984 to Date* –privately published 1988.

30. Digby, Capt P K A – *The History of King Edward VII School 1902-1968* – unpublished manuscript.

31. Ewing, J – *The History of the 9th (Scottish) Division* – John Murray 1921.

32. Forsyth, D R – *Orders of Chivalry, Foreign Decorations and Awards.*

33. Forsyth, D R – *Medals for Gallantry and Distinguished Conduct.*

34. Forsyth, D R – *Decorations to Natal, Cape Colony and Union Defence Force Units 1877-1961.*

35. Franks, N – *Appendices to 'Flying Minnows' by Roger Vee* – Arms and Armour Press 1977 Republication.

36. Gough, Gen Sir Hubert – *The Fifth Army* – Hodder & Stoughton 1931.

37. Hammerton, Sir John (editor) – *'I Was There' The Human Story of the Great War* – 4 Vols Waverley Book Company 1938.

38. Hanbury, D M – *Br James Oblate OSB* – 1953.

39. *History of the Seventy-First Siege Battery South African Heavy Artillery* – no date or publisher.

40. Hogg, J V and Thurston, L F – *British Artillery Weapons and Ammunition 1914-18* – Ian Allen, London 1972.

41. *Honours and Awards, Army, Navy and Air Force 1914-1920* – published by J B Hayward 1979.

42. *In Tribute to SA Forces* – reprinted from *Panorama*, February 1987.

43. Jennings, H D – *The D H S Story* – Davis and Platt 1965.

44. Jenkins, G – *A Century of History, The Story of Potchefstroom* – Potchefstroom Herald 1939.

45. Johnstone R – *Ulundi to Delville Wood* – Maskew Miller 1926.

46. Juta, H C – *The History of the Transvaal Scottish 1902-1932* – Hortors

1933.

47.   *King Edward VII School Magazine* 1914-1922.

48.   Lambert, L – *Combat Report (24 Squadron).*

49.   Lawson, Pte John A – *Memories of Delville Wood, South Africa's Greatest Battle* – Maskew Miller 1918.

50.   Lawson, K C – *Venture of Faith (The Story of St John's College, Johannesburg 1898-1968* – Council of St John's College 1968.

51.   Levyns, J E P – *The Disciplines of War* – Vantage Press Inc 1984.

52.   Liddell Hart, Basil – *A History of the World War* – Faber and Faber 1930.

53.   Liddle, P H – *The Soldier's War 1914-1928 and the Airman's War 1914-1918* – Blandford Press.

54.   *Michelin Guides to the Battlefields 1914-1918 Ypres and The Somme.*

55.   Middlebrook, M – *The Kaiser's Battle* – Allen Lane 1978.

56.   *Militaria* – Official Professional Journal of the South African Defence Force.

57.   *Military History Journal* – official publication of the SA Military History Society.

58.   *Military Medal Society of South Africa Journal.*

59.   Monick, S – *A Bugle Calls* – Witwatersrand Rifles Regimental Council 1989.

60.   *Museum Review* Vol 1 No 1 – SA National Museum of Military History.

61.   *Nongqai Magazine.*

62.   Norris, G – *The Royal Flying Corps. A History* – Frederick Muller Ltd.

63.   Orpen, N – *Gunners of the Cape* – Cape Field Artillery Regimental History Committee 1965.

64.   Orpen, N – *The Cape Town Highlanders* – Cape Town Highlanders History Committee 1970.

65.   Orpen, N – *The History of the Transvaal Horse Artillery 1904-74* – Transvaal Horse Artillery Regimental Council 1975.

66.   Orpen, N – *The Dukes* – Cape Town Rifles Dukes Regimental Council 1984.

67.   *Personalites in South African Motoring and Aviation* – published 1941.

68.   Raleigh/Jones, H A – *The War in the Air.*

69.   Reitz, D – *Trekking On* – Faber and Faber 1933.

70.   Robinson, B – *Air Aces of the 1914-1918 War* – A Harborough Publication.

71.   Rosenthal, E – *General Dan Pienaar, His Life and Battles* – Afrikaanse Pers 1943.

72.   Serowe – *War Memories* – Underhill and Co: no date.

73.   Shaw-Sparrow, W – *The Fifth Army* – Bodley Head 1921.

74.   Shermer, D – *World War I* – Octopus Books 1973.

75. Sharp, John R – *The Aces: World War I Aviation 1914-1918* – published by the editor/author, USA.
76. Shores, Christopher – *Air Aces* – Bison Books.
77. Simpkins, B – *Rand Light Infantry* – Howard Timmins 1965.
78. Singleton-Gates, G R – *Bolos and Barishynas* – Gale and Polden 1920.
79. Smith, J A – *John Buchan. A Biography* – Rupert Hart Davis 1965.
80. Solomon, E – *Potchefstroom to Delville Wood* – The Football Sports Publishers: no date.
81. South African Defence Force Documentation Centre, Pretoria – various document series associated with World War I.
82. *Springbok Magazine*.
83. Stayt, H – *Idle Thoughts from Darkland* – Maskew Miller: no date.
84. *St John's College and the War* – St John's College Archives.
85. Terraine, J – *The Western Front 1914-18* – Hutchinson 1967.
86. *The British Roll of Honour* – Queen Hithe Publishing Company.
87. *The Roll of Honour of the South African Forces in the World War 1914-1919* – Privately printed.
88. *The Story of Delville Wood (Told in Letters From the Front)* – Cape Times: no date.
89. Transvaal Scottish Regimental Museum Document Collection.
90. Tylden, Major G – *The Armed Forces of South Africa* – Africana Museum 1954.
91. *Union of South Africa and the Great War 1914-1918 Official History* – Government Printer, Pretoria 1923.
92. Unpublished Diary of Major A E Lorch DSO MC – SA National Museum of Military History.
93. Unpublished letters and diaries from various sources.
94. Uys, Ian – *For Valour* – Uys Publishers 1973.
95. Uys, Ian – *Delville Wood* – Uys Publishers 1983.
96. Uys, Ian – *Roll Call, The Delville Wood Story* – Uys Publishers 1991.
97. Van der Byl, P – *From Playgrounds to Battlefields* – Howard Timmins 1971.
98. Van der Spuy, Maj-Gen K R – *Chasing the Wind* – Books of Africa 1966.
99. Walker, G Goold – *The Honourable Artillery Company* – Bodley Head 1926.
100. Wallis, J P R – *Fitz, The Story of Sir Percy Fitzpatrick* – Macmillan 1955.
101. Warwick, George W – *We Band of Brothers* – Howard Timmins 1962.
102. Wavell, Gen Sir Archibald – *Allenby: A Study in Greatness* – OUP 1941.
103. *Who's Who in South Africa*.

Index

Murray, Maj C M: 159, 242, 263
Murray of Atholl tartan: 35, 40, 56-57, 279

Nagb el Erajib: 87
Nagb Medean: 87
Nancy: 40, 42, 56, 61, 102-103, 279, 281, 400-403
Nash, Canon: 84, 159, 234
National Party: 420
Nel, Lt W J B: 350, 406
Neville, Lt R E: 341, 343
Neuve Eglise: 341, 343
New Army *see* Kitchener's New Army
New Zealand's contribution to the war: 17
New Zealand Expeditionary Force: 18
New Zealand Stationary Hospital: 351
Nieuport: 284
Nile River: 67, 69
Noor el Bahr, H T: 69
North Midland Farm: 343
North Russian Expeditionary Force/Relief Force: 383, 387, 427
Northern Transvaal Command: 23
Norcutt, Capt H J: 428
Nose, the: 186-187
Noyon-Montdidier sector: 367
Nurlu: 299-303, 305-306, 309, 313

Orpen, Lt H C M: 424
O T C (Officer Training Corps): 333-334, 336
Oise: 284
Old Contemptibles: 115
Oliver, Lt C K: 424
Olivier, Capt E: 421
Oost Pinega: 388
Oriana: 59-60, 98, 131
Original memorial to SA Brigade: 279-280
Ormiston, Maj T: 186-188, 306-307, 315-316, 318, 416
Oxford University: 333-336, 384

Palestine: 331, 443-444
Palmer, Lt J: 424
Park Station: 403-404, 411
Parr, Chaplain S: 353

Passchendaele: 266, 269, 271, 283-284, 341, 406, 423, 429-430, 440-441
Pay: 62, 212, 235, 432-433
Peacock, Capt F: 300, 319, 323, 325
Pearse, Lt T F (later Capt): 181, 304, 417
Perham Downs: 388
Peronne: 122, 172-173, 309, 313, 317
Perry, 2/Lt H: 373
Peters, 2/Lt J: 372
Petersen, Pte A E: 40, 42, 61, 102, 279, 281
Petits Puits: 351
Peyton, Maj-Gen W E: 75, 86-87, 91, 94-95
Philip, Capt A W: 298, 317-318
Phillips, Lt E J: 150, 152
Picardy: 120, 368
Pick House: 345, 349
Pilditch, Lt G: 424
Pill-boxes: 238, 244-245, 252-253, 258, 261, 264, 349
Pimple, the: 182, 186-188
Pipes and Drums: 42, 101, 121, 169, 404
Pithey, Lt C R: 419
Ploegsteert: 106
Plumer, Gen Sir Herbert: 100, 169, 340, 356, 361
Point du Jour: 213
Poona: 23
Porchaux: 372
Pope-Hennessy, 2/Lt B: 351
Poperinghe: 238-239
Poppies: 120, 265
Portuguese: 341
Potchefstroom: 21-23, 25-29, 30-31, 33-36, 37-40, 50-51, 263, 367, 395, 409, 416
Potsdam Redoubt: 252
Potter, George and Co: 38
Pougnet, Capt V N: 300, 384, 412
Power, Maj (Dr) M S: 156, 400, 417
Pretoria: 22-23, 27, 38, 74, 185, 190, 192, 387, 402, 404, 409, 412, 435
Pretoria Citizens' Service Medal: 404
Priluk: 390
Princes Street: 142
Princess Mary: 56
Pyott, Capt I V J: 424
Pyramids: 59, 63